NowIt SpringsUp

Spiritual Insights for Every Day

CAROL DUERKSEN
MICHELE HERSHBERGER
LAURIE OSWALD ROBINSON

Now It Springs Up
Spiritual Insights for Every Day

Library of Congress Control Number: 2007929715

International Standard Book Number: 978-0-9742716-3-7

Now It Springs Up

is

dedicated

to all the families

who are and will pass on to their children

the love of Scripture

and the importance

of the journey with God.

Table of Contents

Acknowledgments

To the people of Sycamore Grove, I say thanks for helping me love the Bible and the journey. I thank my husband, Del, for his encouragement and love through the days and nights of birthing a book. I also thank my daughters Erin and Tara and son JD for their patience and support and for the inspiration they gave me through their own journeys with God. Tara, you pulled me through when the creative juices were drying up. Thanks.

—*Michele Hershberger*

I thank my husband, Alfonso, for his loyal support and affirmation during the yearlong writing process. I also thank my various church families for forming and informing my faith, which has been rooted in a life of Bible reading, study and reflection.

—*Laurie Oswald Robinson*

My thanks to my husband, Maynard Knepp, who said "Find somebody to help you" when I threw out the idea of writing this book, and who gave me the space to spend hours at the computer writing it. I too, am thankful for the church of my childhood, Alexanderwohl Mennonite, and my church family today, Tabor Mennonite, for feeding my spiritual journey.

—*Carol Duerksen*

We all acknowledge the huge role our parents played in planting the seeds of faith in our lives and who showed us what it means to live the Scriptures: John D. and Phyllis Schrock, Paul E. Oswald and the late Dorothy Mae Egli Oswald; Milton and Alice Duerksen.

Special thanks to Kevin Cook, page designer; Nancy Miller, cover designer; Helen Tellez, copyeditor; and Marlene Kropf for her endorsement.

One of the deepest cries of people today is for a meaningful faith that will sustain them in troubled and uncertain times. Although participating in congregational life is essential for healthy spirituality, people also need to nurture their own relationship with God through daily prayer and reflection on scripture if they want to grow to maturity. *Now It Springs Up* offers rich and accessible guidance for that journey.

Three experienced authors, Carol Duerksen, Michele Hershberger, and Laurie Oswald Robinson, have teamed together to offer fresh, engaging reflections on daily scripture readings that follow the rhythms of the Christian year. In addition to thought-provoking biblical meditations, each day's entry includes an invitation to prayer and to action.

What I noticed immediately about the book were two things: the candid, personal voice of each author, and the depth of spirituality reflected in these writings. Each writer has revealed—humbly and vulnerably—how God's Spirit met her and invited her to grow as she pondered the text for the day. Confession and repentance wonder and awe, honest doubts and perplexing questions, and occasional delightful flashes of humor weave their way through these pages.

The spirituality of these writers reflects at least three important commitments. First, what they write is biblical. Each day's meditation begins with scripture. Then, drawing upon the best of biblical scholarship and their own close reading of the text, the writers open up the passages, illuminating the divine-human encounter in each text and making lively connections for us today.

A second feature is the incarnational perspective that shapes their interpretations. The Jesus they follow is not some long-ago, far-away Judean prophet, but a living presence who walks on grimy streets, eats at crowded tables, and weeps with mourners beside a fresh grave. In the same way, the experiences they describe from their lives have a vivid, down-to-earth quality that will invite others to identify with them.

A third feature of the spirituality of the book is its matter-of-fact dependence on the Holy Spirit. These writers expect to hear and respond personally to the Spirit's voice. Though they reveal their struggles and know the bitter taste of failure, they also know the joy of intimate communion with God. The suggestions they offer for prayer and walking in the world encourage us to trust that same active Spirit to work in our lives.

All in all, the approach of *Now It Springs Up* offers a fresh re-interpretation of the ancient Benedictine practice of *Lectio Divina*. This way of praying the scriptures begins with meditative reading and includes patient listening, honest prayer, and active obedience to the Word. Practiced regularly, such dwelling in scripture transforms us. Gradually a new person emerges who looks at life and humanity with the wisdom and compassion of Christ and becomes a winsome sign of God's love and grace in the world.

Who will benefit from this well-grounded resource? Anyone who yearns for a deeper encounter with God will find much here to satisfy that longing. Scattered throughout the collection are entries specially designated for families and children. The suggestions for prayer and action in these entries would be suitable for family worship or even for children's Sunday school classes. I can also imagine this guide being used when people gather for committee meetings or other church business. I will keep the book on my desk so it is readily available for moments of meditation in the midst of busy workdays.

Just as the prophet Isaiah promised, when we call upon God, rivers will flow in desert places and new life will spring forth. With such refreshment, we will become a people of praise who walk in the world with love, trust and hope in God's good future.

Marlene Kropf, Associate Professor of Spiritual Formation and Worship, Associated Mennonite Biblical Seminary; Congregational and Ministerial Leadership, Executive Leadership, Mennonite Church USA

| *Introduction* |

THE CALLING

By Carol Duerksen

Why would three multi-tasking, often overbooked women decide to write a book of 365 devotionals?

We still ask that question, and we still give the same answer: Because we are crazy. And because, much larger in our lives than the craziness, is the strong sense that God's Spirit put in a call, a "text message," if you will, to each of us.

We met. We talked. And, with huge amounts of apprehension and exhilaration, we decided to go for it. 365 divided by 3 was 122 devotions per person. It seemed manageable. We set a day to discuss details, which Michele and Laurie will explain further in the rest of this introduction.

And we began to pray, ponder, study and write.

You're holding the harvest. We trust and pray that the same Spirit who called us and then sat with us at our computers will also sit with you in your devotional times.

THE CHOICE OF SCRIPTURE

By Michele Hershberger

One of my fondest childhood memories is finding my father reading his Bible early in the morning. He sat on his favorite overstuffed chair, reading and underlining as he read chronologically through each Testament. "What do you do with Amos?" I asked him once. "Well, it's in there for a purpose," he said. "It's all in there for a purpose."

It's all in there for a purpose. Believing this, Carol, Laurie and I set out to use parts of the whole biblical narrative as the starting point for our devotionals. We decided not to stick with the easy categories of literature, like narratives or Paul's sermons. We decided to include whole books—and difficult passages. We wanted to experience it all.

Some of the genres were easier than others. And even in the easier genres, some passages were tempting to skip. How do you even begin to write a devotional on I Corinthians 14: 33-39, where Paul speaks about women being silent in the church? The Bible scholar in me wanted to whip into an exegetical frenzy (and you should have seen me in Revelation!) and explain the Greek words and the cultural background for pages on end. But then I would remind myself—this is devotional Bible study. The main purpose is not to scientifically research each passage, but to hear in a fresh way what the Spirit says to us—now.

That being said, this book is different from other devotionals in that we did pay attention to historical accuracy and solid exegetical work. We may not discuss the Hebrew words in the devotional per se, but we did try to do justice to each passage. We tried our best to not make the text mean something for us that it couldn't have meant for the original audience. Not only did we tackle Amos and some of the "gnarlier" psalms, but we also refused to use fluffy interpretations. This is not necessarily a "feel good, five easy ways to get a better spiritual life" kind of devotional. The Bible isn't that simple. And neither are our lives.

Life today is different from my childhood days, when my father read devotionals each morning. That's why I asked my oldest daughter, Tara, to help me write some of my devotionals. I wanted a young adult perspective. I wanted to write devotionals not only true to the original audience, but meaningful in our world today. It is my hope that this is a book for young adults like Tara, early morning die-hards like my father, and anyone who wonders how the Bible applies to their lives.

And that includes children. Because we wanted this book to be family-friendly, we included two devotionals each week that were written especially with children in mind. There's one exception, and that's the story of Joseph—his whole story is written in language that communicates with children. And, just as we've noticed that adults often listen and learn a lot from children's stories in church, we think adults will gather some lessons for life from the devotionals for younger minds.

My father still reads his Bible every morning. And maybe, just maybe with the help of this book, his grandchildren and their children will read it too.

THE CHURCH SEASONS

By Laurie Oswald Robinson

Where I grew up in a small Midwestern Mennonite church, the only dates observed in the church calendar were Christmas Day, Good Friday and Easter Day. But later exposure to other faith traditions taught me that the church liturgical year is multi-layered with many seasons. I learned that Advent precedes Christmas, Epiphany follows Christmas, Lent precedes Easter and Pentecost follows Easter. My exposure to the circular pattern of the church calendar brought new sights, sounds and sensibilities to my faith journey that teased a three-dimensional rainbow from a more flat, monotone expression.

This devotional book strives to follow the church year in a loose way. Our book is not year specific, so we can't place a Christian celebration on a specific date, except for Christmas, which is always Dec. 25, and Epiphany, which is always Jan. 6. Nevertheless, Carol, Michele and I hoped to cover the main themes of the various Christian seasons in devotions that fall generally within the dates of those Christian seasons. Here is a general overview of the seasons:

- **Advent:** The first Sunday in Advent is considered the start of the Christian year. Advent includes the four Sundays before Christmas. It commemorates the anticipation of the Messiah's first coming, as well as the second coming.

- **Christmas:** Christmas Day is December 25 and celebrates Christ's birth but "Christmas" spans 12 days, until Jan. 6, the close of the 12 days.

- **Epiphany:** Celebrated Jan. 6. Epiphany means "manifestation" or appearance" and signifies in the Western churches the coming of the Magi to Baby Jesus. In the Eastern churches, it signifies the baptism of Jesus and his first miracle in Cana.

- **Lent:** Begins on Ash Wednesday and lasts 40 days (not counting Sundays, which are counted as "Little Easters" even during Lent.) The season is penitential and repentant, focused on fasting, confession, devotion and discipline, and it ends the day before Easter.

- **Easter:** Begins on Easter day, the celebration of the risen Lord, and lasts 50 days until Pentecost. The 50 days are meant for celebrating and reflecting upon the explosive, life-giving power of the resurrection. It is based on the great Jewish festival of 50 days. The festival began with the opening of the harvest season two days after the start of Passover and extended until what came to be called the Day of Pentecost.

- **Pentecost:** The final Sunday of Easter is Pentecost, during which the well-known Acts2: 1-21 passage is used. The day focuses on the church as corporate community. It's not about the spirit's action within individual – which if focused on many other times of the Christian year — but about the formation of the church.

For those who want to explore the Christian liturgical year in more depth, a helpful resource is *Calendar: Christ's Time for the Church*, by Laurence Hull Stookey (Abingon Press, 1996). The overview above was gleaned from this resource.

Scriptures

JANUARY pages 21–58

FEBRUARY pages 59–92

Dates in italics are for children and families

MARCH   pages 93–128

APRIL   pages 129–163

Dates in italics are for children and families

MAY pages 164–199

JUNE pages 200–234

JULY   pages 235–273

AUGUST   pages 274–310

Dates in italics are for children and families

SEPTEMBER pages 311–347

OCTOBER pages 348–385

NOVEMBER pages 386–421

1. Exodus 15:22-27
2. Exodus 16:1-12
3. *Exodus 16:13-21*
4. Exodus 16:22-36
5. Exodus 17:1-7
6. *Exodus 17:8-16*
7. Exodus 18:1-12
8. Exodus 18:13-27
9. *Exodus 19:1-9a*
10. Exodus 19:9b-25
11. *Exodus 20:1-17*

12. Exodus 20:18-21
13. Exodus 32:1-6
14. Exodus 32:7-14
15. *Exodus 32:15-24*
16. Exodus 32:25-35
17. Exodus 33:1-11
18. Exodus 33:12-23
19. Exodus 34:1-10
20. Exodus 34:11-16
21. *Exodus 34:17-28*
22. Exodus 34:29-35

23. Exodus 35:1-29
24. *Exodus 35:30—36:7*
25. Isaiah 9:1-7
26. Isaiah 40:1-11
27. Isaiah 40-27-31
28. Isaiah 42:1-4
29. Isaiah 42:5-9
30. Isaiah 44:1-5

DECEMBER pages 422–457

1. Isaiah 45:14-19
2. Isaiah 45:20-25
3. Isaiah 49:1-7
4. Isaiah 49:8-13
5. *Isaiah 49:14-21*
6. Isaiah 49:22-26
7. *Isaiah 50:4-9*
8. Isaiah 52:13-15
9. Isaiah 53:1-6
10. *Isaiah 53:7-9*
11. Isaiah 53:10-12

12. *Isaiah 60:1-9*
13. Isaiah 60:10-22
14. Isaiah 61:1-9
15. Isaiah 64:1-4
16. Isaiah 65:7-25
17. Isaiah 66:18-24
18. Luke 1:1-4
19. Luke 1:5-25
20. Luke 1:26-38
21. Luke 1:39-45
22. Luke 1:46-56

23. *Luke 1:57-66*
24. Luke 1:67-80
25 and 26. Luke 2:1-20
27. Luke 2:21-24
28. Luke 2:25-35
29. Luke 2:36-40
30. Luke 2:41-50
31. Luke 2:51-52

Dates in italics are for children and families

JANUARY 1

IN THE BEGINNING

PLUNGING INTO THE WORD:

John 1:1-5

PONDERING ON THE WAY:

In the beginning … in the beginning. It sounds so special, so full of promise and yet almost scary. In the beginning …

It is the beginning of a new year. And it's strange that most of the world has chosen to begin a new year in the darkest time possible—the dead of winter. We celebrate the birth of Jesus on December 25, and we all smile and admit that this was probably not his birthday, so why at this dark time? Why celebrate the most important birth of all, why create a new beginning—in such darkness?

I really don't have the answer. But I like that we start a new year in darkness because—

Because it reflects my life a lot of the time. God sometimes asks me to see light when there is only a murky black. God sometimes asks me to grope in the darkness and take baby steps forward. God sometimes asks me to have the courage to begin again, even though I'm discouraged and tired and just want to sleep the night away. "The light shines in the darkness, and the darkness did not overcome it." The light, God's light, wins the day every time.

I love the idea that Jesus was born at the darkest of times and that every day after his birth, it keeps getting lighter.

Every day.

—*Michele Hershberger*

PRAYING AND WALKING IN THE WORLD:

- Is God asking you to see light when there is only a murky black? Does that seem fair? Do you need God's help?

- Can you name your darkness? Can you name the light, even if you can't see it? Are there others who can help you? Can you talk to them about it?

JANUARY 2 *(FOR CHILDREN AND FAMILIES)*

LITTLE LIGHTS, BIG LIGHT

PLUNGING INTO THE WORD:

John 1:6-13

PONDERING ON THE WAY:

Elmer … I'll never forget Elmer. He took my cousins and me fishing, even though we were ten and he was the preacher with so many important things to do. And he took us swimming, and he dove off the high board, even though he was almost seventy. The lifeguards got so nervous, and we kids just giggled. Elmer was going to be fine; we just knew it.

But beyond the swimming and the root beer parties and that summer evening when we barbecued squirrel, Elmer was a man of God. Even at the tender age of ten, I knew that. Elmer was more than fun and games. He knew God, and he let God's love flow through him to everyone he met.

He was not the light but came to testify to the light, the true light of Jesus Christ.

If Elmer were here today, he would look at me and say, "Michele, who have you taken fishing lately?" And I would smile and get out my pole.

Thank you Lord, for the Elmers in our world.

—*Michele Hershberger*

PRAYING AND WALKING IN THE WORLD:

- Name the Elmers in your world. Can you rejoice in their witness, at the same time acknowledging they are not the true light?

- Who do you need to "take fishing"?

- **Prepare an interactive prayer station following these steps:**

  1. Have three to four short candles for each person who will participate in this prayer. Place these candles on a table around one tall candle. Have matches ready to light the candles.

  2. Make sure small children sit next to an adult to ensure proper supervision.

  3. Have a Bible open to the first chapter of John.

Steps for the interactive prayer:

1. Ask one person to read John 1:6-7. Say, "Who in your life has pointed you to the Light of the world? Light some of the small candles, and name those persons who have helped you find Jesus."

2. Persons take turns lighting the small candles and naming persons who have been "witnesses" for them.

3. Ask another person to read John 1:8-11. Then light the tall candle as a symbol of Jesus. Say, "But all these persons we have named are not the Light. They each have failed, just as we all have failed. Like the people who lived next door to Jesus, we have failed to recognize him. We have failed to accept him for who he is."

4. Instruct each person to blow out the small candles they lit.

5. Sit for a moment in silence.

6. Read John 1:12-13. Using the tall candle, relight each small candle. In your own words, remind the others how that, when we do follow Jesus as the true Light of the world, then we become God's children. We will never be the Light, but through Jesus, the Light shines through us. It is a light that no darkness can consume (v. 5).

7. Thank God for the Light and for the people who bear witness to that Light.

JANUARY 3

GOD IN THE HOOD

PLUNGING INTO THE WORD:

John 1:14-18

PONDERING ON THE WAY:

One of my favorite paraphrases of these verses begins this way: "And the Word became flesh and moved into the neighborhood."* Into the neighborhood? My neighborhood? A quiet little town in Kansas? But it's just as hard to imagine Jesus in the Bronx or in the old-growth forests of Oregon or on the streets of Montreal. But why not?

Why not?

Another image comes to mind. Now we're not in Montreal anymore, but in the wilds of the Sinai desert. Thousands and thousands of people go marching along in no-man's-land, searching for some Promised Land. The whole scene would be absurd, except for this mysterious pillar that guides them. In the day, it is cloud. By night, pure fire. It both reveals and conceals the divine presence. The pillar is God … God dwelling among them.

Sometimes the pillar stops. And the people scramble to put up tents, especially a huge tent that is their worship space. Their tabernacle. And then, when everything is ready, God "tabernacles" with them. The pillar comes to rest at the mouth of the meeting place. God dwells among them. It is so holy that if a person dares come too close, without the proper precautions, he dies.

Dwelling is personal. And intense.

Too many times in church, I hear all this hoopla about us going up to heaven. "I'll Fly Away," we sing, and we ask people if they know how they too can get to heaven. It's not that I don't believe in heaven, but the whole story of the Bible is a story of a God who wants to come down.

Yahweh walks around the garden saying, "Adam and Eve, where are you?" God walking in a garden looking for people? Doesn't God know where they are? And then in the wilderness, God dwells with the people, tabernacling. And then Jesus comes, the Word, and what does he do? He moves into the neighborhood. And even after Jesus dies and is resurrected and ascends into heaven, the pattern continues.

What happens next? The Holy Spirit descends upon the new believers and they, and we, become—the body of Christ. And finally at the end, it happens again. Do we go up? No. The New Jerusalem comes floating down. And God dwells among his people.

God wants to be in our space.

The powerful Word who made the whole universe loved us so much that he took on flesh. And came to us, in all our messiness and filth and tears and laughter and goofiness. He moved into the neighborhood.

Your neighborhood.

> —Michele Hershberger

PRAYING AND WALKING IN THE WORLD:

- Is the idea of God dwelling in your midst a comforting thought or a scary one? Why?

- Look back at John 1:11-12. Jesus came down, but not everyone received him. God wants to be in your space. Are you a gracious host?

- How has heaven come down to your neighborhood this last month? In what specific area would you like for God's presence to dwell even more fully?

* John 1:14a, *The Message* by Eugene Peterson

JANUARY 4

THE FAMILY TREE

PLUNGING INTO THE WORD:

Matthew 1:1-17

PONDERING ON THE WAY:

Can you imagine the first time the boy Jesus sat down beside his mother and father and asked them about their family history? Did Mary blush? Did Joseph squirm? How do you explain Tamar, who dressed up like a prostitute and seduced her father-in-law so she could have a child? Or how much do you tell the boy about Rahab or Bathsheba? Do you tell these stories in detail, or do you skip the stories altogether?

Now all of those stories, given their context, show women who were trying to be faithful. Tamar turned out to be more righteous than her father-in-law because he would not abide by the laws of levirate marriage, which was her only hope of survival. But still? These stories can seem pretty wild at their first telling.

What does it mean that Jesus came from such a "checkered" background?

I think it means God can use anyone. I think it means God is full of grace.

I think this genealogy—the genealogy of the Son of God—helps me acknowledge my own "checkered" background and realize that God can use me—even me.

—*Michele Hershberger*

PRAYING AND WALKING IN THE WORLD:

Take some time, right now, to write out your genealogy. You can start with your mother and father and go backwards, or start with the earliest ancestor you know and work your way back to you. If you need to, make some phone calls to your relatives. See if you can fill in the blanks.

Look over the names. Think about the stories, the history, represented by each name. Ask yourself these questions:

- Who are you proud of? Who are you angry with?

- Who doesn't quite fit in the family tree and yet, in some strange way, really does?

- Do you need to do something about the skeletons in the family closet? If so, what?

- Can you see God's faithfulness through these people? All these people? How?

- Is it comforting to know that Jesus had less than perfect people in his family tree?

- What are the miracles represented here? How can you say thanks?

JANUARY 5 (FOR CHILDREN AND FAMILIES)

NAMES

PLUNGING INTO THE WORD:

Matthew 1:18-25

PONDERING ON THE WAY:

Adults: This Bible reading is a great one to use with small children, especially as you look into the aspects of naming. Children are intrigued with names, especially their own. Make sure you have some idea of what their names mean before starting this devotional time with them.

Did you know that most names have a special meaning? Sometimes we don't know what these meanings are, but we can look in books and find out a story of how a name came to be and what its special meaning is. For example, my name is _____. And this name means _____. Do you know what your name means?

God gave Jesus two names. See if you can hear them when I read the Bible story. (Read Matthew 1:18-25, or just read verses 21-23.)

What do you think the name *Jesus* means? (He will save his people from their sins.)

What do you think *Emmanuel* means? (God with us.)

Why do you think Jesus had two names?

Names are important. God knows your name, and like Jesus, you are special to God.

—*Michele Hershberger*

PRAYING AND WALKING IN THE WORLD:

- If you had a chance to give Jesus another special name, what would it be?

- What name do you think God would like to give you today? *Beloved? Precious? Blessed?*

JANUARY 6 *(FOR CHILDREN AND FAMILIES)*

GIFTS FOR JESUS

PLUNGING INTO THE WORD:

Matthew 2:1-12

PONDERING ON THE WAY:

Today is a special day, a day we call Epiphany. On this day, we remember the wise men who came from a faraway country to visit the baby Jesus. And they didn't just visit; they also brought some gifts. Do you know what they brought Jesus? (Let the children answer if they can.) And how did they find Jesus and Mary and Joseph? They found him by following a very bright star.

       —Michele Hershberger

PRAYING AND WALKING IN THE WORLD:

- What were some of the special gifts you received this Christmas?

- If you had the chance to give Jesus one thing, what would it be?

- Take some paper and crayons and draw or write what you would give Jesus. Then put the slips of paper in a gift box. Set the box in a special place. End with prayer, asking God to accept your gifts of love.

- **Adults:** Read this passage and think about how God used—pagans. Yes, pagans. The wise men weren't Jewish. And quite frankly, they figured things out better than the people who were born to figure it out (who should have figured it out)—the chief priests and scribes. What does this mean for us? Are we liable to miss the new King too?

JANUARY 7

GOD CRYING

PLUNGING INTO THE WORD:

Matthew 2:13-18

PONDERING ON THE WAY:

Many times—too many times—I've found myself sitting beside the bed of a dying friend. Or standing beside the phone, fingers trembling, trying to dial, because someone's son was killed in a car accident. Someone's beloved son.

I never know what to say in these cases. I'm sorry? I'm sorry for what seems like a needless death? I'm sorry she died too young? I'm sorry you couldn't say good-bye?

I'm sorry you hurt so much?

But it's worse to try to make explanations. Sometimes I get nervous at funerals when I hear people, people with good intentions, trying to soothe the pain of the bereaved with some platitude. Well, maybe there's a lesson to be learned here, some people say. What? God let a wonderful saint suffer excruciating pain so the rest of us could learn some lesson? Is that the only way I'll learn? What kind of a God is that?

What kind of a God would let fifteen or twenty babies die that night in Bethlehem? Yes, I understand that God allows free will, and, yes I know the flight to Egypt fulfilled prophecy, but I still ache. I ache for the parents. I ache for the lives that could have been.

How could the miraculous Birth be tied to such death?

Did the angel come to them too, and no one listened? Did some of the parents get away?

Did God cry that night too? Did God say, "I'm sorry you hurt so much"?

Maybe there are no words to say. No explanations. And we hold out our arms and cradle our grieving friends and fight injustice and close our eyes and see—

God crying.

> —*Michele Hershberger*

PRAYING AND WALKING IN THE WORLD:

- What brings you to tears today?

- What is God crying about today?

- Is it okay to be mad at God? Is it okay not to know why some people suffer? Read through the Psalms and you will find poems of anger and hurt. Do you need to write a poem of anger and hurt to God? God is faithful. God will hear you.

JANUARY 8

SADNESS AND GLADNESS

PLUNGING INTO THE WORD:

Jeremiah 31:15-20

PONDERING ON THE WAY:

Epiphany is the season in the church calendar spanning January 6 until Ash Wednesday, the start of Lent. At a time when many people have packed Baby Jesus away in a storage box as if the story is done, the drama just begins to get juicy.

Today's reading reminds us how quickly the story of the sweet Baby Jesus twists and turns into the possibility of a bitter murder. Jeremiah 31 refers to the weeping of Rachel, the representative ancestress of Israel, at the fall of Jerusalem. This prophecy is inserted in the Matthew birth narrative to refer to Herod's slaughtering of the innocents—baby boys up to age two—in attempts to find and kill Jesus.

But Christian seasons remind us that God's plan for our world transcends the devastations of our humanity. Epiphany celebrates the baptism of Jesus and uses the color green to symbolize life. The word itself means manifestation, or how Jesus manifested himself as God with us, a presence that stares down slaughter and survives.

Because God is with us, we don't need to fear the depression and grayness that can haunt us. Epiphany gives us permission to stare into the blank space where the tree once twinkled and to feel our sadness, as well as our gladness.

Because I know the green of Christ transcends the world of gray, I can admit how sad I was that my mother, the late Dorothy Mae Egli Oswald, was not with me during my first Christmas with my new husband, Alfonso. I can accept that this year I may go to funerals, as well as to baby showers. I can embrace the fact that suffering, as well as celebration, will be part of my days.

And because Epiphany means "to appear," I can choose to see the eternal light appearing in dark winter. Its appearing reminds me that a crying baby, Jesus, came into a world of people who cry so they also can sing.

—*Laurie Oswald Robinson*

PRAYING AND WALKING IN THE WORLD:

- In personal prayer, thank God for the sadness and gladness, grieving and dancing, grayness and greenness in your life. Meditate on how Jesus, God with us, cares about our rejoicing and our weeping and is present with us in all of it.

- Pray for your loved ones and friends who were grieving and suffering during the holidays because of death, divorce, or depression.

- Send an e-mail or snail mail card to someone who needs comfort for the weeping during this Epiphany season.

JANUARY 9

DREAMS LEAD TO NEW ROADS

PLUNGING INTO THE WORD:

Matthew 2:19-23

PONDERING ON THE WAY:

I wonder what Joseph was thinking after Jesus' birth. Perhaps his nights were filled with worries and nightmares about Herod's power. Then suddenly, God brought a dream that contained a map for the Holy Family to find a new road. It offered insights and instructions for a journey that would lead to a peace no longer plagued by Herod.

I also wonder what would have happened if Joseph hadn't listened to the angel of the Lord. Or, how would the story have unfolded—or folded—if Mary and Joseph hadn't listened to the angel of the Lord regarding the coming birth of Jesus? Their receptivity to their dreams led them, and us, into the most unimaginable, but true, story ever told or ever lived.

Sometimes Christians are afraid to listen to their dreams, fearing they are an open door into the occult or will lead into the trickery of New Age materials that don't honor Christ. But there also are many Christian materials today that encourage us to seek the Holy Spirit's insight about what our dreams mean for our waking lives. They often bring insight about that ninety percent of us we don't see as we are experiencing the ten percent of our day-to-day lives.

Perhaps your dreams this January are as mundane as sensing that God wants you to shed pounds or as nail-biting as being called to move across the country or become a mission worker in a foreign land. Perhaps they are revealing something about a deep wound that needs healing or a relationship that needs mending. Whatever may be beckoning you into new lands, Mary and Joseph are good models for teaching us how to be open to new paths that can get us there.

—*Laurie Oswald Robinson*

PRAYING AND WALKING IN THE WORLD:

- Pray for insight about dreams that you remember as being significant. What is God saying about the imagery and feelings you experienced in those dreams?

- Buy a journal and record your dreams, as well as what you sense God saying about those dreams.

- Share your dreams with a trusted friend or family member so the dreams won't melt away but will become a more solid part of your journey with God.

JANUARY 10

WEIRD COUSINS IN THE WILDERNESS

PLUNGING INTO THE WORD:

Matthew 3:1-12

PONDERING ON THE WAY:

We have taken step after step beyond the Christmas story into the events that occurred during the period we call Epiphany. But suddenly, we must leapfrog from Jesus' story into the story of his weird cousin, John the Baptist. Suddenly, we leave safety and head for the wilderness.

If we risk leaving safety for wilderness, we see that the point of Jesus' birth and baptism is not about Jesus. It is about us. What will we do with this story? When the December calendar flips into January, what are we going to do with this baby? Will we allow him to grow up in us to baptize us with the Holy Spirit and with fire?

In my mid-thirties, I attended a series of prayer seminars where I found healing for deep-seated emotional and spiritual wounds. I'll never forget the day God called me to give up the safe Nazareth for the wild desert. A counselor prayed for the darkness that had lived so long in my soul. As I repented of the actions of myself and others that led to that darkness, I felt what seemed like a thick rope uncoil from my stomach. As the counselor's prayers and my repentance pulled the rope up and out of me, the cavern that had been filled with confusion, leading to pain, now became an open space for confession, leading to peace.

Oftentimes when I was comfortable in Nazareth, I didn't see how much stuff I had filling up my soul. It was only when some John the Baptist somewhere called me out of that safety that I saw how much my stuff got in the way of living out my baptism.

How about you? Any weird cousins hanging out in your life, beckoning you into the wilderness?

—*Laurie Oswald Robinson*

PRAYING AND WALKING IN THE WORLD:

- Pray for insight about ways God may be calling you from safety to wilderness and for the courage to follow.

- Find some symbols in nature that remind you of your baptism, and put them next to your devotional materials or in your room.

- Reach out to a child, parent, or neighbor who is experiencing some wilderness.

JANUARY 11 *(FOR CHILDREN AND FAMILIES)*

REAL RABBITS, BELOVED KIDS

PLUNGING INTO THE WORD:

Matthew 3:13-17

PONDERING ON THE WAY:

Have you ever loved a stuffed animal so much that you carried it around with you all the time?

This is what happened in *The Velveteen Rabbit*. It's a story about how a boy loved his stuffed rabbit so much that he slept with it every night. After lots of wear and tear, the boy rubbed off the rabbit's spots and dirtied his pink satin ears.

In the story, the rabbit asks Skin Horse if toys can become real. Skin Horse says that real is what you become when a child loves you. "By the time you are Real, most of your hair has been loved off, and your eyes drop out and you get loose in your joints and very shabby," Skin Horse says. "But these things don't matter at all, because once you are Real you can't be ugly, except to people who don't understand."

The story can remind us of today's Bible story, when John baptizes Jesus. Even though Jesus was the Son of God, worthy to wear purple robes, he asked his cousin, who wore camel hair and ate grasshoppers, to baptize him. As he was baptized, a voice from heaven said, "This is my Son, the beloved, in whom I am well pleased."

Have you ever seen a baptism? What did you see? Do you know why people do this?

Jesus chose to be baptized by his weird cousin, far away from fancy churches. Jesus didn't care about what things looked like on the outside. He didn't care whether John was perfect enough to baptize him, or whether there were big, white towels to dry off with. Jesus cared most about being the Son of God. God calling Jesus "Beloved" shows that God cared most about that too. God's acceptance and love helped Jesus to be himself as he followed God.

It isn't good grades, new sneakers, or popular friends that give us worth. Being loved by God and loving God back is what makes us real kids—kids who are okay being ourselves without needing to be pretty or perfect to be accepted. So, as you take your favorite stuffed animal to bed—the one with all the fur rubbed off—hold it tight and remember that God is holding you tight too, whispering your name, "Beloved."

> —*Laurie Oswald Robinson*

PRAYING AND WALKING IN THE WORLD:

- Find a stuffed animal to hold tight, and ask your mother or father or caretaker to hold you tight as you say your nightly prayers. How does it feel when you are held tight like that? Imagine God holding you tight and calling you "Beloved."

- Talk to another adult about the word *real*. Look it up in the dictionary. Talk about what it means to be a real person. What does it mean to be accepted for who you really are, rather than for pretending to be perfect, without any faults? How do you sometimes pretend to be perfect?

- Read *The Velveteen Rabbit* by Margery Williams.

JANUARY 12

RAZZLE DAZZLE

PLUNGING INTO THE WORD:

Matthew 4:1-11

PONDERING ON THE WAY:

Let me begin by stating the obvious—I am not tempted in the same way Jesus was tempted. I don't get hankerings for bread every time I see a brown stone. I don't want to even think about jumping off the high-pitched roof of my church sanctuary.

I'm not tempted with these things because I'm not divine. The thought of making supper out of rocks from the backyard doesn't even occur to me (for which my family is grateful).

But Jesus was divine. And the devil, knowing that, came to Jesus much the same way he came to Adam and Eve. He came with a question. To Adam and Eve he asked, "Do you want to be divine?" To Jesus, he asked, "Do you think you can be truly human?"

The devil was tempting Jesus to use his divine powers to take shortcuts to shalom, to take the easy road to messiahship, to pull out the divinity card whenever suffering was just around the corner. It was more than stones into bread; it was the temptation to feed the people so they would follow him. It was more than letting angels catch you; it was using any miracle to razzle-dazzle the people into following him. And in the final temptation, in a bald-faced effort, Satan offered Jesus all of the political and military powers on earth. "Go ahead," the devil teased, "force them to accept your peace-loving ways."

And Jesus, bald-faced, called that temptation what it was—worshipping the devil himself.

I wonder, has the church ever tried bribing people into the kingdom? Has it ever sought to razzle-dazzle people into its ranks? Has the church ever worked with the state to gently coerce or downright threaten people to become believers?

Okay, maybe the church has been tempted like Jesus.

And have I ever sought my identity through my special abilities? Have I ever decided who I was by what others thought of me, after I razzle-dazzled them by my big show? Have I ever declared myself beloved because of all of the things I owned, even if it wasn't every kingdom and power?

Okay, maybe I have been tempted like Jesus.

    —Michele Hershberger

PRAYING AND WALKING IN THE WORLD:

- Jesus was tempted to use his divinity in such a way that he could avoid the cross. In what ways does the church try to avoid suffering? In what ways do you try?

- Jesus was tempted to be effective, efficient, practical. He was tempted to bring shalom in a non-shalom way. Does that ever work? Do the ends ever justify the means? If that's true, what does that mean for our temptation to use violence to achieve good ends?

JANUARY 13

GOLD AND RUST

PLUNGING INTO THE WORD:

Luke 4:14-30

PONDERING ON THE WAY:

Perhaps you remember signing yearbooks with the caption beneath a senior picture, "most likely to succeed." You may have envied classmates, those who turned everything they touched into some kind of gold. They got A's on every test, they dated the most popular guy or gal in school, they wore the greatest clothes or drove the sportiest car.

Years later, this same person came home for class reunions far different than when he or she left. They'd lost their hair, their figure, their confidence that everything would go their way. What looked like stardom in high school became like a shooting star because of life's "falls." What began as the gold of youth turned to the rust of the wear and tear of aging.

But it can go the other way too. What looks lowly may become mighty. The people in Jesus' hometown had their opinions of Jesus too. They resented the fact that Jesus, the son of a lowly carpenter in Nazareth, was claiming that the Spirit of God was anointing him to bring the good news to the poor, to proclaim release to captives, to give sight to the blind. They resented it so much, they drove him out of town.

This passage says he passed through the midst of them and went on his way. So too, Jesus calls all of us to be who God created us to be. We may have grown up in a rich or poor family. We may be a flashy star or a hidden team player. We may have self-confidence or fight each day to feel okay about ourself. No matter what our lot in life, God calls us to pass through our days, secure in knowing that God loves us as we are and beckons us into the future, no matter what the past.

—*Laurie Oswald Robinson*

PRAYING AND WALKING IN THE WORLD:

- Reflect on what aspect of yourself in high school gave you the greatest struggle with feeling second-rate and less-than. Reflect on what aspect of your life as an adult makes you feel "rusty" and fallen.

- Pray that God will make you aware of the gold of your inner giftedness and how you may express and share it. Pray for greater focus on the state of your heart, rather than the state of your pocketbook, popularity, or performance.

- Pick one person whose outside appearance turns you off and make it a point to speak with her or him. Spend time getting to know that person on the inside.

- This passage also speaks to us about ethnic arrogance. Jesus' hometown folk weren't ready to kill him until he mentioned how God took care of foreigners to the exclusion of Israelites. How about your congregation? Do you like to think God is only for your people?

- What sermon would get you thrown over a cliff? Do you dare preach it anyway?

JANUARY 14 *(FOR CHILDREN AND FAMILIES)*

BECAUSE I SAID SO

PLUNGING INTO THE WORD:

Luke 4:31-37

PONDERING ON THE WAY:

Like most kids, you've probably asked your parents why you have to go to bed at 8 p.m. on school nights, eat your vegetables, or clean up your room on Saturdays. And like most kids, you roll your eyes when you ask "Why?" and they say, "Because I said so." Sometimes this feels too simple and unfair. But even if you don't like it, you usually do what they ask. You recognize that your parents have a God-given right to guide you as you grow up.

A gospel story shows that people recognized that Jesus had a right to guide events and people. The big word for this is *authority.* He had so much of it that he could even tell demons what to do. In this story in Luke 4, Jesus was in the synagogue, or church, where he saw a man with an unclean spirit, or a demon—a darkness that lived inside of this man.

The demon recognized Jesus and cried, "Let us alone!"

Jesus answered, "Be silent, and come out of him!" And the demon did what he said.

Jesus was special. He stood out above the other teachers and preachers who talked about God. Jesus was special because he was God's Son on a special mission for God—to tell everybody that God loves them. Jesus wants us to do the same thing—to tell people that God loves them. And if we ask "Why?", the answer is simple: "Because God loves you."

—*Laurie Oswald Robinson*

PRAYING AND WALKING IN THE WORLD:

- Talk with your parents about what it means to obey them. Talk about the things you sometimes think are unfair, and which things are okay. Can you understand why they ask you to do the things they do?

- Ask Jesus to help you share Jesus' love with other kids, especially those who may not have loving parents in their lives.

- Draw or paint a picture of the story in Luke 4 for your refrigerator or for the bulletin board to remind you of Jesus' power and special place in your life.

JANUARY 15

GONE FISHING

PLUNGING INTO THE WORD:

Luke 5:1-11

PONDERING ON THE WAY:

With all due respect,
I do need to say
I know about fishing.

My parents fished.
I grew up fishing.
I've studied fishing.
It's what I'm trained to do.

I know when and where
they're most likely to bite.
I know when to be patient.
And when I'm wasting my time.
I know.
I've been there, done that.
With all due respect, Jesus,
I know what I'm doing.

Yes, Jesus?
Uh …
Well, sure
I'll do that.
Can't say I understand why.
But I'll do that.

Oh my!
Okay.
Whatever you say.
A new kind of fishing?
Leave what I know
for the complete unknown?
Trust only you?
With all due respect, Jesus,
I do need to say
Yes.

        —Carol Duerksen

PRAYING AND WALKING IN THE WORLD:

- What "new kind of fishing" is Jesus calling you to do?
- What might you have to leave behind to go fishing with Jesus?
- Pray for Jesus to help you cast out your net to go fishing for souls.

JANUARY 16 *(FOR CHILDREN AND FAMILIES)*

WHO DOES HE THINK HE IS?

PLUNGING INTO THE WORD:

Luke 5:17-26

PONDERING ON THE WAY:

One day, while Jesus was teaching, some guys showed up with a friend of theirs who was paralyzed. They'd heard that Jesus could heal people, so they brought their friend to Jesus to be healed. There was just one problem—the house was so full of people crowding around to hear Jesus, they couldn't get close to him.

Imagine you are those friends. What would you do to try to get your friend in to see Jesus? Any ideas how you could pull it off?

Here's what the men came up with. The houses in those days had flat roofs. They carried their friend up onto the roof, tore open the roof above where Jesus was standing, and then lowered the man who was paralyzed right down in front of Jesus! Pretty creative thinking, wasn't it?

What do you think Jesus did when he saw the man being dropped down in front of him?

Jesus was so impressed with the faith of the friends and their love for their friend, he looked at the man and said, "Your sins are forgiven." This really surprised everyone. The friends were surprised because they'd hoped the man could be healed and walk again. The religious people who were listening were surprised because they didn't see how anyone except God could forgive sins. They started muttering to each other, "Who does he think he is, anyway?"

Why do you think Jesus said, "Your sins are forgiven?" Who did he think he was?

Jesus knew who he was. He's the Son of God, so of course he can forgive sins! He is concerned about our souls **and** our bodies! That's why he performed so many miracles while he was on earth—to show people that he truly was the Son of God. He forgave the sins of the man who was paralyzed, and then he healed him so he could walk again! The man and his friends left the house, amazed at what had happened and praising God big time!

—*Carol Duerksen*

PRAYING AND WALKING IN THE WORLD:

- Who do you know that has received healing—either physical or emotional? Thank God!

- Do you have friends who would do anything for you? Are you that kind of friend?

INCLUDING THE EXCLUDED

PLUNGING INTO THE WORD:

Luke 5:27-32

PONDERING ON THE WAY:

A common thread runs through Luke's Gospel: Jesus included the excluded.

In this story, that thread brings Levi into the kingdom. Levi was a tax collector in a society that subjected its citizens to many taxes. Not only were citizens taxed heavily, but the system didn't prevent the persons collecting the taxes from pocketing a generous amount for themselves. So tax collectors, also known as publicans, were wealthy but despised people.

Jesus found one of those tax collectors, named Levi, sitting at his tax booth and said simply, "Follow me."

Levi left everything behind to obey Jesus. He also threw a party in honor of his new "employer." The only problem was, he invited other tax collectors and persons who were outcasts to be the guests at this party in Jesus' honor. The Pharisees and scribes just didn't get it.

"Why do you eat and drink with the scum of society?" they wanted to know.

Jesus' answer not only made it clear to whom his ministry is extended—it also forced the listeners to decide whether they were well or sick, righteous or sinner. Jesus' answer forces us to contemplate: Am I sitting at the table with Jesus and the outcasts, or am I standing beside the table criticizing?

And by the way, we're not talking cheap grace here. Yes, Jesus included the excluded, but there are also ethical expectations in God's kingdom. The opportunity to repent is a gift from God, and God expects sinners to accept that gift.

—*Carol Duerksen*

PRAYING AND WALKING IN THE WORLD:

- Be honest: Are you sitting at the table with Jesus and the outcasts, or are you standing beside the table?

- Pray about your spiritual health. Are you well or sick?

WORKS CITED

Interpretation, Luke, pages 77-79.

JANUARY 18

DIGGING IN OR DROOLING

PLUNGING INTO THE WORD:

Luke 5:33-39

PONDERING ON THE WAY:

When do you honor the old ways, and when do you celebrate the new?

When do traditions reign, and when is it time for new rituals? The issues we face in our personal faith journeys and congregations are nothing new. Jesus got asked the same questions, and this passage relates one of those times.

Fasting was one of the three good works of Judaism, and the question here was whether or not Jesus' followers were to fast. Jesus didn't give a black and white answer—he said it was a question of appropriateness, of what is fitting for a given occasion. "Not now while I'm here, but later when I'm gone."

Then he told a parable to expand upon his answer. Old wine doesn't belong in new wineskins; old garments aren't used to patch new ones. The disciples (and the early church, as Luke relates in the Book of Acts) had to decide which aspects of Judaism they would bring to their new faith, and which they would leave behind. Rituals of worship needed to grow out of their tradition, as well as their fledgling Christianity. This delicate balancing act could swing dramatically either way—abandoning everything of the past and drooling for all that is new, or digging in heels and refusing to move beyond "We've always done it this way."

This balance seems to involve both defending the faith and expanding the faith, holding on to core values and letting go of rigid thinking, celebrating where the church has come from and enthusiastically making plans to move forward. Our prayer must be that Jesus will guide us on this discovery journey of when "the old is good" (v. 39) and when it's time for new wineskins.

—*Carol Duerksen*

PRAYING AND WALKING IN THE WORLD:

- What aspects of your faith are core values you could never give up? What could you leave behind?

- What are some elements you admire about other denominations? How can you incorporate them into your spiritual journey?

JANUARY 19

THE SUNDAY TIMES

PLUNGING INTO THE WORD:

Luke 6:1-11

PONDERING ON THE WAY:

Three things here,
three simple uncomplicated straightforward
challenging
messages:

People first
Sabbath next
My agenda last

Respect the Sabbath
Rest
Exception being
The needs of people
It's never the wrong day
to help another human

Exception not being
The work
you didn't get done
last week

> —*Carol Duerksen*

PRAYING AND WALKING IN THE WORLD:

- What do you do with the Sabbath? What does it mean to you for the Son of Man to be Lord of your Sabbath?

- Read a book about the Sabbath. Here's a good one that changed what I do on the Sabbath: *Sabbath: Finding Rest, Renewal, and Delight in Our Busy Lives* by Wayne Muller.

JANUARY 20 *(FOR CHILDREN AND FAMILIES)*

FAITH HEALING

PLUNGING INTO THE WORD:

Luke 7:1-10

PONDERING ON THE WAY:

Think about a grown-up you really love and admire. It could be a parent, a teacher, a preacher or another adult who means a lot to you.

Now, imagine that one day you are playing with your friends when someone comes with an important message for you. The message comes from the grown-up you thought of a minute ago.

The message from that adult is simple: "I need to see you. Please come see me now."

Would you say: "I don't believe your message; I need to hear it from the grown-up directly, then I'll believe it"?

Or would you drop everything and go find out why this important adult in your life needs to see you?

You'd probably go. The word from the grown-up is so important to you, you don't have to hear it directly and in person. You go because you know it's important.

In today's Bible story, a military officer has a slave who is very sick. The military man believes that Jesus can heal his slave, so he sends some other officers to go tell Jesus. He doesn't ask Jesus to come see the slave—he simply believes that if Jesus says the word, the slave will be healed. The military man never meets Jesus, but he believes in him so strongly that he knows Jesus can heal his slave.

Jesus is amazed at this man's faith, and he heals the slave.

How does this apply to us today? None of us has met Jesus. We read about him in the Bible, but we haven't met him in person. That's where faith comes in—we have faith that Jesus is with us. We have faith that when Jesus says something, it is true and we need to do what he says.

You would drop everything to go when your favorite grown-ups call you because you have faith in them even when you don't see them. It's the same with Jesus. We may not have seen him in person, but we have faith in him and his word.

—*Carol Duerksen*

PRAYING AND WALKING IN THE WORLD:

- **Adults:** Who do you know who is very sick? Humble yourself before Jesus, knowing that though none of us deserves his attention but that he wants to minister to us. Pray for Jesus' presence and healing in that person's life.

- **Children:** What things frighten you? What has happened in your life that sometimes makes you unhappy? Faith means trusting Jesus even in scary times and even when you are unhappy with life. Can you pray to Jesus about those things?

JANUARY 21

WHAT DO MY FRIENDS LOOK LIKE?

PLUNGING INTO THE WORD:

Luke 7:18-35

PONDERING ON THE WAY:

Is this
what God's Messiah
looks like?

Is this what he does?

The sightless see blue skies,
lepers stroke new skin,
the lame leap,
ears that didn't, hear.
The dead live

Yes!
I like
that kind
of Messiah.
Give me more!

The poor
become heroes?
The outcasts
come in?
The rules breakers
rule?

No,
that's not
what I expect
a Messiah's friends
to look like.

But
if God's Messiah
is doing God's work
in the world,
and I claim to follow
this Jesus Messiah …
then
what do my friends
look like?

   —Carol Duerksen

PRAYING AND WALKING IN THE WORLD:

- What do your friends look like? Do they all look a lot like you?

- John the Baptist was "unusual," and so was Jesus. How "unusual" are you willing to be as you follow Jesus?

JANUARY 22

SELDOM OVERWHELMED

PLUNGING INTO THE WORD:

Luke 7:36-50

PONDERING ON THE WAY:

So … who are you in the story?

I'm Simon, the Pharisee in the story. Seriously, I am.

It's not all bad. Like Simon, I have asked Jesus to come to my house … in the spiritual sense of course. I have given appropriate, albeit surface, hospitality. I've done the things expected of me—in a Pharisee type way. Jesus has spoken to me, just like Simon, and just like Simon I've said, "Teacher, speak." I'm open to learning—you have to give me that.

But, I must admit, I've seldom cried over my past life. I've seldom wept with gratitude over what Jesus has done for me. This unnamed woman sobbed over Jesus before the crucifixion—before the miracle of the resurrection. She didn't need to see *The Passion of the Christ* to be overwhelmed with love and regret and gratitude.

I'm seldom overwhelmed—with anything anymore, much less my faith. Much less Jesus. Don't be too hard on yourself, you may be saying. Anointing someone's feet was more acceptable in that culture, you might be thinking. You're right, of course. But the expensive ointment? Crying so many tears that I could fill a basin and wash mud off his feet? Letting my hair get dirty? Kissing his feet like that?

Let's be honest. It's been awhile since I've been that overwhelmed, that filled with … love.

So what's the problem? I want to know because I don't want to be Simon. Forget all the good stuff, Simon was judgmental and downright rude. Jesus reserved some of his harshest words for people just like him. Their self-righteousness stunk to high heaven as much as any sexual sin imagined.

But how do you get that kind of gratitude? And I do think it's gratitude because, like the parable, the woman's sin already had been canceled. I can picture some earlier time—Jesus touching her hand, lifting up her chin so she could look into his eyes. I can hear Jesus say, "Your sins are forgiven." It's possible she could have been crying because of a huge weight of guilt—maybe it was both—but the love, says the parable, comes from the debt removal. And she had tons of love for Jesus.

So should I sin more, so I can be more grateful? God forbid, says Paul in Romans 6. If that's not the answer (and I'm fairly certain it's not) then what is?

Maybe … maybe I need to see myself as the woman. Maybe I need to open my eyes to my great debt, including my sin of self-righteousness, my sin of harsh judgmentalism. Maybe I need to face my own hypocrisy.

The key to renewed love and gratitude is not sinning more but being more sorrowful for the sinner I am. I need to realize the terrible wrongs I've committed. I need to acknowledge the things I've neglected to do. I need to admit to the times I've judged others and not myself.

Simon was so callous in his attitude toward Jesus that he didn't even provide the basic hospitality his culture deemed right. Oh, is that me? Isn't that sometimes … me?

Your faith has saved you, Jesus said to the woman. What does that mean? And what was Jesus saying to Simon and saying today to me? Your lack of faith (or love or gratitude) has condemned you?

God have mercy on me, a sinner.

—*Michele Hershberger*

PRAYING AND WALKING IN THE WORLD:

- List everything you can glean from the story about Simon. Now list everything you can glean from the story about the woman. Which one are you?

- Find a bottle of cologne or perfume. Then go to a quiet spot and list your sins on paper. Feel the sorrow of each sin. Will you, with God's help, really change? Your sins are forgiven, says Jesus. Pour out the perfume, onto the ground or into the sink. You are pouring it out on Jesus. He smiles with joy and love … and forgiveness—for you. Go in shalom.

JANUARY 23 *(FOR CHILDREN AND FAMILIES)*

PREPARING THE SOIL

PLUNGING INTO THE WORD:

Luke 8:1-15

PONDERING ON THE WAY:

Act out this story with your children:

- Once upon a time, a farmer *(adult or child)* went out to plant his seeds.

- He threw the seed this way and that way *(farmer throws out pretend seed)*.

- Now, some of the seed *(a child as a seed)* fell on the path where people walked, and the ground was hard, and the seeds could not go down.

- So the birds came and ate those seeds up.

- Other seeds *(child as a seed)* fell on some rocks.

- They began to grow *(child starts to "grow")*, but they didn't have enough water, and so they withered away *(child sinks to the ground)*.

- Some other seed *(child as a seed)* fell among the weeds, and when the seeds started to grow *(child starts to "grow")*, the weeds just choked them out *(child falls)*.

- Some other seed *(child)* fell on rich, beautiful dirt—dirt that was very healthy for the seeds.

- These seeds grew and grew and grew *(child grows tall)*, until they made even more seeds themselves.

> —*Michele Hershberger*

PRAYING AND WALKING IN THE WORLD:

Questions for children:

- You are like seeds in that you grow. Your bodies can grow big and strong if you choose to exercise and eat the right kinds of food. Can you name some foods that are good for your body?

- What are some good ways to work your muscles and practice running and moving?

- The thinking and feeling parts of you also can grow healthy and strong. Just like eating healthy food, you can make good choices and help these inside parts grow strong too. You can choose to listen to good stories in books like the Bible and turn away from bad stories, like some of the stories on TV. Can you think of other things you can do?

Question for parents:

- What can you do to "prepare the soil in your own life and in the lives of your children?

JANUARY 24

YOU FELL ASLEEP

PLUNGING INTO THE WORD:

Luke 8:22-25

PONDERING ON THE WAY:

You fell asleep? What's that supposed to mean?

Oh, I know.
You were trying to teach them a lesson.

Not necessarily?
You were tired.

Oh.

Still and all it was
Too much,
a dirty trick.
They obeyed you, didn't they?
Trusted you—
They put out.

Isn't that enough?

Storms come up, I understand
Storms happen, okay yes I know, but
The boat was taking water, Peter was bailing with all he's got
the others too and the wind bit their faces, shrieking
Gales from every direction.
They were shrieking too, screaming your name.
Chilled to the bone.

How can you sleep through that?

See, I can't sleep. Hurricanes dump on me, problems at work, tornadoes touch
down and pick me up.
I look up to see a wall of water coming toward the shore.
A wall of water is my home

(When 200,000 people died from the tsunami that one December,
dripping walls of horror filled their vision too)

Where were you?

Taking a power nap?

Okay. I'm sorry. You did
Wake up. Was your bed sea water-soaked?
Or was it their voices like thunder in your ears?

Or did you sleep at all?

Do you fall asleep on me?
Do you rebuke the tsunamis in my soul or my lack of faith?
Or both?

Do I really want you awake in my boat?
I'm treading water here.

Wake up.

> —*Michele Hershberger*

PRAYING AND WALKING IN THE WORLD:

- On what stormy sea are you adrift?

- What are you more afraid of—the storm, or Jesus sleeping on you? Or a fully awake Jesus?

JANUARY 25

TORTURED

PLUNGING INTO THE WORD:

Luke 8:26-39

PONDERING ON THE WAY:

Some people are plagued. Tortured. Tormented in their minds. There could be a myriad reasons. And for whatever reason, society deems them unclean. They have a bad reputation, a difficult past; they have AIDS or gonorrhea, a mental illness. Maybe they have a demon, a real demon that tortures them night and day.

I would imagine this describes more people than we want to admit. Maybe it's true for me—or you.

There are consequences, of course, for this torment. There is added misery bestowed upon them—upon us—by a well-meaning society. These people get sent away. Punished. Ostracized to the tombs. Stripped naked. Chained up. Asked mean questions. Gaped at.

Ignored.

Was the man in the tombs in Luke 8 unclean because of his demons or the pigs or because of the tombs themselves? Which came first? And was it his fault? Partly his fault? Is it my fault or yours? Does it really matter?

Maybe not.

Sometimes there are legions of problems, layers of stuff that get tangled up in chains of despair. Sometimes it's so complicated you don't have a name anymore.

So along comes Jesus (or Jesus working through one of his followers), and that just adds to the misery. "You gonna torture me too, huh, Jesus?" Is that you talking, Jesus—or the demons?

How can Jesus be both threat and hope? Deliverance and agony? Do I want to be rescued? Really?

And then you watch your demons charge off an embankment and into the sea. Drowned. Gone. What does it mean to be free?

Well, the swineherds in your neighborhood aren't happy. There's money to be made off of misery. Nobody likes to lose money. So they call the others, and there may be more gawking, more fear—you may still be ostracized. And of course, so will Jesus because he messed up the equilibrium. He messed up the balance of clean and unclean people, good and bad. He changed the rules because now you're dressed and calm and in your right mind.

That makes people afraid. They may ask Jesus to leave.

And you'll want to go with him, but he'll ask you to stay—to help the others. And you will. You see, there are lots of tormented, unclean people. And Jesus came to set them free.

—*Michele Hershberger*

PRAYING AND WALKING IN THE WORLD:

- Do you really want to be rescued?

- Would you rather be harassed or ignored? Why?

- Is there an unhealthy disequilibrium in your town? Are people free to change? Do you benefit from the status quo?

- Who are you in this story? Who do you want to be?

JANUARY 26

HEALING IN HIS WINGS

PLUNGING INTO THE WORD:

Luke 8:40-56

PONDERING ON THE WAY:

Did you ever wonder why the woman in this story, the bleeding woman, touched the edge of Jesus' cloak? What an odd detail for the writer of Luke to remember. What happened? Did she trip and fall and then, in desperation, grab the only part of Jesus she could reach? Is perseverance the point of this story? Those who push their way through a crowd will find the healing they need?

It makes for a nice moral, but it's not quite true. Every Torah-observant Jew wore a prayer shawl, and on the bottom edge of the prayer shawl, according to Numbers 15:37, was fringe, or *tzitzit*. Persons were encouraged to hold their tzitzit in their hands—five strands for the five books of Torah knotted four times for the four sacred letters of the name of God—as a tactile way of remembering who they were. They were God's beloved children, always and forever.

So the fringe of a prayer shawl was important, and the Messiah's tzitzit even more so. The Jews believed that Messiah's tzitzit, according to Malachi 4:2, had healing power. Just like the sun of righteousness had healing in its wings, so too would Messiah have healing powers in his *canaf*—his prayer shawl or wings.

The bleeding woman believed Jesus was Messiah. This was no accident, no stumble amidst the crowd. She knew what she had to do—and she did it.

Jesus knew it too, and knew that she had to be called out. Her act of faith and her healing must be made public, for she suffered not only from a physical condition, but from a social illness too. Bleeding women were considered unclean. They could not worship in the temple. And anyone they touched became unclean too.

But not Jesus. Not Messiah. His power was so great that it overcame all impurity, even hers.

Even mine. Even yours. Believe in the Messiah. Touch the fringe.

—*Michele Hershberger*

PRAYING AND WALKING IN THE WORLD:

- Lie on the floor and pray for whatever is dying in your loved ones. Ask in faith, knowing that Jesus hears you.

- Find a scarf or shawl that has fringe on it. Wrap the tassels around your fingers. Feel the threads. God knows that we as humans need physical ways of connecting. Ask Jesus to help you believe.

- If the purity of Jesus can overcome the impurity of a bleeding woman and a corpse, what does that mean for you? Can Jesus pronounce you clean? Will you let him?

JANUARY 27

THE WALLET BIOGRAPHY

PLUNGING INTO THE WORD:

Luke 9:1-9

PONDERING ON THE WAY:

Take your wallet, billfold, purse, or briefcase—whatever is handy and represents you in your everyday life—and do a quick inventory. Empty the contents out on the table or floor and look to see what you have right now.

What things do you see that aren't usually there? What do these things represent? Extra stress? A special joy?

What things are there that are always there—money, credit cards, drivers license, a stick of gum? How do these items represent your discipleship? Should any of these things not be there? What items should be added?

Look again at the story. Have you been sent out? No matter what career you have, are you in the business of proclaiming the kingdom of God? The business of healing? Who has God healed lately—through you?

Why do you think Jesus asked the twelve to leave behind all staffs, bags, bread, extra tunics, and money? What is Jesus calling you to leave behind?

—*Michele Hershberger*

PRAYING AND WALKING IN THE WORLD:

- If a biographer was writing your story today, what story would your wallet tell?

JANUARY 28 *(FOR CHILDREN AND FAMILIES)*

JESUS HELPS OTHERS THROUGH US

PLUNGING INTO THE WORD:

Luke 9:10-17

PONDERING ON THE WAY:

Needed for this story: A loaf of bread or other food item to share together.

What is a miracle? (A simple definition is: when something impossible happens.)

Have you ever made a miracle happen? (No, only God can do that.)

Has God ever asked you to help with a miracle? Listen to this story and try to find the part of the story where Jesus asked his friends to help him.

Read Luke 9:10-17.

What was the miracle of the story? Why did Jesus make this miracle happen? (He loved them.) There are a lot of people in a crowd of more than five thousand. How big does a building need to be to handle five thousand people?

Could Jesus have done the miracle all by himself? Then why do you think he gave the food to his friends to give to the people? (Jesus wanted them to feel his love too—that they were special and important to them.)

Jesus wants to use us today to help him do miracles. One of the reasons we pray is to listen and hear Jesus tell us what he wants us to do.

Let's take this bread and bless each other with it. _____ (name of a child), will you take this and break off a piece for everyone? When you give everyone the piece of bread, I want you to say, "Jesus loves you and I do too!"

—*Michele Hershberger*

PRAYING AND WALKING IN THE WORLD:

- **Adults:** When was the last time Jesus looked at you and said, "You give them something to eat"? Can you trust that Jesus will supply what you need as you minister to others?

- Jesus not only supplies our needs and the needs of others around us. There are leftovers. Name some "leftovers" you are thankful for.

- **Children:** Can you think of someone who might like a visit from you? Do you know of a grandma or grandpa who would love to see you? Maybe you can take them some cookies or a loaf of bread.

JANUARY 29

GROUP SHOWER, PERSONAL BATH

PLUNGING INTO THE WORD:

Luke 9:18-27

PONDERING ON THE WAY:

My baptism day at Manson (Iowa) Mennonite Church was memorable, though incomplete. I still remember the white lace dress, the *Living Bible* engraved with my name in gold letters, the lukewarm water trickling down my hair and dotting the red carpet. I joined the other junior high kids as we made a chorus line in front of the sanctuary.

It seems like my baptism was more like a group shower than a personal bath. The experience held the seed of a committed Christian life. But for me as a thirteen-year-old, it was marked more by communal belonging than personal believing. I feared being left by my peers more than I felt a fervent desire to follow Jesus.

In today's Scripture passage, Jesus seemed to understand the way human beings can flock together rather than stand out and up for what they believe. To draw them out from the group as individuals, he posed two questions in verses 18-21: "Who do the crowds say I am?" and "Who do you say I am?"

They all answered the first question, spouting out such names as John the Baptist and Elijah. Only Peter had the nerve to answer the second question: "The Messiah of God." Jesus answers Peter's confession with his own confession, which he directed to the group (vv. 23-24): "If any want to become my followers, let them deny themselves and take up their cross daily and follow me. For those who want to save their life will lose it, and those who lose their life for my sake will save it."

At thirteen, I couldn't begin to understand this kind of personal commitment and discipleship. God knew this and didn't expect more than I could give. But whether we are thirteen, forty-three, sixty-three, or ninety-three, Jesus calls us out of the nameless chorus line into a face-to-face "dance" with him.

—*Laurie Oswald Robinson*

PRAYING AND WALKING IN THE WORLD:

- Reflect on your own baptism day: Who was there, what did you see, what did you feel, how did it change your life—or not?

- Pray about some ways you can bring the meaning of your baptism into daily life.

- If you are a young person yet to be baptized, seek out an adult to talk about what it means; if you are an older baptized person, seek out a young person whom you can support in the experience.

JANUARY 30

TIDE AND THE TRANSFIGURATION

PLUNGING INTO THE WORD:

Luke 9:28-36

PONDERING ON THE WAY:

When I'm in a more irreverent frame of mind, the Transfiguration scene conjures up for me cheesy detergent commercials. Two women hold up white shirts, one washed with Tide and the other with another leading brand. We are supposed to see the shirt washed with Tide as gleaming, dazzling; and the other shirt as lackluster, a dull white-gray. It is hard to tell which is which, but as North American consumers, we are supposed to believe Tide wins.

Peter, James, and John didn't have anything to compare with Jesus' dazzling white clothing. The commentary in my *NRSV* translation says that "dazzling white" signified the color of heavenly garments. In other words, there was no earthly comparison to heavenly transformation. So to bring this back down to earth, Peter, after seeing Moses and Elijah with Jesus, says in verse 33, "Master, it is good for us to be here; let us make three dwellings, one for you, one for Moses and one for Elijah."

Maybe feeling out of control, he wanted to corral the glory and make it more manageable. But glory can't be contained. In verse 34 we read, "A cloud came and overshadowed them; and they were terrified as they entered the cloud." In the midst of the cloud they heard a voice say, "This is my Son, my Chosen; listen to him!"

Peter got a lot more than he bargained for after his confession of Jesus as the Messiah of God. He got heaven. He got authority. He got a color he had no earthly word for and that no earthly remedy could make as bright. He wanted Tide but got Transfiguration, with which no leading brand of human effort will ever compare.

—*Laurie Oswald Robinson*

PRAYING AND WALKING IN THE WORLD:

- Close your eyes and imagine you were there with Jesus, Peter, James, and John. How would you respond to the dazzling white garment? The glowing face of Jesus? The glory in the shadow of the cloud?

- Pray for God to reveal those areas of life you want to control and contain rather than yield to cross-carrying, suffering, and sacrifice. Then ask for grace to become more open to Transfiguration and less prone to reach for Tide-like remedies.

- Discuss with your faith community how you could mark this Transfiguration event with a ritual, drama, or music during Sunday morning worship or during other gatherings, such as cell or small group meetings.

JANUARY 31 *(FOR CHILDREN AND FAMILIES)*

LITTLE KID, BIG DEAL

PLUNGING INTO THE WORD:

Luke 9:46-50

PONDERING ON THE WAY:

My sister Jane is a grandma. One evening after supper, her children and grandchildren put on a talent show. Cousins and aunts and uncles sang songs and did dances. Caleb, three, shouted, "I want to show you what Grandma taught me the other day!" He wiggled up onto the piano bench and with his index finger pounded hard on middle C. "See!" He beamed. "I can play the piano too!"

Some of the acts included things only big kids could do. But it was Caleb's act that seemed to bring the most joy to his grandma's heart. He didn't play guitar like Uncle Seth or sing like Cousin Neva. But he could share what his grandma taught him.

In Luke, Jesus' disciples argue about who among them would be the greatest. Jesus took a little child by his side and said, "Whoever welcomes this child in my name welcomes me, and whoever welcomes me welcomes the one who sent me; for the least among you is the greatest."

Jesus reminds us that little people are a big deal to him, even though the world sometimes considers a little kid to be a little deal. No matter how tall you are or how many talents you have, Jesus accepts and welcomes you. So when you feel small inside, remember how big you are in Jesus' eyes!

—*Laurie Oswald Robinson*

PRAYING AND WALKING IN THE WORLD:

- How many children are in your family? Are you the smallest, the biggest, or the one in the middle? Pray a prayer of thanks that God made you who you are.

- Draw or paint a picture of today's Bible story and put it on your refrigerator as a reminder that Jesus welcomes you, no matter what your size or talent.

- Ask your parents to take you to visit a big person this week, either a grandparent or an elderly person in the nursing home. As a little kid, you can be a big blessing to an elderly adult.

FEBRUARY 1

FIRE FROM HEAVEN, FIRE IN THE BELLY

PLUNGING INTO THE WORD:

Luke 9:50-56

PONDERING ON THE WAY:

One morning in the Wichita, Kansas, airport, I saw a family saying good-bye to their son, husband, and father. He wore U.S. Army fatigues and cried as he held two daughters in his arms. Tears rolled down their tiny faces as my eyes and those of others grew red with tears, even though he and his family were strangers to us. We knew that if circumstances were different, he could be our father, our brother, our uncle.

As he peeled away from loved ones and boarded the plane for Iraq, I felt angry about soldiers having to leave the haven of family for the horrors of war. Our government sends troops into another country to seemingly spread democracy and freedom. But all this war effort seems to spread is pain and suffering. Like James and John in verse 54, I wanted Jesus to do something drastic to end this killing. I wouldn't want him to command fire down from heaven upon our nation. But I did feel the fire of anger in my belly toward U.S. leaders, and I wanted Jesus to mete out justice.

I believe Jesus would rebuke my anger, just as he rebuked the disciples' desire for revenge against the village that failed to receive him. He was determined to fulfill his mission, as the passage tells us he "set his face to go to Jerusalem." But even though he was radically committed to this direction, his mission would never include retaliation against enemies. Then, and in the days ahead, he modeled what it meant to follow him on the journey with peaceful rather than painful steps.

We know the end of his story; instead of calling down fire on those who crucified him once he arrived at Jerusalem, he spread out his arms and died. But we don't know what happened to the young soldier, and we don't know what to do with the hatred in our own souls. So we pray to walk in peace on this journey with Jesus, the Prince of Peace, even as fires of war—and fires in the belly—continue to burn.

—*Laurie Oswald Robinson*

PRAYING AND WALKING IN THE WORLD:

- Reflect on soldiers and their families you may know personally or have read about in the newspaper. Take some time to pray for peace in their lives.

- Pray for governments around the world to begin choosing to walk their journeys in peace and forgiveness rather than pain and hate.

- Today, model one peaceful action or attitude toward a person or a situation that makes you feel like retaliating.

FEBRUARY 2

FORK IN THE ROAD

PLUNGING INTO THE WORD:

Luke 9:57-62

PONDERING ON THE WAY:

Saint Francis of Assisi, born in Italy around 1181, was a follower of Jesus in the Middle Ages. Saint Francis often is depicted in statuary with birds alighting on his open hands and critters cuddling at his feet. Stories detail how animals of the forest felt no fear of this peace-loving man.

Other parts of his story are less pastoral and more passionate. His choice to follow Jesus through a life of poverty led to a painful encounter with his rich father. Francis stripped himself of his clothes and handed them to his father, saying, "Until now, I have called you my father on earth; now, I desire to say only 'Our Father in Heaven.'" After doing this, he forever left a life of privilege to embrace a life of poverty. He established a following of men, all of whom ministered to the poor and disenfranchised.

In today's passage, Jesus' would-be followers faced a similar fork in the road. They were in the process of counting the cost of being a disciple when Jesus tallied up a shocking score. In verses 59-60 we read, "To another he said, 'Follow me.' But he said, 'Lord, let me first go and bury my father.' But Jesus said to him, 'Let the dead bury their own dead; but as for you, go and proclaim the kingdom of God.'"

Some mission workers in distant lands have missed parents' funerals because they could not get home on time, but this experience is less common in this age of easy travel. Nor is it likely we will have to strip ourselves bare in order to be faithful or to prove a point. Nevertheless, Jesus' intent for each believer seems to be the same; our main priority needs to be proclaiming the kingdom and not pursuing our comforts. Like Saint Francis, Jesus' father is now our father, which makes heaven our final home.

—*Laurie Oswald Robinson*

PRAYING AND WALKING IN THE WORLD:

- Spend some time in prayer and reflection today about what "creature comforts" distract you from proclaiming God's kingdom. Pick one of those comforts to forego this week as a way to be mindful of faithful people who sacrificed for Jesus.

- Go to your local bookstore or library and choose a book on the saints to read this month in preparation for Lent.

- Who in your world is facing struggles with their family because of faith issues? If this person is in your community, reach out to them this week. If they live far away or in another country, write an encouraging note via snail mail or e-mail.

FEBRUARY 3 *(FOR CHILDREN AND FAMILIES)*

GOOD SAMARITAN SWIMMING

PLUNGING INTO THE WORD:

Luke 10:25-37

PONDERING ON THE WAY:

When I was in junior high, my Caucasian family invited an African-American child from Omaha, Nebraska, to spend time in our home in Iowa. In the privacy of my house, we giggled until midnight, played with my cousins and enjoyed picnics with my parents. Our different skin colors didn't matter. We were just two young girls enjoying the summer.

That feeling changed the day we went swimming at the town pool. I became self-conscious about our new friendship. Sheila's* dark skin contrasted with the dozens of white bodies splashing in the water. I brought a person into our community who was very different from us, maybe even seen as weird. Did that make me a weirdo too?

Sheila stepped onto the high dive and yelled, "Watch, Laurie!" Even though I was up to my chin in cold water, I felt hot and embarrassed. I must choose: Would I answer her or would I ignore her? Somehow, I found the courage to yell back, "Way to go!"

Perhaps that choice is like the choice the good Samaritan made in today's Bible story. The Samaritan people were outcasts in the eyes of Jews. But the Samaritan is the one who stopped to help the wounded man along the roadside. His kindness perhaps was rejected later when the wounded man became well and found out he had been helped by an outcast. But the Samaritan took a risk anyway.

Sheila wasn't a total stranger, nor was she wounded. But in choosing to respond to her rather than ignore her, I took a risk. Sometimes Jesus calls us to take a risk when we want to save face. Becoming a weirdo for the sake of befriending someone who is considered weird isn't cool in the world's eyes. But in Jesus' eyes, it is being a good neighbor.

* name changed

—*Laurie Oswald Robinson*

PRAYING AND WALKING IN THE WORLD:

- Reflect on what it means to take a risk in befriending someone who has no friends. Look up the word *risk* in the dictionary to help you understand what that means.

- Ask Jesus to help you become more of a good neighbor in your school and in your community.

- Is there someone in your school who has no friends? Take a risk and ask them to come over for pizza and a movie at your house some evening within the next month.

FEBRUARY 4

MARY, MARTHA, AND MYERS-BRIGGS

PLUNGING INTO THE WORD:

Luke 10:38-42

PONDERING ON THE WAY:

Personality tests reveal the way one "does life." For example, the Myers-Briggs test has four categories: introversion-extroversion, intuitive-sensing, feeling-thinking, and judging-perceiving. Friends or lovers who want to deepen their relationship take the tests to discover whether they are an ENFP (extrovert, intuitive, feeling, perceiving) or an ISTJ (introvert, sensing, thinking, judging), or any of the other combinations.

It's a tool that can help them work on understanding and complementing each other. In the first category, for example, introverts get energy from being alone, and extroverts get energy from being with others. In the fourth category, judgers like to nail things down, whereas perceivers want to gather more and more information before making decisions.

In today's passage, Martha was perhaps an E and J who chatted with a dozen people a day, worked her fingers to the bone, and crossed tasks off her to-do list. Mary, probably an I and a P, sat at the feet of Jesus, gathered information about her Savior, and daydreamed about a poem she could compose in her journal about this amazing man.

After Martha complains to Jesus about Mary, it seems Jesus prefers Mary's personality over Martha's. But verses 41-42 seem to point to the problem of worry rather than a preference for being versus doing. He says, "Martha, Martha, you are worried and distracted by many things; there is need of only one thing. Mary has chosen the better part, which will not be taken away from her."

What is the "better part" Jesus is talking about? I have a hunch it is the part of any personality type focused on staying in the moment, being present to the present, setting aside worries about tomorrow in favor of attention to God's movement today. That kind of attention doesn't only belong to the P's of this world. It can belong to anyone who lets go of self to listen to Jesus—whether in the hubbub of action or the quiet of contemplation.

—Laurie Oswald Robinson

PRAYING AND WALKING IN THE WORLD:

- Reflect on what is worrying and distracting you today. During prayer, open and lift up your hands, imagining you are placing all your worries in God's hands.

- If you haven't taken the Myers-Briggs personality test, do so. If you have, take a short refresher about your preferences. Then thank God for creating you as you.

- Take some time today to sit at Jesus' feet in silence, listening for whatever he has to say. Don't act on it. Just absorb it for today.

FEBRUARY 5

YOUR OWN LORD'S PRAYER

PLUNGING INTO THE WORD:

Luke 11:1-4

PONDERING ON THE WAY:

Most of us know the Lord's Prayer by memory, but I dare say, few of us pray it every day. And even if we did, perhaps its familiarity keeps us from truly thinking about what it means.

My personal version of today's verses would look like this:

> God,
> Show me yourself.
> Show me how you are in control of the world
> Because it's not looking very good right now.
> Show me that somehow your purposes are being worked out
> Because, to be honest, it just isn't very obvious.
>
> Thanks for providing me with food.
> Help me to make wise choices in feeding my body.
>
> Forgive me
> For being more interested in being forgiven
> Than in forgiving others.
>
> Keep me from the damage I can do to myself
> And the violence the forces of evil can bring upon me.

Eugene Peterson's version in *The Message* goes like this:

> "Father,
> Reveal who you are.
> Set the world right.
> Keep us alive with three square meals.
> Keep us forgiven with you and forgiving others.
> Keep us safe from ourselves and the Devil."

The disciples asked Jesus to teach them how to pray. We should do no less.

—*Carol Duerksen*

PRAYING AND WALKING IN THE WORLD:

- Pray the Eugene Peterson version of the Lord's Prayer. Pray it at least once every day this week. As you pray, pause after each line. What is each line saying to you, your life, each day?

- Write your own version of the Lord's prayer.

FEBRUARY 6 *(FOR CHILDREN AND FAMILIES)*

BREAKFAST SPIDERS?

PLUNGING INTO THE WORD:

Luke 11:5-13

PONDERING ON THE WAY:

Do you like to eat fish? Or would you prefer a hamburger? Or maybe macaroni and cheese? What is your favorite food?

Imagine asking your mom and dad for that favorite food. You hear them in the kitchen, making the meal. You wash your hands, sit down at the table, your mom or dad comes out of the kitchen with a covered pot and sets it down in front of you. You take off the lid and see ... A SNAKE!

Imagine telling your mom or dad that you'd like some scrambled eggs for breakfast. They smile and go to the kitchen and start making breakfast. When they call you to the table for breakfast, you look at your plate. What do you see? A BIG NASTY SPIDER!

Does this seem very strange? Would your parents play a trick like that on you?

This is a story that Jesus told. Do you have any idea what point he was trying to make with that story?

Jesus is saying that parents give their children good gifts, not bad gifts. And then he goes on to say that if parents, who are human and make mistakes, want to do their best for their children, how much more will God, who is perfect, give good gifts to his children!

Now, what do you think is the best gift God could give you?

The best gift God can give us is God's Spirit in our lives. God's Spirit isn't something you can see, touch, taste, or smell like food—God's Spirit is something you feel inside your heart. And just as you ask your parents for good food, you can ask God for the Spirit in your heart, and God will answer your prayer.

—*Carol Duerksen*

PRAYING AND WALKING IN THE WORLD:

- Adults, make a gratitude journal of God's gifts in your life. Next time you are tempted to be negative or focused on what you don't have or what is going wrong, go to your gratitude journal.

- Have you asked God for the Holy Spirit to inundate your life?

- Ask God to help instill in you the same level of trust that a child has with loving parents.

FEBRUARY 7

SWEEPING YOUR SPIRITUAL HOUSE

PLUNGING INTO THE WORD:

Luke 11:14-28

PONDERING ON THE WAY:

Inquiring minds want to know! But **what** they want to know may change, depending on culture and context. Inquiring minds in today's world, when we see magical or unusual events, ask: "Did it really happen? How did it happen?" Inquiring minds in the day of Jesus didn't question if or how. They asked, "Who did it? Whose power was it?"

When asked "Who did it?" in this healing story, Jesus had an opportunity to answer with logic, with a comparison, and with a challenge. Logically speaking: "Why would Satan work against himself?" Comparatively speaking: "What power do exorcists use?" And finally, the challenge: "If I work by the finger of God, then the kingdom of God has come."

Culture and context don't figure as heavily into the next segment of this passage. Jesus says that when we "clean house" in our spiritual lives, we must fill the empty rooms with good, or the bad will return sevenfold. That principle of humanity hasn't changed through the generations. Getting rid of sinful influences in our lives is only half the battle—we must replace them with positive input. An empty house won't remain empty. Something will move in. If we don't want seven uglier friends to take up residence, we'd better invite the beautiful people in first.

—Carol Duerksen

PRAYING AND WALKING IN THE WORLD:

- Take some time to sweep out your spiritual house. Invite Jesus, the healer, to walk through the rooms with you. What does he see in the room where you eat? Where you interact with your family? Where you sleep? Where you relax? What does he want to clean up?

- Now, what does Jesus want you to put back into those rooms? Go through each room again, redecorating it with the Jesus touch.

FEBRUARY 8

WOE TO YOU!

PLUNGING INTO THE WORD:

Luke 11:37-53

PONDERING ON THE WAY:

My friend invited me to dine with her the other day, so we met, gathered up our pizza, salad, and sodas and took our places at the table. We talked, as we often do, about faith. We talked about people whose beliefs are similar to ours and those whose faith perspectives are different from ours.

And she said, "I know some people who are very liberal and accepting of others, but the thing is, they aren't at all tolerant of people who don't agree with them." And we talked about that. How is it that, whether we fit into the "liberal" or "conservative" box or any number of places in between, we can't give other people the space to believe differently? How is it that we lose our self-critiquing ability?

That's what Jesus is critiquing in this passage: the Pharisees' inability to do self-evaluation and correction. And the very fact that Luke relates this story proves that the problem continued into the church of Luke's time. Luke reports this mealtime conversation in the hopes that the church of his day will take notice for themselves.

So now we read it more than 2000 years later. Much has changed. And some things haven't changed at all.

—Carol Duerksen

PRAYING AND WALKING IN THE WORLD:

- Read the passage again. Take notice of it for yourself. Put yourself at the end of Jesus' "Woe to you!" Forget about the people you think should be on the receiving end of that phrase. Leave that up to God. It's not like God hasn't seen this from God's people before.

FEBRUARY 9

HOURS IN THE DAY

PLUNGING INTO THE WORD:

Luke 12:13-21

PONDERING ON THE WAY:

The organizational skills
of one certain middle-class woman
came to the attention of her supervisor
who
promoted her
and she
started climbing
the ladder.

It did mean
extra work
of course.
Longer hours
but that's what you do
to climb.

Sundays
became catch-up days
for shopping, laundry
and personal errands.

Family meals
happened in the new SUV
along with a DVD.

She tried not to think about work
in the new hot tub
beside her husband
at the end of the day
But she did.

The church wondered
could she organize
the yearly benefit auction?
She certainly could,
but she declined.
There just aren't enough hours in the day
she said.

Her last hour
alone
in the SUV
coming home late
from work,
She never had a chance to react
to the drunk driver
coming head on.

—*Carol Duerksen*

PRAYING AND WALKING IN THE WORLD:

- How do you spend your hours?

- Imagine someone is writing your obituary. What would be written about how you spent your life? Are there changes you'd like to make now?

- Are you "rich toward God"?

FEBRUARY 10 *(FOR CHILDREN AND FAMILIES)*

I CAN SLEEP ON WINDY NIGHTS

PLUNGING INTO THE WORD:

Luke 12:35-40

PONDERING ON THE WAY:

Our Bible story today is about staying awake, but I'd like to tell a story about a boy named Victor who stayed asleep.

Victor wanted to earn some money, so he went to a cattle show, hoping that a farmer would be looking for a boy to help him on his farm. Sure enough, there were farmers looking for hired hands, but there were also other boys hoping to be hired.

A farmer came up to Victor and asked, "What do you know about farm work?"

Victor answered, "I can sleep on windy nights."

"What?" the farmer asked.

"I can sleep on windy nights," Victor repeated.

Well, that didn't impress the farmer at all—he figured Victor must be stupid or something, and he left to go talk to other boys.

But he was so curious about Victor that he came back. Victor looked strong and honest, so the farmer thought he'd be a good hired hand on his farm. He asked the question one more time, and again Victor said, "I can sleep on windy nights."

The farmer decided to hire Victor even if he didn't understand what he was talking about. And Victor was great—he did a really good job with the animals and the other farm chores.

But one night something happened. During the night, a huge windstorm came up, and it woke the farmer. He began to worry about his cattle, his haystacks, and his barn. He hurried to Victor's room to wake him.

"Wake up!" he shouted. "Can't you hear the wind? We have to go see what's happening to the cattle and the hay and the barn!"

But Victor was sound asleep, and he wouldn't wake up.

"I'll fire him in the morning!" the farmer said as he stormed out of the room and out into the farmyard.

He ran to the barn. He expected to find doors banging and being torn off their hinges. But the doors were all closed tight and bolted shut.

What about the cattle? He expected to find them out in the wind, but when he opened the barn door, he found them standing calmly in their pens.

What about the haystacks? He expected to find them blown away. Instead, he found them covered with a big tarp, and nothing had blown away.

He searched his whole property, always expecting to find something wrong, and always everything was all right.

He finally went inside, dripping wet from the horrible rain and wind storm. He went to Victor's room and looked in. Victor was still sound asleep.

And then he knew the meaning of Victor's words, "I can sleep on windy nights."

Victor was so faithful in his work, he had nothing to worry about.

> —*Carol Duerksen* *Based on a story from* Uncle Arthur's Bedtime Stories, Volume One, *by Arthur S. Maxwell, copyright © 1950, Review and Herald Publishing Association.*

PRAYING AND WALKING IN THE WORLD:

- Our Bible story is about being ready for the return of Jesus. Because we don't know when that will happen, just like Victor didn't know which night the storm would come, it is important that we are always prepared. What does that mean—to always be prepared?

- Adults: One answer of what it means to "be prepared" could be found in Micah 6:8: "Do justice, and to love kindness, and to walk humbly with your God."

  How prepared are you?

FEBRUARY 11

MUCH GIVEN, MUCH REQUIRED

PLUNGING INTO THE WORD:

Luke 12:41-48

PONDERING ON THE WAY:

I have been blessed beyond measure or comprehension. Here is my short list.

My parents infused us with unconditional love and discipline, with humility and self-confidence. I simply can't find fault with the atmosphere they surrounded us with as children. (My perspective was quite different as a teen, but that's another story.)

Today I am blessed with a husband of twenty-five years who also loves me unconditionally, gives me both space and support, and brings laughter and vitality into the life of this introverted writer. Together, we own 120 acres of Kansas prairie paradise that's inhabited by wildlife, as well as lots of not-so-wild life that we have invited to live with us.

We are members of Tabor Mennonite Church, a congregation that has nurtured and supported us, given us a setting to worship God, and given us opportunities to share our gifts.

We have seventeen former exchange students who immensely enriched our lives and are now living (some with their own children) in Germany, Norway, Sweden, Hong Kong, and Czech Republic.

Maynard and I both enjoy our jobs. We both experience excellent health.

I could go on and on. Much has been given to me. Jesus says that "from everyone to whom much has been given, much will be required."

Lord, help me to keep my part of the deal.

—Carol Duerksen

PRAYING AND WALKING IN THE WORLD:

- Make a list of what God has given you. How have you been blessed? How are you giving back? What more could you do?

- Thank God for everything on your list and for those things you have been giving back. Ask God to work in your heart and mind to continue to find new ways to give.

- Reflect on how you have been using your gifts to build the kingdom of God and to be ready for the return of Jesus.

FEBRUARY 12

REPENT

PLUNGING INTO THE WORD:

Luke 13:1-9

PONDERING ON THE WAY:

At that very time there were some present who told him about the
three thousand trapped in the World Trade Center on
September 11, 2001.
He asked them, "Do you think because
these people suffered in this way they were
worse sinners than the other New Yorkers,
working in their shops or traveling on the subway?

"No, I tell you, but unless you repent, you will perish as they did.

"Or what about those eighteen miners
caught in an underground explosion—do you think
they were worse offenders than
the others living in West Virginia? No, I tell you
but unless you repent, you will all perish as they did."

Jesus made his point and, after the fig tree story, started to walk away.
But I stopped him and said, "What about the children
starving in Darfur or the AIDS crisis or the war in Iraq with all those
civilians being killed and—"

"Exactly," he said.
Repent.

—*Michele Hershberger*

PRAYING AND WALKING IN THE WORLD:

- Is it okay to ask God why certain people suffer? Is it okay if you don't receive a full answer?

- Are you like the fig tree, given an extra year of grace? Will God ever say to you, "Enough already!"?

- Is God fifty percent merciful and fifty percent holy? Or seventy percent holy and thirty percent merciful? Can God be one hundred percent of both?

FEBRUARY 13

EIGHTEEN YEARS

PLUNGING INTO THE WORD:

Luke 13:10-17

PONDERING ON THE WAY:

So why couldn't Jesus have waited one day? I've always wondered that. The woman, stooped by a spirit—who knows what—had waited eighteen years. What's one more day? Really?

The official religious leaders were so angry. Why mess with their minds like this? Why pour salt in the wound? Why would you purposefully heal on the one day you weren't supposed to?

Why not take the woman aside and whisper, "Meet me here tomorrow, same time. I'll heal you then."

Why not?

Because he is Lord of the Sabbath.

That's why.

Because it had been eighteen years.

That's why.

—Michele Hershberger

PRAYING AND WALKING IN THE WORLD:

- What does Sabbath mean to you?

- What are some of the religious rules in your life that might miss the point if you aren't careful? What are you going to do about it?

- Who in your life has suffered long enough? Can you bring this person to Jesus, no matter what day it is?

REMEMBERING SARAH

PLUNGING INTO THE WORD:

Luke 14:1-6

PONDERING ON THE WAY:

I will always remember Sarah. She lived next door to me years ago—a big woman, with just a touch of five o'clock shadow on her chin and cheeks. I remember her smile, made more comical by a couple of missing teeth. She usually wore a silk kerchief on her head, and loose strands of gray hair would dance around her face when it was windy. I remember the knock-knock jokes and the way she laughed. I smile thinking of those times.

But it wasn't always that way. I used to dread the sound of her approaching steps. Looking back, that's a terrible thing to admit, but those heavy footsteps and her laugh always caught me at the wrong time. Was there ever a right time? Sarah seemed needy. She would stay for an hour, and the conversation would wander hither and yon, and I had three little ones to watch and a house to clean and so many other more important things—it seemed—to do.

Sometimes I wished she had some specific problem, some exact tragedy or situation that we could solve together, with the help of Jesus, of course. We would pray and I would give her a hug—wonderful soul that I was—and she would get better, not so needy, and my heart wouldn't sink every time I heard her laughter on the front porch.

It was her neediness that haunted me—the realization that her troubles and her need for attention were chronic, somehow never ending.

I wonder if that is how the Pharisees felt when they saw the man with dropsy. Every day he stood at the edge of their patio, at the edge of their conversations. Needy. Dropsy was a chronic disease. People got better for a while, only to come down with all the symptoms again the next month, or maybe the next. Why did he come, just within their view? And did he come only on this day, when Jesus was their guest? Or did their hearts sigh with heaviness as they saw him almost every day?

But on this day, they were not watching the man with dropsy as much as they were watching Jesus. Watching him closely, the Scriptures say. But Jesus noticed the man. So he asked them if the law allowed for the healing of this man on the Sabbath. They were silent—an act of shaming in that culture. So Jesus healed him and sent him away. Then he said, "If one of you has a child or an ox that has fallen into a well, will you not immediately pull it out on a sabbath day?" Again, they had nothing to say.

I can only imagine what the Pharisees were thinking that day. Maybe they were only concerned with tricking Jesus. Or maybe they simply put the Sabbath laws—strictly interpreted—above the welfare of a sick man. But maybe they were just tired, like me, tired of a chronic disease, of a person who will come back for more, tired of being so drained by the unending need.

At least Jesus healed the man with dropsy. Nobody healed Sarah, really, although I prayed for it, prayed for some unnamed miracle that would make her someone new.

But there was healing. There was a miracle. The miracle happened in me. Sarah taught me how to slow down. She showed me about the danger of needing to control everything, although I need further healing in this area. Sarah gave me love when I was cranky and ill-tempered. She helped me learn to let go of dirty dishes in the sink and unfinished work. She taught me that it wasn't my job to fix people.

Yes, there were times, even after my "healing," that my heart sank when I heard her footsteps on the porch. And yes, sometimes I had to set boundaries—which is a good thing—and say, "No, Sarah, I can't talk today." But in the long, slow process of conversations around the dinner table and the long, slow process of Jesus living in Sarah, I began to be healed of my chronic disease.

Will I always struggle with busyness and the need to control, the desire to put things ahead of relationships? Yes. You see, I'm pretty needy. But am I better, because of Sarah? Yes. And that is a good thing.

So I never forget Sarah. And I smile whenever I think of her.

> —*Michele Hershberger*

PRAYING AND WALKING IN THE WORLD:

- Who are the Sarahs in your life? Is it possible that you are needy as well?

- What things, even religious things, come before relationships in your life?

- On this Valentine's Day, pray for love to share with those who are lovely in different ways.

FEBRUARY 15

JESUS AND MARTHA STEWART

PLUNGING INTO THE WORD:

Luke 14:7-14

PONDERING ON THE WAY:

Jesus seems inconsistent in this passage. Or at the very least it seems like he's trying on a new role. Hi, I'm Jesus and I'm here to help you gain more honor—the subtle way! Just sit in a significantly less honorable seat at the banquet and watch your hosts seat you properly—and in public too!

Since when has Jesus taken on Martha Stewart? Since when does Jesus dole out handy social tips? And should I humble myself strictly so that I will someday be exalted? Should external rewards ever be my motivation for my good deeds?

Well? Maybe. I am looking forward to spending eternity with the Lord. Is that an external reward? Are the rewards Jesus is talking about different from the typical rewards here on earth?

You and I will be repaid at the resurrection. We will be exalted—for our humility—at the end of the ages. Can we wait?

Jesus was asking his listeners—is asking us—to wait. To see things in a different perspective. In Jesus' day, reciprocity was an important value. If you were invited to a banquet, you were expected to reciprocate in an equal or greater way. People invited only those who could help them out socially, people who had the means of returning the favor.

Things haven't changed much, have they?

But Jesus advises his followers to invite the poor, the crippled, the lame, and the blind—people unable to repay. But that's okay, because the heavenly Father will make up for it. And you and I, we will be hosting others for the right reasons.

So, who are you having over this Sunday noon?

—*Michele Hershberger*

PRAYING AND WALKING IN THE WORLD:

- So, who are you having over this Sunday noon?

- Does true humility have its own reward? Is there a special gift that people marginalized by society can bring, if only we ask? Are we humble enough to receive from the poor and the blind and the lame?

THE GREAT DINNER PARTY

PLUNGING INTO THE WORD:

Luke 14:15-24

PONDERING ON THE WAY:

This Scripture passage is a delightful one to act out with children. The retelling that follows uses both children and adults as various characters. Adapt the passage and characters as needed.

One day Jesus told this story, *"Someone gave a great dinner and invited many people."* Ask your child/children to quickly "prepare" a meal. This should include making the "food" and setting the table. If appropriate, use real food like slices of apples and crackers.

"When it came time for the dinner, he sent out his helper to say to the people who had been invited that it was time to come." Send one of your children to the door to call, "Time to eat!" or another mealtime ritual you use.

"But the invited guests began to make excuses." Have another child or an adult play the part of one of the guests. Say, *"Let's go ask our guests why they aren't here yet."* Coach the guests to make excuses. Some examples of excuses would be, "I have to go play ball right now," "My favorite TV show is on and I can't come," or "We just bought a puppy and I have to take care of him."

"So the helper came back to the house and told them that nobody was coming to the party. The people making the dinner were so sad." Encourage the children to look sad.

"Then the people making the dinner got mad. This isn't right!" Encourage the children to march around the room showing anger.

"Then they got an idea—a great idea. They decided to invite other people to their party. They invited people they had never had supper with before. They even invited people who were not their friends." Ask the children to role-play going to the door and inviting others in. An adult can be one of the new guests. Spend time eating the food and having your party. After eating, ask your children if they can think of names of people they could invite over for a real dinner sometime.

End by saying this: *"When Jesus asks us to come to his party, we shouldn't make excuses. Nothing is more important than being with Jesus. And we also should be willing to invite all people to come and eat with us. All people can be our friends."*

—*Michele Hershberger*

PRAYING AND WALKING IN THE WORLD:

- Talk about some people you can invite to play at your house and maybe share pizza with you.

- Are there new people at your church you could invite to eat food with you? Are there new students at your school?

- How would you feel if everyone else got invited to a party and you didn't? Remember that God invites everyone to his party.

- Take time to pray and thank God for food and friends.

FEBRUARY 17

HAVE YOU CONSIDERED THE COST?

PLUNGING INTO THE WORD:

Luke 14:25-35

PONDERING ON THE WAY:

Imagine yourself buying a new house. What are some of the things you would do before you signed the papers? Or think about starting a new business or deciding to enlarge your family. What are the considerations you would make before attempting these major moves?

Is it any different with your faith? How big is the decision to follow Jesus? For some of our spiritual ancestors, the decision meant persecution and death. For all of our spiritual ancestors, it meant stepping out into the unknown, seeing only one step at a time, walking blindly—by faith.

Have you considered the cost?

—*Michele Hershberger*

PRAYING AND WALKING IN THE WORLD:

Begin this time of meditation with prayer. Ask God to get rid of whatever preoccupations that may keep you from hearing from the Lord through this Scripture passage. Then, read the verses slowly several times. What is Jesus saying ... to you?

Use these questions to help you focus:

- What does it mean to hate your father and mother? Does Jesus want you to despise your parents and family? Or is there some other meaning? Be careful not to soften the text. *Hate* is a powerful word. Jesus asks us for everything.

- How does the parable just before this passage (Luke 14:15-24) help us interpret this text? Buying a piece of land or cattle or the first year of marriage were excuses men could use to avoid going out to Holy War in the Old Testament. In this parable, these same excuses are used to avoid the master's invitation to a banquet. And this time, the excuses are insufficient. This banquet is even more important than Holy War. But who would want to miss out on a grand banquet anyway?

- What does it mean to carry your cross? What is true cross bearing? Surely it is more than bad allergies or extra stress at the office or children who are particularly cranky some afternoons. Should we Christians expect to suffer? What does it mean if we are not suffering because of our identity as followers of Jesus?

- Did you sit down and count the cost before committing yourself to following Jesus? Have you ever considered becoming a missionary? Selling all your possessions? Being martyred for your faith? Do you have what it takes to finish the tower you started?

- Take a moment to list on a piece of paper all of your most prized possessions. Then put a checkmark by the items you think you couldn't give up for God. Does a pattern emerge? What does it mean for you if you have things you wouldn't give up for God? Do these things enslave you? If not, then why wouldn't you give them up for the kingdom of God?

- What means the most to you? Why?

- Do you trust that there is a grand banquet for you?

End this time with prayer. Remember that, on at least one level, none of us has what it takes to "finish the tower." We all need the grace and strength freely given to us by the Spirit to do this impossible work. We live in the paradox of complete grace and complete commitment. They go together.

May God be with you as you build your tower.

FEBRUARY 18 *(FOR CHILDREN AND FAMILIES)*

PARTY ANIMALS

PLUNGING INTO THE WORD:

Luke 15:1-7

PONDERING ON THE WAY:

Materials needed:

- A paper plate for each person

- Crayons, pieces of white or black yarn, scissors, and glue

- A Popsicle stick for each paper plate

- Bible or the script that retells the story (below).

Before reading the Bible story, use the supplies you gathered to make sheep faces. Use the crayons to make eyes, a nose, and a mouth. Then glue hair on the sheep. Finally, glue a Popsicle stick on the back of each plate. Use these faces to help you act out the Bible story.

Once upon a time, there was a farmer who had a hundred sheep. That's a lot of sheep. Let's see if we can count to one hundred *(practice counting if you want to)*. But one day, he counted and ... oops! One sheep was gone! *(Have one "sheep" go and hide.)* What should the farmer do?

Well, he took right off and went up the mountain to look for his lost sheep. He looked in the caves *(look in "caves")*, and he looked in the forest *(look in a "forest")*. He looked in the bristle patches *(look somewhere else and say "ouch!")*, and he looked in the meadows. Finally, after walking and walking, and looking and looking, until his feet hurt and his eyes were sore—finally, he saw a little white head wagging *(your lost sheep can wag her head)*. And he ran and scooped up his precious lost sheep and took her *(or him)* in his arms and carried her all the way home *(role-play all these actions)*.

And when the farmer got home, guess what happened! They had a party! Everyone came, and they had cake and ice cream. The band played, and everyone said, "Yippee!" *(Direct the other sheep to dance and celebrate and say, "Yippee!")*

—*Michele Hershberger*

PRAYING AND WALKING IN THE WORLD:

- How long do you think Jesus would walk to find you? I think he would walk and walk until he found you.

- Is there an older adult, like a grandma or grandpa, who would like to see your sheep face? Can you plan on sharing this story with them?

- The farmer cared about every single one of his sheep, just as Jesus cares for every single person in the world. Take some time to thank Jesus for this great love.

FEBRUARY 19 *(FOR CHILDREN AND FAMILIES)*

A PENNY AND A PARTY

PLUNGING INTO THE WORD:

Luke 15:8-10

PONDERING ON THE WAY:

In today's Bible story, Jesus describes how a woman has ten coins but loses one. She lights a lamp, sweeps the house, and searches until she finds it. She throws a party for her friends and neighbors to celebrate how the lost coin was found.

You may have a piggy bank to help you save your pennies for a special treat or for Sunday school offering. It might not seem like a big deal if you were to lose one penny out of the bank, since the bank probably holds lots more.

Today's story isn't just about the woman losing and finding one penny. Jesus told the story to help us think about how God feels when God finds a person who is lost. Many parents teach children about how God created them and how Jesus saves them from their sins. But when those children grow older, they forget or ignore this message. As a result, they lose their connection to God, to themselves, and to other people.

God throws a party in heaven when just one of these lost persons is found. God wants all the people God created to be part of God's community. One by one, all the pennies add up in a piggy bank. And one by one, all the persons who are found by God increase God's happiness.

—*Laurie Oswald Robinson*

PRAYING AND WALKING IN THE WORLD:

- Talk with your parents about how they came to be found—how they heard the message of God's love and Jesus' forgiveness.

- Pray about what it means for you to be "found."

- Make friends with someone in your neighborhood who doesn't have a place to go for Sunday school. Invite that friend to your Sunday school sometime this month.

FEBRUARY 20

WAITING FOR A WAITING FATHER

PLUNGING INTO THE WORD:

Luke 15:11-32

PONDERING ON THE WAY:

Our family needed help to heal some extended family hurts, so some of us attended a family therapy session together. Our counselor mentioned a helpful book, *The Return of the Prodigal Son: A Story of Homecoming* (Image, 1992). The late author, Henri J. M. Nouwen, says Luke 15 depicts the universal search for "home" and the need for transformation: moving from being a self-centered "son" or "daughter" to becoming a compassionate "mother" and "father." Nouwen, a counselor, said that all human beings are searching for home in their own way. Once we have come home, all of us need a waiting, welcoming parent rather than a harsh judge, no matter what we've done.

It is this kind of waiting father that we see in verse 20: "But while he was still far off, his father saw him and was filled with compassion; he ran and put his arms around him and kissed him." This response was unthinkable in the Jewish culture. The son didn't ask to be bailed out of credit-card debt—he asked for a third of his father's total assets. This could justify rejection or ambivalence.

In that day, passionate abandon was undignified behavior for a man of Middle Eastern culture. But none of this stopped the father's wild, lavish, forgiving welcome. The father focused on the healing of the homecoming rather than the hurting of the exile.

In the landscape of our lives, there may be loved ones who long to come home but cannot as long as they sense withholding rather than welcome. Looking out your front window, do you see a loved one far down the road who is waiting for a welcoming father or mother? Perhaps it's time to unlock the door and run first.

       —Laurie Oswald Robinson

PRAYING AND WALKING IN THE WORLD:

- In your prayer time today, ask God to show you when you have been the prodigal, the elder brother, and the waiting father or mother.

- Reflect on which "prodigals" are waiting for you to become a welcoming father or mother so they can risk coming home. Which friend or family member most needs your welcome this week?

- Purchase *Return of the Prodigal* for your library, or borrow a copy.

FEBRUARY 21

CORN COUNTRY AND TRUE CROPS

PLUNGING INTO THE WORD:

Luke 16:1-15

PONDERING ON THE WAY:

Growing up in Iowa's corn country meant I was surrounded by farming. My father, a dealer for John Deere implements, was one of those rare birds in our church who didn't have the roughened hands of a farmer. He used his hands to provide good tractors and combines at a fair price.

Four decades ago in our community, those people striving to have a good business were sometimes seen as seeking dishonest wealth—rather than the true riches of a good spiritual life. Money and spirituality did not go hand in hand. But times have changed. Both business and money are seen in a different light in our wider church. We understand that a right use of money can be integral to the growth of God's kingdom.

It's difficult to discern what Jesus' parable about the dishonest manager is telling us about money. But it's clear that dishonesty is never right (v. 10). And it's clear that somehow we are to use our money to help connect people to a loving Master. In the heavenly economy, does God want debts reduced, even removed? Yes. And even on earth, God wants people to have a second chance. That's why God established Jubilee, a set of laws in the wilderness, where every seven years, debts were canceled, land lay fallow, and slaves were freed. Does God care about people in financial trouble? Is God concerned that we may enthrone the money god in our hearts? Yes. Yes.

It wasn't vocational choices that determined whether Dad or the farmers would be enslaved to their wealth, whether it came from crops or from selling farm equipment. When the offering plate passed down the pews, it wasn't smooth or rough hands that determined the gift's value. It was the condition of the heart. And only God could discern whether these hearts nurtured and harvested crops of true value.

—*Laurie Oswald Robinson*

PRAYING AND WALKING IN THE WORLD:

- Reflect on the demographics of your community or church. What professions are considered as being service-oriented, and which ones are considered to be more self-serving? Is vocational choice ever seen as the measure of one's spirituality? If so, is this a good marker?

- Reflect on whether you ever have judged someone on their stewardship. In your prayers today, ask God to replace a harsh spirit with more open attitudes.

- Assess an area where money has an enslaving quality in your life. Take one small step this week to bring this area into more balanced stewardship.

FEBRUARY 22

A HOLY EQUATION

PLUNGING INTO THE WORD:

Luke 16:19-31

PONDERING ON THE WAY:

As the youngest of a large clan, I have witnessed the diverse parenting styles of my siblings who have teenage children and grandchildren. A theme threading through all the styles—no matter how lenient or strict—are the words, "You will have to live with your choices." Those little sermons rarely stopped nieces and nephews in their tracks as they ran with breakneck speed into a bad choice. But when the race was run, many of those young people limped home, broken and searching for a second chance.

Today's passage is also about choices. The rich man who wore purple robes and ate sumptuous foods chose not to care for Lazarus. In the afterlife, the failure to heed the Old Testament command to care for the poor snagged the rich man. When he faced the consequences of his choice, he wanted to right the wrong. But he didn't get a second chance.

This passage is easily confusing. We could focus on heaven or hades and try to predict who is going where. We could think the text is saying that only the poor will enjoy eternal life while the rich will suffer. But the most balanced message seems to give us a holy equation: choice = deeds = destiny. Pop culture and cyberspace tease us into thinking that image, not substance, matters most. But Scripture shows us it's not words or intentions that shape our destiny. It's what we do with God's commandments that matters in God's kingdom—in this life and the next.

—*Laurie Oswald Robinson*

PRAYING AND WALKING IN THE WORLD:

- Reflect on what choices in your life make you like the rich man who wears purple robes, closes his eyes to the poor, and fails to see how his deeds today shape his tomorrow. Or, if you are a Lazarus, consider how your choices make you blind to God's goodness, even though you may live with scant material resources.

- In the areas identified from above, pray for the wisdom and strength to make different choices.

- Do you have a Lazarus in your life? If so, what does this Lazarus need? Is there something you can do to bring material comfort? Or, if you are a Lazarus, is God calling you to bring some spiritual cheer to someone who may have everything money can buy but is still lonely and unhappy?

FEBRUARY 23 *(FOR CHILDREN AND FAMILIES)*

COOKIES, FISHING, AND THANKS

PLUNGING INTO THE WORD:

Luke 17:11-19

PONDERING ON THE WAY:

Many of our parents teach us how to be polite. For example, to ask for something, we say "please." When we receive it, we say "thank you." When Grandma bakes us our favorite cookies, or when Daddy takes us fishing, it's good to thank them. We can give them a hug or kiss and tell them how good their kindness felt to us.

We can't see God. But it's still good to say please before we ask something in our prayers and to remember to thank God when that prayer is answered. Jesus tells a story in today's Bible passage that helps us think more about this. In the story, there were ten lepers—people who were covered with sores. They called out to Jesus for healing—"Jesus, Master, have mercy on us!"

Jesus healed them all. But nine of them went on their merry way without saying thank you. Only one leper returned. He praised God with a loud voice, fell at Jesus' feet, and said thank you.

How about you? What has God done for you that you have forgotten to praise and thank God for? You can't give God a hug as you do your grandma or dad. But you can sing a praise song or pray or simply say, "Thank you, God. That really was great."

—*Laurie Oswald Robinson*

PRAYING AND WALKING IN THE WORLD:

- Write a list or draw a picture of all of the good things God has done for you and your family.

- Spend several minutes with your family in a prayer of thanksgiving for these good things.

- Is there anyone you have forgotten to thank for doing something good for you? Find that person this week and say, "Thank you! You really made me feel good."

FEBRUARY 24

LAST-DITCH PRAYER

PLUNGING INTO THE WORD:

Luke 18:1-8

PONDERING ON THE WAY:

There are many situations when I say a last-ditch prayer: "God, if you don't do something about this, then nothing will get done." Such was the case when, after years of living in New York City, I wanted to come home to the Midwest where I grew up. But I had no prospect of a job. Nothing on the horizon indicated such a huge move would be possible.

For months, I prayed God would take me home, closer to my extended family. And for months, nothing happened. But one day I got a phone call, out of the blue, from an editor of a Mennonite publication. He asked if I would interview for a possible position. Within a few weeks, I was hired. And in a few short months, I had moved from the city to the prairies—within driving distance of my father and most of my siblings.

Whereas my plight didn't involve injustices like the widow in today's story, I felt powerlessness to deal with distance and lack of resources. In the Jewish culture, widowed women were some of the most powerless people in society. But this powerless woman received help from a powerful judge. She was rewarded not for her peskiness but for her willingness to honestly and constantly confess her smallness to someone bigger.

Though lowly, we can continue to pray to our God on high. Though our heads may tell us we are a lost cause, we do not have to lose heart. We can keep in constant, persevering prayer even in the midst of deep ditches with no relief in sight. This is the kind of faith the Son of Man hopes to find on the earth when he comes. Will he?

—*Laurie Oswald Robinson*

PRAYING AND WALKING IN THE WORLD:

- In your journal, list three times when you prayed "last-ditch" prayers. Describe in words or convey in images how God's power overcame your powerlessness.

- Spend some time in prayer, asking God to grant a deeper understanding of God's justice in an unjust world.

- If you have children in your life, reassure them that adults and their heavenly Parent intend to take care of them—especially when they feel the most powerless.

FEBRUARY 25

PARABLE OF THE HUSBAND AND WIFE

PLUNGING INTO THE WORD:

Luke 18:9-14

PONDERING ON THE WAY:

In our home, today's passage could be renamed "The Parable of the Husband and Wife." After years of living as a single woman, I find it easy to accuse my new husband of insensitivity or short-sightedness. When Alfonso does things I don't understand, or fails to do things I think should be done, our home's mood defaults to a "temple atmosphere."

Like the Pharisee in the temple, I can thank God that I am not like other people, especially like my bumbling husband. Adding insult to injury, I make a list of all the things I do right. It gives me a sense of entitlement about why God should answer my prayers to change Alfonso—and leave me unchanged.

But the tax collector in the temple gives us another model of prayer. Instead of standing in a prominent place like the Pharisee to thank God for his piety, he stood far off and beat his breast, crying, "God, be merciful to me, a sinner." The parable ends by telling us that the tax collector, and not the Pharisee, was justified before God.

Centuries of Christians have uttered an ancient prayer, taken from this passage and others. It's called the Jesus Prayer, and it goes like this: "Jesus, Son of God, have mercy on me, a sinner." As I round bend after bend in the learning curve of marriage, I am learning to repeat this prayer silently when the temptation to criticize overtakes me. The prayer doesn't fix our conflict, but it leads me away from my rigid piety and makes a humble pliability more possible.

—*Laurie Oswald Robinson*

PRAYING AND WALKING IN THE WORLD:

- If you are married, pray for insight about when you are tempted to be like the Pharisee. Pray a prayer of thanksgiving for the times when God has graced you with humility.

- If you are single, pray for the grace to be humble and pliable in all your relationships.

- Together as a married couple, or in a small group of singles and married couples, read and discuss the book by Jim Roberts, *Deliberate Love* (N.L. Euwer & Co., 2004). It is available at 6101 Buena Vista, Fairway, KS 66205-3229; jimroberts@deliberatelove.com.

FEBRUARY 26

JUST BE A BABY

PLUNGING INTO THE WORD:

Luke 18:15-17

PONDERING ON THE WAY:

Jesus spent a lot of time trying to define God's kingdom for the disciples. He told parables, made analogies, demonstrated with his actions, and used teachable moments. Our passage today is one of those teachable moments.

People were bringing infants to him. "Bless my baby, Jesus," they requested. The disciples got impatient. In their opinion, Jesus had more important things to do. Kingdom business was in process, and children got in the way. Giving time and attention to them didn't bring immediate results.

We know from other accounts of the disciples that they often were focused on people earning their way into the kingdom. Jesus had to keep reminding them that's not how it works. In this case, he said that the kingdom must be received as a little child would receive it.

And how would that be? They simply receive. Little children don't earn or achieve in order to receive. They are loved because of their vulnerability. They are valuable because they have earned nothing, yet they mean everything to those who love them.

So it is with God's kingdom. We receive God's love without working for it. We receive God's unconditional love because we are God's beloved children.

—*Carol Duerksen*

PRAYING AND WALKING IN THE WORLD:

- On a scale of 1 to 10, are you more of an "achiever" (10) or a "receiver" (1) when it comes to God's kingdom? How is God speaking to you about that?

- When do you get impatient with how others are "bringing in the kingdom"?

- Are you ever too goal-oriented and not vulnerable enough in your spiritual life and commitments?

- Pray about your times of impatience and places where you may need to change your spiritual focus.

FEBRUARY 27 *(FOR CHILDREN AND FAMILIES)*

ABOUT THAT CAMEL AND NEEDLE

PLUNGING INTO THE WORD:

Luke 18:18-30

PONDERING ON THE WAY:

Note to adults: If you are reading this to a small child, it will help to have a sewing needle and a picture of a camel available. If you really want to have fun with this, take the child to the zoo to see the camels, take a needle with you, and make the comparison.

Take a look at the camel. It's a big animal, isn't it? It's a tall, kind of funny looking, unique animal.

Now take a look at the needle. It's very small. Notice that on one end of the needle there's a very small hole. That's called the "eye" of the needle, and it's where you put the thread so you can sew something.

Now let's imagine something you are going to try to do. You will try to put the camel through the eye of the needle. That's right—put a big camel through the little hole in the needle. Could you do that?

It's impossible, right? It's actually kind of silly to think about that, isn't it?

Did you know that Jesus talked about a camel going through the eye of a needle? He said that it's just as hard for a rich person to get into the kingdom of God as it is for a camel to get through the eye of a needle.

Well, most of us are rich, compared with the rest of the world. So this makes it seem impossible for us to be in God's kingdom. That's exactly what the people said when they heard Jesus make this statement. They asked Jesus, "Then who can be saved?"

And you know what he said? He said, "God can do anything! Nothing is impossible with God!"

None of us can be good enough to earn our way into God's kingdom, but because God can do the impossible, God loves us even when we don't deserve it. And you know what? That is even more amazing than seeing a camel walk through a needle!

—*Carol Duerksen*

PRAYING AND WALKING IN THE WORLD:

- **Prayer:** Jesus, I can't imagine how a camel could get through a needle. That's impossible! And I also can't imagine how big your love is for me. That's impossible for me to understand too. But I know it's true, and I thank you for that. Amen.

- **Adults:** While it is true that God can do the impossible, we also must heed the warning of Jesus written here. Money and possessions, in and of themselves, are not evil, but it is so easy to love those things and put our faith in them instead of God. And then we are a stuck camel.

- If God asked you today to sell everything you have and give it to the poor, could you do it? What **is** God asking of you?

FEBRUARY 28

WALKING TALL

PLUNGING INTO THE WORD:

Luke 19:1-10

PONDERING ON THE WAY:

small man
short
on friends
long on cash
curious about a man
who preaches a different way

surprised man
out on a limb
the Great Teacher
wants to dine
with him?

broken man
made whole
his household too
those he defrauded
the poor
all know salvation
spreads beyond
one heart

small man
walking tall
—*Carol Duerksen*

PRAYING AND WALKING IN THE WORLD:

- In which areas of your life are you "small"?

- Where do you need to go out on a limb to meet Jesus?

- How are you participating in the salvation of persons, your community, the world?

- Write a note or call someone who "walks tall" and is an inspiration to you.

MARCH 1

PROPER GREETINGS

PLUNGING INTO THE WORD:

Romans 1:1-17

PONDERING ON THE WAY:

I don't know about you, but I'm getting lazy when I write and answer e-mails. Sometimes I just start writing. No "Dear so and so." Sometimes not even the person's name. I just get to the point.

Paul, on the other hand, did it right. Not only did he begin his letter to his friends in Rome with a proper greeting, his greeting had meaning: "Grace to you and peace from God our Father and the Lord Jesus Christ."

The normal, customary Greek greeting was *chaierein*. This word meant "greetings." Paul utilizes a wordplay on the Greek greeting, changing it to *charis*, which means "grace." Then he follows that immediately with "peace," or shalom, the standard Hebrew greeting.

What is Paul doing here? He's being wonderfully "politically correct" according to Jesus Christ. (Would that be PC according to JC?) Paul is beginning his letter with a greeting that combines both Hebrew and Greek, Jew and Gentile. In the greeting, the words do not merge, but neither do they stand alone. They stand side by side, symbolizing Paul's theme for this whole letter: God's redeeming love is for everyone.

It is a greeting to read, own, and cherish. And I dare say, Paul would be pleased to see it show up on our e-mails.

But we need to take note of another not-so-politically-correct phrase in this passage. In verse 16, Paul makes a blunt statement, and he doesn't really care what people think or how they might take it.

"I'm not ashamed of the gospel," he says. "This is who I am—take it or leave it!"

So here we have instructions on how to live: We live as unashamed ambassadors of Jesus, and we offer grace and peace to each other.

—*Carol Duerksen*

PRAYING AND WALKING IN THE WORLD:

- **Pray:** Jesus, give me words of grace and peace to share with the friends I know and the friends yet to be made as I share your love.

- How do you begin and end your e-mails? Consider using a greeting and salutation with meaning. Or add a verse or quote at the bottom that has special meaning for you.

MARCH 2

A NOTE FROM OUR PARENT

PLUNGING INTO THE WORD:

Romans 1:18-32

PONDERING ON THE WAY:

My dear children,

The problem began with Eve and Adam. Despite my warnings, they thought it would be good to have just a little more power and control. They wanted to be lord over themselves, and that is a big problem. When people replace me with their own version of a god, we have a problem.

It's called sin. The same thing happened when Moses went away to get my instructions on how to obey me and live a good life. The people got tired of waiting for him and wanted a god to worship. They threw their gold into a fire and, according to Aaron, "out came this bull calf." Yeah, right.

You people today may not be worshipping golden calves, but you have your own gods. It isn't a question of whether or not you will have a lord over you—it's a question of who or what it will be. And let me tell you, when I am not the Lord of your life, I am not happy.

I could send punishment and plagues on you like I did on the Egyptians, but instead, I'll just leave you to your own devices. Go ahead. Just keep on thinking you are the lord of your life. Keep on abusing each other emotionally, mentally, physically, and spiritually. You'll pay the bill. You'll live—and die—with the consequences. Just let me know if you want a change of heart. I'll be waiting.

Your Tough-Love Parent,

God

> —*Carol Duerksen*

PRAYING AND WALKING IN THE WORLD:

- This passage calls us to confession. Find a place where you can be alone for at least fifteen minutes. Light a candle, quiet yourself, and allow God's Spirit to bring to mind the idolatry in your life. How have you replaced God? What are your "golden calves"?

- Pray this prayer every day: Jesus, be the Lord of my life.

MARCH 3 *(FOR CHILDREN AND FAMILIES)*

EVERYBODY NEEDS A FRIENDLY SOCK

PLUNGING INTO THE WORD:

Romans 2:1-16

PONDERING ON THE WAY:

This is a story about a black cat named Slickfester Dude and a Siamese cat named Tjej (Tjej is Swedish for *girl* and it's pronounced Shay.) Slickfester and Tjej were real cats, and Tjej really did these things. Slick's conversation with me is, of course, imaginary.

"She's doing it again," Slick told me one evening as he jumped up onto the bed next to me. Downstairs, I could hear Tjej making cat noises.

"Sounds like she's got her sock," I said to Slick, who rolled his eyes.

"She is so strange," he said.

Moments later, Tjej showed up in the bedroom. In her mouth was a rolled up pair of socks. She set them down, said a few words, and lay down beside them.

"When did this all start?" Slick wanted to know.

"When she was a kitten she played with socks she found in the clean-laundry basket," I explained. "She carried them around like a doll and talked to them."

"But she's not a kitten anymore. So what's her problem?"

"Actually, she quit for a while, until she had kittens of her own. Then she started again, as if to teach them about playing sock."

"I saw one in the food dish one day," Slick said. "And another time, it was in the water pan."

"I know. She treats them as if they're alive. Like they're friends."

"I saw one on the bed next to her grown-up son, Lloyd. Does that mean he's doing it too?" Slick sounded quite disgusted.

"I don't think so. I saw Tjej put that sock there, next to him, while he was taking a nap," I said. "In fact, she did that to me once."

"She gave you the sock?"

"Yep. I was taking a nap, and when I woke up, the sock was lying against my arm. As if Tjej was giving it to me to be my friend."

"Very peculiar," Slick said. "It's probably because she's Siamese."

"What do you mean by that?"

"Weird cats, those Siamese."

"Any weirder than black cats?"

"What do you mean by that?" Slickfester Dude sat up straight and glared at me.

"I mean, all of you cats are unique and special because of what's inside of you, and your color or breeding isn't what's important."

"Well, it's what's inside of that Siamese that's strange."

You Finish the Story:

- What would you say to Slickfester about his attitude toward Tjej?

- What do you think Slick should say to Tjej?

    —*Carol Duerksen*

PRAYING AND WALKING IN THE WORLD:

- Do you ever think that people who are different from you are strange or stupid? Do you ever say bad things about people who are different from you or you just don't understand?

- Jesus said that we shouldn't judge other people. Just as we wouldn't want others to say bad things about us, we shouldn't say bad things about them. **Pray this prayer:** Jesus, forgive me for thinking and saying bad things about people I don't understand. Help me to be kind to them. Amen.

"Everybody Needs a Friendly Sock" is excerpted from *Slickfester Dude Tells Bedtime Stories* by Carol Duerksen, copyright © 1997 by WillowSpring Downs.

MARCH 4

YOU ARE HERE

PLUNGING INTO THE WORD:

Romans 2:17-29

PONDERING ON THE WAY:

Read this passage again. Substitute *Christian* for the word *Jew* in verse 17. When you come to verses 21 and 22, substitute the sins that you are most critical of in others. Then take a good hard look at yourself. Often, the things we are most critical of in others are the issues we fight within ourselves. At the same time, the areas where we are quickest to point our fingers are the areas farthest away from our understanding or experience.

Why is it easier for us to find the Bible passages that address someone else's sins than those that speak to our own?

—*Carol Duerksen*

PRAYING AND WALKING IN THE WORLD:

- Find a place that is totally dark. Take a candle, lighter, and your Bible with you. Begin your quiet time in the dark. Realize that it is you in the dark. It is not the people you criticize for their actions and their beliefs—it is you and only you. Pray about the darkness and brokenness in your life. When you are ready, ask for forgiveness and healing. Light your candle. Pray for God's Spirit to give you the light to search your heart.

- Read Psalm 51:1-17.

MARCH 5

CHOSEN FOR A MISSION

PLUNGING INTO THE WORD:

Romans 3:1-8

PONDERING ON THE WAY:

What does it mean to be God's chosen people? And this is not just a question for

Jews, nor is it just for American Christians who may believe that God loves America more than any other country. It's a question for all of us—a crucial question.

There seem to be two options. As my colleague Marion Bontrager helped me understand, some people interpret the word *chosen* in the Bible as "God's favorites." Others see God's election as being chosen for a mission. People who see the Israelites/Jews, and consequently themselves as Christians, as God's favorites read the Bible differently than people who see themselves and the Jews as chosen for a mission.

Paul wrestles with this issue in the book of Romans. What advantage, he asks in chapter 3, is there in being the chosen ones? Keeping all the laws, going through the painful process of circumcision, enduring the ridicule of so many others—was all that for naught? These are legitimate questions, especially as Paul and the other apostles argue for inclusion of the Gentiles, all the other peoples of the world who haven't had to do any of those rigorous tasks.

There is a great advantage, Paul claims, but not the advantage typically assumed. The Jews are not God's favorites, but rather God's chosen missionaries. As Paul looks at the sweep of the biblical story, he remembers passages like Genesis 12:3, when God chose Abram and said, "In you all the families of the earth shall be blessed." He looks at the exodus event and sees that all the slaves were rescued (Exodus 12:38).

Paul remembers how the people tried to throw Jesus off a cliff when he reminded them that God's grace was for people like the widow of Zarephath and Naaman the Syrian (Luke 4). And Paul remembers his own dramatic conversion on the road to Damascus. Part of that conversion meant accepting a brand-new thought—that the inclusion of the Gentiles was part of God's plan all along. The Israelites, beginning with Abraham, were chosen to be the conduits through whom God's blessings would come to all.

But that doesn't mean it's easy, or even gratifying. Being chosen for the task of helping all people become God's people can have its pitfalls.

Christians today can feel the same way. We can get caught up in enjoying God's blessings and forget our true calling—to be a vessel of God's love wherever we are, to help others find God and become part of his people.

How do you see yourself? God's favorite or chosen for a mission?

> —*Michele Hershberger*

PRAYING AND WALKING IN THE WORLD:

- In this text, Paul also tackles the thorny issue of sin and God's grace. If our unfaithfulness serves to illuminate and highlight God's justice and mercy, then should we be punished for our sin? Do you think that is a valid argument, even if Paul doesn't? Why or why not?

- How does your congregation see itself? As God's favorites or chosen for the task of bringing God's love to others? List your church programs. How many of them have nurture of Christians as their primary role? How many have outreach as their primary role?

MARCH 6

SPANISH MOSS

PLUNGING INTO THE WORD:

Romans 3:9-20

PONDERING ON THE WAY:

My family drove from Missouri to Florida one year for a vacation. We headed south into Louisiana and Mississippi and saw beautiful scenery that took us far beyond the cornfields around our hometown. The most amazing sight for us, however, was the Spanish moss that grew on almost every tree. It was like driving through a curtained garden, where every tree was decorated with a delicate, lacy veil of green. I secretly wished we lived in a more southern climate so we could have Spanish moss on our trees too.

Then we researched the plant. This intricate lace, so beautiful, is deadly to most trees. It is a parasite, sucking the life out of whatever it attaches itself to. The moss is so attractive, yet its presence is so devastating. I no longer wished for Spanish moss in my front yard.

In many ways, that is what sin is like. From a distance, it looks so attractive. Before we understand it, we think it can't be half-bad. It might even look downright good. But, when it attaches itself to our lives, we start to get sucked dry. The law helps us see this reality, to understand sin for what it is, maybe even before sin attaches itself so deeply into us. That is a gift. Through the resurrection power of Jesus, we can break free from the power of sin. That too is a precious gift.

—*Michele Hershberger*

PRAYING AND WALKING IN THE WORLD:

Paul uses Old Testament passages to help his readers see sin in all its variegated ugliness. Use the questions below, adapted from these scriptures, to search your own life. Confess your sins to God. Ask for God's divine intervention to help you truly repent—that is, change your ways. Trust God to forgive you out of his great mercy and love for you.

1. Where do you lack understanding?

2. How do you need to seek God more?

3. To whom have you been unkind?

4. What unloving words have you spoken? What lies have you told? Who has been hurt by your words?

5. What are you bitter about?

6. How have you been an accomplice in shedding blood?

7. Is anyone miserable because of you? Have you ruined anyone?

8. How have you forsaken the way of peace?

9. Do you have little or no fear of God? Why?

Now say a prayer of thanksgiving to God, who is faithful to forgive your sins. God is newfound freedom. Go in the strength and mercy of God.

FAITH OR FAITHFULNESS?

PLUNGING INTO THE WORD:

Romans 3:21-31

PONDERING ON THE WAY:

How are we saved? Many people use this passage to help them answer this age-old question. Part of the discussion centers around verse 22.

It can be translated from the Greek in two ways:

1. "… the righteousness of God through **faith in** Jesus Christ for all who believe."

2. "… the righteousness of God through **the faithfulness of** Jesus Christ for all who believe."

So, does it matter? Perhaps it does.

Faith in Jesus Christ is something we do. While not specifically good deeds, like obeying Torah, having faith in Jesus does involve a choice, a decision. Do I trust

Jesus? It is something I can choose to do and can look back and say yes, I have done this or no, I have not.

The second way of translating verse 22 emphasizes Jesus' actions instead of ours. And how was Jesus faithful to God? We can look back on his life, his teachings, and his nonviolent submission to the authorities who crucified him to see incredible faithfulness. It was his faithfulness, faithfulness that carried him all the way to a cruel death on a cross, that saved us, and that still saves us.

How would you translate the verse?

On one hand, "faith in Jesus" can become just one more thing we do, or need to do, in order to "get saved." "I believe" can become a way of earning God's favor. We can get just as legalistic about using just the right words that prove we have faith as we can about reading the Bible seven minutes every day.

On the other hand, we do need to make a choice to follow Jesus. God will not force us into relationship as a follower of Jesus. We must choose to leave a way that leads to death, turn around, and follow the way of life. That is the most important choice we will ever make.

Part of the confusion lies in our Western understanding of the word *faith*. Today persons tend to see faith as saying yes intellectually to a set of truth statements, and that believing in something can be separated from actions. The ancients saw faith differently. They saw no dichotomy between beliefs and actions. Having faith in God meant trusting God enough to obey. This obedience came not because of any effort to win salvation or God's favor, but rather as the natural result of one's trust.

Faith was almost … a verb.

So perhaps we should cling to both translations, claiming the truth that each proclaims. It was the faithfulness of Jesus, nothing else, that saves us, and even our poor attempts of faith are nothing but bits of sand on a vast seashore. But we do have a choice to make—the choice to follow because we believe. We follow not because we have to or so that through our following we earn a ticket to heaven, but because—we do.

Do you?

Is faith a verb in your life?

> —*Michele Hershberger*

PRAYING AND WALKING IN THE WORLD:

- Which translation of verse 22 are you more comfortable with? Why?

- How can you start "faithing" more?

MARCH 8 *(FOR CHILDREN AND FAMILIES)*

TERESA TRUSTS

PLUNGING INTO THE WORD:

Romans 4:1-25

PONDERING ON THE WAY:

Faith is a big, grown-up word. What do you think it means? Maybe it's easier to think of a story.

Once there was a girl named Teresa. Teresa's mother told her that if she cleaned up her room, she would get to go to the store and buy an ice cream cone. Teresa believed her mom, and so she obeyed her—and of course she got some ice cream. Teresa had faith in her mother. She trusted that her mom would do what she said she would do. Teresa knew it would be good to obey her mom. When Teresa trusted and then obeyed her mom, that is called faith.

Sometimes faith is easy. Teresa's mom and dad had always loved Teresa and had always made the best decisions for Teresa. Teresa had faith every morning that her mom and dad would fix her a good breakfast. And every morning they did. After awhile, Teresa's faith in her parents was so strong that she obeyed them even when they didn't promise her an ice cream cone or some other wonderful treat. Teresa knew that her parents loved her and wanted the best for her, and so, knowing that, she obeyed them without question, at least most of the time.

That is how faith works with God. God loves us and always has the best in mind for us. So we can trust God and obey God. Trusting and obeying put together equals faith. Christians, like Teresa when she got older, stop doing things for God just so they get rewarded. They start obeying God because it's the natural thing to do. It feels right. When you know God has the best in mind for you, and you know how good God has been to you in the past, always taking care of you, then—it's easy to trust God.

In our Bible story today, Abraham and Sarah show faith in God. They trust what God says and then do what God says. They obey because they really do believe God's words. They obey because they love God, and they know God loves them.

This is an exciting way to live. This is a joyous way to live.

—*Michele Hershberger*

PRAYING AND WALKING IN THE WORLD:

We are to trust God the way Abraham and Sarah did. Let's practice some trust. Here are some things you can do to show you trust your parents. Which things would you like to try?

- Jumping off the edge of the bed or the couch into Daddy's arms.

- Being blindfolded and letting Mom lead me around the living room.

- Eating new foods that Mom promises are good for me.

MARCH 9 *(FOR CHILDREN AND FAMILIES)*

DOCTOR DAN

PLUNGING INTO THE WORD:

Romans 5:1-11

PONDERING ON THE WAY:

(Read this story for your children as a way to interact with Romans 5:1-11. After discussing the questions, read Romans 5:1-11 aloud.)

High up in the mountains there was a small village where people lived, much like you and I live in our towns and cities today. They had some of the same problems you and I have, but they also had a specific problem that was horrible to live with. There was a disease that inflicted the people, causing them to die a slow and painful death. This disease was not well-known or widespread, but it had killed many of the people. Yes, to the people of this town, this disease was the worst of all enemies. The sickness took the lives of young and old, rich and poor alike. There was no cure.

That is, until one day when a doctor from a neighboring town discovered one. His name was Doctor Dan. This kind physician lived close to the village. Doctor Dan watched the people suffer, and his heart went out to them. So he worked for ten years to develop a medicine that would fight the disease that hurt so many in the village.

What was so strange, however, was that the people hated this doctor. All the years that he worked on a cure, they laughed at him and called him names, like Dr. Dumbbell. They didn't want to cooperate when he asked them questions about their sickness, and some even tried to kill him.

But despite their mean actions toward him, Dr. Dan kept working. Finally, after days and days of working without stopping, the medicine was ready. The doctor sent it to the pharmacy in town, free of charge, even though making the medicine cost him everything he had in the bank.

Some people took the free medicine and were saved from death. Others refused, not trusting the doctor's word that this medicine was really good for them. They continued to get sicker and sicker, until they finally died.

—Michele Hershberger

PRAYING AND WALKING IN THE WORLD:

- Why do you think the doctor kept working on a cure for the disease even though the villagers were mean to him?

- Can you think of stories in the Bible where God did something wonderful for the people even though they didn't deserve it? (God rescuing the slaves from Egypt, Jesus coming to show us God's kingdom, which ended up with his death on the cross.)

MARCH 10

A QUESTION FOR EVERY DAY

PLUNGING INTO THE WORD:

Romans 5:12-21

PONDERING ON THE WAY:

Who are you more like? Adam or Christ?

This is a legitimate question. You might think it's presumptuous to put yourself in the same category as Jesus, but do you really want to be like Adam? Isn't that what we're being saved from?

Through one man, Adam, came death. And death starts—really—before you die. What are the things or relationships in your life that feel life-draining? Name them. Be specific.

Through one man, Christ, came life. And again, Paul is talking about much more than eternal life with Jesus. This abundant life starts now. What are the things and relationships in your life that are life-giving? Name them. Be specific.

—Michele Hershberger

PRAYING AND WALKING IN THE WORLD:

- The examen, one of the ancient spiritual disciplines of the church, asks two questions every day. To do the examen, you find a quiet space and time and ask yourself, "What am I least grateful for today?" and "What am I most grateful for today?" Then you pray about the answers that come to your mind, asking forgiveness for the ways you have hurt others and God, and expressing gratitude and joy for those things and relationships that come to you as blessing.

- Practice the examen as part of your prayer time for the next seven days. You may see a pattern emerging, certain types of situations that bring you sadness and joy. If you practice the examen for a longer period of time, you will notice even more patterns. What is God trying to tell you as you notice these patterns?

- Who are you more like—Adam or Christ?

MARCH 11

A BURYING CEREMONY

PLUNGING INTO THE WORD:

Romans 6:1-14

PONDERING ON THE WAY:

We live in a transitional world. We live with a promise that has not yet been completely fulfilled. We live after the resurrection, where death and sin were surely defeated, and yet we live in the midst of both death and sin. We know who wins in the end, but we still live in the heat of the competition.

My sins, your sins, have been buried with Christ. I have been given—you have been given—the same resurrection power over sin that raised Jesus from the dead. We are not slaves to sin any longer.

But … but … I still sin—sometimes. It doesn't make sense, I realize that, but the truth of the matter is that I still struggle. Now, thanks to the wonderful grace and power of God, I am more victorious over sin now than even five years ago. I can see the evidence of God's transforming work in my life.

But I still sin. I do.

Maybe you do too.

So, we need a burying ceremony.

—*Michele Hershberger*

PRAYING AND WALKING IN THE WORLD:

- Take a piece of paper and a pen or pencil. Find a shoebox, and grab a handy shovel or spade from the garden. You know what to do. Write them down. Include all those sins done against you, as well as the ones you've committed. Bury them. Throw dirt over the grave. (If you have no place to bury the box, prepare to burn your paper.)

- And celebrate victory!

MARCH 12 *(FOR CHILDREN AND FAMILIES)*

SLAVE BOY TO FREE MAN

PLUNGING INTO THE WORD:

Romans 6:15-23

PONDERING ON THE WAY:

A story about a slave boy, Olaudah Equino, helps us understand what *slavery* means. Olaudah was born into a wealthy West African family in 1740s in a land now called Nigeria. When he was eleven years old, slave traders captured him and brought him to America on a slave ship. He was packed with about four hundred other Africans into a tiny lower deck. The hot and smelly air made people very sick, and many of them died at sea.

When the ship got to America, Olaudah was taken north to a plantation in Virginia. There, he was sold to a navy lieutenant. The boy became a sailor and spent much time in England, where he educated himself. After seven years, he was sold again to a captain in the West Indies. The captain sold Olaudah to a Quaker merchant from Philadelphia. He began to work on a slave ship, where he traded glasses and other objects on the side to save about $3,700, enough to buy his freedom.

After he became free, he helped free slaves around the world. He did this by writing his life's story, which became a best seller. He became England's leading spokesperson for blacks and helped to end slavery. He died in 1797, and ten years later Britain and the United States outlawed slave trade.

As today's verses show, when we have Jesus in our hearts, we are no longer like the slave, Olaudah, who wasn't free to make choices about his life. Jesus frees us from our old master, sin, which makes us do bad things. And then he gives us power to choose to serve God. With Jesus in our hearts, we become like the free man, Olaudah, who could choose to do good.

—*Laurie Oswald Robinson*

PRAYING AND WALKING IN THE WORLD:

- Discuss what would happen to you if you became a slave boy or slave girl. How would that change your life? How did it change Olaudah's life?

- In your prayers today, thank God for the freedom Jesus gives you to serve God.

- Is there a friend at school whose ancestors were slaves? If so, ask this person to tell you the family's story.

- Read a book or watch a video about slavery.

MARCH 13 *(FOR CHILDREN AND FAMILIES)*

LOCKED OUT BUT STILL LOVED

PLUNGING INTO THE WORD:

Romans 7:1-6

PONDERING ON THE WAY:

On the last night of Bible memory camp at an Iowa lake, our cabin counselor turned out the lights. As she did so, she gave me the eagle eye and said, "Don't even think about trying to sneak out of the cabin tonight. If you do, I will lock the door."

Even though she was a beloved friend and longtime babysitter for our family, I cared more about my fun than her feelings. I giggled for a while with the other girls, who fell asleep. Then I slithered out of my sleeping bag and snuck out. I joined my other friends scampering throughout the campgrounds, as was the custom on the last night of camp.

If you've ignored rules or been unkind to a friend, verse 5 can remind us why: As human beings, we tend to do things that aren't good for us or other people. The Bible calls this part of us the "flesh." It cuts off our relationship with God and others. Verse 6 tells us that the new Spirit life in Jesus helps us make more loving and kind choices.

My counselor had the new Spirit life of Jesus inside of her. Even though she locked me out (and I had to sleep on a bench all night), we talked about our broken trust. She said she was disappointed in me but still loved me and wanted to renew our friendship. By doing that, she modeled what it means to choose life rather than death.

—*Laurie Oswald Robinson*

PRAYING AND WALKING IN THE WORLD:

- In your prayers today, ask Jesus to show you when you have been unkind or disrespectful to others. Ask for forgiveness.

- Also in your prayers, ask Jesus for a bigger dose of his new Spirit life, which can help you make better choices next time.

- Think of one person to whom you need to say "I'm sorry." Find that person and do it, either in person or in a homemade card.

MARCH 14

SNEAKING AROUND

PLUNGING INTO THE WORD:

Romans 7:7-25

PONDERING ON THE WAY:

I felt deep relief the first time I snuck into a Catholic church to receive ashes on Ash Wednesday. Lent, the six-week season before Easter, fosters reflection and repentance. It felt wonderful to visibly acknowledge that I am weak and sinful and that death is my lot. Anabaptist tradition isn't void of the need for repentance from sin. But in earlier times, the Mennonite church wasn't prone to mark these realities by church-year rituals.

Today, some Mennonite congregations provide ashes, and I no longer sneak to find them. Walking a journey through Romans during Lent is also a good way to come into the light of day regarding the phrase used during Ash Wednesday services: "Remember that you are from dust and to dust you shall return." Romans 7 says that to be human is to be in tension between death and life, sin and righteousness, the dust of human flesh and the flame of Christ's Spirit. During Lent we stop denying this conflict, embrace our helplessness, and reach out for our true source of help.

Verses 24-25 openly admit our state: "Wretched man that I am! Who will rescue me from this body of death? Thanks be to God, through Jesus Christ our Lord!" This is the balance of the Christian story: We are in the depths of powerlessness against sin; but Christ rescues us out of the pit through his power.

Until we feel the powerlessness of our pit, we will never feel our need of his power. Romans 7 helps us stop hiding our dustiness. We need to let the light of the Son reveal how dust has collected on our lives and to allow this season to be the hands of housecleaning.

—*Laurie Oswald Robinson*

PRAYING AND WALKING IN THE WORLD:

- In your prayers this week, search out some "dustiness" in your life. In God's presence, allow yourself to see it and accept it.

- Then surrender your dustiness into God's care and let that surrender lead you to new humility about your foibles and frailties.

- Find some helpful resources regarding the Lenten season. One suggestion is Laurence Hull Stookey's book, *Calendar: Christ's Time for the Church* (Abingdon Press, 1996).

MARCH 15

ABBA MOMENTS

PLUNGING INTO THE WORD:

Romans 8:1-17

PONDERING ON THE WAY:

Saturday morning came uncomfortably the day after my husband and I had a conflict the evening before. He held me as I coiled into a tight little ball. No matter what he said, I could not let go of my irrational fear of abandonment that followed my inappropriate anger and resentment from hours earlier. After talking and praying, we got to the root of my fear, followed by reassurances of his faithful presence. But even after his kind assurance, it was hard to trust his love.

That meltdown took all weekend to resolve. But it was only a symptom of the existential human disease Romans 8 describes; that is, as humans we are so easily enslaved to our fears of abandonment—based on faulty performances and a sense of unworthiness and condemnation. If we remain under the law, we are condemned. And condemnation and the abandonment that comes with it are scary. These fears block us from being open to the Spirit of adoption as sons and daughters of God, an adoption based not on what we do but who we are.

As wary and wounded adults, we may feel it is impossible to become like trusting children who openly cry out to God in the spirit of verses 14-16: "For all who are led by the Spirit of God are children of God. For you did not receive a spirit of slavery to fall back into fear, but you have received a spirit of adoption. When we cry, 'Abba! Father!' it is that very Spirit bearing witness with our spirit that we are children of God."

These verses don't promise the magic of making every adult like a child, or healing all the childhood memories of abuse for those who suffered so. But they do promise that there is another way—the law of the Spirit. Through the Spirit, we are transformed and start "performing" because we want to, because we have been adopted.

God doesn't abandon us to our performance-based fears. Rather, this God turns abandonment into "Abba moments" of presence.

> —*Laurie Oswald Robinson*

PRAYING AND WALKING IN THE WORLD:

- Reflect on those moments you have felt abandoned in your life, either by God or others. How does today's passage cause you to think or feel differently about those experiences? Journal your responses to this question.

- In your prayers this week, take one or two of those situations and invite Jesus' presence into that abandonment. Journal what you hear God saying to you.

- Is there a person in your life who needs to be reassured of your unconditional presence in the face of some earlier conflict? When you are prayerful and centered, offer that reassurance.

MARCH 16

TRANSLATION

PLUNGING INTO THE WORD:

Romans 8:18-27

PONDERING ON THE WAY:

At a Mennonite World Conference event, a half dozen people of various ethnic groups are enclosed in booths. They are translating the speakers' messages into words the diverse audience can understand. This image comes to mind when reading Marjorie Hewitt Suchocki's book, *In God's Presence* (Chalice Press, 1996). She speaks of our interrelatedness with God, others, and God's creation—a view that gives intercessory prayer new impact. In Kansas, I pray in English for someone in Burkina Faso who speaks an African dialect. And I can be certain God hears and answers those prayers.

In a mysterious but real way, solidarity in the Spirit transcends words. God, the intercessor, and the one prayed for become one—despite differences in culture and racial-ethnic backgrounds. We even are connected to God's physical creation. Today's passage explores this mystery of our interrelatedness within the universe. Verses 22-23 say, "We know that the whole creation has been groaning in labor pains until now; and not only the creation, but we ourselves, who have the first fruits of the Spirit, groan inwardly."

These groans are described as sighs too deep for words—but they are never in vain. Suchocki defines prayer as God working with the world the way it is, to bring it toward what it can be. This links with Romans 8, which says God won't let creation fall into the abyss of pain and suffering. God won't let our fellow believers go without hope. Instead, a glorious promise of eventual wholeness infuses our human prayers with heavenly hope. This hope is found through the Spirit, who translates our sighs into God's goodwill.

—Laurie Oswald Robinson

PRAYING AND WALKING IN THE WORLD:

- Think of several people for whom you have prayed recently. Did they live near you or far away? Did it feel different to pray for those who are close to home than for those who lived in another state or country? If so, how?

- After some reflection, pray for those people again. With eyes closed, imagine you are all interconnected by a web of God's love. See in your mind's eye how the sound of your prayers reverberates through the entire web and reaches the person you want God to touch.

- This week, think of one suffering person for whom you have felt compassion but whom you have felt powerless to help. Based on the encouragement from today's devotional, offer your sighs to God, trusting the Spirit's translation.

- How do you see God's physical creation "groaning"? How has humanity contributed to that? What can we do to bring wholeness back to creation?

MARCH 17

THIRD TIME'S A CHARM

PLUNGING INTO THE WORD:

Romans 8:28-39

PONDERING ON THE WAY:

A poster of Romans 8:31 graces the wall of the bedroom of my sister and brother-in-law: "If God is for us, who is against us?" It's not unusual for couples to put positive reminders on their wall. But given the journey of this couple, it is a deep mark of faith. This marriage was the third one for both of them. Despite repeated devastations and disappointments, they chose to believe that God was divinely shaping a new fidelity—not threatened by their human frailty but strengthened by God's faithfulness.

The faith of this couple in God's faithfulness is a good model for us during Lent. In experiencing Lent's reminders of our powerlessness, depravity, and disconnection, it is good to dwell in verses 28-39. They powerfully promise that nothing can separate us from the love of Christ. And more than that, they assure us that trials don't have the power to victimize us. Rather, we can be victorious in the abiding presence of Christ.

Wary friends and family counseled this couple against marriage. But after five years of dating and indepth counseling with their pastors, they felt God calling them to commit to a love relationship based on faith rather than fear. Years down the road, this couple has abided in Christ's presence through trials and tests of blended family and midlife adjustments. Since their decision, they are increasingly certain God is causing all things to work together for good. Their faith is embracing Christ's promise to never leave them despite the human heartbreak they suffered. And God's faithfulness is transferring words on the wall into the ways of their hearts.

—*Laurie Oswald Robinson*

PRAYING AND WALKING IN THE WORLD:

- Reflect on lifestyles that may easily be viewed as being beyond God's presence and grace. What do today's verses say about your perspective? How do these Scriptures seriously change that perspective?

- In today's prayers, ask God to show you areas in your own life where you feel separated from God's love and grace. Recommit those areas to God in light of today's promises.

- Memorize all or portions of Romans 8:28-39.

MARCH 18

SONS AND FATHERS

PLUNGING INTO THE WORD:

Romans 9

PONDERING ON THE WAY:

My husband was born out of wedlock and adopted by a stepfather. It wasn't until his mid-thirties that he met his biological father. In this short visit—the first and only—my husband couldn't begin to bond with the person who should have carried him to the park on his shoulders, taken him to a baseball game, and gone camping. Instead, my husband lived with an abusive stepfather who did not fill in the empty spaces.

Even after suffering these early wounds, my husband is one of the most gentle and caring persons I know. Some of the credit for this miraculous wholeness can be attributed to his mother, who raised him in the faith and faithfully prays for him every day. She knows her son belongs to a loving and present heavenly Father, despite the absence and abuse of earthly fathers.

Today's passage explores what it means to be a true son or daughter of God. In the Jewish world, being a descendant of Abraham and Sarah, through Isaac, marked you as belonging to God's family. The other descendants of Abraham (Ishmael's descendants) didn't count. But the writer of Romans says it's more complicated than that. What makes us part of the family of faith is not bloodline and flesh but the promises and the mercy of God (v. 9). It's not that Abraham's descendants were void of a relationship with God. The disconnection came when they established ties to God through human exertion rather than by God's mercy (v. 18). God will raise up descendants from whomever God chooses.

My husband can't stop being a son of his biological father. But until the bonds are established through loving a relationship, they will forever be strangers. No matter what our earthly parentage, culture, or ethnicity, God's merciful adoption transforms those who weren't beloved into the beloved children of the living God.

—*Laurie Oswald Robinson*

PRAYING AND WALKING IN THE WORLD:

- Reflect on your experience with your earthly father or father figure. How did this relationship succeed or fail in reflecting the love of the heavenly Father?

- If you have "father deficits," pray for a greater capacity to be adopted and beloved by God. If you have a healthy relationship with a father, either alive or deceased, thank God for his wholesome ability to mirror God's love accurately.

- Befriend a child who you know doesn't have a strong father figure. This week, plan one activity that can convey a sense of fatherly love.

MARCH 19

A MEDITATION FOR LENT

PLUNGING INTO THE WORD:

Romans 10; Deuteronomy 26:1-11

PONDERING ON THE WAY:

Road sign for the day: Caution—Lent ahead. Beware of too much self-examination.

What? Isn't that what Lent is all about?

To a point.

What is happening in our Deuteronomy passage? The children of Israel, grateful for God's gifts from the land that God gave them, are to recite the story of God's redemptive dealings with them, beginning with their ancestor Abraham. Note the tone of this recitation. It's all about God. God gave the land to us, and that land is now bearing fruit. God heard our cries, God delivered us, God brought us to this land. So now we are bringing this fruit because God blessed our harvest.

Now fast-forward to the early church. Paul writes that the fulfillment of what God had in mind with his chosen people has now been embodied in Jesus Christ. This Christ, as described in Romans 10:5-13, is the culmination of the story of God's chosen people—the people who recited the legacy of God's involvement in their lives. What legacy are the new Christians to recite?

The legacy of salvation. "Confess with your lips that Jesus is Lord and believe in your heart that God raised him from the dead, [and] you will be saved."

Note the tone of Paul's words. It's all about God. It's about not seeking to establish our own righteousness, but submitting to God's righteousness. It's about Christ being the key to God's relationship with us, not our own works and efforts. And that's where the caution comes in. When we become preoccupied with ourselves during Lenten self-examination, we are on the road to a dangerous self-idolatry. We can't diagnose and then "repair" ourselves without God's grace. We can't make the wrongs right under our own power.

Lent is about self-examination to the point of the cross. Then it's all about what God did on that cross, and in the tomb three days later.

　　　—Carol Duerksen

PRAYING AND WALKING IN THE WORLD:

- Confess your areas of self-idolatry.

- Read Deuteronomy 26:5-9, substituting the story of your life, your family, your ancestors. Then read verses 10-11 and decide how you will express your gratitude to God for the bounty with which you have been blessed.

MARCH 20

TORN OFF AND GRAFTED IN

PLUNGING INTO THE WORD:

Romans 11:1-32

PONDERING ON THE WAY:

　　What does chosen mean?
　　God chose Abraham's family—at least his family through Sarah—
　　But what does that mean?

　　If it means being God's favorites,
　　I'll pass.
　　Abraham's family tried so hard—and failed …
　　Only so the unchosen people could get in?

　　"We tried so hard … it was as if
　　God hardened our hearts, blinded our eyes,
　　So despite our efforts,
　　We were doomed.
　　Is that what chosen means?"

If it means chosen for a mission,
A light to the Gentiles
Then … maybe.
God is sovereign, to choose how
God will choose.
Who am I to question?

Perhaps I am
The branch torn off,
With others taking my place.
Perhaps I am the one grafted in.

Perhaps … we all have been chosen.

—*Michele Hershberger*

PRAYING AND WALKING IN THE WORLD:

- How have you been disobedient to God? From what do you need to repent? What response do you offer to God for the grace you have received?

- Venture into a commentary: Locate a Bible commentary in a library or from your pastor. Read what it says about this passage or another passage that is particularly challenging for you.

MARCH 21 *(FOR CHILDREN AND FAMILIES)*

IT'S ALL ABOUT GOD

PLUNGING INTO THE WORD:

Romans 11:33-36

PONDERING ON THE WAY:

Today, let's learn a phrase that will help us praise God. Here's the phrase:

From God
And through God
And to God

Are all things.

To God be glory forever!

Learn this with your children. Say it with them every day until it is written on your hearts—not only the words, but the understanding of the words.

—*Carol Duerksen*

PRAYING AND WALKING IN THE WORLD:

- **Discuss:** What things are *from* God? What things are *through* God? What things are *to* God?

- Listen to a song from one of your favorite Christian CDs about the all-encompassing power of God.

- Turn to the Psalms and read one that expresses the same thoughts found in Romans 11:36. Offer this psalm as your prayer of praise to God.

MARCH 22

FAITH SHAPES

PLUNGING INTO THE WORD:

Romans 12:1-8

PONDERING ON THE WAY:

Heaven forbid

Cookie-cutter Christians

Shaped in the exact same mold

Same

Same

Same

Yet when your faith shape

Conflicts with mine

I cringe

I critique

I cry, "Foul!"

So what is it exactly
That I want?
I want sister and brother Christians
Who believe mostly like me,
Whose diversity is interesting
But never challenging,
Whose understanding of the Bible
Resonates with mine.
Not cookie-cutter
By any means.
Just the same dough
At least.

God forbid
I get
What I want.

   —*Carol Duerksen*

PRAYING AND WALKING IN THE WORLD:

- This passage is loaded with potential for personal growth. During this Lenten season, which areas of your life do you want to work on? Presenting your body as a living sacrifice? Renewing your mind? Thinking of yourself as full of worth because of Jesus, but not more highly than you should because of the sin in your life? Acknowledging and using your gifts? Acknowledging and appreciating the gifts of others?

- Catholics use the Rosary to give structure to their prayers. Create your own "structure" with which to pray during this Lenten season. Perhaps it is a rope with knots; perhaps you pray through the alphabet with each letter representing a person or situation; perhaps it is a prayer shawl with each color representing a certain prayer.

MARCH 23

TO DIE OR LIVE FOR PEACE

PLUNGING INTO THE WORD:

Romans 12:9-21

PONDERING ON THE WAY:

When my husband traveled to Burundi in Africa as part of a Mennonite Central Committee project, he met two men whose lives give testimony to this passage.

One of them, Norman, was a university student in Burundi when war broke out in Burundi and Rwanda. Some students who were in his Bible study were killed in the tribal war between the Hutus and Tutsis, and many of the remaining students went into hiding. Norman refused to take sides because he was committed to peace, and he refused to go into hiding. He helped his fellow students hide by taking them their belongings and other necessities at night to avoid being seen. He was committed to helping all victims, regardless of their ethnicity.

When told that he must join the fighters, Norman refused, saying, "We are all God's children; there is no sense in killing." As a result, he was dragged out of his college room and beaten severely.

Norman survived the beating and the war, and has co-founded Help Channel Burundi—a "Food for Work" organization that is providing hope to many people in Burundi. God has honored his faithfulness to the way of peace, and Norman's life continues to be a blessing to many.

Which is more difficult—to die or to live for one's beliefs in the way of peace? Norman is prepared to do both.

And you?

—*Carol Duerksen*

PRAYING AND WALKING IN THE WORLD:

- Watch a video about someone who valued peace over violence. Ghandi and Dr. Martin Luther King Jr. are obvious choices. *End of the Spear* is another good option.

- This is a great passage to memorize. Do the whole thing, or choose a section that talks about what you need to work on the most in your life.

- Pray for peace in relationships and in the world.

MARCH 24

GOD AND GOVERNMENT

PLUNGING INTO THE WORD:

Romans 13:1-7

PONDERING ON THE WAY:

The thought of not paying the percentage of my federal taxes that goes to the military machine has crossed my mind more than once, but I haven't had the courage or the conviction strong enough to follow through. At the same time, my husband and I have a very dear friend who is in the Air Force National Guard, and he has had the courage and conviction to go where he is sent, including the Middle East and Kuwait. We both read the same Bible, we follow the same Jesus.

Our passage today addresses the authority of the government. Several things are clear:

- Christians cannot frivolously disregard civil authority.

- Governments are agents of good, bringing order to what would be chaos without them.

- Governments should be supported with our taxes.

- Governments should not demand the total loyalty of a person—that loyalty belongs to God.

This passage, however, does not answer the basic question: *How do we know when the government has overstepped its boundaries and moved from being an agent of God to being an enemy of God?* That question remains to be discerned, based on our reading of the Bible and our perspective on what the government is doing; and like my friend and I, we may come out at different places.

One more thing is sure: The lordship of God is not limited to those areas that fit in the "religious" category. God is the God of the whole creation, and nothing in that creation, whether religious or secular, is beyond the power of God. This is one of the areas where I need to say to myself: "God is so much bigger than my ability to understand, and that's good news."

—*Carol Duerksen*

PRAYING AND WALKING IN THE WORLD:

- Pray for your government authorities—local, state or province, national. If you're used to doing this already, pray for an aspect of government you don't usually think about. If you don't do this on a regular basis, start the habit today.

- Does being subject to the governing authorities mean you have to do whatever they say? Do they have the right to persecute you when you commit civil disobedience because you follow Jesus? What do you think? How do Acts 4:13-22 and Acts 5:29 speak to this?

MARCH 25 *(FOR CHILDREN AND FAMILIES)*

LOVE IS LIKE A STACK OF LAUNDRY

PLUNGING INTO THE WORD:

Romans 13:8-14

PONDERING ON THE WAY:

Assemble the following items:

- A Valentine heart or something similar that portrays the feeling aspect of love
- A plate of food
- A stack of clean laundry

Ask the children to identify which of the items represent love, and why.

Talk about it, based on the following thoughts:

It's easy to think of love as just a good feeling you have for someone else. That is one aspect of love. But the love Paul talks about in the Bible is much more than that. To love somebody is to want good things for them and to help make good things happen for them. For example, the plate of food and the clean laundry represent love because these are some of the things people *do* for each other—provide them with food and clean clothes. It's easier to do loving things for people we love than for those we don't like, but Jesus wants us to actively do loving things for people we don't like.

—*Carol Duerksen*

PRAYING AND WALKING IN THE WORLD:

- Pray with your children, asking God to help you love people you may think are "unlovely."
- Talk about examples of *doing* love. Share examples of when you have acted on love even when it didn't feel fun, or talk about things you could do in the future.

MARCH 26

AUNT THELMA AND COMMUNION

PLUNGING INTO THE WORD:

Romans 14:1-12

PONDERING ON THE WAY:

So I said to Aunt Thelma—what is it
With these new people in church—you know,
The woman with the red hair and those bratty kids?

Thelma looked at me and sipped her cup of lukewarm coffee—
(She can be so irritating sometimes)
Oh, she said,
The ones who won't take
The bread and wine with us at Easter?

It's communion, Thelma, and it's grape juice—you know that.

But Thelma, they sit in the front row
And they move their hands funny when we pray.
I don't like it. Is there something wrong with the way
We do communion, now that's what
I'd like to know.

Thelma looked at me
Hard.
Have you been over to help them get settled in?
Have you had your ear to the ground to help her get a job?
Have you offered to babysit those kids?

That's what I'd like to know.
                              —*Michele Hershberger*

PRAYING AND WALKING IN THE WORLD:

- If Jesus were sitting across the kitchen table from you, what kind of conversation would you have with him about the red-haired woman with those bratty kids? What words would Jesus have for you?

- "We do not live to ourselves." Is that statement true for you? What sins do you need to confess right now?

MARCH 27

THEOLOGICALLY RIGHT OR GOOD?

PLUNGING INTO THE WORD:

Romans 14:13-23

PONDERING ON THE WAY:

When you stand before the judgment seat of God, some glorious—or scary—day, will you want to be commended for being theologically right ... or theologically good? Will you want to be known for your adherence to correct doctrine or for your compassionate behavior? Will you be more likely to reflect God's holiness or God's mercy?

Now wait a minute (you might be thinking), God's holiness and mercy can't be separated! There isn't any real dichotomy. Goodness is an integral part of rightness.

Yes. Exactly.

But you and I live in a world full of sin. We live in a world of inadequate understanding where people disagree about right doctrine and appropriate behavior. Sometimes Christians work with slogans like, "Unity in the essentials and freedom in the nonessentials." That's a fine idea, but it doesn't address the problem. Everyone agrees that we should stand firm on the core beliefs of the faith. But no one can agree what those core essentials are!

Paul lived in the same kind of world. And so, when the issue of whether or not to eat meat placed before idols came up, Paul had a complex situation on his hands. Paul himself agreed with the "strong," those who understood that the meat was clean food. But he positioned himself on the side of the "weak." The ones with the correct doctrine didn't love their brothers and sisters enough. And if Paul had to place a priority on one thing or another, he had to go with this: being good over being right.

Sound radical? Sound theologically correct?

Didn't Paul care about faulty theology? I think he did. But he also understood that right beliefs don't guarantee a pure heart. And are they really the right beliefs if there is no love for the weak brother or sister?

When you stand before the judgment throne on that glorious, scary day, what will God say? Will you rather be theologically right or theologically good?

—*Michele Hershberger*

PRAYING AND WALKING IN THE WORLD:

- What are the essentials of the faith for you? How are your core beliefs connected to God's call to love others, even those in your congregation with whom you disagree?

- Choose an issue the larger church is struggling over today. Now imagine yourself before God's throne. Which scenario would you rather face—God accusing you of being too lenient or too harsh with a brother or sister in Christ?

- How can an insistence of right belief actually be an act of mercy? Can you think of an example?

MARCH 28 *(FOR CHILDREN AND FAMILIES)*

WELCOMING

PLUNGING INTO THE WORD:

Romans 15:1-13

PONDERING ON THE WAY:

After reading the Scripture passage silently to orient yourself, talk to your children about Gentiles. For young children, it is enough to understand that back in the days of Jesus, Gentile was the name given to everyone who was different from you, if you were a Jew. And some of the Jews were mean to the Gentiles, because they were different.

Ask the children these questions:

- Do you know anyone who is different from you? How are they different?

- Is being different a good thing or a bad thing?

- Why do you think some people are short and other people are tall? Is it better to be one or the other?

- How are you different from other children?

Then say something to this effect: Everyone is different in one way or another, because God made us all special. So being different is a good thing. And Jesus tells us in our Bible verses today that we should be extra welcoming to people who are different from us. What does it mean to welcome people?

—Michele Hershberger

PRAYING AND WALKING IN THE WORLD:

- If you have younger children, you may want to make a pretend dinner and invite imaginary people in for a meal. If you have older children, you may want to make a list of specific things your family can do to provide welcome to people in your town who may feel as if they don't belong.

- **Adults:** Paul says you should welcome others as Christ has welcomed you. How did Christ welcome you? Did you deserve this welcome? How can you welcome people in a similar way to Christ's welcome? Who would Jesus invite in if he lived in your neighborhood?

MARCH 29

WHAT'S YOUR AMBITION?

PLUNGING INTO THE WORD:

Romans 15:14-22

PONDERING ON THE WAY:

If you were to take a personality test today, would you score higher on confidence or cowardice? Would you have higher scores on shyness or arrogance?

Paul would have scored high on confidence on the day he wrote this part of the letter to the Romans. Maybe even borderline arrogance. "I myself feel confident about you … that you yourselves are full of goodness" (v. 14). "I have reason to boast of my work for God" (v. 17). "I have fully proclaimed the good news of Christ" (v. 19).

How many pastors do you know who talk like that?

But there's more to the story. There's some ambivalence squeezed in between the confident lines. "Nevertheless on some points I have written to you rather boldly [because you needed it] … by way of reminder" (v. 15). Even the boasting is qualified. Paul boasts. "in Christ Jesus," and he speaks of nothing except what Christ has accomplished through him (v. 18).

It's all about Jesus, not Paul.

Maybe that's why he can be so confident.

—*Michele Hershberger*

PRAYING AND WALKING IN THE WORLD:

- Make a list of the things you feel confident to do. Then make a list of things you don't have confidence doing. Do you do anything on this second list anyway?

- Paul says that his ambition is to "proclaim the good news." In one sentence, what is your ambition? Can you boast about this ambition?

- In what ways can you boast about what Jesus is doing through you?

MARCH 30

TRAVEL PLANS

PLUNGING INTO THE WORD:

Romans 15:22-33

PONDERING ON THE WAY:

I was devastated. All my work, all my planning seemed to be all for nothing. I had intended to be a pastor, at this same church, for the next ten years. My husband and I would be able to keep the children in one school, one neighborhood, with one set of friends. Life would be hard at times, yes, but predictable and relatively safe. I had paid my dues. I had been a careful planner. And now this?

I won't go into detail about the reasons my plans changed. It's enough to say that I was disappointed and angry with God for a while.

Paul also planned for his future. Paul wrote about these plans in Romans 15:22-33. He made plans—but he held them loosely. Paul didn't seem to get upset when they didn't work out. And as we read between the lines, it's obvious that it didn't always work out.

"This is the reason that I have so often been hindered from coming to you ..." Obviously his earlier plans didn't materialize.

"But now, with no further place for me in these regions …" What does it mean to have no further role in the place where you had been?

Paul planned to go to Spain, stopping off at Rome along the way. He hoped to receive a warm welcome by the Roman Christian community and to be officially sent off and blessed by them. But by his very writing of these goals, was there a tinge of worry that this might not come to fruition? He already had been somewhat sidetracked. He needed to go to Jerusalem to deliver a love offering from the Macedonian church to the Jerusalem believers. It was a joyous task, but nonetheless, not the specified goal.

And Paul knew that he needed the prayers of these Roman brothers and sisters. There were forces at work that would derail him from his plans, especially as those plans served his true purpose—to proclaim the gospel.

Scholars tell us there is no evidence that Paul ever made it to Spain. He did go to Rome, but that was under other circumstances. He was led there in chains, where he met his death (Acts 28). Did he ever get to go? Did he ever fight back waves of disappointment when his plans fell flat?

I fought back the waves—a lot. We moved across the country. I thought my life was over, or at least the life I had come to love. I couldn't see into the future, or maybe I didn't want to. But God saw. And God took care of me.

I will never say that God caused me to stop pastoring. But God took what seemed negative and fruitless and used it to give me many new opportunities. Many new doors flung open. My future looked bright, despite my unfulfilled plans.

"I appeal to you, brothers and sisters, by our Lord Jesus Christ and by the love of the Spirit, to join me in earnest prayer to God on my behalf …"

Lord, help me to plan.

Lord, help me to submit to your will.

—*Michele Hershberger*

PRAYING AND WALKING IN THE WORLD:

- Write a "travel plans" letter the way Paul did. Be as specific as possible.

- Take this letter and hold it up to God. Give God your plans, your dreams, your goals.

GREETINGS OF LOVE

PLUNGING INTO THE WORD:

Romans 16:1-27

PONDERING ON THE WAY:

Most children like creative names, and this passage is full of them. Read the passage aloud, and ask your children to count how many names you say. It doesn't matter whether the names represent people Paul wants to send greetings to or people who are sending greetings with Paul. (I counted thirty-five.) Have fun with the pronunciations!

Explain to the children that greeting someone is like saying hi in a special way. Ask them to think of special ways we say hello to each other. All of the people Paul wanted to greet helped him do his work, which was caring for the church. *Who are the people who help us in the church? How many can we name?*

> —*Michele Hershberger*

PRAYING AND WALKING IN THE WORLD:

- Set out crayons, marker, and paper and make greeting cards for friends and/or people who help your family. The children can send them to Sunday school teachers, pastors, and other church workers.

- If your names have any special meaning, talk about that with your children. Is there a reason you gave your children their names? Tell the story behind these names.

- If you could choose a name for yourself, what would it be? Why?

APRIL 1

SPILT COFFEE AND TEARS

PLUNGING INTO THE WORD:

Luke 19:28-44

PONDERING ON THE WAY:

It was one of those early mornings, too early, when everything seemed to go wrong. I was going on three hours sleep at Chicago's O'Hare Airport, groggy and feeling sorry for myself.

Ah, I thought, *I'll treat myself to a fancy coffee.* Usually one to avoid the overly sweet java jolts, I grinned as I waited in the long line. I was going to pay more than four dollars for sixteen ounces, and I was going to enjoy every drop. I was worth it.

I walked in triumph with my trademark coffee. Now, if I were only sporting a cell phone, I'd really be hip.

Then it happened. In my hipness, I forgot to watch for the moving walkway. My step at the end of the floor slowed down but I didn't. Pair that with an even slower moving elderly lady and—you guessed it—my almost full caramel machiatto went everywhere.

I was upset. Notwithstanding sticky brown goo on the woman and me—she was very understanding—I had lost it. My expensive coffee. Most of all, I lost my coolness.

I wanted to cry. Lack of sleep and wounded pride and four dollars down the drain all worked to make my lower lip quiver just a bit.

With the help of several paper towels and inward scoldings, I regained control, sat down in an airport seat, and opened my Bible—to Luke 19:28-44.

I celebrated looking hip? I almost cried over spilled coffee? What's wrong with this picture?

The disciples and others were celebrating Jesus as he rode into Jerusalem on a colt. On one hand, this was right and good to do. Jesus was the king and did deserve their praise. Why, if they had not cried out in praise, the very stones would have shouted.

And yet, looking ahead in the story, this same crowd would yell, "Crucify him!

Crucify him!" by the end of the week. They were right to praise Jesus, but they were shouting accolades for the wrong reasons.

They thought Jesus was cool.

They thought Jesus would save them from Roman rule. They thought he would whip up some new miracles and whip out a sweet life for everyone. They thought Jesus was hip—by their own definition of it.

How many times do I see and praise the cultural Jesus, the hip Jesus, a strong Jesus on America's side, a Jesus who supports the good life for me—a Jesus made in my own image?

Then Jesus went to a place where he could see the city and—he wept. He wept for what he knew was coming.

When's the last time I wept over innocent people being crushed by the system, cried about the oppression of the poor, felt righteous anger about people physically or sexually abused?

Or is spilt coffee what I truly care about?

God have mercy on me.

God have mercy on me.

—*Michele Hershberger*

PRAYING AND WALKING IN THE WORLD:

- Why do you praise Jesus? Are they the right reasons?

- When's the last time you wept for a people who could not recognize the time of their visitation from God?

APRIL 2

THE POWER OF A SECRET

PLUNGING INTO THE WORD:

Luke 22:1-6

PONDERING ON THE WAY:

Families know the power of a secret. One person withholds information about a destructive event. As a result, the entire family system suffers from a silence that gains power by privately growing more intense in the shadows. Often, this can happen when a family member experiences abuse from a parent or a sibling. The longer the pain is hidden, the more power it has to destroy lives by shame, guilt, and despondency.

The religious leaders and Judas—whom they agreed to pay for his betrayal of Jesus—also kept a secret. It involved Judas's plan to betray Jesus into their hands. This was to be done in a setting where no crowds could cause an uprising. The leaders were not courageous enough to capture Jesus in broad daylight. They were afraid of Jesus' popularity with the people, and so they chose a coward's way out.

In this season when we are focusing on Christ's crucifixion and resurrection, we can see how his courage overcame their cowardice. His dying in the light of day on the cross canceled Judas's secret plan carried out in the secluded garden. The power of his resurrection canceled the power of the secret.

—*Laurie Oswald Robinson*

PRAYING AND WALKING IN THE WORLD:

- If you know of family secrets in your generation or those past, how did they shape your family?

- Pray that Christ's light and resurrection will shatter the power of that secret to shape your family in unhealthy ways.

- Share with a friend or family member what you have learned during your Lenten reflections about Christ's power in your life.

APRIL 3 *(FOR CHILDREN AND FAMILIES)*

CHRIST PICKS HIS TEAM

PLUNGING INTO THE WORD:

Luke 22:7-34

PONDERING ON THE WAY:

Have you ever felt the pain of being picked last for your gym class dodgeball team? Or, have you felt the pride of being chosen as team captain? Either way, your heart races faster when it's team-picking time. It feels more like a popularity contest than a true test of ability.

Think about the last time you were picked—or not picked—for a team. How did it feel to be chosen, or not? Talk about those feelings right now with the adults helping you to do this devotional.

Perhaps today's Bible story can help us think about this. A few days before Jesus was crucified, he had a special meal with his friends. In one way, these friends were special because they had been picked for a wonderful job. They were picked to spread God's love to everyone. In another way, these friends were just like you and me—sometimes scared, sometimes not so good at sports. Sometimes they even fought with each other, like in verse 24.

But great performers or perfect people aren't who Jesus seeks to be his followers. Jesus looks for kids and adults who are the kind of leaders who serve rather than wait to be served. When they see a need for someone to be loved or cared for, they reach out and help without expecting trophies or praise.

Jesus himself is the "captain" who models what that means. He tells his disciples that he is the one among them who serves. So if you want to know what being a good captain or team player is all about, look to Jesus, the greatest coach ever.

>   —*Laurie Oswald Robinson*

PRAYING AND WALKING IN THE WORLD:

- Pray that Jesus will help you be a good captain or team player on God's team of servant-hearted people.

- Find three servant-hearted people in the New Testament and write a story or draw a picture of their lives.

- Be a servant to someone in your neighborhood who needs help with yard work or other duties.

APRIL 4

THE SWORD OF CRISIS

PLUNGING INTO THE WORD:

Luke 22:35-38

PONDERING ON THE WAY:

As soon as I graduated from kindergarten, I knew in the depth of my Mennonite bones that Jesus was a peaceful Savior who called us to be peaceful people. But through the years, I discovered that people shaped by the Mennonite subculture struggled with the fact that good conflict resolution precedes good peacemaking. I observed that members of our congregation could be against going to war but still be at war with each other. Patterns of unexpressed anger often turned into passive-aggressive behaviors. By the time I had graduated from high school, I saw a string of pastors and families grapple with the messiness of unresolved conflict.

Today's short passage can help us better understand the link between conflict resolution and pacifism. On first reading, it seems Jesus is abandoning his peace-loving ways and condoning the use of swords. But Bible scholars say Jesus used *sword* to symbolize "crisis." In veiled language, Jesus attempted to alert his disciples to the coming crisis of his capture and crucifixion, and their need to be ready.

Jesus' challenge to his disciples sheds light on our discipleship. Do we grasp the sword of conflict as an inevitable part of being human and being Christian? If not, it may be time to substitute a more conflict-aware peacemaking for our one-dimensional pacifism.

—Laurie Oswald Robinson

PRAYING AND WALKING IN THE WORLD:

- Ask God to reveal whom you have felt anger toward recently. Has a fear of conflict kept you from acknowledging this anger? If so, admit your fear to God now.

- Ask God to help you accept and resolve your anger rather than run from it and shove it under the rug of resentment.

- Within your congregation or community, find one person with whom you have been at odds, and work toward mutual resolution of the conflict.

- Look at the next passage, Luke 22:39-53. Reflect on how Jesus used the sword in this passage. How does this text help interpret today's passage?

APRIL 5

MORE ALARMING THAN BLOOD

PLUNGING INTO THE WORD:

Luke 22:39-46

PONDERING ON THE WAY:

Several years ago, the Mel Gibson film, *The Passion of the Christ,* swept the world like wildfire. People of many faiths, Christian denominations, and theological bents argued the merits and demerits of Gibson's portrayal of Christ's last week. One scene gripped me more than all the others. It was of Christ praying all alone in the garden without the support and solidarity of his sleeping disciples.

Gibson's rendition showed how the devil appeared to Jesus through an evil character, tempting Jesus to abandon his life's call to suffer and to die. Chills ran up and down my spine as I watched Jesus battle this demon by sweating drops of blood. Yes, the blood was alarming. But even more alarming was the lethargy and sleepiness of the disciples in the face of such pathos. It's hard, on this side of the resurrection, to understand how they could fall into such prayerlessness during Jesus' crisis.

Most alarming of all was the link between their behavior and my own. Struggles and battles are waged around me every day for the wholeness of my soul and the souls of my loved ones or strangers. Somewhere, near or far, someone is sweating through situations that can be symbolized through drops of blood: soldiers in Iraq, divorcees, prodigal daughters and sons, unemployed parents, abused children. And yet, prayer times for these people are so hard to schedule and much harder to keep.

No matter what one thinks about Gibson's take on Jesus' passion, today's passage reminds us we cannot afford to fall asleep in the midst of the struggle. Drops of blood are a far cry away from the dreams of sleep.

—*Laurie Oswald Robinson*

PRAYING AND WALKING IN THE WORLD:

- Reflect on the patterns of your prayer life. Where are they strong and consistent? Where are they weak or inconsistent?

- Begin with today's prayer time to establish a pattern that is more consistent, even if it is only a few minutes each day.

- Seek a prayer partner with whom you can meet somewhat regularly for prayer and intercession. If you currently have one, mutually establish a new pattern that could enhance your partnership for the benefit of God's kingdom.

APRIL 6 *(FOR CHILDREN AND FAMILIES)*

A YUCKY KISS

PLUNGING INTO THE WORD:

Luke 22:47-53

PONDERING ON THE WAY:

It's natural to give our moms and dads kisses. We give kisses before we go to school, before we go to bed, before we go to a week of camp. And some kisses happen out of the blue—after we get a bike for our birthday, when Mom bakes us cookies, when our grandparents bring us an unexpected gift of a doll or fishing pole.

Today's Bible story tells us that Judas, one of Jesus' twelve disciples, kissed Jesus. But it wasn't the good kind. It was the yucky kiss of betrayal. Judas's kiss was a sign to the religious leaders that Jesus was the man they were to capture and later crucify.

This story about a yucky kiss can help us think about what kisses mean. In our culture, a kiss is a sign of affection, kindness, and loyalty. Jesus deserved that kind of kiss from Judas. Instead, he got a kiss that was opposite. That kiss betrayed their friendship and eventually led to Jesus' death.

But it's just like Jesus to turn the story around, from hate to love. In response to this cruel kiss of death, he stretched out his arms and gave his life—not only for Judas, his friend turned enemy, but for the whole world.

> —*Laurie Oswald Robinson*

PRAYING AND WALKING IN THE WORLD:

- Give your family kisses of kindness and thanks every day.
- Use some modeling clay to create the scene of Judas's yucky kiss.
- Have you hurt a friend? Ask for forgiveness from God and from your friend.

APRIL 7

PETER, OUR MIRROR

PLUNGING INTO THE WORD:

Luke 22:54-65

PONDERING ON THE WAY:

Throughout my Christian journey, I've heard more stories about Peter than any other disciple. Preachers, group leaders, and laity seem to have a love-hate relationship with this disciple. He mirrors so well our experiences of being first hot, then cold, then lukewarm in our walk with God. No matter how hard Peter tried or how hard we try, it seems the cycle of faith and fear plays over and over again.

Peter's humanness may intrigue us because it reveals our own waffling; one day we stand on the rock of Christ and our faith, the next day we sink in the shifting sands of ambivalence and fear. Christ named Peter as "the rock" on whom Christ would build his church. But even the dignity of this name failed him during his time of trial.

Who of us does not cringe in our souls when we read how Jesus turned to look at Peter after the final denial and the cock's crowing. What love and pain must have poured out of the Master's eyes. What tears of remorse and self-hatred must have poured out of Peter's.

Peter mirrors our own experience. But the Lord's look can penetrate the surface of our behaviors to understand the source of our fears and weakness. If you are shifting on the sands of life today, remember that Jesus' look can lead you to the stable rock of his love.

> —*Laurie Oswald Robinson*

PRAYING AND WALKING IN THE WORLD:

- Close your eyes and imagine that you are Peter. Listen to your three denials. Listen to the cock crowing. Watch the Lord look at you in pain and love. How does that look make you feel? Pray for forgiveness for your denials of the master.

- Now close your eyes and imagine you see the Lord look at you after your denials. What do you see in his eyes? Pray for the openness to receive the love of the master.

- For a family movie night, rent *The Passion of the Christ* or some other movie about Christ's passion. (**Note:** *The Passion of the Christ* includes graphic violence.) Discuss the movie's strengths and weaknesses. Discuss the nature of the relationship between Peter and the Lord.

APRIL 8

DARK NIGHT OF THE SOUL

PLUNGING INTO THE WORD:

Luke 22:66—23:25

PONDERING ON THE WAY:

St. John of the Cross, a well-known sixteenth-century saint, experienced "the dark night of the soul." He wrote poems and books to describe it. The dark night is when a believer feels deserted by God. What once felt fulfilling now leaves one empty. It's not that the Christian has stopped loving God. It feels more like God has stopped loving the Christian. In his writings, he explored the Christ's paschal mystery— through death to life—and strove to model what it meant to deny himself, pick up his cross, and follow Jesus.

Sandra Cronk, in *Dark Night Journey* (Pendle Hill Publications, 1991), encourages believers to welcome this dark night, because it helps us to grow deeper. She writes of how Christ experienced the dark night during crucifixion. It was a total stripping of glory, power, knowing, and strength. It left only mockery, shame, loss of friends, and humiliation. It even marked God's desertion of his Son, leaving Jesus with the awful choice to save or not to save himself. In verse 35 of today's passage, we hear the taunting crowds: "He saved others; let him save himself if he is the Messiah of God, his chosen one!"

The Messiah showed us that the dark night of the soul was the only way to fulfill his call as a chosen one. We are chosen to follow his example, even though we are eager for Lenten fasts to end and the sweet smell of Easter lilies to begin. We want to move quickly from the death of sin to the life of redemption. But Christ, St. John of the Cross, and Cronk testify that the only way to life is through death. It is not the darkness we must fear; it is our fear of the darkness that most often keeps us from the light.

> —*Laurie Oswald Robinson*

PRAYING AND WALKING IN THE WORLD:

- Sit in a dark room in silence, reflecting on the times you have experienced a dark night of the soul. What did you learn during that season of your life? Write or draw your answers in a journal or sketch book.

- Ask God to reveal to you what desire for fulfillment keeps you from embracing your emptiness. Ask for the grace during this Easter season to do less shopping, watching television, and multitasking and more resting, praying, and being quiet.

- Read *Dark Night of the Soul,* John of the Cross's classic. Other reading on the dark night and deeper prayer include: *Beginning to Pray* by Anthony Bloom (Paulist Press, 1970); and *My Only Friend Is Darkness: Living the Night of Faith* by Barbara Dent (Ava Maria Press, 1988).

APRIL 9

AS GOOD AS IT GETS

PLUNGING INTO THE WORD:

Luke 23:26-43

PONDERING ON THE WAY:

So this is the end of a very unusual life. The Son of God, who arrived on earth in an animal shelter, is going to leave his earthly life hanging between two bandits. It doesn't get more ironic than that.

Unless, of course, you consider the story of what he did in between. The Lord of the universe lived an ordinary life for thirty years. Then he spent three years getting himself in trouble with the Religious We Are Right, hanging out with the unlovely people of society, performing miracles, and teaching about a way of life that just didn't make sense. In the end, he was just more trouble than he was worth, so the Jewish authorities hung him on a cross.

Between two bandits. And even there, like in his birth and in his life, some believed and some didn't. One guy cries out with all the sarcasm he can muster: "Well, Mr. Messiah! This would be a good time to pull off a miracle for yourself and for us too!"

Despite his haze of tormenting pain, the other man sees Jesus clearly, understands who he is and where he is going. He knows he wants to go there too.

And Jesus said to that man, "Come along, my friend, come along."

So it is that while Jesus was dying for the sins of all humanity, he was welcoming one sinner into the kingdom. While he was literally carrying the cares of the world on his shoulders, he was speaking to the heart of one man. It doesn't get more amazing than that.

But it does. Because now he sits at the right hand of God, interceding for us, desiring our homage, welcoming us one at a time into the kingdom.

And that's as good as it gets.

—*Carol Duerksen*

PRAYING AND WALKING IN THE WORLD:

- **Prayer:** Jesus, be in my heart when I awake, and in my thoughts when I fall asleep. Then, in between my rising and my retiring, be in the story of my life.

- Watch one of the videos that have been produced about the life of Jesus.

APRIL 10

GETTING CLOSE

PLUNGING INTO THE WORD:

Luke 23:44-49; Hebrews 10:19-22

PONDERING ON THE WAY:

If you've ever taken the opportunity to read the Pentateuch (the first five books of the Bible), you know they are packed with the Law—things people were supposed to do and not do in order to have a right relationship with God. These laws included myriad instructions on who could approach God in the holy of holies in the tabernacle, and how that should be done. The Levites communicated with God on behalf of the rest of the people. Average folks couldn't get close. In fact, if you didn't belong there, getting too close to the holy of holies meant instant death, on the spot.

Then someone else died. Jesus, the Son of God, died, and when he did, the curtain in the temple ripped in two. The sacred space was exposed, the symbolic place for God's presence opened up. Jesus became our high priest. God invited us, because of his beloved Son's sacrifice, into a one-on-one relationship with the Lord of the universe. Now, rather than getting too close resulting in death, getting close results in life!

Now, we belong there. Praise God!

—*Carol Duerksen*

PRAYING AND WALKING IN THE WORLD:

- Locate a piece of cloth that you will be ripping in two. Take time to prepare your heart to pray, then slowly rip the cloth. As it tears, thank God for (1) God's unending and unfathomable love for all of humanity and (2) Jesus' death and the life we are offered as a result of his death and resurrection.

- Holding the two pieces of cloth, imagine how it feels to walk into the holy of holies—the presence of God. How does that feel for you? What do you want to say to God? What might God want to say to you?

APRIL 11

AND THEY OBSERVED THE SABBATH

PLUNGING INTO THE WORD:

Luke 23:50-56

PONDERING ON THE WAY:

The last verse of yesterday's passage tells us that the women who followed Jesus from Galilee stood at a distance, watching the horrific death of their friend. This is the man who had changed their lives and whom they supported financially (see Luke 8:1-3). The trauma of seeing him tortured and hung on a cross had to tear their hearts apart.

Today we read that they followed Joseph as he took Jesus' body down from the cross, wrapped it in linen cloth, and placed it in a tomb. Knowing where the body lay was important to them because they wanted to return with the burial spices and ointments.

But before they did anything, they observed the Sabbath.

Nothing—not even the death of Jesus—disrupted their obedience to keeping the Sabbath.

Does this seem strange? Everything stopped for the Sabbath? Even the burial rites for Jesus' body?

Compared to today's laissez-faire attitude by most Christians toward the Sabbath, yes, it seems surprising. But in that time and that culture, it wasn't an issue for the women. The Sabbath meant rest and worship. It's what you did. No questions asked.

And so, in shock and dismay, they rested and worshipped with their faith community. Their world torn apart, they drew strength from the familiar. The hopes they may have had for the new kingdom ushered in by the Jesus Messiah had been dashed, and they found comfort and stability in the traditions they had known since birth.

The women didn't know that the next morning their despair would turn to joy and their mourning into dancing. Their lives would be uprooted again in amazing, confusing, exciting, and challenging ways. For now, for this day, they rested and waited.

—*Carol Duerksen*

PRAYING AND WALKING IN THE WORLD:

- What is your relationship with the Sabbath? Are there changes you feel you should make?

- What faith traditions do you have that give you stability?

- In what areas are you being stretched in your faith journey?

APRIL 12 *(FOR CHILDREN AND FAMILIES)*

JEREMY'S EASTER EGG

PLUNGING INTO THE WORD:

Luke 24:1-12

PONDERING ON THE WAY:

Jeremy was born with physical and mental problems and also a sickness that meant he would not live very long. Still, his parents wanted to give him as normal a life as possible, so they sent him to a Catholic elementary school. By the time he was twelve, Jeremy was only in second grade. His teacher got quite irritated with him because he squirmed in his seat, drooled, and made grunting noises. Once in a while he talked clearly, but mostly, he didn't seem to be getting anything at all.

When spring came, the children began to talk about Easter. The teacher told them the story of Jesus. Then she handed out large plastic eggs to the children and told them to take the egg home and bring it back with something inside that showed new life.

The teacher figured Jeremy didn't understand what she said, and she planned to talk to his parents that evening and explain the assignment. But she forgot, and the next morning her classroom was full of excited children and their plastic eggs.

In the first egg, the teacher found a flower, and she praised the little girl who had brought it. "A flower is a sign of new life," the teacher said.

The next egg had a plastic butterfly in it. "We know that a caterpillar changes into a beautiful butterfly," she said. "Very good!"

Next, the teacher found a rock with moss on it. She explained that moss also showed life.

Then the teacher opened the fourth egg. The egg was empty! *It's probably Jeremy's egg,* she thought to herself. *I just wish I'd called his parents and explained the assignment.*

She set the egg aside so she wouldn't embarrass Jeremy. But it didn't work.

Suddenly Jeremy said, "Aren't you going to talk about my egg?"

Flustered, the teacher said, "But Jeremy—your egg is empty!"

He looked into her eyes and said softly, "Yes, but Jesus' tomb was empty too!"

Time seemed to stop. The teacher couldn't believe her ears. Finally she said, "Do you know why the tomb was empty?"

"Oh, yes!" Jeremy answered. "Jesus was killed and put in there. Then his Father raised him up!"

Three months later, Jeremy died. The people who came to pay their respects at the mortuary were surprised to see nineteen eggs on top of his casket, all of them empty.

—Carol Duerksen, based on a story by Ida Mae Kempel

PRAYING AND WALKING IN THE WORLD:

- What are the signs of Easter's new life in your life?

- Get a plastic egg. Open it up, hold it in your hands, and pray for the joy of the resurrection of Jesus to fill your heart.

APRIL 13

WHERE WAS GOD?

PLUNGING INTO THE WORD:

Luke 24:13-35

PONDERING ON THE WAY:

Do you remember where you were when the Twin Towers got hit? When the Challenger exploded? When President Kennedy was assassinated? When you received the news of the death of a loved one?

Emotional traumas like these sear their impressions on our hearts and minds. The unimaginable becomes reality. We can't fathom what has happened. One of the things we need to do is talk about it. And one of the things we often ask is: Where was God?

As the two disciples walked to Emmaus, they rehashed the tragic death of their leader and friend Jesus. They still couldn't believe it. If Jesus was indeed the Messiah, then what happened? Where was God?

So they walk and talk, and a stranger joins them. The stranger asks what they're talking about, and they're dumbfounded. How can anyone not know what happened in Jerusalem? The two disciples painstakingly and painfully recall the events for the stranger's benefit, ending with the confusing yet potentially amazing news that Jesus was actually alive.

And of course he was, right there, walking with them.

Where is God when tragedy and catastrophe strike? Does unbelievably bad news make us unbelievers? No. Jesus walks with us through the fire, through the gunshots, through the valley of the shadow of death. Never forget it: Jesus walks with us.

> —*Carol Duerksen*

PRAYING AND WALKING IN THE WORLD:

- Read Psalm 23 as a prayer.

- Recall a time when you needed comfort and a listening ear, and someone was the "ears of Jesus" for you. Write a thank-you note to that person.

- Who needs you to walk through a valley with them?

APRIL 14 *(FOR CHILDREN AND FAMILIES)*

NO GHOST

PLUNGING INTO THE WORD:

Luke 24:36-49

PONDERING ON THE WAY:

Begin this time by asking children what they think about ghosts. Include the following questions: Are ghosts real? Do ghosts have skin and bones? Can a ghost eat?

Depending on the age of your children, either read verses 36-43, or tell the story in words your children will understand. Include the following:

People thought Jesus was dead and that they were seeing a ghost. But Jesus had risen again—he was alive! The people needed proof, so he asked them to touch him—a ghost doesn't have skin and bones. Then he did another thing that ghosts don't do—he ate!

Jesus really did live on the earth, die, and arise from the dead. He went back to live with God, and here's the cool thing: Jesus is both with God and with us. We can't see him the way the disciples did, but we can feel him in our hearts and see what he does in our lives.

—*Carol Duerksen*

PRAYING AND WALKING IN THE WORLD:

* Sing the children's song "Into My Heart," or pray the words of the song together:

    Into my heart,

    Into my heart,

    Come into my heart, Lord Jesus.

    Come in today,

    Come in to stay,

    Come into my heart, Lord Jesus.

* **Adults:** This passage contains the verses known as the Great Commission. The Great Commission tells us what the good news is, the people who are to be told the good news, and the power that will be given to them to help spread the gospel. How does your life intersect with this commission? Do you feel the good news in your heart? Are you living it out? Sharing it? Knowing the power of the Holy Spirit? Pray for this commission to become your personal experience.

* What proof do you need today that Jesus is alive and well in the world and in your life?

APRIL 15

BOOKENDS

PLUNGING INTO THE WORD:

Luke 24:50-53

PONDERING ON THE WAY:

A week ago, we looked at the bookends of Jesus' earthly life. Today, we see the bookends of Luke's Gospel. Using Luke as the writer, the Holy Spirit did a beautiful job of drawing parallels at the beginning and end of this book.

Jesus leads his followers out of Jerusalem, blesses them, and then disappears from the earth and returns to be with God. His followers, who are on cloud nine themselves, return to Jerusalem, to the temple, to spend time there worshipping and praising God. They know that they have witnessed something truly amazing. The Holy Spirit is at work, and they know that more marvelous things lie ahead.

Rewind to the beginning of Luke's Gospel. Zechariah is in Jerusalem, in the temple, worshipping God. He receives a surprising visit from an angel, promising him and his wife, Elizabeth, a son in their old age. The Holy Spirit is at work, and Zechariah will experience more miraculous things in the future.

I can't help but wonder: If we would bookend our days, our weeks, our months, and years with the reminder that the Holy Spirit is working, and marvelous things lie ahead, how different the story of our lives in between those bookends might be.

—*Carol Duerksen*

PRAYING AND WALKING IN THE WORLD:

- Choose a prayer you will use to bookend your days, morning and evening. Change the prayer every few weeks.

APRIL 16 *(FOR CHILDREN AND FAMILIES)*

DO YOU BELIEVE?

PLUNGING INTO THE WORD:

John 11:1-27

PONDERING ON THE WAY:

For parents to read silently: Young children have a wonderful gift of faith. They can and do—believe. Sometimes we may get alarmed when their belief in God and Peter Rabbit fall into the same category, but that's to be expected. They do believe in Moses, but they also feel certain about the tooth fairy. We older ones know better; we work hard to sort the truth from make-believe. Yet at times we get so stuck on the particular explanations of the Gospel miracles that we impede our ability to just believe. Seeing the stories afresh in the eyes of children can help us recapture a strong faith.

Begin your family time by asking these questions:

1. Do you believe in miracles?

2. Who sends us miracles?

3. What miracles have you seen lately?

Then retell the story in your own words, or read the following aloud. Encourage your children to act out the story as you tell it.

Now a certain man named Lazarus was very sick. Oh, his head hurt so much *(they hold their heads and grimace)*. He lived with his sisters, Mary and Martha. And his sisters knew what to do—tell Jesus. So they sent some friends to run and tell Jesus *(children run and tell Jesus)*. Jesus loved Lazarus, but he walked too slowly *(children walk slowly)* so that by the time Jesus got to Lazarus's home, Lazarus was dead *(Lazarus falls over)*. His friends put Lazarus in a tomb *(move Lazarus to a new place)* and put a big stone over the tomb *(use pillows)*. Lazarus was there for four days before Jesus came.

Mary and Martha saw Jesus coming to their house, and one by one they ran to meet him *(children run to Jesus)*. They didn't understand why Jesus didn't get there sooner. But Jesus said, "Don't worry. Everything will be all right. I am the resurrection and the life."

Now ask the children: "What do you think the word resurrection means?" After hearing their answers, help them see that resurrection means that someone who is dead is alive again. Ask them, "So what do you think is going to happen to Lazarus?" Try to coax out of them: "Jesus will bring him back to life!" Ask them to listen as you finish the story.

Jesus cried a little bit, because he saw how sad Lazarus's friends and sisters were *(sad faces)*. But then he went to the tomb and he said, "Take away the stone!" *(Children take away the pillow.)* Then Jesus prayed to God *(children do this)* and called out, "Lazarus, come out of there!" And Lazarus walked out of the tomb! *(Lazarus rises up, and everyone cheers and claps.)*

End your time together as a family with prayer, thanking God for being the resurrection and the life.

        —*Michele Hershberger*

PRAYING AND WALKING IN THE WORLD:

*   Have crayons and paper ready for the children if they want to draw the story.

*   Use modeling clay and build a tomb with a big stone in front of it.

*   Don't be afraid to discuss issues of death with older children. They may want to talk about why Christians don't come back to life now, or they may wonder where people go after they die. Be sensitive to their questions. Reassure them that God loves them and takes cares of people after death.

APRIL 17

WHY JESUS WEPT

PLUNGING INTO THE WORD:

John 11:28-44

PONDERING ON THE WAY:

You stayed away two extra days
I'd have rebuked you too—softly
of course, I'm half scared of you

But that's exactly why I'm so mad—
because I do believe in your supernatural power.
I know you could have healed him.

Why did you let his sisters weep?

Why did *you* weep, Jesus?

Did you stay away just so there'd be a miracle to do?
That's kinda hard to swallow.

I'm wrapped up in my own burial cloths—questions that keep
Winding their way through my brain, restricting movement
Pressing my flesh between strips of muslin—
Dried, caked blood of old hurts, festering sores
of doubt.

It's getting hard to move.
The stench is pretty bad.

Why do you weep, Jesus?

Maybe I just can't understand why you were gone those two days,
maybe I just have to
Let it go.

Let it go and just (Is he calling my name?)—
Believe.

> —*Michele Hershberger*

PRAYING AND WALKING IN THE WORLD:

- What grave clothes are tying you up right now? Can you hear Jesus calling you out of the cave?

- Is it okay to question Jesus? Is it okay to wonder why perfectly good people suffer so much? Does it help to read in this story that Jesus wept?

- Do you need God's help to just—believe?

- Tear some muslin or cotton cloth into long strips, the kind of strips that one might wrap around a corpse in the time of Jesus. Take a black felt pen and write down on these strips all of the things that bind you up. Ask yourself what problems, situations, or relationships keep you from enjoying life, from free movement. Pray and ask Jesus to unbind you and let you go, just as he did Lazarus.

APRIL 18

IN THIS YOU REJOICE

PLUNGING INTO THE WORD:

1 Peter 1:1-9

PONDERING ON THE WAY:

"Although you have not seen him, you love him; and even though you do not see him now, you believe in him and rejoice with an indescribable and glorious joy...."

I've sat by the bedside of several dying souls in my time as a pastor. There was nothing more precious, more sacred than those moments of waiting, moments of quiet, moments of peaceful preparation for the transition into a brand-new world.

Sometimes my friends suffered bodily. They would groan, they would close their eyes to keep from crying out, they would bite their lips. But I would look on their faces, etched with pain, and see beyond that to a dignity, a perseverance, but more than that. There was hope on their faces, even as their eyes remained closed.

"Though you are in much pain, yet you believe...."

But Peter wasn't writing to cancer patients in hospital wards. He was writing to Jewish believers scattered throughout a wide geographic area. He was writing to people suffering for their faith, people who risked their lives calling Jesus Lord. "Though you are in fear of your physical life, yet you believe...."

And not only believe, but rejoice! "In this you rejoice, even if now for a little while you have had to suffer various trials...."

In this you rejoice? What is there to rejoice about in the midst of persecution? What is there to rejoice about when you are slowly dying in pain or you are grieving a loved one or suffering from depression?

Believe—and rejoice?

Rejoice, says Peter, for by his great mercy, God has given us a new birth into a living hope through the resurrection of Jesus Christ from the dead.

Resurrection hope—like Paul and Silas in the jail in Acts 16. They have nothing to sing about. They have nothing to sing about. They're sitting in this stinking dungeon, the innermost part of the dungeon. There is filth, human filth, and rats, and it's so dark you aren't sure what you're sitting in, and the flesh on their backs is gaping open. The blood flows down and mixes with the mud. And we say, well it's okay, it's okay because God's gonna send an earthquake and they are going to be set free, but they don't know that yet. They don't know that yet. Silas' eye is swollen shut, and Paul's lip is huge, one tooth gone. They might die—they meet with the magistrate in the morning, if they don't bleed to death by then—they are probably going to die, and they ... sing. They sing.

"Although you have not seen him, you love him; and even though you do not see him now, you believe in him and rejoice with an indescribable and glorious joy...."

—*Michele Hershberger*

PRAYING AND WALKING IN THE WORLD:

- What is your dungeon? Do you dare sing to God like Paul and Silas? Can you sing despite your pain and doubt?

- Is it okay if you can't rejoice and sing? What about all those lament psalms that cry out in sorrow and anger to God. Is that part of our faith too?

APRIL 19

LIVING IN THE VALLEY

PLUNGING INTO THE WORD:

Ezekiel 37:1-14

PONDERING ON THE WAY:

So who are you in this story? Which part do you relate to the most? Those dry bones, brittle and hopeless? They were so depleted, they proclaimed hopelessness even after the miracle of resurrection had begun! Are you that dry?

Or are you faithful and fearful Ezekiel? Has God used you lately to bring about resurrection to the people you care about? Has God asked you questions that are impossible to answer? Has that power made you tremble as you watched?

Are you in the middle of a miracle? Bones and sinews together, but not much else? Do you feel caught in a group of corpses, waiting for the breath of God to make you come alive?

Is it scary to be waiting for life? Called for a mission? In the middle of transformation? Wherever you find yourself—whoever you are in this story—know that God is there too.

God is knitting your life back together. God will put the finishing touches on. You don't have to know all the answers. Your incredulity at the miracle won't stop it from happening.

There is no degree of death God can't breathe new life into.

God cared enough about dead people to send a vision to Ezekiel to bring this good news—"Nothing's too dead for me." The exile to Babylon was an open grave but also, ironically, the place of new birth, a second chance to be God's people, a burst of grace that made skeletons walk.

The God who cared that much back then ... is the same God today.

Really.

—*Michele Hershberger*

PRAYING AND WALKING IN THE WORLD:

- Spend some time in silence before God. Really listen to hear where God thinks you are in this story. Are you dry bones? Ezekiel? Or in the messy middle of renewal? God is where you are. God can help you no matter who you are in this story.

- Name the valley. Count your dry bones. What is draining life right out of you now? What does God say about this?

- Who is your Ezekiel? Have you thanked this person lately?

APRIL 20 *(FOR CHILDREN AND FAMILIES)*

SOFT HEARTS, HARD HEARTS

PLUNGING INTO THE WORD:

Jeremiah 31:31-34; Ezekiel 36:25-28

PONDERING ON THE WAY:

After reading the two Scripture passages, ask your children what they think a "heart of stone" means and what a "heart of flesh" means. Which one would be harder? Which one would be softer?

Pass around a small stone. Ask the children if it is alive. "What makes something alive? What do living things do that nonliving things can't do? How could you make this stone come alive? Is that possible?"

Talk about how only a miracle could make the stone come alive. Say, "The Bible verses today talk about God's people having a heart of stone. Do you think that's a good thing or a bad thing? They didn't really have hearts made of stone, but this was a special way of saying that the people were mean and naughty. Do you feel hard inside when you disobey someone? How does it feel inside when you are mean to someone else? Hard or soft?"

Continue by saying: "It's impossible to make this stone come alive or become soft. But that's what God said would happen to the hearts of the people when God was there. What do you think it means to have a soft heart?" (If they are stuck, suggest things like being willing to listen or to change, obeying parents, being kind, etc.)

—*Michele Hershberger*

PRAYING AND WALKING IN THE WORLD:

- Give everyone one stone and some modeling clay. Let the children shape the clay into hearts. Direct each one to talk about how their hearts were soft at times and hard at times this last week.

- Pray and ask God to do a miracle and soften the hard places in your heart.

APRIL 21

COFFEE, SUDOKU, AND JOY

PLUNGING INTO THE WORD:

1 John 1:1-4

PONDERING ON THE WAY:

Sometimes the oddest things make me happy. Well, *happy* is perhaps too strong a word ... *content* maybe. Or maybe the word is—*joy*.

And it's usually the little things. The perfect cup of coffee on a cool morning. The surprise of wildflowers along the roadside. A good joke. Sudoku. Time to just sit.

I was taken by the joy in 1 John 1:1-4. And it wasn't so much about coffee and wildflowers, although there is nothing wrong with those things. But the people writing (note the "we") in this passage found joy in things more odd than even Sudoku. They found it in knowing something with certainty, something they had seen and touched, which leads to another joy, having something to share with others, something that matters. They had something that fights evil and brings people together, something that changes the world.

They knew where they were going. They knew what brought fellowship.

They were sure about Jesus. Wow.

That beats coffee any day.

—*Michele Hershberger*

PRAYING AND WALKING IN THE WORLD:

- What brought you joy in the last twenty-four hours? Are there other joys God would like to give you?

- Do you have hot-coffee-on-a-cool-morning joy? Do you have the deeper joy of 1 John 1:1-4? It's okay to have both. Which kind of joy do you need the most?

- Is it weird to think about church work—evangelism, writing, nurturing congregational life—as complete joy? Should it be weird?

- What are you certain of? What would you like to be certain of?

- How can Jesus deepen your joy today?

APRIL 22

LIGHT A CANDLE FOR GOD

PLUNGING INTO THE WORD:

1 John 1:5-10

PONDERING ON THE WAY:

Let's light a candle for God
for God is light.
Now, is that the bright
light of the TV screen,
bare light bulb of interrogation,
"light of my life, you make me whole,"
cold light of a gas station at midnight
blinking, we ask how to find our way?

Or are you
Soft light in a baby's eyes,
Warm glow of afternoon sun on vincas
Hot glow of the sanctuary Pentecost morning?

This light, your light
pierces my darkness,
reaches back to the dingy corners of
My soul
for musty misdeeds stacked in the back room
for filmy residue of doubts,
the monsters under my bed.

Your light drives them out—
but I have to squint sometimes.

I will not say I have no sin …
But I will say the darkness is less now and that I still
"welcome darkness my old friend, I've come to"—

Light a candle and curse the darkness
And start walking toward
You.

  —Michele Hershberger

PRAYING AND WALKING IN THE WORLD:

- We don't have to be perfect. In fact, 1 John tells us we must admit we sin. But we are to walk in the light. What does that mean for you?

- Light five or six candles. Let each candle represent a darkness that God has sent away with his light. Pray with gratitude for this grace.

APRIL 23 *(FOR CHILDREN AND FAMILIES)*

CAVE OF THE WINDS

PLUNGING INTO THE WORD:

1 John 2:1-14

PONDERING ON THE WAY:

When I was ten years old, my family took a vacation to Colorado where we visited Cave of the Winds. As we walked deeper and deeper inside the cave, the guide turned off all the lights. Even though I was grasping Dad's hand, I felt very scared. It was so dark, I couldn't see his hand, but I knew he was there because of his strong grasp.

Caves are very, very dark places. Have you ever explored a cave or visited a cave on vacation with your family? What did it feel like to be in that darkness? Were you scared?

In the deepest part of the cave, there is no ounce of daylight—and that's where we were. When the guide lit a candle, it cast light on Dad and me. I breathed easier. Not only could I feel Dad's hand, now I could see it, and that helped me feel less scared.

Today's Bible story tells that even though we don't live inside caves, we can live in the kind of darkness we find in such places as Cave of the Winds. If we hate other people—doing bad things to them and saying bad things about them—then it's like we're living in a dark cave, all by ourselves, without having someone to hold our hand.

But if we love other people—being kind, caring, and sharing—then it's as if we're walking in the daylight outside the cave. In this daylight, we can walk side by side, hand in hand, safe in the love of God we show each other.

—*Laurie Oswald Robinson*

PRAYING AND WALKING IN THE WORLD:

- Go inside a dark closet and shut the door. What does it feel like to be in that dark place? Now, ask your mother or father or another adult to join you in the closet and hold your hand. What does it feel like? Then open the door and stand outside in the lighted room, joining hands with them. What does that feel like?

- In your prayers today, thank God you can live in God's love and feel safe in the company of others who love you. Light a candle during this prayer to remind you that God's love helps you walk in the light, side by side with family and friends.

- Find a book about caves and discuss how a light can fill the darkness in caves; or explore a cave during a family outing.

APRIL 24

"COVER GIRL" FOR JESUS

PLUNGING INTO THE WORD:

1 John 2:15-17

PONDERING ON THE WAY:

The late Mother Teresa, who founded Missionaries of Charity to serve the poorest of the poor in Calcutta and around the world, did not seek fame. But she received it. By the early 1970s she was an international celebrity. Her face appeared on the cover of many prestigious magazines and newspapers. Her fame is attributed to in the 1969 documentary *Something Beautiful for God* by Malcolm Muggeridge and his 1971 book of the same title. In 1979, Mother Teresa received the Nobel Peace Prize for her ministry. She refused the conventional ceremonial banquet and asked that the $6000 prize be diverted to Calcutta's poor, claiming the funds would feed hundreds of needy people for a year.

In 1999, Gallup ranked Mother Teresa as the "most admired person of the twentieth century." At the time of her death in 1997, Missionaries of Charity had more than 4000 sisters, an associated brotherhood of 300 members and more than 100,000 lay volunteers. They operated 610 missions in 123 countries. These included hospices and homes for people with HIV/AIDS, leprosy and tuberculosis; soup kitchens; children's and family counseling programs; orphanages; and schools.

If today's Scripture passages were the focus of a Christian magazine, Mother Teresa's face would shine from the cover, and her story would embody chapter 2, verses 15-17. Mother Teresa knew the world and its desires are passing away. And because she knew this fleetingness, she achieved fame that passes the test of time. She reminds us that it's not the world's goods but goodness grounded in God that makes us truly rich.

—*Laurie Oswald Robinson*

PRAYING AND WALKING IN THE WORLD:

- Reflect on what a reporter would say about your life in a story written for a Christian publication. Journal your answer.

- At what junctures would your story jibe with verses 15-17? At what junctures would it diverge?

- Read *Something Beautiful for God* for your personal or family reading time.

- Watch the movie *Mother Teresa* from Fox Family Films.

APRIL 25

"I WISH WE'D ALL BEEN READY"

PLUNGING INTO THE WORD:

1 John 2:18-29

PONDERING ON THE WAY:

The Jesus Movement swept North America when I was a teenager in the mid-1970s. Those years followed the freewheeling spirit of the 1960s. Our society's new freedoms were not free. They cost. People indulging in unfettered lifestyles paid a price in bondages, and they sought to break them through Jesus' love and power. The unraveling of society evoked a rash of end-time talk and spiritual renewal.

Such songs as "I Wish We'd All Been Ready" filled Bible studies with images of the last days; youth services replaced ancient hymns and formal preaching with praise lyrics and speaking in tongues; and flocks of young people wept at revival altars everywhere.

In our troubled world, we hear a new rash of end-time talk. And it sounds eerily familiar to today's passage of Scripture. Written about a hundred years after Christ ascended into the heavens, the author in verse 18 tells readers that it is "the last hour" and that many antichrists have already come. The author encourages believers to beware of those who would deceive them about their faith and lead them away from solid teaching about Jesus.

The writer says the ability to discern truth from falsehood occurs when believers accept the anointing they received from the Holy One, Jesus Christ. The Spirit of Jesus abides within them and will be their teacher. It seems 1 John is advocating for a balance: holding to outward tenants of faith as well as to the inward teaching of the Spirit. Being ready for Jesus' return is a good blend of truth that comes from without and from within. True freedom lies not in being a groupie or a lone ranger but in being connected to Christ and community.

—*Laurie Oswald Robinson*

PRAYING AND WALKING IN THE WORLD:

- In your quiet time today, reflect on the 1960s. Were you alive then and, if so, did that era shape who you are today?

- Pray for the discernment of the Holy Spirit on any spiritual issue with which you are currently grappling. Couple this with seeking counsel from your brothers and sisters in Christ.

- Identify a young person who desires to try his or her wings in new forms of worship. Dialogue with that person about different worship styles and share what worship means to you.

OSWALD FAMILY PHOTOS

PLUNGING INTO THE WORD:

1 John 3:1-10

PONDERING ON THE WAY:

A tradition at our Oswald family reunions is filling a table with old family photos we dig out of closets and cedar chests. One photo shows me how much Cousin Joanne looks like Aunt Helen; another shows me how much Nephew Seth looks like Grandpa Paul. A present-day reunion mirrors the past and also predicts the future.

The clan's youngest members will follow in some of the footsteps of their ancestors; what seems like a new direction is a well-worn pattern. The seed of behavior planted generations ago still grows. I long to share coffee with Great-Uncle Sam who died after I met him only once, or enjoy supper with Grandma Elizabeth, who died when I was two. Pictures tell me I share their facial features. I wonder how many of their dreams, fears, and hopes beat in my own heart.

In 1 John 3, we read how a seed of God's love is planted in us as children of God. God's likeness is etched into our features, even though what we will be is not yet revealed fully. Verse 2 says that we can know one thing for sure: When he is revealed, we will be like him. In our psychologically aware world, we speak of how we need to break unhealthy generational patterns. In God's family, that is unnecessary, as our heavenly parent passes on patterns that are healthy. As God's seeds flower in our souls, they lead us away from sin and into right living.

—Laurie Oswald Robinson

PRAYING AND WALKING IN THE WORLD:

- Reflect on the stories you have heard at family reunions. What aunt or uncle or grandparent do you most identify with? Why? What qualities of theirs do you share? Are they healthy or unhealthy? Sinful or life-giving?

- In prayer today, ask God to help you receive fresh revelation about God's attributes. Ask for greater ability to mirror those features and attitudes.

- Plant a few seeds in a pot you can place next to your quiet-time place or office desk. Watch them grow and think about how God's seed is growing inside of you.

APRIL 27

CRASH

PLUNGING INTO THE WORD:

1 John 3:11-24

PONDERING ON THE WAY:

Crash won the Oscar for best picture at the 2006 Academy Awards. The film took top honors by portraying a 36-hour period in Los Angeles. It showed how the life of a white officer in the Los Angeles Police Department collided with the lives of African American, Middle Eastern, and Hispanic characters in such a way that highlights bigotry.

A pivotal scene shows how the police officer sexually abuses a woman. A day later, he is called to a crash site where she is pinned inside a car. When she recognizes her former abuser, she resists letting him pry her from the twisted metal. But in the face of death, she chooses to trust his help. And he saves her from the fire that would have killed them both.

This film does not end with hopelessly rampant racism. It shows how changes in characters bring redemption to their attitudes. Today's passage brings—in the face of hatred and evil—the redemption of Christ's modeling. Human beings are prone to parrot the hatred and evil of Cain. But Christ shows us what love is—laying down his life for us. And so we can lay our lives down for each other.

We may not practice the kind of overt bigotry portrayed in *Crash*. But in equally harmful ways, we may exercise false power and superiority because of education, wealth, color, privilege or religion. First John reminds us we don't have to remain in this "death," a life void of mutual relationships. Like the police officer, we can make new choices and reach out to our brothers and sisters who may experience needs different from ours. It will mean risking former attitudes that seem to keep us safe but really are very dangerous.

—*Laurie Oswald Robinson*

PRAYING AND WALKING IN THE WORLD:

- Reflect on the subtle but harmful ways social status gives people a false sense of power. List them in a journal or notepad.

- Hold the list in your open hands as you pray. Ask God for forgiveness for the times your superiority caused others to "crash" into marginalization or isolation.

- Find one person on your list and ask forgiveness for your silent but deadly attitude.

- Watch the movie *Crash*. (Warning: this film has strong language.)

APRIL 28

DIVINE MERCY, A TRUE PROPHECY

PLUNGING INTO THE WORD:

1 John 4:1-6

PONDERING ON THE WAY:

Because of how mystics experience God, they easily can be seen as "false prophets," a term used in today's passage. Mystics receive revelations directly from God through meditation and intuition or other states beyond normal consciousness. Because these means bypass more widely trusted, intellectual ways of knowing God, church leaders are not quick to declare such revelations as true inspirations helpful for the entire church.

Some mystics, such as Saint Faustina, are recognized as true prophets. She was a member of the Congregation of Sisters of Our Lady of Mercy in Poland. In 1931, she received revelations from Christ regarding his mercy for all people. Before she died in 1938, she left a diary describing a vision of Jesus clothed in a white garment. He raised one hand in blessing; the other hand touched his garment at the breast. Two large rays—one red and the other pale—shone from the opening. Jesus told her to paint the image with the inscription, "Jesus, I trust in you." The pale ray stands for the water that makes souls righteous; the red ray stands for the blood that is the life of souls. He told her the rays come from the depths of his most tender mercy at the time his agonizing heart was opened by a lance on the cross. He told her that those who dwell in the shelter of these rays will receive God's mercy and comfort and find healing.

Some sectors of the Catholic Church observe "Divine Mercy Sunday" the Sunday after Easter. They recognize that her inspiration passes 1 John's test for truth: "Every spirit that confesses that Jesus Christ has come in the flesh is from God." In the early church—as today—some people denied the incarnation, the belief that Jesus was fully human and fully divine. They fail to believe that Jesus came from God into our world to show us who God is and to restore our broken relationship through the mercies of God. God used Faustina as a twentieth-century messenger of this mercy in a miserable and merciless world.

—*Laurie Oswald Robinson*

PRAYING AND WALKING IN THE WORLD:

- Reflect about the times you've had an unusual image of God come to you in your prayer times, or have had a friend or member of your family or church family share such a vision. What was your attitude about it?

- Pray you will become more open to Christ's living water and God's ocean of mercy by any means God chooses for you.

- Read Faustina's diary, *Divine Mercy in My Soul* (Congregation of Marians of the Immaculate Conception, 1987).

APRIL 29 *(FOR CHILDREN AND FAMILIES)*

GO, CHICKEN FAT, GO!

PLUNGING INTO THE WORD:

1 John 4:7-21

PONDERING ON THE WAY:

I still can see and smell and feel that morning gym class as a third-grader at Manson Elementary School in Iowa. All one hundred pounds of me huffed and puffed my way through the gym-class jumping jacks, as more than thirty thin little girls squeaked their tennis shoes across the shiny wooden floor.

Arms and legs moved in time to the 4/4 beat of an exercise record, a favorite of our gym teacher, Mrs. Shay. One little girl I thought was my friend pointed at me and started laughing as the record blared, "Go, you chicken fat, go!" She led a chorus of other girls who all pointed at me and said, "Go, Laurie, go chicken fat!" For what seemed like eternity, they hooted at me, until Mrs. Shay put brakes on the abuse. "Stop it, everyone!" she shouted, as my little spirit crumpled inside my big body and my tears washed the gym floor.

Most boys and girls have been both the teaser and the teased. At such times, it's easy to be afraid of being all alone, or feeling guilty we made someone else feel alone. But today's passage tells us that no one has to be afraid to be alone. God loves us all with perfect love. It's the kind of love that knows that no matter how fat or skinny, no matter how good or bad at gym, we are always lovable.

And because all of us are lovable, God asks us to love one another. We don't see Jesus on our school gym floors, but he is there, caring about how we treat each other. The way we know if we love a God we can't see is to love our friends we can see.

—*Laurie Oswald Robinson*

PRAYING AND WALKING IN THE WORLD:

- When you have you been the teaser? When have you been the teased? What did each time feel like? Discuss with your parents what your feelings were and how you would like to deal with these situations next time they happen.

- In your prayers, ask God to help you know how to love others for being lovable, not for how they look or what they do.

- Next time in gym class, have fun without comparing who is "the best."

APRIL 30

THE BIBLE AND BROTHER

PLUNGING INTO THE WORD:

1 John 5:1-21

PONDERING ON THE WAY:

Christians believe they are to love God. It goes without saying, doesn't it? Of course Christians love God!

Maybe it goes without saying, but sometimes, it also seems to go without "doing." What does loving God actually mean? What is the active aspect of loving God?

According to verses 1-5, the active aspect of our love of God is threefold.

First, we believe that Jesus is the Christ. We believe that Jesus is the Son of God, and we are not embarrassed to say that and to live in that reality. In a day when truth is being questioned, this is a truth upon which we stand firm.

Second, we obey God's commandments. Here it gets sticky. Different interpretations of God's instructions for life as found in the Bible have resulted in the huge variety of denominations, all of which call themselves Christians. We are called to be faithful—to the Spirit of God within us and to the discernment we experience in the body of believers. We strive to obey God's commandments, knowing that we will fail at times but also knowing that's not a reason not to try.

Finally, we love each other. Loving each other goes hand in hand with loving God. When we don't love our sisters and brothers, we have dropped the hand of God. That's not a good place to be. And loving doesn't mean the casual "love" we sign at the end of a letter. Loving means sacrifice, going the second and third mile, loving those who don't love us. Need more specifics? Read what Jesus said and did for three years on the earth.

As I write this, my cat, named Brother, has planted himself in my open Bible on the table beside me. I realize that I am often more patient with him and give him more attention than I do many of my brothers and sisters in Christ. I realize I have much to learn, and much to do, when it comes to loving God.

—*Carol Duerksen*

PRAYING AND WALKING IN THE WORLD:

Meditate with the following prayer, personalizing it, repeating it, using it in ways that are meaningful to you:

Lord God, I love you.

Walk with me as I strive to know, understand, and do your commandments.

Give me your heart for my brothers and sisters. Use me as a vessel of your love for them. I can't do this by myself. Help.

In the name of Jesus the Christ, amen.

MAY 1 *(FOR CHILDREN AND FAMILIES)*

GOOD JOB, GOD!

PLUNGING INTO THE WORD:

Genesis 1:1—2:3

PONDERING ON THE WAY:

Can you think of a time when someone has told you, "Good job!"? Maybe it was when you did well on some schoolwork, or you cleaned your room, or you were extra nice to your brother or sister.

Can you imagine somebody saying "Good job!" to God? Have you ever said it? Let's try it.

Parents, read the Bible story to the children. After each day, pause and say, "Good job!" with your children. If you want to make it more fun, give God a high five along with the words!

—*Carol Duerksen*

PRAYING AND WALKING IN THE WORLD:

Children of God of all ages, take the opportunity today to experience and appreciate God's creation. Spring is exploding in nature—this is a wonderful time to celebrate the creation story. Take a walk in your neighborhood, yard, park or countryside. Thank God for everything you see. If you have children with you, say with them: "God made this. Good job, God!" Realize that God made everything—even manmade things were created from materials that the Creator put into place. Reflect on the amazing variety and complexity of God's work.

WHAT I KNOW FOR SURE

PLUNGING INTO THE WORD:

Genesis 2:4-25

PONDERING ON THE WAY:

Today's reading is the second account of the creation story. Yesterday's reading tells of a world created by God, and the last thing created is humanity. In today's passage, God creates a man, then the garden, the animals, and finally Eve.

Which one is true?

The truth, I believe, is this: God created everything. I don't know how, or in what order, or how long it took. I don't need to know.

Some people treat these two chapters as a historical account of what actually happened. Others treat them as a mythological story. The third option is to say that this text is a proclamation of God's deliberate and decisive involvement with creation. Creator creates creation. These three words are inseparable, and they say it all. The subject of the sentence is never separated from the object, and the object is never separated from the subject. And the verb connecting them refers to a special action by God and the special relation that binds these two parties together. Creator creates creation.

The second truth I see in these two chapters is the paradox of a God who is both transcendent and imminent. God is both "above and beyond" anything we can imagine or comprehend. At the same time, God is close enough to walk in the garden with us. God is over all creation, yet God is inside of us.

And that's what I know for sure.

—*Carol Duerksen*

PRAYING AND WALKING IN THE WORLD:

- What are your thoughts about these two accounts of creation?

- What do you know for sure about how the world was created?

- What do you know for sure about the Creator?

- Theologians have written books about these two chapters—you've just read the *Cliff Notes* version of two pages in the *Interpretation* commentary by Walter

Brueggemann. If you are interested in digging deeper into an understanding of biblical texts, I'd highly recommend this series of commentaries because they are easily accessible to lay persons like myself who want to know more about God's Word.

MAY 3 *(FOR CHILDREN AND FAMILIES)*

THE BLAME GAME

PLUNGING INTO THE WORD:

Genesis 3:1-19

PONDERING ON THE WAY:

Do you ever say, "He started it!"? Or do you ever say, "She made me do it!"? Do you ever blame somebody else for something that you chose to do?

Would you believe that people have been blaming somebody else since the beginning of people on this earth?

God made the first two people on the earth, Adam and Eve. They were getting along great in the big beautiful garden that God gave them to live in.

Then one day a sneaky snake who could talk told Eve that she should eat some fruit from a special tree. The only problem was that God told Eve and Adam not to eat from that tree. The snake told Eve she'd be really smart if she ate the fruit—as smart as God, in fact. That sounded good to Eve, so she ate some of the fruit, and then she asked her husband if he wanted some too. He said, "Sure, why not?" and he ate some too.

Of course, God found out, and they were in big trouble. And you know what Adam said when God asked if he'd had some of the special fruit?

He said, "Eve started it!"

And you know what Eve said? "The snake made me do it!"

It's true that other people can get us into trouble, but most of the time we have a choice, just as Adam and Eve did. We can choose to do what is right. If we choose to do what we know we should do, then we don't have to play the "blame game." Because really, there are much more fun games to play!

—*Carol Duerksen*

PRAYING AND WALKING IN THE WORLD:

- When do you blame somebody else for something?

- **Adults and children:** Sometimes we want somebody else to look bad as a way to help us look good. That isn't right. God doesn't say "Good job!" to us when we put others down in order to raise ourselves up. Ask God to forgive you for the times you've done that. Pray for a sense of self-worth that comes from knowing you are a creation of God, not from putting others down.

MAY 4

GREENER PASTURES

PLUNGING INTO THE WORD:

Genesis 3:20-24

PONDERING ON THE WAY:

Yesterday we talked about the blame game being as old as humanity itself. Here's another thing about us that hasn't changed since the beginning: We always want more, more, more. But the grass isn't always greener on the other side of the fence.

Eve thought that having more wisdom sounded great, and if she could get it in the process of eating some delicious fruit, why, that was just too good to pass up. Adam agreed. They had it all—a beautiful garden, all the food they needed, and a relationship with God. But they wanted more. And the consequences of their greediness and disobedience? They got kicked out of the garden paradise. The grass definitely wasn't greener on the other side.

Our North American culture feeds our desire to want more, and it feeds *on* our desire to want more. It tells us that having more stuff will make us feel good, so we buy more stuff and fuel the materialism furnace.

The other side of the issue, as my husband would say, is that the production of goods gives people jobs, so keep on buying! (Maybe that's why it's okay for him to have a motorcycle, but he frowns when I want another llama. People manufacture motorcycles. Llamas make more llamas.)

See, there you have my confession. Both the motorcycle and the llama are luxury items. We just wanted something more.

—*Carol Duerksen*

PRAYING AND WALKING IN THE WORLD:

- What about you? Are you happy in your paradise? Or are you always jumping the fence into what looks like greener pastures?

- When you do get more, what are the consequences? Less peace of mind? More work and less time for relationships? Is life better when you have more?

MAY 5

IN COLD BLOOD

PLUNGING INTO THE WORD:

Genesis 4:1-16

PONDERING ON THE WAY:

One of the contributing editors to *With* magazine sent me a story the other day. After reading it, my first thought was to reject the story. It was just too violent, too graphic, too bloody. It's bad enough that teens see this stuff in movies and on television. They don't have to read it in *With*.

The only problem was, the story was paraphrased straight from the Bible. You just read it. Cain lures Abel into a field and murders him in cold blood. The first human being born on the earth murders the second one. How horrible is that?

The first people on the earth have control issues, and now the next generation succumbs to jealousy and hatred. You'd think God would throw up those big creative hands and say: "I give up! I've only started, but I give up!"

God was angry, to be sure. Cain got consequences, no doubt. Sin results in separation from God, and Cain was separated from his land and became a wandering fugitive. But God didn't give him the "eye for an eye" treatment. God actually protected Cain from anyone who might try to kill him.

The inherent ability to do violence to each other lies within each one of us, and we all do it, whether in word or deed. We are all sinners. Yet somehow God's ability to lift us up goes above and beyond our tendency to fall.

—*Carol Duerksen*

PRAYING AND WALKING IN THE WORLD:

- To whom do you do violence? How? Ask God for forgiveness.

- Can you take the next step? Can you ask the person for forgiveness?

- How do you feel about capital punishment? Is it legal in your state?

FROM REVENGE TO LOVE

PLUNGING INTO THE WORD:

Genesis 4:17-26; Matthew 5:38-48

PONDERING ON THE WAY:

Buried in this recounting of who bore whom and who did what is the beginning of a terrible tradition. Lamech boasts to his wives that he "killed a man for wounding me, a young man for striking me."

Yes, a young man's life was snuffed out because he hit Lamech. The terrible tradition that started was called the Law of Lamech, and it meant unlimited revenge. Unlimited revenge was the law of the land when Moses issued a new law, and that was "an eye for an eye." This limited revenge was certainly better than the Law of Lamech and prevented people from handing out a punishment greater than the injury warranted.

Then Jesus came along with new instructions to replace the law of "an eye for an eye." Matthew 5:38-41 gives the new law from Jesus, which is actually a return to Paradise (God's original, ultimate will): His followers are to love their enemies and do good to them. From unlimited revenge to unlimited love—that's quite a journey for humanity to travel. Our calling to "be perfect as your heavenly Father is perfect" seems to be asking a bit much!

The word *perfect* comes from a Greek word that means "end," "goal," or "limit." Usually it means "attaining to the end—complete maturity." In this case, since the comparison is made between God and God's children, the meaning is expanded to include more than "maturity." The perfection Jesus is talking about is a God-like quality of love and kindness, even for those who don't deserve it. It isn't a matter of being completely without sin, but it is a case of working at attitudes and actions toward others. It isn't something we can do alone, but the grace of God who loves us when we don't deserve it also can give us the strength to offer that grace to our enemies.

—*Carol Duerksen*

PRAYING AND WALKING IN THE WORLD:

- Pray for the people who fit into your "enemy" category.

- Sing or listen to a song that describes the unlimited love of God.

Credits: *NRSV Harper Study Bible,* copyright © 1991 by Zondervan, Grand Rapids, Michigan.

MAY 7

GOD DESTROYS THE EARTH

PLUNGING INTO THE WORD:

Genesis 6:5-22

PONDERING ON THE WAY:

It was every inclination of the thoughts of our hearts.
Even God can have regrets.

Start over. Cleanse the earth.

Like a dream breaking onto the shore of consciousness,
We tried to recreate what was lost. All will be well.

It is every inclination.
We succeed and we move on.

There is wickedness breaking onto the shores of consciousness.
Even God has regrets. What have we done?

We try to start over, to cleanse the earth.

Who will we find favor with?
Every inclination of the thoughts of our hearts.
Falls … like the rain.

Complex designs; memories of the fallen.
Shifting forms blurring in the rain, the constant rain.

One day I thought I saw a bird fly through gray sky
But nothing is out there.
One day I thought I saw an angel walking toward me,
Like a dream breaking onto the shore of consciousness.

There is endless possibility, but in the rain, nothing develops.
The waves keep crashing, but we are not yet clean.

Now we do not need God to destroy the world.
We can do it ourselves.

Like a dream, we try to recreate what was lost.
We are lost. We will never find Eden again.

—*Michele Hershberger*

PRAYING AND WALKING IN THE WORLD:

- There is evil all around us today. As much as we try to amend our ways, we still have evil inclinations. Do you think God is still questioning creating us?

- God has never sent another flood to cover the earth, but there are still natural disasters. While we try to recreate paradise, what natural habitats are we destroying? While we seek natural resources, what environmental assets are we draining?

MAY 8 *(FOR CHILDREN AND FAMILIES)*

FUN WITH NOAH!

PLUNGING INTO THE WORD:

Genesis 7

PONDERING ON THE WAY:

Advance preparation:

- Healthful snacks

- One or two blankets and chairs that can be used as an "ark"

How many of you know who Noah is? *(Parents, if your children don't know the story, take time to tell it to them now.)*

Let's be Noah and all the animals we can think of. First, we need to build the ark. What is an ark? *(a big boat)*

We have to build a really big boat. *(Get out the blankets and chairs and assemble the "boat.")*

Now we have to get food for the animals. Who will get the food? *(Have children put your snacks inside the tent.)*

Now it's time for the animals to come in. You be an animal and make its sound and move the way that animal moves, and I'll try to guess what animal you are. Okay? *(They become animals. If you have two children, have the animals come in together into the boat, two by two. Then, they go back out and become a different animal.)*

Do you think we thought up all the animals in the world? We surely didn't. God cared for all the animals and fed all the animals and made sure they had everything they needed. And do you know what? God cares for us like that too. *(Take time now to sit inside the boat and eat your snacks.)*

> —Michele Hershberger

PRAYING AND WALKING IN THE WORLD:

- When you get scared, think of how Noah must have felt, living through a flood. God took care of Noah, and God can take care of you too.

- What is your favorite animal? What is your least favorite animal? Do you have a pet? On the ark there were all of those creatures and thousands more too.

- God cares about animals. In Bible times, Noah helped God take care of them. How can you help God care for the animals?

- **Adults:** Noah found favor with God and thus was charged to save his family and all the animals. What can you do to save a part of your local and global environment?

MAY 9

WAITING AND WAITING

PLUNGING INTO THE WORD:

Genesis 8

PONDERING ON THE WAY:

My daughter was once in the musical *Children of Eden*, a retelling through song and dance of the first nine chapters of Genesis. The first act focuses on Adam and Eve, Cain and Abel, and their struggles. The second act is about Noah and his family. Tara played Noah's wife, so of course, the second act was my favorite.

There were songs to introduce the family members, a ballet for the animals boarding the huge "ark," and an intense number featuring a solo by Almighty God to represent the start of the flood.

And then there was a scene about how bored the family was on the ark. And then a few songs about how the food was running out. Then a touching dance about the desperation of life on the ark, followed by a climatic scene full of anger and betrayal, because life on the ark was so hard. You get the idea.

Noah's family had to be bored after forty days of rain, but that was just the beginning. The water kept rising for 150 days. That's five months. When you get bored, think about having to live on a boat with animals from February to July. But that's not all, folks. Only a short three months after the ark came to a rest, the other mountaintops appeared. Finally, on the twenty-seventh day of the second month of the following year, the earth was dry and they got to leave the ark.

It's common to believe that Noah lived on the ark for forty days. Isn't that what all the cute songs say? But it was more than a year on that ark. They were hungry and tired and fed up with the animals and their noises (and smells). Really, that boat was no picnic.

Perspective is everything. On one hand, Noah and his family were living through terrible times—awful, boring, stinky, scary times. But what was the alternative? Being dead at the bottom of the sea.

I wonder how many times I see myself desperate in a floating zoo instead of blessed in an ark of grace. I wonder how many times I'm bored instead of grateful. It's so hard to wait when the days are long and painful—or boring. Can I see a glimpse of the sun in the midst of the rain? Can I see God saving me as I bob up and down on the water?

—*Michele Hershberger*

PRAYING AND WALKING IN THE WORLD:

- Noah and his family were very patient, but the wait was well worth it. What are you willing to wait for and pray about for forty days? One hundred fifty days? What is worth a week of prayer and waiting?

- Sometimes our prayers are like the dove. They don't work the first time, but the next time or the time after that, they do. What are some "doves" that have come back to you? Do you have a "dove" on your hands right now?

MAY 10 *(FOR CHILDREN AND FAMILIES)*

RAINBOWS AND COVENANTS

PLUNGING INTO THE WORD:

Genesis 9:1-17

PONDERING ON THE WAY:

After the flood, God made a covenant. A covenant is a promise. God made a covenant with Noah and his family, promising that there would never be another worldwide flood. God also promised that Noah's family would have lots of children and refill the earth with people. There would always be summer, fall, winter, and spring, and the people of the earth would always be able to eat meat and vegetables for food. God really takes care of his people.

The people made a promise too, as part of the covenant. Noah's family and all of their children and their children (that means you and me too) would take care of one another and the earth. God had us promise this because God loves us and wants to keep us safe.

God put a rainbow in the sky as a sign that God would never destroy the world again. This was the seal of the covenant between God, humans, animals, and the whole earth. Every time we see a rainbow, it is a reminder of the promise God made to never destroy the earth and the promise humans made to take care of creation.

—*Michele Hershberger*

PRAYING AND WALKING IN THE WORLD:

- God has promised to take care of us, and we are called to care for God's creation. That means being careful about the way we treat the earth and not using too many of its resources. What are you doing, or what can you do, to be careful with earth?

- Get out crayons, markers, or paint and draw rainbows. Then you can remember the promise that rainbows represent.

- What is your favorite color? Do you think God has a favorite color?

MAY 11

SIN AND A CHOICE

PLUNGING INTO THE WORD:

Genesis 9:18-29

PONDERING ON THE WAY:

It took a year and more than one backed up sewer, but God finally had purged the earth of all its evil influences. Noah and his family could now live flawless lives and create a race of super-righteous humans. It could be the new Eden.

But something went wrong.

Wait, what? I know you're experiencing whiplash. After all this trouble, all this cleansing of the evil, almost immediately, Noah is drunk, Ham is mortally shamed, a third of the future population is cursed, and millennia of feuds and wars are instigated. Oh, and Noah lived 950 years.

This seems impossible. Noah, what were you thinking? What happened to Eden? If sin comes only from outside sources, then Noah and his family would be sin-free in a utopia of happiness. That's not the case. Sin can come from the inside too. Noah had sin inside of him.

A store owner might be well-off, but greed may cause her to siphon funds. A married man may love his wife, but lust might cause him to cheat. Idolatry, profanities, vanity, overworking, disrespect, lying, murder—we as humans have the capacity to sin within our hearts without any outside help. Yes, in many cases, outside sources may influence our actions, but there is always a choice. That choice comes from within us.

What will you choose?

We can do only so much to combat the outside forces. Some are out of our control; some can be ignored or transformed. The sin that comes from within us is a completely different monster, and we have to fight it in a different way. Be aware of those internal forces. We cannot fight them alone. But we can give them to God.

—*Michele Hershberger*

PRAYING AND WALKING IN THE WORLD:

- What are some outside forces that lead us into sin? What are internal forces? Which are more powerful?

- Spend time in prayer thinking about a sin that plagues you. Acknowledge your brokenness before God. Give God your problems and worries.

MAY 12

LA TORRE DE BABEL

PLUNGING INTO THE WORD:

Genesis 11:1-9

PONDERING ON THE WAY:

The humans are at it again. Here we have people like Tarshish, Rodanim, Casluhim, Uzal, and Jobab, all direct descendants of the godly (if occasionally drunk) Noah. This one big family decided to build a nice city. It would have a nice big tower, the biggest in the world. Look out, Sears Tower, this city would really make a name for them.

This doesn't sound like such a bad plan—science, industry, innovation, the advancement of their small civilization. In today's day and age, we all appreciate success and tall towers. They wanted a home, they wanted everyone to stay centralized, they wanted improvement and, eventually, indoor plumbing. These seem like relatively benign desires to us in our world of constant developments. So what does God have against good architecture?

Nothing. This story deserves a closer look. They wanted to reach the heavens, and in their time heavens meant the literal domain of God. They didn't understand the cosmos as we do now. They wanted to reach the level of the Almighty. They wanted fame and immortality. With their unified language, their science could feed on itself and grow.

God stopped the advancement of their wicked knowledge. As in the garden, the people were guilty of pride. They thought too much of themselves and began a competition with God Almighty.

This story needs a closer look. Or maybe we need a closer look at ourselves. It seems okay to us now to make names for ourselves and build our skyscrapers or our empires, our fame and fortune. After all, God didn't disrupt the Renaissance or any other age of enlightenment, including our present technology boom. But does that make our pride acceptable now? No. The very action condemned in this passage is condoned in our society. Society may not understand what is so bad about a great tower. That is the point at which we begin to think our understanding of the world is greater than God's.

¿Y somos preparados tratar con las repercusiones? I didn't think so.

God wants us to be humble. God wants us to acknowledge God's sovereignty and accept our shortcomings and faults. All that we do is through God. All of our gifts and talents are from God.

—*Michele Hershberger*

PRAYING AND WALKING IN THE WORLD:

• Of what are you too proud? Make a list.

• Are there things in your life that you are trying to control (trying to be like God)? Make a list of all the things you worry about. Go back over your list and mark all the ones that you can't do anything about. Give those to God.

• How does pride kill off a community, even if it doesn't cause us to speak another language?

MAY 13

KNOWING GOD

PLUNGING INTO THE WORD:

Exodus 13:17—14:9

PONDERING ON THE WAY:

The word *know* is the most frequently used word in Exodus. No, I'm not counting *a, the, will, are, and, toaster* or any other frequently used words. "Know [nō] verb: to believe firmly in the truth or certainty of something, to realize something, to have a thorough understanding of something."

God is very concerned that the people know the One who rescued them from Egypt. In the pillar of cloud and fire—God is. Though the Israelites cannot see God directly, they can see *something*. The presence is there. God is. God guides and protects them, keeping them always from danger and toward the Promised Land. The Israelites know and trust that presence, the cloud and the fire. God takes care of them so they may know that the Lord God is Lord.

God also is concerned that the Egyptians know him. The text describes the hardening of Pharaoh's heart and the resulting battle as the means by which the Egyptians will know who is truly God. I struggle with this part of the story. God hardened Pharaoh's heart so that many Egyptians would die, but somehow they also would know the Lord—when it's too late! I can understand the need for a demonstration of God's power so the slaves can begin to trust God, to have appropriate respect and even healthy fear. But to harden the heart of a king and then knock him down for it? Isn't that grossly unfair?

So … maybe I don't know the Lord as much as I think I do. Maybe there are some things I don't understand. Maybe my questions about free will and God's sovereignty, and why innocent people die and undeserving people get rescued are unanswerable. At least for now. Maybe they are my pillar of cloud and fire. I can see God, and yet I can't.

Maybe knowing the Lord doesn't equal having it all figured out.

Can I trust the pillar ahead of me, trust it enough to take a step forward? Can I trust even when the army is behind me, closing in? Can I, in those moments, know the Lord?

Lord, help me know you.

—*Michele Hershberger*

PRAYING AND WALKING IN THE WORLD:

- In the pillar of cloud and fire, God is both revealed and hidden. You sense something, but can't quite see God. What is your pillar?

- In what ways does God reveal God's self to you? To others?

- What is your first response when you look back over your shoulder and see the army advancing?

- Pray and ask for help to know—really know—the Lord.

MAY 14

LEAVE THE LAND, FACE THE WATER

PLUNGING INTO THE WORD:

Exodus 14:10-18

PONDERING ON THE WAY:

Six months into my new marriage, I discovered that liberation from former loneliness was not a freeway into the bliss of instant companionship. In front of me loomed some growth curves. After forty-five years of being single, becoming a partner was a tough transition. I feel deeply called to marriage. But some days the responsibilities of caring about another person tempt me to reminisce about roads with fewer hairpin curves and steep hills.

My marriage lacks the drama of the parting of the Red Sea and the death of an entire army. Marital conflict has not come close to such a scenario! But comparisons could be drawn about attitudes and tensions. The Israelites delivered from the Egyptians' tyrannies felt delighted about release into a new future but also desirous to return to an earlier life.

They cried to Moses, "It would have been better for us to serve the Egyptians than to die in the wilderness." They didn't want the Egyptians—they wanted their out-of-Egypt situation to be less like an unknown wilderness and more like a predictable home.

Moses saw through their overdependence on human comfort and their lack of dependence on God's provision and said, "Do not be afraid, stand firm, and see the deliverance that the Lord will accomplish for you today." The Lord told Moses to be the first to go forward by lifting up his staff and stretching his hand over the sea to divide it. God's provision would not come free. It would cost risk and cooperation. The Israelites were not to fight. They were to stand still—completely trusting: "The Lord will fight for you."

I am the more anxious one in our marriage; my more laid-back husband often takes the first step in trusting. He often models the belief that the Lord who brought us out of separateness into union will help us forge a healthy togetherness. But the sea parts only as we stop looking at the land behind us and face the water in front of us.

—*Laurie Oswald Robinson*

PRAYING AND WALKING IN THE WORLD:

- Reflect on the times you came to the shores of your own "Red Sea" and were tempted to turn around and go back to the land you left. What did you choose? How did those choices affect your ongoing spiritual journey?

- Pray for the courage to stretch out your hand of faith over what looks like an impossible situation.

- Do you know someone who is enslaved within an Egypt-like situation or feels abandoned in an unknown wilderness? Spend some time helping—in mutual, respectful ways—to strengthen that person's faith and trust.

MAY 15 *(FOR CHILDREN AND FAMILIES)*

RED SEA TSUNAMI

PLUNGING INTO THE WORD:

Exodus 14:19-31

PONDERING ON THE WAY:

Do you remember where you were the day after Christmas in 2004? It was the day
a huge tsunami—a tidal wave caused by an earthquake—traveled across the Indian
Ocean. Eventually a huge wall of water taller than your house hit the coastline,
killing more than 280,000 people and destroying towns, villages, and resorts.

In today's Bible story, we read about another huge wave that could be called a
tsunami. Moses and the Israelites fled Egypt and its cruel ruler and came to the Red
Sea. God told Moses to stretch his hand across the water. The sea parted with walls
of water on the right and the left, and God's people crossed the dry sea floor. But the
ruler and his army weren't so fortunate. God told Moses to stretch his hand across
the Red Sea again, and the two walls of water crashed and drowned all the soldiers
and their horses.

The crossing of the Red Sea was the original and best example of how the Israelites
were to wage war—by letting God do it in a miraculous way. When God said, "Be
still and you will see" (vv. 13-14), God wasn't kidding.

But God kills people?

It's not wise for Christians to think God sends tsunamis to kill people. Nor would it
be wise to label God as violent, even though people died in today's story. Perhaps it's
good to reflect on verse 31, which tells us how "the people saw the great work that
the Lord did."

And because of this miracle, it says, the people trusted God.

As humans we don't easily understand natural disasters or miracles. But we do know
that God, who creates the oceans, is more powerful than its biggest waves. And
God can be trusted to not let us drown in our tough times, no matter how big. Just
as God made a pathway through the sea for the Israelites, God will make a path
through our problems.

            —*Laurie Oswald Robinson*

PRAYING AND WALKING IN THE WORLD:

- What problem are you facing right now? Talk about it with your parents or
  another loving adult.

- Together, pray that God will make a path through this problem through the
  power of God's grace and wisdom.

- This Bible story can be found in such movies as *The Prince of Egypt*. Rent this
  movie—or another movie about Moses—and discuss how God's power is used
  for good in people's lives.

MAY 16

FEARS INTO FAITH

PLUNGING INTO THE WORD:

Acts 2:1-13

PONDERING ON THE WAY:

Many people don't know that New York City has more than fifteen Mennonite congregations flung throughout the city of eight million people. Each year when I lived there, from 1986 through 1998, the congregations gathered for a multicultural celebration hosted by the New York City Council of Mennonite Churches.

No matter their background, participants experience the language, culture, and worship of people who are Latin-American, Caucasian, African-American, Ethiopian, and Asian. You can hear the English interpretation of a Spanish sermon, see the gently swaying bodies of an Ethiopian choir, and hear children from many lands sing the same song.

I'd write or call home about these days, always conveying the amazement of this modern-day Pentecost. I often got the feeling that my family and friends couldn't quite believe this scenario. And to be honest, it bordered on a surrealistic experience for me too!

Today's passage contains a similar kind of feeling about the rush of violent wind and tongues of fire, which both united the new people of God and echoed the birth of the old people of God at the exodus. Some considered the infilling of the Holy Spirit and the ability to understand one anothers' languages as God's power; others saw the same event as a drunken brawl (v. 13). The one view was full of faith; the other view, full of fear.

Whatever fears we had about one another in the city, that annual gathering went further than anything else in our urban experience to transform those fears into faith. Individually, we were tiny candles, dwarfed by the city's neon. Together, we became a huge fire of God's heat and light, renewed in the Spirit's empowerment.

—*Laurie Oswald Robinson*

PRAYING AND WALKING IN THE WORLD:

- When was the last time you were in a culturally mixed setting during worship?

- What did you learn about unity amidst diversity in God's family?

- Ask God for a new humility that recognizes that your light of faith burns brighter when joined with others in the fellowship of the Spirit.

- If you are part of an urban, multicultural fellowship, invite a person to your worship service who has never had such an opportunity. If you live in a homogeneous setting, expose yourself to a more diverse worship event.

TODAY IS YOUR LAST DAY

PLUNGING INTO THE WORD:

Acts 2:14-21

PONDERING ON THE WAY:

During a period of my life that was full of anxiety, I received counseling from a therapist who helped me understand "mindfulness," or staying present to the present moment. She helped me to lessen anxiety by three steps: paying attention to my thinking and altering it toward a positive end; praying to a God who is present; and being grateful for circumstances unfolding each day, even though some circumstances are less than pleasing or happy.

The idea of being mindful about each day is introduced in today's passage. Peter's speech to the Pentecost crowd focuses on the "last days." Two millennia later, many biblical scholars interpret "last days" to mean the "day of the church," which began at Pentecost. Peter quotes from Joel, an Old Testament prophet, who, even though he lived thousands of years before the disciple, was discussing what would happen in the last days.

Joel and Peter gave their perspectives in very different ages, yet they seemed to think it was important to be open and mindful about what is possible when God pours out the Spirit on all flesh: Your sons and daughters shall prophesy, your young men—and women—will shall see visions; your old men—and women—will dream dreams.

The ability to prophesy, envision, and dream blossoms when people are attuned to God's Spirit in the present and entrust the past and the future to God. Whether we are living in the last days is not nearly as important as living the present day as if it were our last.

—*Laurie Oswald Robinson*

PRAYING AND WALKING IN THE WORLD:

- In your quiet time today, reflect upon one event you are anxious about regarding the past and one event you are anxious about regarding the future. Record these anxieties in a prayer journal or notebook.

- Take time to entrust these situations to God, asking for the grace to live in today only and to be open to how God's Spirit wants to work in your life now.

- Identify a young person, as well as a middle-age and an older adult, whom you can encourage to be more open to God's Spirit working in their life today.

MAY 18 *(FOR CHILDREN AND FAMILIES)*

SIX OR THREE THOUSAND

PLUNGING INTO THE WORD:

Acts 2:22-41

PONDERING ON THE WAY:

I was a third-grader at Bible memory camp when I accepted Jesus Christ into my heart. A missionary talked about Jesus being our Good Shepherd who saves us from sin—from doing and wandering into bad things. Animal facts about sheep tell us they need continuous care and need to be led to good grass and water. Sheep are easily attacked by wolves and other wild animals. And sheep tend to stay in flocks and follow a leader—whether a good one or a bad one.

In hearing how the Bible compares people to sheep, I realized I had strayed from God's green pastures and was lost. I needed Jesus to carry me on his shoulders when I was tired and rescue me from dangerous cliffs. So I accepted Christ as my personal Savior amidst about a half dozen other little girls who went to a room in the back of the chapel to pray. The missionary asked each girl to pray in her own words, inviting Jesus into her life.

Today's Bible story tells us that when Peter preached, three thousand people at one time invited Jesus into their lives. They were the first people to become Christians after Jesus died and rose again into heaven. Six girls asking Jesus into their hearts in the twentieth century seems very different from the three thousand people accepting Christ in the first century. But for more than two thousand years, the message has been the same: If you are lost and need care, the Good Shepherd will find you and carry you home to food, water, and safety.

—*Laurie Oswald Robinson*

PRAYING AND WALKING IN THE WORLD:

- Talk with your parents or other adults about what it means to ask Jesus into your heart. If you feel it is the right time, ask your parents to help you pray to Jesus, telling him you are lost and want to be found.

- Memorize Psalm 23, or read it and create a crayon picture of the psalm.

- Find a book about sheep and shepherds. Discuss why sheep need a shepherd to care for them and keep them safe.

- **Adults:** Peter emphasized the importance of repentance. And repentance means more than "I'm sorry." For what do you need to repent?

MAY 19

BREAD BASKETS AND SUNDAY PLATES

PLUNGING INTO THE WORD:

Acts 2:42-47

PONDERING ON THE WAY:

The concluding communion service of an annual gathering of Mennonites in Canada included children in a very special way. Leaders had schooled the children in how to carry bread *very carefully* to the tables. "Remember what we practiced," the leaders chimed. The children carted baskets of bread as if they were rare treasures. They set the baskets next to glasses of grape juice on the tables and silently walked away.

Their reverence and respect are virtues adults need in relating to brothers and sisters in Christ. As we partook of the bread and cup of Christ at that gathering, I felt at one with the larger North American body. It was not the amount or kind of people, or the configuration of those gathered, that bonded us. It was the unifying forces of reverence and respect that made us all children linked within God's family.

The first believers also knew the unifying power of the gathered family of God. No sooner had they given their lives to Christ than they gave their lives to one another. They shared bread, possessions, and time with glad and generous hearts. They spent much time together in the temple, but that fellowship overflowed into their homes.

Take a cue from the first church and invite guests for Sunday dinner instead of going to a restaurant after church. Make time to push back chairs and talk over coffee and tea. In breaking bread, you also may be breaking society's pattern, which keeps us so busy that we no longer have time to *very carefully* care for one another. In that caring table time, Christ is present, helping us to reverence and respect one anothers' stories and lives.

—*Laurie Oswald Robinson*

PRAYING AND WALKING IN THE WORLD:

- Reflect on how many times you have invited guests into your home for meals in the last six months. How do you feel about the frequency?

- Pray the Lord will widen your sense of hospitality and help you make changes to enlarge your meal table.

MAY 20 *(FOR CHILDREN AND FAMILIES)*

CONES AND COINS

PLUNGING INTO THE WORD:

Acts 3:1-10

PONDERING ON THE WAY:

Do you like ice cream? What's your favorite flavor?

I'll never forget when I bought a vanilla ice cream cone at a snack stand in Africa. I was there for a big church meeting of Mennonites. As I licked my cone, I saw a young African girl and her blind grandfather. Her tiny hand thrust a tin cup toward me. They were poor and needed money to buy food. Her brown eyes asked me to put coins in her cup so her family could eat.

As I looked into her hungry eyes, I realized that many of us in North America eat three meals a day plus snacks in between, but many families in this country in Africa could only eat supper three times a week.

I found some coins and put them in her cup. I was crying. I didn't want the ice cream anymore. I was sad.

Why do you think I felt that way? How do you think you would feel in the same situation?

Today's Bible story tells us about Peter and John, who didn't have money to give people. But they did have something else. They were filled with the riches of Jesus. Jesus saves people from their sins; he heals them from sickness; and he fills them with joy and peace. Jesus' power flowed through Peter and John, and the crippled man was healed.

No matter how little or how much money we have, Jesus' riches never run out. Jesus wants us to share the life he gives us with others. Even if we don't live in Africa and can't be there to help the girl and her grandfather, we can be more careful about how we live at home. We can buy and eat just what we need, instead of too much.

We can pray daily for people who don't have enough food. We can send money to organizations like Mennonite Central Committee.

People can be poor in more ways than not having enough money. Sometimes they don't have enough love and care from their families, and that affects how they act. We can let Jesus' love flow through us and be more kind to kids at school who don't look or act the way we do. Whether it is with our money, actions, or prayers, Jesus wants us to care for one another.

—*Laurie Oswald Robinson*

PRAYING AND WALKING IN THE WORLD:

- Do you know where Africa is? Ask your parents to help you find this continent on a world atlas or map. Find out what Mennonite Central Committee is doing in Africa to help people who don't have enough food or who are sick (see www. mcc.org).

- Save money to send to Mennonite World Conference or MCC, organizations that serve Mennonites around the world, or another organization your parents help you find. Maybe you can skip a can of pop or an ice cream cone and put that money in your savings bank.

- **Adults:** Identify ways you can give of your time, talent, and treasure to support God's family around the world.

MAY 21

WOULD YOU EXPECT ANYTHING LESS?

PLUNGING INTO THE WORD:

Acts 3:11-26

PONDERING ON THE WAY:

Sometimes when I read this story, I wince. I love it that the lame man is healed. I love it that Peter tells everyone the story of Jesus and makes all the right connections. I love the courage that he and John show, it's just that—well—why can't those kinds of miracles happen now?

Why am I more inclined to put money in the lame man's hand than take his hand and lift him up? Why don't we stand in the courtyard like Peter and proclaim the miracle for all to see?

Sometimes miracles do happen, if only we see them through eyes of faith. Even my own life story is full of miracles just like this.

My sister Ann was born with a hole in her heart. The doctors gave her little chance to live. Hope lay in open-heart surgery, where the doctors could repair the hole. But that was a very serious operation to perform on a newborn or even a six- or nine-month-old baby. We knew Ann had a better chance of survival if we could postpone surgery, so that's what we asked for in prayer.

And God answered our prayers. As the months rolled into years, and the pattern of postponement progressed from weeks to months to years, we began to live with the normalcy of Ann's condition. We asked for no specific healing from God.

Then when Ann turned fourteen, all the bad symptoms showed up again—blue lips, fainting—signs that the hole was getting larger and that surgery was needed. We took her to the cardiologist, who confirmed those suspicions and gave Ann a catheterization, a procedure that gave us a picture of the hole. So we gathered again as a family and congregation and prayed. What did we pray for? We prayed for the surgery to be postponed, just like before.

And how did God respond? By healing her heart completely. By closing the hole with flesh. The doctors took another catheterization, right before surgery, just as a way to prepare them for the operation. They were amazed, speechless. The hole had practically grown shut overnight.

And why not?

I love it that God gave us more than what we prayed for. I know that sometimes God doesn't seem to give us the miracles we want. But it's also true that God isn't dependent on just the right amount of faith before miracles can happen. Faith is faith, whether our faith feels tiny or not. It's not about us—it's about God.

So maybe we shouldn't be afraid to ask. And maybe we shouldn't be surprised when it happens—even when bigger miracles than expected happen.

> —*Michele Hershberger*

PRAYING AND WALKING IN THE WORLD:

- What do you expect from God? Is it possible that you expect too little and therefore receive less than what God wants to give?

- Sometimes God seems to say no to our request. Or perhaps the Spirit urges us to pray not for a specific miracle but for peace and strength to live through our trials. Is it hard to keep praying? We are to be faithful to God in these situations too.

- **Prayer:** God of Abraham and Sarah, you are my God. Lord of life-changing miracles, you are my Lord. Jesus, you are my daily strength and my hope for tomorrow. Lord, I believe! Help my unbelief.

MAY 22 *(FOR CHILDREN AND FAMILIES)*

EXTRAORDINARY!

PLUNGING INTO THE WORD:

Acts 4:1-22

PONDERING ON THE WAY:

We all want to be special. We want to be good at something—whether it's sports, music, schoolwork, dance, computers, video games, or something else. We don't want to be just "ordinary." We want to be special.

What are some of the things you do well?

Peter and John were two guys who did some amazing things in the early church. They healed people and preached, and thousands of people came to know Jesus because of their preaching. They were really good at what they did!

But you know what? The Bible says that Peter and John were "uneducated, ordinary men." They hadn't been to college to learn how to be doctors and heal people. They hadn't been to a special college to learn how to preach.

Do you have any idea why they were so good at preaching and healing?

The answer is simple: They were friends and followers of Jesus. Jesus gave them the power to heal. Jesus gave them the power to preach. And he gave them the courage to stand up for their beliefs. Having Jesus in their lives made these ordinary men extraordinary!

—*Carol Duerksen*

PRAYING AND WALKING IN THE WORLD:

* Even when we feel ordinary, Jesus is our friend and helps us feel special. Let's pray to Jesus right now: *Jesus, it's me, (child's name). I want to be your friend. I want to feel special because you are in my heart. Thank you for loving me. Amen.*

* **Adults:** What difference does Jesus make in your life? Make a list. Tell someone else. Spend one day noticing everything that is affected by the presence of Jesus in your life. Then try it for another day, and another …

MAY 23

CRAVING THE BOLDNESS

PLUNGING INTO THE WORD:

Acts 4:23-31

PONDERING ON THE WAY:

Imagine this: your faith is getting you into trouble with the authorities—and it's the kind of trouble that could lead to death. What would you pray for? God's protection? I think that's what I'd pray for. The need for self-preservation would come to the front very quickly.

But not Peter, John, and the new believers. They prayed not for protection but for boldness. They didn't pray that the authorities wouldn't find them—they prayed that the authorities *would* notice the signs and wonders done in the name of Jesus. They prayed for boldness, for the strength not to back down in the face of threats, and for the power to give witness to their new life in Jesus. They knew what the consequences could be, but they were more concerned about earning the consequences than avoiding them.

God honors their request. The building shakes, and they are filled with the power of the Holy Spirit. They do indeed preach God's message with boldness.

—*Michele Hershberger*

PRAYING AND WALKING IN THE WORLD:

God, it's not that I'm asking
for a period of persecution
here in North America
(although it could be what we need)

It's just that I crave the boldness
the single-mindedness
the focus on faith
that we read about in Acts.

So I ask for your Spirit
to do what is right
for this time and this place
in the life of the church.

Bring it on
and give me the boldness
to go where your Spirit leads.

　　　—Carol Duerksen

MAY 24

OUR IMMORTALITY IDEALOGY

PLUNGING INTO THE WORD:

Acts 4:32-37

PONDERING ON THE WAY:

What is it about money? Why does it hold so much power over us? Why is it so hard to talk about in our churches? Why does it break up marriages and divide families? After all, "you can't take it with you."

Maybe not. But you can leave it behind, and anthropologist Ernest Becker has observed that might be why it's so powerful. Becker notes that as a belief in God and other traditional sources of immortality declined in Western culture, money assumed a god-like quality in our lives and also became a ticket to leaving a legacy after our death. We can't take it with us when we die, but we can leave it to our offspring. We can leave it to an institution to erect a building bearing our name. In Becker's words, money is our "immortality ideology"—our modern way to ensure that, after we die, our name and achievements will live on.

As Christians with a different view of immorality, we shouldn't fall into that trap, should we? We should be able to turn loose of our hold on money and give it freely, right? We should be willing to live as the new believers did in today's passage.

Not. Why not?

Because it's not what we're being taught by the church. From children to adults, we are not being instructed in simpler lifestyles and open sharing of our resources. It's not what our culture is pressing upon us. Most of us would rather join our neighbors in the "more is better" mode.

I'm the first to admit, that's my reality. Just this morning I saw a friend's new lush, green lawn and I wanted it. He planted special grass seed that does well in the shade. I want my yard to look like that. It'll cost money to transform my "mowed weeds" area to that kind of lawn, but it's so beautiful. Will I ask my Christian brothers and sisters if this is a good way to spend money? No. I'll do what I want to with my money.

And that's exactly what the early believers did. The difference being, what they wanted to do was to share everything.

—*Carol Duerksen*

PRAYING AND WALKING IN THE WORLD:

- Do you talk to others about what you do with your money? Do you think it's none of anyone else's business? Why or why not?

- Pray for God to talk to you about your money.

THE STRUGGLE TO BE FAITHFUL

PLUNGING INTO THE WORD:

Acts 5:1-11

PONDERING ON THE WAY:

When I read the story of Ananias and Sapphira, my first questions are: Does God require us to give everything? Is that why Ananais and Sapphira died? Was their sin that they didn't give everything or that they lied in order to look better in front of the other believers?

I believe it was the lying that got them in trouble. And then I wonder: Who did they think they were fooling? How stupid of them to try to deceive the apostles!

Many of us are guilty of deceiving our brothers and sisters in the faith, as well as ourselves. Have you ever said, "I'm just getting by" or "I'm not very well off, especially compared to so-and-so."

Why do we say that? Are we justifying materialism, greed, coveting, and the desire to acquire? I think so. Maybe the deceit isn't as obvious as the lies that struck down this unfortunate couple, but it's still there.

Does it seem a bit strong that Ananias and Sapphira died for their deceit? Yes. Their church family was certainly scared after what happened. But the church had been called to be different—testifying to the fact that Jesus called his believers to live together in self-sacrifice and servitude. If lies, greed, and deceit were allowed to go on without consequences, the church itself would die.

The early church was made up of people like you and me, dealing with the same human tendencies we have. They struggled to be faithful to their newfound relationship with Jesus. We struggle to be faithful too—some of us in the newness of faith and some of us because it seems "old hat."

May God be patient with us.

—*Carol Duerksen*

PRAYING AND WALKING IN THE WORLD:

- How can greed kill you? How can deceit kill you?

- What are your biggest struggles in terms of being faithful? Journal and pray about them. If possible, share them with someone you trust who will pray for you and help keep you accountable. Do the same for that person.

MAY 26

SELLING SKELLY ON SUNDAY

PLUNGING INTO THE WORD:

Acts 5:17-42

PONDERING ON THE WAY:

My dad, John Schrock, used to own several Skelly gas stations. It was our livelihood, how my parents put bread on the table. It was also the time of the infamous "gas wars." One day my father received a mandate from headquarters to keep his gas stations open on Sundays. My father owned his stations but had a special partnership with the mother company that supplied him with gas. That company could cut him off—whenever they pleased.

So mandates were to be taken seriously. But for my father, keeping the Sabbath was also a priority. He tried to talk to his superiors, but they didn't understand his concern to obey God. They gave him an ultimatum—either open the stations on Sunday or find yourself another gas supplier. My dad countered with this offer, "If I can sell as much gas as other stations that are open seven days a week, making my quota for gas sales, will you let me keep the Sabbath the way I want?" They knew my dad to be a good businessman, and they knew it would be hard for him to increase his gas sales substantially while staying closed on Sundays. So they agreed, insisting my father make his quota right away.

Dad never opened on Sundays. And, for reasons that are beyond explanation, he sold more gas, enough gas to satisfy the men from Skelly.

It may seem like a small thing. But my father understood what Peter and John knew to be true. There are times when you must obey God rather than the human authorities. When the human law violates God's laws, there is only one choice.

On some things you can't compromise. Period.

> —*Michele Hershberger*

PRAYING AND WALKING IN THE WORLD:

- What are some other issues where human laws conflict with God's laws? What should you do when your employer says you must lie for the company if asked—or lose your job? What should you do when your country asks you to fight in war, and Jesus tells you to love your enemies?

- Pray for courage—the courage to speak and teach the good news of Jesus' life, death, and resurrection; the courage to be dishonored for speaking the name of Jesus.

MAY 27 *(FOR CHILDREN AND FAMILIES)*

CHURCH WORKERS

PLUNGING INTO THE WORD:

Acts 6:1-7

PONDERING ON THE WAY:

Discuss this question with the children: *Who works in our church?*

The most obvious answer is the people who get paid for their work in the church, such as the pastor and the custodian. But, as we read in today's Scripture passage, there are many other people God calls to work in the church besides those who are paid for their work.

Make a list of all the people who do something in the church. You can do this by thinking of the different responsibilities and who does them; or you can go through a church directory and look at the names and think of the things this person does, or has done, in the church.

Isn't it amazing how many people are involved? Certainly the pastor isn't the only person who works in the church! A church needs people to change light bulbs, dust the pews, pay the electricity bill, order Sunday school materials, make food, teach, visit sick people, plan worship services, and many other things. A church is like a family that lives in a house—the house needs to be taken care of, and so do the people who live in the house.

Ask the children: *What's your favorite part of church? Is there work you can do in church? Is there work you might like to do when you grow up?*

> —*Carol Duerksen*

PRAYING AND WALKING IN THE WORLD:

- Choose some people in your church who don't often get thanked for their work, and make some thank-you cards for them.

- **Adults:** Using your annual report book or another listing of the ministries and organizations of your congregation, pray your way through the work of your church. Take your time, praying for perhaps one ministry a day.

MAY 28

STEPHEN, THE FIRST MARTYR

PLUNGING INTO THE WORD:

Acts 6:8-15

PONDERING ON THE WAY:

It's a well-known fact that Stephen was the first Christian martyr. In fact, in Bible Bingo this answer would probably only score a double, barely enough to send the teammate who could name the last king of Judah sliding into the metaphorical home plate.

However, there are still many questions about Stephen. Who was he? Why was he arrested in the first place?

Stephen was a young Greek-speaking Jew, "a man full of grace and power" (Acts 6:8). He was a miracle worker like his predecessor, Peter, and a great orator like his successor, Paul.

So, why did opposition arise in the first place? This guy seems truly angelic, a New Testament all-star, the kind who gets straight A's, is class president, and probably a natural at sports.

Stephen came under fire for some of the same reasons Jesus did. The Jews who railed against Stephen claimed he dishonored their temple and law. The Old Testament Law had become an obsession to them—law and tradition were prized over spirituality. Stephen upset the establishment because he accepted unclean Gentiles. Stephen was an upstanding Jew; he loved Torah. But he found a grace that had been lost in the Law somewhere along the way. He found the fulfillment of Torah.

He found Jesus.

Though we may not be in immediate danger of a trial of our faith, how do we compare with Stephen? Do we upset the establishment by our words or actions? In many countries, this does happen. Thousands of Christians have died for their faith over the centuries—more in the twentieth century than in all the previous centuries combined—and they still struggle for freedom of religion today. They can't take their religion lightly. It is a matter of life and death.

Is it for us?

—*Michele Hershberger*

PRAYING AND WALKING IN THE WORLD:

- In what ways are good institutions corrupted by hate or greed? Can these institutions be restored to their original purpose? How can we as Christians help restore them?

- Are rigid laws and church traditions still valued over our actual relationship with God?

- In what ways do Christian ethics oppose widely accepted societal norms? How does the Christian lifestyle line up with our cultures? How does it differ?

- Pray for Christians across the world who are persecuted for their beliefs in places like Indonesia, Colombia, Iran, and Algeria. Pray for religious freedom in Iraq, Afghanistan, the Middle East and for continued tolerance and acceptance throughout the world.

MAY 29

MORE THAN KNOWING THE STORY

PLUNGING INTO THE WORD:

Acts 7:1-53

PONDERING ON THE WAY:

I have a friend who loves genealogies. She used to make diagrams charting not only her family tree, but also the history of each family member. Like my friend, I come from a tradition that loves family history and church history, especially if they overlap: *Your great-great-uncle planted the church where your first cousin once removed is now the bishop. Isn't that great!* Well, yes, it is, but that's not the point.

Stories are extremely important in Jewish culture. The Bible is made up almost entirely of stories. A retelling of the entire history as Stephen delivers it in this chapter is not rare. Biblical precedents include Deuteronomy 26:5-10; Joshua 24; Psalms 103, 104, 105, and 106. Clearly, history is important. Our story gives us identity and stability. It shows us the way we should go. It illustrates God's faithfulness … despite our unfaithfulness.

That was Stephen's point. He showed the people that throughout their history God took care of the Israelites even though the people rejected Moses, turning from his guidance many times in the wilderness. Stephen attacked the establishment by drawing comparisons between the early dismissal of God's messengers—like Moses—and the rejection of Jesus. You didn't get it with Moses, and now you've rejected Jesus too.

You didn't learn your lesson. The story is important—knowing your story is so important. But ironically, as Stephen pointed out to his accusers, you can know the story and the Law well and still be the ones least faithful to it.

It's good to know the story, but it can't stop there. Are we faithful to the story? Do we let it transform us? Would we—do we—recognize the prophets in our midst today?

> —*Michele Hershberger*

PRAYING AND WALKING IN THE WORLD:

- Write down your faith story. You can start with your personal testimony or trace your ancestor's faith journeys.

- What patterns emerge? Are they good or bad?

- Do you see your story as a continuation of your family's story? Of the biblical story?

MAY 30

FORGIVENESS

PLUNGING INTO THE WORD:

Acts 7:54—8:2

PONDERING ON THE WAY:

I am amazed by his courage. I'm almost envious of his visions and the indwelling of the Spirit. I wonder what went through his mind as they dragged him out of the city. But more than anything else, I stand speechless at Stephen's ability to forgive. Just like Jesus. "Father, forgive them for they know not what they do." "Lord, do not hold this sin against them." That kind of forgiveness—that is what catches me the most.

Real forgiveness is hard to do. It isn't just accepting someone's apology and then letting the resentment build up in you. It isn't forcing yourself to say the words when every part of your being screams otherwise. It's not forgetting their sin. If you have been badly hurt, that's not possible to do right away. But it is letting go, over and over again.

A friend of mine likens it to dribbling a basketball. If you keep reminding yourself of all the awful things done to you by the other person, it's like you are continuing to dribble a basketball, and every time your hand touches it, the ball comes back to the same height. But if you stop replaying the grievances—and forgive—it's like the basketball that gets no new energy from your hand. The ball bounces back—almost to the same height as before—and the ball will continue to come up. But gradually the bounce gets weaker, until the ball is silent on the floor. When we forgive, the ball of resentment will come back up. If we don't feed it, like the basketball, it gradually will lose its momentum.

Forgiveness takes a long time. I don't know how Stephen's story would have been different if his persecutors had just tortured him without killing him. Was it easier to forgive them, knowing he would soon die? Does Jesus give a person special strength in high pressure times like this? I don't know. I do know that I cannot forgive without the supernatural power of Jesus helping me. And I know I want to forgive, because I want to be free.

As free as Stephen.

—*Michele Hershberger*

PRAYING AND WALKING IN THE WORLD:

- How high is the basketball of resentment bouncing in your life right now? If you have some hard things to forgive, give yourself grace and time. Ask Jesus to help you. Find others who can be supportive. If you are nursing resentments that you really should let go, then stop dribbling. Ask Jesus to help you stop dribbling.

- In what situations do you need courage? What visions from God do you need to see? What "coats of injustice" have been laid at your feet? Ask God to give you that courage, that vision.

MAY 31

VENDING MACHINE PRAYER?

PLUNGING INTO THE WORD:

Acts 8:9-25

PONDERING ON THE WAY:

Even if we don't like to admit it, most of us love magic. We are fascinated by it, from Harry Potter books to Las Vegas specials on television. It's not that we believe in it—we know it's all special effects, lighting, smoke and mirrors, quick fingers, or chemicals. But despite reason and enlightenment, we still flock to magic shows, adore the epic summer blockbuster, pay hundreds to have the neighborhood's best fireworks display, and even practice card tricks to astound our nieces and nephews.

Simon wanted to capitalize on the people's eternal love of magic, mystery, and sorcery. He also wanted something for nothing. He tried to buy the power of the Holy Spirit from the apostles, not knowing that God's power can never be for sale.

As children, our parents care for us though we can offer little in return. As children of God, we receive blessings we have not earned. God takes care of our basic needs, and God grants providence if we only believe and ask. That asking is called prayer.

Why do I pray? Do I want magic? Blessings for free? Say the right prayer, or pray enough, and presto, I get my miracle. God does grant miracles, but if I expect to get my every desire every time I pray, I am being like Simon in this story. Prayer doesn't work like a vending machine.

On the other hand, I can't make the opposite mistake—not believing in the power of prayer at all. God has the power to do absolutely anything, and our prayers are part of that. Prayer has led to many incredible recoveries, salvation, healing. God might not help us win the lottery, but through prayer God can help us be better people, better Christians. God can heal our wounded souls.

Prayer isn't just about asking, granting, and receiving. Prayer is our way of communicating with the Almighty. Through prayer we can confess our sins and shortcomings. Through prayer we share our troubles and search our hearts for answers. Prayer is a way of cleansing our souls by bringing everything to God. When we use prayer to truly speak to God, we are not asking for something for nothing, we are opening ourselves to a meaningful relationship with God.

—*Michele Hershberger*

PRAYING AND WALKING IN THE WORLD:

- What is prayer to you? Is it magic, or is it a method of confession and meditation? How do you bring your prayer requests to God?

- Have you ever been guilty of failure to believe in the power of prayer? Meditate on some of the ways in your life or the lives of your family and friends that God has answered prayers.

JUNE 1 *(FOR CHILDREN AND FAMILIES)*

JESUS LOVES EVERYONE

PLUNGING INTO THE WORD:

Acts 8:26-40

PONDERING ON THE WAY:

When my daughter Tara was small, we lived in a neighborhood with people who were different from us. Many of them came from countries other than the United States. One of Tara's friends was named Julie. The first time Julie came over to play, she would not talk to me. She would not answer my questions. She seemed friendly, and she did not seem shy. I couldn't understand why she didn't talk. Finally Tara poked me in the ribs and said, "Mother, quit talking to Julie. She doesn't understand a word you're saying!"

I couldn't believe it! Julie spoke Russian, and Tara spoke English, but that didn't seem to matter to them. They had a wonderful time playing. They rode their bikes together, played with dolls, went to the park, and played on the swings. Even though they were different from each other, they still had fun.

In the Bible, there are many stories of people who believed in Jesus. In this story, a man hears the good news of Jesus and believes in him for the first time. This is a very happy story because the man was able to feel God's love.

Something is different about this story though. It is about a man who is not a Jew. He is one of the first non-Jewish people (called Gentiles) to believe in Jesus. Some people thought that only Jews could be followers of Jesus. But in this story a Gentile becomes a Christian.

Sometimes we are afraid to be friends or to share with people who are different from us. Some people may look different or go to different schools. They may even speak a different language. But Jesus still loves them. And we should too.

—*Michele Hershberger*

PRAYING AND WALKING IN THE WORLD:

* Sing the song "Jesus Loves the Little Children." Think about the children you know who may look different or act differently than you. Jesus loves those children very much.

- Look at a map of the world. It's a very big place. Find your country and your state. Find a country you've never been to or heard of. Jesus loves people in your country and in places you have never been.

JUNE 2 *(FOR CHILDREN AND FAMILIES)*

SAUL'S CONVERSION

PLUNGING INTO THE WORD:

Acts 9:1-19

PONDERING ON THE WAY:

Read this simplified version of the story and have the children act it out. Older children may read the parts of Saul, Jesus, and Ananias. Possible actions will be represented in parentheses.

Saul was a man who didn't like Christians. *(Make a "mean" face—scowl.)*

He traveled to Damascus to find Christians to put in jail. (Walk toward "Damascus.")

Then a bright light came from the sky, and Saul fell to the ground. (Fall to ground, cover eyes with hands, etc.)

A voice from heaven said, "Saul, Saul, why do you persecute me?"

And Saul said, "Who are you, Lord?"

And the voice said, "I am Jesus, whom you are persecuting. But get up and enter the city, and you will be told what you are to do."

Saul was blinded. (Continue to cover eyes, grope around.)

His friends took him to Damascus.

In that city there was a Christian named Ananias. (One child can become Ananias.)

The Lord sent Ananias to help Saul.

Ananias was scared because Saul had been mean to Christians. (Show fear.)

But he trusted in the Lord and went to see Saul. (Move to the child portraying Saul.)

He put his hands on Saul. (Put hands on Saul.)

He said, "Brother Saul, the Lord Jesus, who appeared to you on your way here, has sent me so that you may regain your sight and be filled with the Holy Spirit."

Saul could see again and he was happy. (Jump and shout for joy.)

Saul was baptized. (Demonstrate baptism or simply hug or shake hands to show friendship in Christ.)

—*Michele Hershberger*

PRAYING AND WALKING IN THE WORLD:

- **Adults:** What does it mean to be Ananias in this story? How can you show love for people who persecute you? Do you have enough faith to accept a former enemy into your home?

JUNE 3

CHANGE IS INEVITABLE

PLUNGING INTO THE WORD:

Acts 9:20-31

PONDERING ON THE WAY:

People have always been resistant to change. It can be scary. Unsettling. Downright terrifying.

Now, by change I don't mean a small change like a vacation (though it can be a nice *change* of pace or a *change* of scenery). Change doesn't simply mean an upgrade. Changing phone companies, tires, or brands of diapers (isn't it time for a change?) won't really make a big difference in your life. We're talking big changes, bigger than tuning your radio dial from rock to country (no one should be forced to do that).

We're talking transformation.

Accepting Jesus into your life causes a big, life-altering change. Getting married, switching jobs, and having children all make a huge impact on your life and change not only your daily routine but your entire way of living. And though change can be good, it also can be very hard. Adjusting to new changes can take a long time, and there is always resistance, even from within yourself.

If it is real change, there are always "change-back" messages. By "change-back," I mean verbal and nonverbal messages others give us to persuade us to go back to the old way of life. Even when our friends and family want this change, they may give "change-back" messages because sometimes even good news is hard to take.

Paul received some fairly harsh "change-back" messages. It isn't surprising that the Jews wanted to kill Saul for his seeming betrayal of their great cause. In one sense, they understood Saul's conversion better than the disciples did. But what about the "change-back" messages from the disciples? The disciples were afraid of Saul and didn't believe that he was one of them. Maybe this reaction was justified, but then again, did they not serve a God who could turn any life around? Isn't this the very miracle they wanted to see, had prayed to see?

Why is it so hard to allow others to change for the better? Why is it so scary when we ourselves find new freedom and hope?

Can we really change ourselves? Isn't that God's business to do? Are we letting God change us? Are we letting God change others? Or are we too afraid?

—*Tara Hershberger*

PRAYING AND WALKING IN THE WORLD:

- Think of the ways your life has changed dramatically. Were they intentional changes? Have they been for the better? Reflect on how other people have reacted to your changes.

- Have there been people in your life who have helped you through a change, like Barnabus helped Paul?

- Think of one change you really would like to make. Pray about it. Tell a friend who can help keep you accountable. Start!

JUNE 4 *(FOR CHILDREN AND FAMILIES)*

HELEN AND TABITHA

PLUNGING INTO THE WORD:

Acts 9:32-43

PONDERING ON THE WAY:

When she was nineteen months old, Helen Keller got sick, and when the illness was over, she couldn't see or hear anymore. Her parents hired Annie Sullivan, a teacher for the deaf and blind, to teach Helen how to communicate. After months of no progress, a miracle happened. Annie pumped water over one of Helen's hands and spelled "water" in sign language. Suddenly, Helen made her first connection between words and what they stood for. Helen learned how to communicate through sign language and Braille, a system of raised dots that helps blind people to read. A movie, *The Miracle Worker,* tells us the story of Annie and Helen and how they worked together to overcome Helen's disabilities.

Today's Bible story tells us about another miracle. Peter, one of Jesus' disciples, came to Joppa, where he heard about Tabitha. She sewed clothes and did good things for people. But she got sick and died. Peter believed Jesus' power could raise Tabitha from the dead. He knelt down and prayed, and Tabitha rose and opened her eyes.

We don't hear of Jesus' modern-day disciples raising people from the dead. But Helen's story reminds us that Jesus' miracles still happen. God's power flows through doctors, teachers, nurses, and scientists to heal sick people of their diseases and to help disabled people gain abilities.

God's power also helps kids grow in their relationship to God. You aren't Helen or Tabitha, and your Sunday school teacher isn't Peter. But you can help one another see and know God in new ways, just as Annie helped Helen "see" water.

—*Laurie Oswald Robinson*

PRAYING AND WALKING IN THE WORLD:

- Talk to your parents about the kinds of modern-day miracles you see all around you. List them on a piece of paper. Thank God for miracles!

- Watch *The Miracle Worker.* Talk with your family about how you could be friends with someone who has a disability.

JUNE 5

STRETCHING THE SHEETS

PLUNGING INTO THE WORD:

Acts 10:1-18

PONDERING ON THE WAY:

As a Caucasian woman, the last thing on my mind was the color of Alfonso's skin. He was the Panamanian man I fell in love with. All I could see was the color of his love for me—a bright light, bringing new hues to my life. But as we announced our engagement, some people questioned whether our biracial relationship could work in a discriminating world.

Our relationship presented the same kind of challenge found in today's Bible passage. Cornelius, a non-Jew who worshipped God, was shown in a vision to send for Peter, a Jewish believer in Jesus, in Joppa. Peter was to come to the home of

Cornelius in Caesarea. But to get Peter there, God first appeared to Peter in a strange vision. In the vision, animals of every kind—including those considered "unclean" by Jews—were lowered down on a sheet to the roof where Peter was praying.

The voice in the vision told Peter to get up and kill and eat these animals, but Peter protested. As a Jew, he could not touch the unclean. The voice said, "What God has made clean, you must not call profane." In the midst of his puzzlement, Cornelius's messengers arrived and called Peter to come down.

The story continues into tomorrow's devotions. But today we can focus on how the sheet that stretched above Peter's head was the first step in stretching Peter's community beyond people he had always considered "okay."

God didn't have to haul me up to a rooftop to marry Alfonso. I willingly ran into his life. And as our wedding approached, I watched how our union was stretching our communities' previous borders to create a wider, more accepting space. I felt joy as I saw how those persons who at first doubted this relationship began to delight in its goodness.

—Laurie Oswald Robinson

PRAYING AND WALKING IN THE WORLD:

- Reflect on the ways you are bound by the perimeters of the particular "rooftop" where you have lived your life. List three of those ways in your journal.

- In each of these three situations, pray to the Lord to stretch your sense of community beyond your current limits.

- Identify one person you have not considered "okay" or "clean." If this person is in your community, find one way this week to be more open to this person. If the person lives far away, pray for his or her welfare.

JUNE 6

GOLFING AND FOLLOWING GOD

PLUNGING INTO THE WORD:

Acts 10:19-23

PONDERING ON THE WAY:

Golf is a strange game—overthink your putt, and you may miss the cup. Swing randomly on your drives, and your ball may sail too far from the fairway. It's a balancing act between taking time and hitting now, between being careful and taking risks.

Following God is a bit like that, as Peter discovered in today's Bible passage. He spent a long time listening to a voice in a vision telling him it was okay to eat unclean animals. And then suddenly, out of the blue, three men appear. They ask him to come down from the roof and to go with them to the home of Cornelius, a non-Jew considered unclean by Jews.

Peter had but a second to choose. Would he remain on that roof, a refuge from the unknown, or would he come down to face the strangers? We know from the story that the voice in the vision asked him to get up and go down "without hesitation." Peter heeded the invitation and went down. A clue he did this in openness rather than fear was that he invited the men into his house before they set out for Joppa.

But what appeared to be a split-second decision had been seasoned by careful listening and reflecting upon the vision he had experienced. Anyone who has watched Tiger Woods during a televised golf tournament knows that what looks easy and smooth has been shaped by countless hours of practice swings. So it is for Peter. So it is for you and me. Golfing or following God takes careful practice and courageous risk.

—Laurie Oswald Robinson

PRAYING AND WALKING IN THE WORLD:

- Reflect on the ways you best hear God: in Bible reading, through prayer, in dreams, through "visions" you receive during worship services? Which ways seem more credible than others? Do some ways give you reason to pause and overthink whether or not you heed the messages?

- In today's prayer time, ask God for increased balance, enlarging your ability to both listen carefully and to risk courageously.

- Who is the equivalent of the three messengers in your life? In what ways this week can you be more open to their invitation to go with them?

JUNE 7

LORD OF ALL

PLUNGING INTO THE WORD:

Acts 10:24-48

PONDERING ON THE WAY:

Lord of all

(a poem in a time of war)

> In this time of war, your creatures
> declare you God of only their nation.
> The "chosen ones," they send bombs
> to fortify oil rights and to secure borders.
> They profile those who do not look like them
> as terrorists and as those "unclean."
> Those who die in these devastations
> are children and innocents,
> whose mangled bodies and spilled blood
> cry out to the Lord of all—"have mercy
> on this merciless killing."
>
> Eons ago, your vision hits Peter
> like a bombshell: he is to befriend the "unclean,"
> the Gentiles who are not safe or acceptable.
> But the wreckage left by the vision's voice
> brings Peter to his knees before an impartial God,
> a God who though not punitive is to be feared
> as the only One in the universe who dares
> to speak peace in a time of war;
> the only One who shows mercy
> in the wreckage of mercilessness.
>
> Today, Peter's story hits us unaware
> like bombs shot between Lebanese and Israelis
> because of bad blood and hostages held;
> and like U.S. tanks gunning through Iraqi desert,
> searching for ghosts of rumors that
> weapons of mass destruction may exist.
> In midst of these ghost-like howls,
> we hear a clear voice proclaiming:
> "Jesus heals all who are oppressed."

That means me and you and
enemies and strangers in the Middle East—
all of us who cry for mercy
in this time of merciless war.

—*Laurie Oswald Robinson*

PRAYING AND WALKING IN THE WORLD:

- Reflect on your views of peace during wartime. Who or what shaped them? Have they changed since 9/11, the destruction of the World Trade Center Twin Towers in New York City, and the unfolding events since then?

- Pray that a godly fear of the Lord of all nations will replace the fear you may feel about nations that are at odds with the United States.

- Identify one family in your community whose son or daughter is serving in the military. Reach out to that family with a "thinking of you" card, or with a phone call, offering to pray for that family and its loved one. Then identify one community or person whose loved one was killed in a recent war. If they live in another country, pray for peace in their land.

JUNE 8

GRACE AND GRUNT WORK

PLUNGING INTO THE WORD:

Acts 12:1-19

PONDERING ON THE WAY:

A decade ago, prayer powerfully shaped my life. At a time when I struggled to be free of spiritual bondage, the prayers of God's people loosened chains that kept me sexually confused and emotionally wounded. As a result, I soared with wings of new freedom to be the person God created me to be in Christ. But it took years of spiritual disciplines to solidify the freedom of that earlier miracle. The pathway toward long-term healing often led from mountaintops of grace into valleys of "grunt work." God often asked me to add footwork to prayer's wings. God asked that as I believed in God's miracle prayer power, I needed to work out what God worked in.

Peter also was released from bondage when God's people prayed. On the eve before Herod planned to kill him, Peter, bound by chains, slept between two soldiers as guards kept watch at the prison door. No sooner had miracle prayer power broken Peter's chains than he had to apply earthly discipline—he had to listen to the angel who said, "Fasten your belt and put on your sandals." After Peter complied, the angel said, "Wrap your cloak around you and follow me." But even after he followed the angel out into the clear, Peter still thought he experienced a vision, rather than reality. It was only after Peter passed the first and second guard that he was convinced the Lord had sent a rescuing angel.

There are many times when we balk at the disciplines required to fully develop a life infused with God's grace. But like Peter, those earthy tasks help us tap into how very real and solid God's miracles are. The feet God asks us to put to those prayers lead us out of dark prisons into the light of day. Putting on our sandals at God's beckoning helps us know we are walking on solid ground and not sinking sand.

> —*Laurie Oswald Robinson*

PRAYING AND WALKING IN THE WORLD:

- Reflect on one time when you were sure someone's prayers brought miracle power into your life. What convinced you it was the power of prayer and not mere coincidence? What kind of "feet" did God ask you to apply to prayer's wings?

- In today's prayers, pray for both God's miracle working power in a weak area of your life and the courage to apply daily disciplines to cooperate with God in strengthening that weakness.

- Think of three persons you know well who struggle with areas of weakness. For one month, pray daily or at least consistently that God would break chains of bondage, whether they are emotional, spiritual, physical, or intellectual.

JUNE 9

HEARING AND HEEDING

PLUNGING INTO THE WORD:

Acts 13:1-3

PONDERING ON THE WAY:

In reading about the birth of the Mennonite church in New York City,* I discovered the story of the late Elizabeth Foth, born and raised in Whitewater, Kansas. She was bound for India as a mission worker, but setbacks brought her to New York instead in 1923. Without support from a mission board, she depended on Sunday school classes and churches to support her first ministry in the slums of Red Hook in Brooklyn. She knocked on doors, conducted Bible studies and youth programs, and did hospital visitation.

In the 1930s, she founded a storefront mission and was sixty-two years old when the mission closed. In the next two decades, she led children's meetings in Brooklyn's public housing, worked in Hell's Kitchen on Manhattan's west side, and birthed a tract ministry on Coney Island's beaches. She carried a sign with Scripture messages and shared the gospel among the crowds. In her last years, she visited hospitals, where she read the Bible and prayed with sick people. She also was a volunteer counselor at the Billy Graham pavilion at the New York World's Fair. At 87 years of age in 1971, she ended 46 years of active ministry on the city streets.

Elizabeth heeded a call before the phrase "culture of call" became popular. This culture is shaped by recognizing people's gifts and encouraging them to use them. Today's Scripture passage describes how the first culture of call developed. As the early church worshipped and fasted at Antioch, the Holy Spirit said, "Set apart for me Barnabas and Saul for the work to which I have called them." Then after fasting and praying, the church members laid hands on the two men and sent them off.

The first-century church did something the twenty-first-century church often can overlook because of its busyness: taking time to worship and to listen to the Holy Spirit. As it listened, the church not only knew which people to send but also realized their mission was to be shaped by God—not by the church's agenda. Their mission was to follow God's mission. In the days when a single woman striking out for New York City was a rarity, Elizabeth heard and heeded God's call to leave the prairies for the drama of the city streets.

God tapping on our eardrums is the first step toward heeding a personal call or tapping on someone else's shoulders—sometimes the most unlikely person. As our hearing improves, so will our heeding. Often that heeding is followed by risk. When Elizabeth took that risk, the lives of countless city people and the life of the church were forever changed.

—*Laurie Oswald Robinson*

* *Mennonite and Brethren in Christ Churches of New York City*, Richard K. MacMaster (Pandora Press, 2006).

PRAYING AND WALKING IN THE WORLD:

- Reflect on the last time you heard and heeded a call for your own life. Reflect on the last time you took a risk to call someone else to use their gifts. How was the experience similar or dissimilar to today's passage?

- Sit in restful silence today for longer than your usual time. Pray for guidance on how to better hear God's calls in your life and the courage to heed them.

Journal about a specific call you've been hearing but have been afraid to heed. List one or two beginning steps toward heeding that call. List one or two risks the heeding of this call would bring. Commit your heeding and your risking to God.

• In your family life at home or in your congregational family, explore new ways those communities may experience more quiet or silence for listening for God's calls. Also explore how to free one another to take more godly risks in gift-calling and gift-using.

JUNE 10 *(FOR CHILDREN AND FAMILIES)*

CRAYONS AND CROOKED LINES

PLUNGING INTO THE WORD:

Acts 13:4-12

PONDERING ON THE WAY:

During my first day of first grade, I wanted to please my teacher by drawing a perfect picture with my new crayons. I was so nervous that the flower did not look like a flower. The sun did not look like a sun. And the straight lines were very crooked. I cried, sure I would never come back to first grade ever again. Of course, my mother and father made me go back. But I will never forget the feeling of shame that, somehow, what I wanted to get so right had turned out so wrong.

Today's Bible story tells us that one of Jesus' disciples, Paul, saw how a magician named Elymas tried to turn another man away from having faith. Paul scolded him: "Stop trying to make crooked the straight paths of Lord." Paul knew that God never led people to walk in crooked, confused paths, even though people sometimes chose that. As a result of the magician's crookedness, he turned blind and needed to be led around by the hand.

There is no shame in drawing a less than perfect picture. But even as a little girl, I could tell a straight line from a crooked one. That's what happens when we learn about Jesus and walk with him in the ways of faith. The more we know him, the less we will want to follow someone who tells us crooked stories or asks us to do something we're not supposed to do.

—*Laurie Oswald Robinson*

PRAYING AND WALKING IN THE WORLD:

- Draw two crayon pictures of straight lines, circles, and squares. In the first picture, draw them in messy ways. Make the straight lines crooked and make the circles look more like squares. Then, draw a second picture that looks more clean and clear. Put these pictures on your bulletin board to remind you to follow Jesus in right ways.

- In your prayers, ask God to help you to know when someone is telling you a crooked story or asking you to do something wrong.

- Who do you know in your neighborhood or school who tries to get you to do things you know Jesus or your parents have told you not to do? Tell your parents about that and pray with them about the situation.

JUNE 11

HOW TO GROW GOD'S KINGDOM, PART 1

PLUNGING INTO THE WORD:

Acts 13:13-52

PONDERING ON THE WAY:

Tell the stories
the spiritual stories
of the people
different cultures
ethnicities
theological backgrounds
Tell the stories
but always ask
and always ponder
What did God do?
Where was God?
Where are you?
Who are you?

How do you know
you are God's child?
How has Jesus
set you free?

Tell the stories.

>   —*Carol Duerksen*

PRAYING AND WALKING IN THE WORLD:

- Do you know the stories of your spiritual family tree?

- Are you passing them on to the next generation? Is your congregation?

JUNE 12

HOW TO GROW GOD'S KINGDOM, PART 2

PLUNGING INTO THE WORD:

Acts 14:8-20

PONDERING ON THE WAY:

Do the good news!
Work to bring healing
of bodies, minds, souls
and always give credit
where credit is due.

Don't give up
When they beat you up
Even then
Run back to the city
Instead of running for your life

It's not about you!
It's all about God!

Do the good news!

—*Carol Duerksen*

PRAYING AND WALKING IN THE WORLD:

- What are you doing to share God's good news with hurting people across the street and around the world? How about your congregation? Does healing and hope fill your walls and spill out?

- Pray for healing and hope to fill and spill out of your soul and the walls of your congregation.

JUNE 13

HOW TO GROW GOD'S KINGDOM, PART 3

PLUNGING INTO THE WORD:

Acts 14:21-28

PONDERING ON THE WAY:

Step out.
Take risks.
Get into trouble.
Earn persecution.

Your soul
will grow
and so will the kingdom.

—*Carol Duerksen*

PRAYING AND WALKING IN THE WORLD:

- Do you agree with this devotional? Why or why not? If so, what are next steps for you?

- William H. Willimon writes this in *Interpretation,* a New Testament commentary, about the author of Acts: "Luke would not have known what to make of a church no longer in the business of making more disciples." Sit with that awhile. Now what?

JUNE 14

GOOD ARGUMENTS

PLUNGING INTO THE WORD:

Acts 15:1-21

PONDERING ON THE WAY:

Disagreement within the Christian church regarding theological interpretations is as old as the church itself, and today's passage is a perfect example. What can we learn from the early church about handling arguments?

In the *Interpretation* commentary on Acts, William H. Willimon cites three elements of the process of working on disagreements:

- The first is **new revelation**. In verses 7-11, Peter alludes to his experience with the vision as told in Acts 10:1—11:18. God is doing a new thing here with the Gentiles. New revelation is one part of the discernment process.

- The second element is **experience**. In verse 12 we read that everyone listened as Barnabas and Paul told of the signs and wonders God was doing among the Gentiles. Their experience played a powerful role in deciding the issue at hand.

- The third element is **Scripture**. Following the telling of the experiences, James brings Scripture into the discussion. New revelation and experience must be tested with Scripture.

A healthy congregation or denomination, according to Willimon, can have a "good argument" when these three standards determine the boundaries for the debate. If a strong, common, binding faith exists, if there are "bottom line" values that people can agree upon, then they have the resources to work on controversy without being destroyed by it.

—*Carol Duerksen*

PRAYING AND WALKING IN THE WORLD:

- What have you personally learned through new revelations, experiences, and study of the Scriptures?

- Pray for your own ability to experience "good arguments," as well as for your congregation and denomination.

JUNE 15

LOVE THOSE LAWS

PLUNGING INTO THE WORD:

Acts 15:22-35

PONDERING ON THE WAY:

The first ecumenical church council ever conducted was over. Believing that the Holy Spirit had been an active part of the council, the apostles and elders sent representatives out with a letter to state the outcome of the meeting. The letter stated the "bottom line" issues for the Gentile Christians to follow that had been decided by the attenders.

The congregation at Antioch read the letter and ... "rejoiced at the exhortation." They rejoiced at both the new freedom and the new laws they had been given. They rejoiced at the boundaries that had been discerned for them. They rejoiced because they felt cared for and affirmed in their faith.

—*Carol Duerksen*

PRAYING AND WALKING IN THE WORLD:

- If you are a leader who discerns and "carries letters," pray for God's wisdom and guidance in your role within the congregation and the wider church.

- If you are a follower who hears what has been discerned by others, pray for the ability to trust and respect decisions made on behalf of the body of believers.

CHOCOLATE AND PEANUT BUTTER

PLUNGING INTO THE WORD:

Acts 15:36-41

PONDERING ON THE WAY:

Luke loved peanut butter. He put peanut butter on everything—on apples, bananas, sandwiches, pancakes, toast, celery, and in his cereal. Luke ate just plain peanut butter as a snack.

Luke's friend Matt did not like peanut butter at all, but boy did he love chocolate! Matt couldn't get enough chocolate. He drank chocolate milk, put hot fudge sauce on his pancakes and in his cereal, and ate any kind of chocolate candy he could get his hands on. For his birthday party, his parents had a small chocolate fountain on the table, with chocolate dripping down, and all kinds of food to dip in the chocolate. Matt was so happy, he almost forgot about his presents!

Luke was at Matt's birthday party—he wasn't so impressed with the chocolate fountain. He asked Matt's mom if she had any peanut butter he could eat. She did, so he took a bowl of peanut butter to the table with him.

Matt saw Luke's peanut butter and started to make fun of him. "Hey, Luke, this is my party, and it's a *chocolate* party!" he said.

"So? I don't like *chocolate,* and your mom gave me peanut butter!" Luke answered.

The guys kept arguing for a little bit, and then Matt took a piece of apple, dipped it in the fountain, and, when Luke wasn't looking, he smashed it into his bowl of peanut butter.

Luke was furious. "You ruined my peanut butter!" he glared at Matt.

Matt and Luke's friends wondered what was going to happen next. Then Brittany, who was sitting next to Luke, picked up the apple from Luke's bowl—the apple that was now dipped in chocolate *and* peanut butter. She took a bite, and a big smile spread across her face.

"Oh, that's good!" she said.

Can you guess what happened next?

Yes, soon all of the kids were dipping their food into both the peanut butter and the chocolate, and loving it! Even Matt and Luke tried it and said it was pretty good.

In our Bible story today, we heard how Paul and Barnabas had a big disagreement, but it ended up being a good thing because there were more people going out to tell others about Jesus! Sometimes God uses disagreements to create new ideas and make things better than they were before!

—*Carol Duerksen*

PRAYING AND WALKING IN THE WORLD:

- Can you think of examples when God has used disagreements for the best in the long run?

- What are some disagreements in your family? How can God use them for the good?

- **Adults:** Who of your brothers and sisters in Christ has really disappointed you? Can you turn that disappointment over to Jesus?

- **Prayer:** God, when we disagree or argue, give us patience with one another and help us trust you to work it all out for good.

JUNE 17 *(FOR CHILDREN AND FAMILIES)*

WHO'S OLD ENOUGH?

PLUNGING INTO THE WORD:

Acts 16:1-5

PONDERING ON THE WAY:

Ask your children to help you make a list of people who they would say are "doing God's work." When you have the list completed, ask children to guess the age of the people on the list, and write that number beside the person's name. (You may help if you have a better idea about the person's age.)

Ask: How old does a person need to be to do God's work?

Say: The Bible doesn't tell us how old Timothy was when he began working with Paul as a preacher, but the Bible does tell us he grew up in a Christian home (2 Timothy 1:5). God was part of his life, even as a child. There's another story in the Bible about God speaking to a boy named Samuel.

Share the story of Samuel with your children, as found in 1 Samuel 3:1-18.

Say: There isn't a certain age that a person has to be to do God's work. God loves us all, from the day we are born, and as we get older, we can do different things for God.

—*Carol Duerksen*

PRAYING AND WALKING IN THE WORLD:

- How do you think God can use you?

- **Adults:** Timothy came from a "mixed faith" home—his mother was a believer, but his father wasn't. I have a good friend who grew up Catholic and abandoned her faith when she married an atheist. When they had three sons, she decided to study all faiths in order to educate her boys so they could make decisions for themselves. What happened? In the process of her studies, she became a believer again herself.

  Never underestimate the power of planting the seeds of faith. Timothy's mother planted them in her son, and he became Paul's righthand man. My friend inadvertently planted them in her heart, and they have been growing and producing fruit for many years!

  In whom are you planting seeds of faith?

JUNE 18

FOLLOWING THE SPIRIT

PLUNGING INTO THE WORD:

Acts 16:6-10

PONDERING ON THE WAY:

I am completely blind.
I try to follow because my only alternative is stagnation.
I am afraid of the unknown; of what I cannot see
I want to follow, but I am blind.

There is a voice.
There is a breeze.
There is a hand on my arm.
I am led because I cannot see.
I follow though I am afraid.
This is trust.

I am a child.
I am young and I cannot resist my impulses.
I do not know what it is to follow.
I want adventure.

There is a song.
There is a sign.
There is my strong belief.
I am led because I do not know.
I follow though I am too small.
This is obedience.

I am the undeniable leader.
I know everything.
I am the one taking charge.
I want others to follow me.

There is a change.
There is an instinct.
There is a whisper in my dreams.
I am led because I am headstrong.
I follow though I had my life planned already.
This is submission.

I am a leader.
I am a follower.
I am a minister, a teacher, a parent, a doctor.
I am a sinner.

There is a vision.
There is a flickering light.
There is the Spirit.
I am led.
I follow.
This is the Way.

                    —*Michele Hershberger*

PRAYING AND WALKING IN THE WORLD:

- One of the great saints of the church, St. Ignatius, developed a prayer called the prayer of examen. In this prayer, one looks back over the last twenty-four hours and answers these two questions: What has been the most life-giving? What has been the least life-giving? There can be variations to these questions, such as: What am I most grateful for? What am I least grateful for? Take time now to do the prayer of examen. If you are with others, share your answers to the two questions and listen to their answers. Then pray for one another.

- Consider doing the examen for a month. Given this longer period of time, you may see patterns developing, the same types of situations or people bringing you joy or sorrow. Let God speak to you in these patterns. What painful things need to change? What joyful things need to be encouraged?

JUNE 19

RISKY HOSPITALITY

PLUNGING INTO THE WORD:

Acts 16:11-15

PONDERING ON THE WAY:

Lydia did everything right. She was worshipping God, which, as a Gentile, was an accomplishment, an act of determination on her part. The Jews didn't stop her from being a God-fearer, but people probably didn't go out of their way to welcome her either. But she saw something in the God they spoke of, and she wanted to be a part—even if she couldn't be on the inside track. Is that why she and the others gathered by the river to pray?

She also did everything right business-wise. She was a successful dealer in purple cloth, a female entrepreneur in a culture that many times made it harder for women to be in business, let alone be successful. And she was successful. She was the head of her household.

And she took every risk. After she and her household were baptized, Lydia urged Paul and his traveling companions to stay at her house. They hesitated, at least for a moment, because the text said that she prevailed upon them. She insisted. Did she have a hunch that Paul would stir things up in town? That they possibly could damage her fine reputation? Was she ready to host a band of rebels who might end up in jail? Would she risk so much for this newfound faith when she herself had not experienced that much welcome?

Yes. She was ready. It was worth the risk.

God, help me be like Lydia.

—Michele Hershberger

PRAYING AND WALKING IN THE WORLD:

- Sometimes we see hospitality as some bland "have your friends over for Sunday dinner" spiritual discipline, hardly worth our attention. But in the biblical narrative, hospitality usually involved risk—lots of it. Taken any risks lately?

- Hospitality implies both giving and receiving. Lydia received as much or more than she gave. What did you receive the last time you shared your home, food, and company?

- Ask God to open your eyes to more hospitality opportunities. Ask God for courage, wisdom, and peace as you take risks.

JUNE 20

BOUND OR FREE?

PLUNGING INTO THE WORD:

Acts 16:16-40

PONDERING ON THE WAY:

Who is captured in this story and who is free? It's a legitimate question.

The girl knows the truth. "These men are slaves of the Most High God, who proclaim to you a way of salvation." She has it—she communicates it. But she is enslaved by demons. She knows the truth, but it can't yet make her free.

The men who own the girl are free, of course. They are even free to bend the law to get Paul and his companions thrown into jail. Nobody messes with their easy money. But that's just it—how do they sleep at night, knowing they are taking advantage of a sick child? How free are they from the power of greed?

Paul and Silas are free, until they mess with the status quo. Then they are falsely accused, publicly humiliated, beaten to a pulp, and unceremoniously thrown into jail. They sit, chained and bleeding, in a dank dungeon. Yet they sing. And their singing is so real that the other prisoners notice. What drives these two to sing praise to God while bleeding and in chains?

The jailer? He feels free until the earthquake hits, and then he knows he's a dead man. Although it is no fault of his that the earth shook, he knows he'll take the fall for the prisoners' escape. He feels captive to his fate, so he decides to take fate into his own hands. He raises his sword to end it all.

There is no freedom in that.

But wait, Paul calls out. You don't have to do that. Look, we are all here. Sure enough. All the other prisoners, faced with the choice of physical freedom and spiritual freedom, choose well. They want the freedom that Paul has.

They choose God. They choose real freedom.

Are you bound … or are you free?

—*Michele Hershberger*

PRAYING AND WALKING IN THE WORLD:

- Who do you identify with the most in this story? Why? What do you need to do to become more free?

- It's amazing that the other prisoners stay. There is a reality more real than our physical lives. Do you have this reality? All you need to do is pray to receive it.

JUNE 21

SECULAR VOICES SPEAK THE TRUTH

PLUNGING INTO THE WORD:

Acts 17:16-34

PONDERING ON THE WAY:

One of my favorite movies is *Rent.* I just can't get enough of the touching "Seasons of Love" or the addicting eight minutes of "La Vie Boheme." One of my daughters even posts the lyrics of "Life Support" at the end of all her e-mails:

There's only us. There's only this.
Forget regret, or life is yours to miss.
No other road. No other way.
No day but today.

And I always cry when Angel dies. Movies can manipulate your emotions, sure. But this is more than that. It's not that Angel's character is irresistibly endearing. It's that this is real life for someone. The love that each couple shares, the love among all of the friends, is real. They care for one another. They show compassion even to the least in society, the way Jesus did.

Rent shows us an unorthodox family who hold one another closer than many traditional Christian families do. So while we might wonder at some of the problems and sins of the movie, we also have to grapple with the truth of their love for one another. Other secular movies can teach us truth too. *Chocolat* is a movie about redemption and grace. *Pay It Forward* is about helping one's neighbors and selfless giving. This is just the beginning. Secular movies, music, and books can hold meaningful truths for us today.

Paul tries to evangelize the Athenians by approaching them on their own level, in terms they would understand. He speaks to them about their own desire for the divine, their own longings for God. He uses the words of their poets. He uses their own reverence for an "unknown God." He comes to them in a secular context with a message of everlasting truth.

Fill a city like Boston with a couple more universities, make every citizen so concerned with their world that everyone votes, give them an intense religious fervor and put them in togas and you have a modern-day Athens. Intellectuals like the Athenians may seem hard to reach because they already have a strong set of beliefs, but despite all of their intellect, they still want more. To quote a little more *Rent*:

> *I find some of what you teach suspect,*
> *Because I'm used to relying on intellect.*
> *But I try to open up to what I don't know,*
> *Because reason says, I should have died three years ago.*

Faith is still undeniable, no matter how much we rely on intellect. God is still there. And God can work and does work and move and live in the secular world. No matter what the context, religious or secular, these truths are irrefutable.

—*Michele Hershberger*

PRAYING AND WALKING IN THE WORLD:

- What places are the Athenses of today? Coffee shops, movie theaters, universities? This is where Paul would be.

- What are some books, music, or movies that have impacted your faith?

- List the last five movies you have seen. What are some truths hidden in the text? If there is no positive moral, then perhaps you need to rethink your "to rent" list.

JUNE 22 (FOR CHILDREN AND FAMILIES)

WHAT IS A MISSIONARY?

PLUNGING INTO THE WORD:

Acts 18:18-28

PONDERING ON THE WAY:

In this story there are several people who work as missionaries. In fact, in the whole book of Acts there are many missionaries.

Miriam was a wonderful missionary. She went to Thailand and Vietnam to teach the English language to children and adults. She would do fun things with her new friends too. She would tell them about Christmas, and together they would make Christmas ornaments and learn funny songs like "The Twelve Days of Christmas." In Vietnam, Miriam had to be careful to not say anything about Jesus and the Bible unless people asked her questions. Then she was free to tell them what they wanted to know. And many times, Miriam's life was so different—so much kinder and gentler—that the Vietnamese people did ask her how she was different. And then she could tell them about Jesus.

She lived there for a long time, helping people and telling them about Jesus. When she came back to America, she became an elementary school teacher in Philadelphia. She still taught English to children whose families were new to the United States, and so they spoke a different language. During school and after school, she helped people and told them about Jesus. So even though she lived in her hometown, she was still a missionary.

—*Michele Hershberger*

PRAYING AND WALKING IN THE WORLD:

- Are there any missionaries from your church? Do you know a missionary personally? Ask your parents to tell you missionary stories.

- What are ways you can be a missionary by helping others?

JUNE 23

SUPERHEROES AND ALTER EGOS

PLUNGING INTO THE WORD:

Acts 19:1-22

PONDERING ON THE WAY:

What I wouldn't give to be Superwoman! First of all, superpower gives a person immunity to fashion faux pas. Mismatched clothes? Too-tight outfits? Capes? In the world of superheroes, that's all kosher. Second, I already have an alter ego—just plain old me—developed. Last, who wouldn't want unlimited power?

It goes without saying that I would be able to fly. I'd never get tired, of course. I'd have X-ray vision. And, obviously, I'd use my powers for good. I would stop time, so I could save people from shootings or car accidents. I could make food grow faster so no one would be hungry. Yes, I could do all these things single-handedly if only I were a superhero.

Only, I'm not a superhero. For some reason, God doesn't work through caped avengers or any other flying altruists. God works through regular people; and the power isn't theirs, it's God's.

God worked through Paul in incredible ways. Aprons that touched Paul had miraculous properties. That's amazing. Even Superman would be jealous of that legendary power.

There were several who tried to do the same miracles by themselves. They wanted to do good by driving out demons. But they did it without God. They didn't put in time praying or waiting. They didn't want sweat or tears. They wanted easy power. They wanted to be superheroes. But God doesn't work through superheroes in capes and tights. God works through their alter egos, the regular people.

Too many times I ask for easy power, but God doesn't want that. God wants me to do the work, to make the sacrifice, to pray, to devote my life. Too many times I want to be a superhero, but God doesn't want that. God wants me.

> —*Michele Hershberger*

PRAYING AND WALKING IN THE WORLD:

- Do you also struggle with the desire for easy power? It is easy to wish for good things, but harder to work toward their fulfillment.

- Do you believe that Jesus can work in your life to perform miracles? Perhaps he already has. How can a strong relationship between you and God facilitate God working through you to others?

JUNE 24 *(FOR CHILDREN AND FAMILIES)*

IDOLS

PLUNGING INTO THE WORD:

Acts 19:23-41

PONDERING ON THE WAY:

In Paul's time, many people believed in other gods. If you have seen the movie *Hercules,* then you know about some of these gods, like Zeus. Thousands of people thought that these gods were real. They made idols, which are statues made of bronze, silver, or gold, dedicated to the gods. They worshipped the idols instead of the one true God, the same God who created the world and sent his Son, Jesus, to save us from our sins.

Today we can have idols too, even if we don't bow down to figures made of bronze, silver, or gold. Whatever we put our trust in instead of God is an idol for us. For example, some people trust that money will save them or that the country's army will keep them safe.

Think of the movies you've watched. Are there idols in the movies? Who or what do people trust in the movies?

When we love something more than God, that is an idol too. We might love our things, like video games, more than God. We might love having just the right clothes more than we love God. We might love winning a soccer game more than we love God.

If you are old enough to spell, look at the word *idol* and write it this way: "I-do-l" and imagine that the "l" stands for "love." So, the word *idol* stands for "I do love." What do you love? Love God first, above everything else.

—*Michele Hershberger*

PRAYING AND WALKING IN THE WORLD:

- What could be some of the idols in your life?

- Try to watch less TV or play fewer video games, or whatever your idol might be. Instead, read good books, play with your brothers and sisters and friends, or do things with your parents.

- **Adults:** Worship of idols is no small problem in today's society. Though we don't have statues dedicated to other gods, we have made gods out of money, power, fame, the military, etc. List on paper all the things that may be considered idols in your life. Pray about the things listed. Then, write Jesus at the top of your paper. Put the paper in a place where you will see it daily. Let it help you put these idols in their rightful place, below the lordship of Jesus.

JUNE 25 *(FOR CHILDREN AND FAMILIES)*

THE BOY WHO DROPPED OFF

PLUNGING INTO THE WORD:

Acts 20:7-12

PONDERING ON THE WAY:

Have you ever had a broken arm, or do you know somebody who has? Doctors set the broken arm in a cast, friends sign names and draw pictures on it, and in a few weeks the cast comes off. Except for the hot itch under the cast, it's not so bad, and everything turns out okay.

Our Bible story talks about a boy, Eutychus, who fell out of a window and died. Eutychus, along with a lot of other people, was listening to Paul preach all day about Jesus. Eutychus was sitting in an open window. He got sleepy—that happens sometimes in long church services, doesn't it? Unfortunately, when Eutychus dropped off to sleep, he literally dropped off the window, three stories to the ground below.

Poor Eutychus. He needed more than a cast. He needed his life back! Paul laid his body over him and prayed. Jesus' life flowed through Paul into Eutychus and brought him back to life!

It's hard to imagine an all-day worship service or a dead boy coming back to life. Even so, miracle stories remind us that for more than two thousand years, Jesus' life has flowed through his followers and has drawn people to church. You are one in a long line of children who have heard the story of Jesus. Whether you hear it in an hour of Sunday school or church, or whether you are like the boy who sat still for a day, Sundays are special times. They're when people gather to worship Jesus and care for one another, just as Paul cared for this boy.

—*Laurie Oswald Robinson*

PRAYING AND WALKING IN THE WORLD:

- Talk delete with your parents about why going to church on Sunday mornings or another time of the week is important for you as a family.

- In today's prayers, thank God for your pastors and Sunday school teachers who help bring Jesus' life to you and your family each week.

- Do you have a friend at school whose family doesn't take him or her to Sunday school? Invite this friend to your church.

JUNE 26

STEP THREE

PLUNGING INTO THE WORD:

Acts 27:1-12

PONDERING ON THE WAY:

Twelve-step programs help people deal with addictions to drugs, alcohol, food, and people. The steps lead addicts away from these dependencies into dependency on God. For example, the 12-step program helps quell my compulsions to be perfect and to please others, tendencies born from a lack of self-acceptance and fear of abandonment.

Step 3 reminds me I can make decisions to turn my will and my life over to the care of God. In God's abiding presence, I stop needing to control people's perceptions of me, and I can refocus my gaze on Christ. His faithful acceptance frees me to offer my unvarnished self to others.

Often crisis and fear evoke control tendencies in people, as seen in today's Bible passage. Paul was on a ship bound for Rome. It likely would fail to reach the city before fall storms struck. Paul told the centurion in charge of the ship that they shouldn't finish the journey—there could be loss of cargo and lives. The centurion listened to the ship's pilot, who disagreed with Paul. The pilot and other shipmates believed that the harbor where the ship was docked was not suitable for spending the winter. So they took a "chance that somehow they could reach Phoenix, where they could spend the winter" (v. 12).

Tomorrow's devotional tells us whether the willful centurion made the right decision. But for now we reflect on the attitudes of the centurion and pilot, who "took a chance." It no doubt felt risky to trust Paul too, though one wonders if control issues blocked the centurion's ability to hear a prophetic word from a man of God.

In our storms, does a need to control cause us to take a willful chance rather than a godly risk? Could heeding Step 3 avert danger and make us more open to God's promptings?

—*Laurie Oswald Robinson*

PRAYING AND WALKING IN THE WORLD:

- Reflect on one time you felt afraid and tried to over-control the situation. What was the result?

- In today's prayer time, ask God for a new ability to cast the troubles of your life into God's care.

- Seek out a friend or relative who is involved in a 12-step program. Encourage this person in their recovery efforts. If you are involved in a 12-step program, ask a friend or relative to support you.

JUNE 27 *(FOR CHILDREN AND FAMILIES)*

"I TOLD YOU SO!"

PLUNGING INTO THE WORD:

Acts 27:13-26

PONDERING ON THE WAY:

Has anyone ever said "I told you so" to you? Maybe you rode your bike after dark and ran into a ditch and got hurt. Or maybe you ate too much candy and got a stomachache. Or maybe your parents told you that if you were mean to kids in school, you would be hurt in the process. You didn't listen, and you lost some friends.

In today's Bible story, some passengers on a ship didn't listen to advice either. Paul told a ship's crew not to sail for Rome, because winter storms were coming. They didn't listen to Paul and sailed anyway. They got caught in a storm and began to throw things overboard to lighten the ship. They were ready to throw all their food overboard when Paul said, "You should have listened to me" or "I told you so!"

Just as parents show kindness and help us solve the problems we make for ourselves, Paul also helped the scared passengers. An angel of God had told Paul that nobody would die on the ship, and Paul gave that message to the people on the ship. This time they listened, and they hoped they would be saved from the storm.

Our mistakes may not make us drown at sea. But if listening to advice from our parents can keep us from a bike accident, or Jesus' teachings can help save a friendship, then it may be worth taking them seriously before we have to hear, "I told you so!"

—Laurie Oswald Robinson

PRAYING AND WALKING IN THE WORLD:

- Remember a time when you heard "I told you so!" How did you feel? What did you do? How could you have avoided hearing those four words?

- Ask God for a soft heart to hear and follow the advice of parents and Jesus in the Bible.

- Draw or paint a picture of today's Bible story. Be sure to draw expressions on the faces that show how happy they were that they would not drown!

JUNE 28

SAVING YOUR SHIP

PLUNGING INTO THE WORD:

Acts 27:27-44

PONDERING ON THE WAY:

Anabaptists value practicing mutual care for one another and care for the world. This value is shaped by being part of a long legacy of people who follow Jesus by being his hands and feet in this world. We strive to love one another as Jesus has loved us.

Sometimes, though, focusing too much on others can keep us from taking care of ourselves. As I serve within the wider church, I see how easy it is for faithful workers in God's vineyard to forget that Jesus is the vine and we are the branches. We strive to produce fruit by focusing longer and harder on our neighbors, near or far. Soon the drought of overwork causes us to feel dry and empty, cut off from the Holy Spirit's flow of life.

Those of us who are over-functioning would do well to reflect on Paul's advice during the ship's harrowing journey in Acts 27. After fourteen days of fasting, he urges them to "take some food, for it will help you survive; for none of you will lose a hair from your heads." Their remedy for saving themselves was deprivation. Paul's remedy was nourishing their own selves to remain strong for challenges ahead. In an act reminiscent of Jesus' breaking of the bread during the last supper, Paul took bread, gave thanks to God in the presence of all, broke it, and ate—and they joined him in eating.

Perhaps we are tempted to deprive ourselves of much-needed soul food—rest, reflection, and renewal—in order to save the "ship" of our homes, communities, and world. We confuse practicing balanced self-care with being selfish. Paul reminds us it is our unbalanced survival mechanisms, not appropriate self-preservation, that threaten a safe and spiritually healthy journey.

—Laurie Oswald Robinson

PRAYING AND WALKING IN THE WORLD:

- Reflect on the times you deprived yourself of much-needed rest in order to serve your family, church, or the world. What was the result?

- Pray for renewed balance to practice good self-care as well as servant-hearted other-care.

- On a slip of paper you can easily see during the week, write down one way you commit to self-care this week in an area you have been neglecting. Ask a friend or spouse to hold you accountable for this commitment.

JUNE 29

GODLIKE OR GOD?

PLUNGING INTO THE WORD:

Acts 28:1-10

PONDERING ON THE WAY:

As a child, I was awed by slideshows of visiting missionaries. On muggy summer Sunday nights, our church family descended into the cool basement to see "exotic" movies of faraway places and people. Afterwards, we enjoyed big bowls of homemade ice cream as we lavished our visitors with attention and respect.

The Malta natives also were intrigued with Paul, who landed on their island with the bedraggled, shipwrecked crew. As he tended a fire in the cold rain, a viper struck him, and they considered him as good as dead. When he lived, they changed their opinion about him; at first they thought he was a murderer, and then they considered him a god.

Their discernment about him was dependent on outer signs. Because of this shallowness, they could not discern that the reason he survived the viper's poison—and later cured people by prayer and the laying on of hands—was because God's Spirit lived inside of him. It was God, and not Paul's godlike performance, that drove his dramatic life.

I see now that it wasn't so much the missionaries' exotic stories but rather their humble trust in Jesus that evoked awe in my young heart. Giving up their lives in adverse conditions for the gospel's sake was dramatic. But more inspiring was recognizing how Jesus inspired them to serve Christ in their neighbor. Looking only skin deep robs God's people of the deeper truth—Christ in the heart is what allows us to be his hands in this world. It is the person of Jesus, not personalities, that we are to worship.

—Laurie Oswald Robinson

PRAYING AND WALKING IN THE WORLD:

- Make a list of the mission workers you support through prayer and financial resources. Name one outer character or personality trait you most admire about each of them.

- In your prayers for these mission workers, thank God for how the life of Jesus within their hearts nurtures this outer personality and character trait. Pray that the Holy Spirit strengthens their sense of the Christ within who empowers their service.

- Next time a visiting mission worker comes to your community or congregation, carve out time to attend their presentation and to thank them for how they have allowed Christ to shape their life.

JUNE 30

CHAINED

PLUNGING INTO THE WORD:

Acts 28:11-31

PONDERING ON THE WAY:

Saul turned Paul, often bound by chains,
preaches Jesus Christ
who can free us from bondage

skeptical disbelief eclipses perception
as dull hearts sing of what we knew before
he came to utter Isaiah's verse

fat with this world's overfeeding,
we spurn heaven's nourishment
in favor of earthly lyrics

we feed each other the false
and chafe at our chains
even as we clutch their steely comfort

tirelessly Saul turned Paul brings us hope
of the gospel that could bind us to the God
of healing, of turning toward the new

but we turn away, choosing instead
the dull throb of bondage and gorging
on our mute, lifeless songs

—*Laurie Oswald Robinson*

PRAYING AND WALKING IN THE WORLD:

- What new word from God are you avoiding? What are you gaining by this avoidance? Reflect and/or journal about this avoidance.

- Pray this week for the courage to face truths you have been avoiding. Ask for God's mercy to soften your hard heart and to unstop your dull ears. Ask for the grace to have your own Saul-turned-Paul renewal.

- Write out a verse or spiritual saying that can help dislodge resistance to becoming the new person God is calling you to be. Put this verse or saying on your bedroom or bathroom mirror to remind you God wants to unbind you from "chains" that impede growth.

I WANT TO BE A TREE

PLUNGING INTO THE WORD:

Psalm 1

PONDERING ON THE WAY:

Given a choice
Chaff or a tree
Which would you be?

Blowing in the wind
With roots firmly planted,
Or blown by the wind
At the mercy of each gust.

Given a choice
Chaff or a tree
Which would you be?

Me?

I want to be a tree!

I want to be a tree
Planted by a stream
Loaded with luscious fruit
Wearing leaves that never wither.

None of that chaff blowing in the wind
Needlessly

Without direction.
Not me.
I want to be
A tree.

What's that you say?

Delight in the law of the Lord?
Day and night?   ·

I'd have to check my schedule.

Given a choice …

    —*Carol Duerksen*

PRAYING AND WALKING IN THE WORLD:

- How could you plant yourself more deeply into God's word? One week, when I wanted to memorize a Scripture passage, I put it on sticky notes on the instrument panel in my car. Now, don't be reading entire Scripture passages while driving and blame me when you have an accident, but maybe you can use drive time constructively.

- In this psalm, the wicked are self-centered and find their energy for life within themselves. The righteous are centered around God and God's Word. Which areas in your life do you need to change from being self-centered to being God-centered?

- Spend some time standing with a strong, healthy tree. Pray for God to feed your roots and to help you "meditate on the law of the Lord day and night."

- A very ancient art, practiced at one time by all Christians, is the technique known as *lectio divina*—a slow, contemplative praying of the Scriptures that enables the Bible to become a means of our union with God. Use *lectio divina* with Psalm 1 or another passage of your choice.

The first step in this practice is the reading/listening. *Lectio* is reverential reading and gently listening for a word or phrase in the passage that is God's word for us this day.

In the second step, called *meditatio,* once we have the word or passage that speaks to us in a personal way, we "ruminate" on it. The image of a ruminant animal quietly chewing its cud was used in antiquity as a symbol of the Christian pondering the Word of God. Christians have always seen a scriptural invitation to *lectio divina* in the example of Mary "pondering in her heart" what she saw and heard of Jesus. For us today these images are a reminder that we must take the word into ourselves—memorizing it, gently repeating it to ourselves, allowing it to interact with our thoughts, hopes, memories, desires.

The third step is *oratio,* or prayer. This prayer is both a dialogue with God and a consecration in which we allow the Word that we have taken in and on which we have been pondering to touch and change our deepest selves.

The final step is *contemplatio.* In this time of contemplation, we simply rest in the presence of the God, who used the Word as a means of inviting us into God's presence. We practice silence, letting go of our own words, simply enjoying the experience of being in the presence of God.

JULY 2 *(FOR CHILDREN AND FAMILIES)*

HOW BIG IS GOD? HOW BIG ARE YOU?

PLUNGING INTO THE WORD:

Psalm 8

PONDERING ON THE WAY:

What is the most amazing thing to you about nature? Is it the tall Rocky Mountains that sometimes reach into the clouds? Is it the brightly colored clouds in a Kansas sunset? Is it the soft cuddly puppy or kitten that you love to hold? Is it the millions of stars you see in the clear night sky?

God created the earth and everything in it—the sun, moon, and stars. It's hard to imagine how big God must be in order to make all of that. And if it's hard to imagine a God that big, it sure makes us feel like a tiny speck of nothingness, doesn't it?

We are tiny specks compared to the tall mountains and the stars, but guess what? This psalm says that we are made "a little lower than God." Even though there are many parts of nature that are bigger than us, we are closer to God's heart than anything else. Now *that* is amazing!

What should we do with that kind of amazing attention from God? We praise God! We say, "How great is your name in the earth!"

—*Carol Duerksen*

PRAYING AND WALKING IN THE WORLD:

- If you can get to a place where you can see the sky clearly after dark, go outside and look at the stars. How do you feel compared with all of the stars? How does God feel about the stars? How does God feel about you?

- Draw a picture or write a poem that completes this sentence: God is so huge that _____.

- Go for a walk in a park or pasture. Pay attention to the big and the tiny aspects of nature around you, and thank God for everything you notice.

JULY 3

LEFT TO TELL, PART 1

PLUNGING INTO THE WORD:

Psalm 13

PONDERING ON THE WAY:

We all have our down times, trials, and tribulations. We have times when we can really resonate with this psalm. But I dare say, none of us has experienced the depth of despair and desperation that Immaculee Ilibagiza did as a survivor of the 1994 Rwandan Holocaust. I will be sharing parts of her story during four devotionals this week, as recalled by Immaculee in her book, *Left to Tell.*

Immaculee grew up along with her three brothers in a loving family in beautiful Rwanda—a country of lush rolling hills, sparkling lakes, green valleys, and mist-covered mountains. For the first twenty-three years of her life, she could "sing to the Lord, because he has dealt bountifully" with her.

Her parents, Leonard and Rose, were both teachers who believed that education was the answer to poverty. They were highly respected members of the community, and her father had a reputation for being an educated, enlightened man who was fair to everyone. A problem in the village usually resulted in the people asking Leonard to help find a solution. Devout Roman Catholics, Leonard and Rose were known for practicing what they believed. They volunteered in a variety of community projects and often opened their home to families that temporarily needed a place to stay.

Leonard and Rose gave testimony to their faith in another significant way; they ignored the social and political realties around them and taught their children that everyone is born equal. While their country struggled with civil war and violence between Tutsi and Hutu tribes, and even after their house was burned by Hutu extremists in 1973, Immaculee's parents never said a disparaging word against Hutus. They believed that evil drove people to do evil acts, regardless of their tribe or race. They refused to classify one tribe as bad.

But in 1994, the tribal warfare between the Tutsis and Hutus exploded into a massacre beyond anyone's imagination. Immaculee found herself crying with the psalmist as he laments, "How long must I bear pain in my soul, and have sorrow in my heart all day long? How long shall my enemy be exalted over me?"

To be continued …

—Carol Duerksen

PRAYING AND WALKING IN THE WORLD:

- Contemplate your childhood. Which part of this psalm best describes your childhood? (Bear in mind, enemies don't have to be people who are out to kill your body. Abuse and abandonment are examples of enemies that can bring destruction to your soul.)

- If your childhood involved dark times of the soul, have you sought healing? Do you need to now?

- If your childhood was bountiful, have you thanked those who helped make that possible?

JULY 4

LEFT TO TELL, PART 2

PLUNGING INTO THE WORD:

Psalm 22

PONDERING ON THE WAY:

Immaculee and two of her brothers were spending Easter vacation with their parents. Despite the political tension hanging heavy in the air around them, they had a good time sharing about school, work, and the activities of their village.

Immaculee felt safe with her parents, but she noticed that her brother Damascene seemed anxious and uneasy. When she asked him what was wrong, he told her that he'd seen the Hutu killers nearby. Not only that, but he knew that the killers carried a list of the Tutsi families in the area, and their family was on the list.

Despite Damascene's urging that the family leave their home immediately, their father wouldn't hear of it. He insisted that things were getting better with the government, and peace would be there soon.

Several days later, fearing for her safety but refusing to leave himself, Immaculee's father sent her to a pastor's house to hide until the troubles were over. All she had with her were the clothes on her back, a rosary given to her by her father, and her government-issued ID card saying she was Tutsi.

Along with seven other women, Immaculee would end up spending ninety-one days crammed together in a small bathroom in Pastor Murinzi's home while hundreds of machete-wielding killers hunted for them, sometimes literally on the other side of the wall.

Verses 1-2, 14-17, and 19-21 of this psalm describe physical, mental, and emotional suffering similar to what these eight women endured. This is a psalm of petition to God for deliverance from life-threatening troubles. It includes the appeal to God for help and praise to God when help arrives. It is also a psalm of prophecy for the suffering and victory of Jesus on the cross.

—*Carol Duerksen*

PRAYING AND WALKING IN THE WORLD:

- Pray for people in your life, as well as people around the world, who live in fear. Think of specific persons and ask God to be with them and to deliver them.

- Recall times when you have experienced God's deliverance. Thank God, and resolve to be willing to share those experiences with others.

- In what ways is your government putting fear into the lives of innocent persons? What can you do to stop it?

- The damage people do to each other with words may not kill the other physically, but a lot of harm still can be done. Do you violate others with your words?

JULY 5 *(FOR CHILDREN AND FAMILIES)*

SUBSTITUTE SHEPHERDS

PLUNGING INTO THE WORD:

Psalm 23

PONDERING ON THE WAY:

What do you know about sheep? Let's try a quick quiz, just for fun. See if you know the answers.

True or False

1. All sheep have wool.

2. Sheep can't defend themselves.

3. Sheep love to eat nice green grass.

4. Sheep can have problems with insects.

Answers

1. **False.** There are twenty breeds of sheep that have hair, like goats, rather than wool.

2. **True and false.** Some sheep have horns they can use to defend themselves, and a mother sheep might butt something with her head if it is threatening her baby lamb. But in general, sheep don't have the ability to defend themselves if something attacks them and wants to kill them.

3. **True.** But they also can overeat on some grass and get sick and die.

4. **True.** Flies and other insects can bite them on their faces because they aren't protected by wool.

In Palestine, when this psalm was written, shepherds were people who had the job of taking care of the sheep. Today, in North America, we use "substitute shepherds" like llamas, donkeys, and dogs to protect sheep herds from being attacked. These shepherds usually do a pretty good job of protecting the sheep, but …

Can you imagine a llama telling his sheep not to eat too much green alfalfa?

Can you imagine a donkey putting oil on a sheep's head to protect it from flies?

This could happen in an animated movie but not in real life. There are some things a substitute shepherd just can't do.

Sometimes we don't realize that Jesus is the shepherd in our lives. We think we have everything we need, and we don't really pay attention to Jesus, even though he is paying attention to us. Jesus takes care of us when we are feeling down and when we are feeling happy. Jesus is with us in the good times and scary times. Jesus is with us and takes care of us like a good shepherd. He's not a substitute. He's the real thing.

—*Carol Duerksen*

PRAYING AND WALKING IN THE WORLD:

- Choose one of the verses in this psalm and create a painting that shows what it means for you.

- **Discuss together:** What would be a modern-day example of someone who protects and guides us? If you were to write this psalm today, what might you say instead of "The Lord is my shepherd"? "The Lord is my _____."

- **Adults:** If you'd like to read a wonderful book about the shepherd and sheep, check out Phillip Keller's book, *A Shepherd Looks at Psalm 23*.

JULY 6

LEFT TO TELL, PART 3

PLUNGING INTO THE WORD:

Psalm 25

PONDERING ON THE WAY:

Immaculee Ilibagazi and seven other women spent ninety-one days in a tiny bathroom in Rwanda, hiding from their own neighbors who were determined to find them and chop them to death with machetes. What did they do during the long days and nights when any noise at all could give them away?

Immaculee prayed. At times she could focus so intently on God that hours would pass like minutes. Other times she was haunted and taunted by internal voices, telling her they would be discovered, tortured, and murdered. Her prayers were much like those of David in verses 1-3 and 16-21 of this psalm. She pleaded for forgiveness for her sins and doubts, and she begged for protection from the killers. Immaculee had nothing left to hold onto except her faith.

And then one day, a battle began within her heart. Her prayers felt hollow, and she knew why; she couldn't pray to a God of love when her heart was full of hatred for the killers. God wanted her to forgive the murderers.

Immaculee struggled for a full week. Day and night, in that bathroom, she prayed, but she couldn't believe that the killers deserved forgiveness. Then one night she heard a woman screaming and a baby crying. The woman's screams ended, and Immaculee knew she'd been killed. The baby cried all night. The next day the cries were feeble and further apart. By evening, there were no more cries.

Immaculee prayed for God to receive the child's innocent soul, at the same time asking, "How can I forgive people who would do such a thing to an infant?"

The answer came back as clearly as if it had been spoken aloud: *"You are **all** my children … and the baby is with me now."*

Those words opened Immaculee's heart. She realized that the killers were like children. They didn't understand how badly they were hurting themselves, their Tutsi brothers and sisters, and God. They would suffer the consequences of their actions, but their souls weren't evil. Despite their horrible actions, they were children of God, and she could forgive a child.

Immaculee prayed that God would lead the killers to recognize the horrible error of their ways before they died themselves, and then she prayed the prayer, "Forgive them, they know not what they do."

—Carol Duerksen

PRAYING AND WALKING IN THE WORLD:

- Who has hurt you beyond what you have been able to forgive? Are you willing to seek counseling, pray, and struggle within your heart until you can honestly and completely forgive that person? Are you able to tell the person?

- When have you heard God's words to you as clearly as if they were said aloud? Did you listen? What happened?

JULY 7

LEFT TO TELL, PART 4

PLUNGING INTO THE WORD:

Psalm 27

PONDERING ON THE WAY:

Immaculee survived the Rwandan Holocaust, only to shed endless tears as she traveled back to her home village to find it plundered, her parents and two brothers brutally murdered. As neighbors related the sadistic details of her family members' last moments of life, her heart raged with hate and the desire for revenge. Again and again, she prayed for God to forgive her evil thoughts, to help her forgive and even love the killers.

God did send peace to Immaculee. The deep sadness was still there, but it was sadness without the bitterness or hatred. Immaculee began to look forward. She persisted until she got a job at the United Nations building in Rwanda. She met U.S. citizen and UN employee Bryan Black there, and they were married in a traditional

Rwandan ceremony. In 1998, they moved to New York City, and they now have two children, Nikeisha and Bryan Jr. Immaculee works for the UN in Manhatten and has established the Ilibagazi Foundation to help others heal from the long-term effects of genocide and war.

As I read Psalm 27, I can't help but see the parallels between this psalm and Immaculee's story. King David and Immaculee both experienced the most desperate down times of life, as well as the soaring highs of knowing that the Lord is their stronghold and nothing can take that away. Immaculee writes, "God saved my soul and spared my life for a reason: He left me to tell my story to others and show as many people as possible the healing power of His love and forgiveness."

We can do no less.

> —*Carol Duerksen*

PRAYING AND WALKING IN THE WORLD:

- Memorize verses 13-14 of Psalm 27. A large part of faith is *believing in advance* that you will see the goodness of the Lord, even when it seems impossible.

- What is your faith story? Are you telling it? How can people hear about God's healing power if we aren't telling our stories?

JULY 8

ALL IS WELL?

PLUNGING INTO THE WORD:

Psalm 30

PONDERING ON THE WAY:

Things weren't always good for David. True, he was a king, but he had his share of problems. Let's just say it wasn't all psalm-writing and giant-slaying. When he wasn't playing his harp, he got himself into some serious moral and political quandaries. This is a psalm of deliverance, so it wouldn't have been written if there was nothing from which to be delivered. David hit bottom during a period of prosperity. He had become self-satisfied, smug, and overconfident.

We've all been there, Dave.

Walter Brueggeman explains that there are three stages of life as a follower of God represented in Psalms. First there is *orientation,* in which everything is just great. As long as you are faithful, God will provide. This is the childhood chapter. Go to church, sing happy praise songs, and life will be sugar and spice and everything nice (and/or snakes and snails, whichever you prefer). This is the honeymoon phase of believing in God. Verses 6 and 7a represent this theology.

Next is *disorientation.* In this stage, something bad happens and praise songs aren't enough to help. Perhaps it is a death in the family, loss of job, divorce or, in many cases outside of America, forced conscription or invasion. People in this phase can become disillusioned, bitter, or resentful. It is good to remember that this phase is common. In fact, most of the psalms are laments. In verse 7b through 10, we see David struggling.

Finally there is *reorientation.* This is where the mourning turns to dancing. We turn back to God and are healed. We remember that only through God can we be saved. There is a danger in this—that we may regress to the orientation mindset, in which everything will be perfect. God doesn't promise perfection. Wise, reoriented people know that. They also know that though they go through trials and tribulations, the Lord is with them.

Look at verses 5, 11, and 12. They are a testament to God's grace and an allusion to the promise of eternal life and glory. It is through God that all things are possible, no matter which phase of our walk we are in.

—*Michele Hershberger*

PRAYING AND WALKING IN THE WORLD:

- Where are you in this psalm? Rejoicing and singing praises? Immovable and prosperous? In the pit? Dancing with joy?

- How can you reach out with sensitivity to people who are struggling in life or with their faith?

JULY 9 *(FOR CHILDREN AND FAMILIES)*

POTATOES IN MY EARS

PLUNGING INTO THE WORD:

Psalm 37

PONDERING ON THE WAY:

When I was a little girl, I would hear certain phrases over and over again: "God loves a cheerful giver." "Sit up straight." "A penny saved is a penny earned."

My dad would say, "If you don't wash your ears better, I do believe potatoes are going to grow in there."

My dad was being silly—I knew that—but I checked in the mirror just in case.

Do your parents do that too? Would you check in the mirror for potatoes? Your parents, grandparents, or teachers all are wise people. They give us lots of advice or wisdom. They have learned a lot through all the experience they've had following God in their daily lives.

There are lots of wise people in the world. They say things like:

- "Where there's a will, there's a way."

- "An apple a day keeps the doctor away."

- "One good turn deserves another."

- "Actions speak louder than words."

- "Practice makes perfect."

Have you ever heard these sayings? Can you or your parents think of any other wise sayings?

This psalm is full of wisdom and good sayings. It has lots of advice in it too. These sayings are about God. They say that as long as we trust God and are righteous, then we will be blessed.

> —Michele Hershberger

PRAYING AND WALKING IN THE WORLD:

- Can you find some of the wise sayings of this psalm? (Hint: verses 3, 27, 28.)

- Memorize one of the verses of Psalm 37, or parts of the verse. It will help you remember to be good.

- Can you think of other sayings or proverbs? Can you make up a brand-new one?

- **Adults:** This is clearly an "orientation" psalm. Are there promises made in this passage that haven't been true for you? Be honest, but remember that the story of your life is not complete yet. Our understanding of what we need is different—sometimes—from God's understanding of what we need.

ODE TO A STEAMING KETTLE

PLUNGING INTO THE WORD:

Psalm 39

PONDERING ON THE WAY:

> The teapot whistles on the stove
> And I burn inside
> Victim of a scorching tongue
> Was she once burned too?
> Teapot trembling, too hot, waiting for further instructions
> But now I boil in my seat
> I sing in my rage
> A silent siren
> The air moist with my venom …
> At myself
> Turn down the heat God
> I cannot bear your gaze
> Your grazing fire of purity
> I must escape
> The whistle
> The bubbling
> The silent noise
>
> God, what can I do?
>
> Make a cup of tea.
>
> —*Michele Hershberger*

PRAYING AND WALKING IN THE WORLD:

- List some times when it is appropriate to speak up for someone or something. List times when it's better to stay silent.

- Reflect on some times when you either have shot off your mouth at the wrong time or left something unsaid. How can you rectify that situation?

JULY 11

BAD THINGS HAPPEN

PLUNGING INTO THE WORD:

Psalm 42

PONDERING ON THE WAY:

The first phrase of this psalm always launches me into the song, "As the Deer Panteth for the Water." So I read the rest of the passage with that stuck in my head. That's not a bad thing. It has a nice, melancholy melody and a beautiful harmony line. But it is almost too pretty for this psalm. I need a song that's sad enough to make me cry or perhaps annoying enough to make me pull my hair out. This is a lament; this is sackcloth and ashes.

The psalm is subtitled "the sorrow of the godly." A believer is separated from God. Where is God? Why does this happen? Is it okay for godly people to suffer? They do, because bad things do happen to good people.

I have a friend who is a go-getter, an adventurer; someone who's always up for fun and excitement. Or at least, he was. As a Christian, he gave generously and always helped people. When he gave street beggars money, we thought he was naïve, but he always said he was simply doing unto others.

Maybe his trust in people was too naïve. He got an ear-piercing and came into contact with the AIDS virus via a dirty needle.

What made it worse was the way he was treated because of his disease. People accused him of all sorts of immoral activities. Few understood and even fewer would help him.

When he died, we—his family and friends—were devastated. He was a person who always wore a smile and could be counted on to cheer me up on a bad day. He had done nothing to deserve his fate, but it came anyway.

It's hard to trust God when these things happen. This experience hurt my walk with God. I wanted to know why this happened. Where was God? Why wasn't this stopped? Why do bad things happen to good people? Why? Then I remembered my friend's attitude throughout the ordeal. He too struggled with faith. He too asked why. But whenever people asked him for help, he still gave generously. He still did unto others. He still attended church, and through his prayers he found peace.

I still don't know why bad things happen to good people. But they do. And good things happen to bad people. But I know that no matter what, we can still find peace through God. We can still have an impact on the kingdom. We are always children of God.

—Michele Hershberger

PRAYING AND WALKING IN THE WORLD:

- Make a prayer station to go with this psalm. First, fashion a complaint box or a suggestion box for God. Then, write things down and stuff the box with as many "suggestions" as you can think of. Now, can you walk away from the box for two weeks?

- Reflect on an experience you have had with an unfair situation. Did it happen to you or to a close family member or friend? How did you, or he or she, reconnect with God? Or have you?

- What phase of life is the writer of this psalm going through? Orientation or disorientation?

- What kinds of things separate you from God? Usually it is a type of sin. If you feel separated from God, ask for help in reconnecting.

- Do people ask, "Where is your God?" What do you tell them?

JULY 12

PRAYING FOR OUR ENEMIES

PLUNGING INTO THE WORD:

Psalm 43

PONDERING ON THE WAY:

Psalm 43, at least verse 1, is not a psalm quoted much in my congregation. As a member of a peace church, I belong to a people who don't feel right about calling down lightning on personal enemies or even national enemies. It doesn't sound WWJD enough.

On one hand, that's a good reaction. Jesus wouldn't and didn't cry out with the anger displayed in many psalms. His words were, "Father, forgive them, for they don't know what they're doing."

Upon closer inspection, however, maybe verse 1 isn't so bad. I do have enemies, from the people who just irritate me to the more malignant evildoers who really threaten me. Shouldn't I be honest about my fear and my anger with the God who knows every corner of my soul already? I do want vindication sometimes, and I can't get past those feelings until I admit they exist.

And who's doing the vindication anyway? In this psalm and in every other psalm that speaks of vengeance, the psalmists, every time without exception, call on God, and only God, to repay the oppressor. Only God is to decide when and how—and who—is to be repaid and receive their fair due.

Only God is wise enough. Only God is holy enough.

Only God loves enough.

We have enemies. We are angry. That's the truth.

But we aren't wise enough, pure enough, to vindicate ourselves. That's not our job. We can never see the whole picture clearly enough.

But God can. Tell him. Tell him now.

> —*Michele Hershberger*

PRAYING AND WALKING IN THE WORLD:

- Who are your enemies? Pray for them. Use Matthew 5:43-47 for guidance.

- Is it okay to be angry as Christians? Is it okay to dislike someone?

- What is your holy hill (v. 3)? Where do you find hope and joy in God?

JULY 13

EMPTY SACRIFICE VS. TRUE WORSHIP

PLUNGING INTO THE WORD:

Psalm 50

PONDERING ON THE WAY:

There are plenty of people who call themselves "Christians" and yet do not attend church. The reason? There are many reasons, but an oft-cited excuse is that the church is full of hypocrites. After all, everybody sins, even the most pious church-goer. And yet every Sunday, the pews are filled with people—sinners—singing praise to God. Doesn't that seem hypocritical?

In this psalm God—the ultimate and true judge—writes a complaint against the people. Ritual and sacrifice had become entwined with true worship, and then slowly ritual came to replace true worship. God is not angry that the people give sacrifices, but the sacrifices cannot replace praise and obedience. God doesn't need the burnt animals; God needs thanksgiving and glory. God doesn't hate ritual in worship; God hates ritual by itself—ritual without a changed life.

God cares about what's inside our hearts. We can go to church as often as we want, but unless we go in a spirit of humility and love, we might as well be going to a museum or a park. Like the Israelites' empty sacrifice, worship without the right spirit is empty worship. No worship can be true without praise, confession, and practicing justice.

Now, I'm not suggesting that you don't go to church. Whenever we go to church we go with mixed motives, and rarely out of the pure joy of worshipping God. We go nonetheless in order to connect with God despite our sin, to confess our shortcomings, and praise God for God's steadfast love. We may never quite hit the mark, but we keep trying. Just remember: God cares about what's in our heart. We must match our inside feelings to our outer signs of reverence.

—*Michele Hershberger*

PRAYING AND WALKING IN THE WORLD:

- If God were writing a complaint against you, what would it say? Take some paper and write it down.

- Spend time in prayer and openly confess your sins to God.

- What are ways you can intentionally prepare your heart to match the worship you give outwardly?

JULY 14 *(FOR CHILDREN AND FAMILIES)*

KING DAVID'S SIN

PLUNGING INTO THE WORD:

Psalm 51

PONDERING ON THE WAY:

How would you feel if someone took your favorite toy? How would you feel if you were the one who took someone else's favorite toy?

Brandon knows the feeling. He took Troy's best mini car while they were both on the playground. It was bright red, brand-new, and had extra-fancy wheels. Brandon wanted it so much. He could see himself playing with that car in his own backyard, every single day.

But every day that bright red car sat on Brandon's window sill. Why? Because Brandon felt bad that he took it. Troy was his friend. What would Troy think if he knew? Was Troy searching his own bedroom and backyard, worried about where the car was?

It wasn't fun at all to play with the car. In fact, when Brandon touched it, he felt sick inside.

This psalm was written by King David after he had done a very bad thing. David's sin was like Brandon's—he took what belonged to somebody else. This sin hurt many people's lives, and it also hurt David for the rest of his life.

God always knows our sins, and God is always sad when we sin. God wants us to be happy, healthy, good people. When we tell lies, or disobey, we pull farther from God. That's why God is sad about sin. But God loves us very much and will forgive us when we tell God we are sorry.

—*Michele Hershberger*

PRAYING AND WALKING IN THE WORLD:

- Think about times when you have disobeyed your parents, told a lie, stolen something, or done something else that was wrong. Pray to God and tell God about that sin. Ask for forgiveness and for help in not doing it again.

- Watch the Veggie Tale video, *King George and the Ducky.*

JULY 15

WORSHIPPING WITH THE "ENEMY"

PLUNGING INTO THE WORD:

Psalm 53

PONDERING ON THE WAY:

A Muslim man cried as he spoke during an interfaith peace service. As I listened, emotions jarred my heart. For months, I'd absorbed news from CBS and *Time* about fighting in Iraq and about the war on terror. My heart was muddled about people portrayed as the "evildoers,"—words we find in today's Scripture passage.

The tenderness and sincerity of this man made me realize that the media can never tell the truth about the real "war"—the one we wage in our hearts. There are more ways to kill than with guns or smart bombs. They are the ways we use to "kill" the human potential to connect with God and each other, ways as small as judging the choice of a person's clothes or as huge as judging a race of people on the actions of its extremists.

Today's psalmist is contemporary in his lament about people who disregard God and terrorize each other. He distinguishes "fools" from "evildoers." Fools say in their hearts, "There is no God." Evildoers know there is a God but act as if there is not. They "eat up people as they eat bread." They commit acts of violence as easily as they eat breakfast.

The psalmist had two categories, but in verse 2 we see that God has only one criterion: Do they seek me? This psalm reminds us that God desires people who place their trust in God's sovereignty and not in weapons, politics, or stereotypes.

My Muslim brother challenged me to let God scrutinize my heart with a searchlight of love and truth. Would I come out of the bunkers of my own littleness and fear and seek God alongside him? Could we plead together for God's mercy and tenderness in our merciless and terrorizing times?

> —Laurie Oswald Robinson

PRAYING AND WALKING IN THE WORLD:

- Reflect on the news reports you listen to each week. Which ones most tempt you to mistrust people of other races and be merciless toward them?

- In prayer this week, invite God to search your heart and remove hidden weapons of judgment, stereotyping, and fear.

- Befriend a person of another faith in order to share how your relationship to Jesus helps you seek God in these troubled times. Invite that person to describe what draws them to seek God.

JULY 16 *(FOR CHILDREN AND FAMILIES)*

STICKS AND STONES

PLUNGING INTO THE WORD:

Psalm 58

PONDERING ON THE WAY:

I was a fat little kid whom neighbor kids loved to tease. I'd often run home to Mom, wailing about how Darla or Nicky or Peggy called me "Fatty" or "Piggy." I often yelled back, "Sticks and stones may break my bones, but words will never hurt me." But the truth was that their name-calling cut my heart into a million little pieces.

The writer of today's Bible story felt a lot like I did as a kid. The psalmist wanted God to "break the teeth" in the mouths of the wicked. My playmates weren't wicked, but their teasing made me want God to get them back. I wanted them to stop saying words that hurt me—much worse than sticks and stones ever could.

Have you ever been called names, like "Dummy" or "Jerk"? Have you ever called someone else names? Verse 11 reminds us that there is a "God who judges on the earth." We don't need to judge people for their actions—no matter how bad they have hurt us. We can give God the job of judging. And we can ask God to help us forgive those who call us names or to forgive us for hurting others with our words.

—Laurie Oswald Robinson

PRAYING AND WALKING IN THE WORLD:

- What names have you been called? Ask God to help you forgive those who have hurt you.

- What names have you used for others? Ask God for forgiveness for hurting others. Find a way to tell someone that you are sorry for calling that person a bad name.

- **Adults:** Ask God to help you vent—appropriately. Can you admit to your anger so you can move on and receive healing? Remember, just as in this and every psalm, you must let vengeance be the Lord's. It's God's business to judge, not yours.

JULY 17

GOD ALONE

PLUNGING INTO THE WORD:

Psalm 62

PONDERING ON THE WAY:

Serenity

God, I pour out my heart to you
A million grains of sand
sifting into your hands,
result of my searching
for a rock of refuge
in people, places, things.

In vain the search ends
dashed against hard rocks
of disillusionment, delusion
in panicked distress
I wait for you to save me
from my restless driving.

Finally safe in the fortress
of your trustworthy embrace,
I give up my lovers
of low estate, of high esteem
their breath lighter than thin air
where I have floated too long.

In your arms I rest—
no longer tossing, turning
in stormy surf or endless sky,
but grounded on your
power and steadfast love
I wait for you in trusting silence.

—*Laurie Oswald Robinson*

PRAYING AND WALKING IN THE WORLD:

- Reflect on how much time you've spent in the last month waiting in silence to receive strength and comfort from God. What has most distracted you—people, places, or things?

- In your prayer time, confess your misplaced trust and renew your commitment to trusting God, your rock, refuge, and fortress.

- Take an hour—at one time—sometime this month to wait on God in silence. Make arrangements beforehand with your family, friends, or workplace to carve out space to do this, and schedule it in your calendar.

JULY 18

NIGHT WATCHES

PLUNGING INTO THE WORD:

Psalm 63

PONDERING ON THE WAY:

I sat in the 3 a.m. dark, where blipping lights signaled that fluid was pumping into my dying mother. My siblings and I took turns sitting with Mom, who had descended into a coma. The nurses said people in a coma can hear you speak to them, even though they can't respond. Knowing time was very short, I held her hand and read aloud from my tattered *Living Bible*. I prayed. I sang. I named my unrealized dreams. I whispered pleas for forgiveness.

We'd been estranged over a longstanding issue. A day before she descended into this mute darkness, when she was still responsive, we forgave each other. I felt assured of our restoration. But I still rambled on with the monologue of a grieving daughter.

The writer of this psalm knew the grieving that comes with loss. At one time, he had spent time in the safety of the sanctuary, beholding the Lord's power and glory. But now that he was hunted and haunted by his enemies, he found himself in a dry and weary land where there was no water. But still, in the darkness and silence of this desert, in the middle of the night, he declared his trust in the Lord's help and the cool shadow of the Lord's wings. In the black hole of nothingness, he clung to the Lord's hand.

I clung to Mom's hand in the desert of her fainting flesh, eaten away by congestive heart failure. But I still sensed the Lord's assurance. His steadfast love was better than life, and it would outlast Mom's labored breathing. Soon, she would bend near the crystal clear rivers, drinking in waters, dancing in the healthy heartbeat of God.

—*Laurie Oswald Robinson*

PRAYING AND WALKING IN THE WORLD:

- Do you see the paradox in verse 8? The psalmist clings desperately to God, and all the while God is already holding him.

- Reflect on the times loved ones or close friends have died. How did the Lord's comfort and light reach you? Journal the ways you struggled to be assured of the Lord's presence and promises in the desert of death. Recall how the Lord finally broke through to you.

- Praise the Lord for how he outlasts life and death, bringing to you and your loved ones the promise of his presence forever.

- If you are in a period of mourning a loved one, allow the Lord's steadfast love to bring you waters in the dry and weary land. If a relative or friend is in mourning, reach out. Don't push an agenda—just be there.

ONIONS AND GOD'S BANQUET

PLUNGING INTO THE WORD:

Psalm 73

PONDERING ON THE WAY:

I've often forgiven those who have hurt me or asked forgiveness from people I've hurt. Sometimes, years later, God asks me to revisit another layer of that painful experience to clear up leftover residue I didn't know still existed. The revisiting wounds my pride—I felt I had done a good thing in dealing with the issue once. I feel like a big onion my mother peeled for soups and stews, shedding tears as she peeled.

Today's passage reminds us we carry many layers of resentment and self-pity, both from the past and the present. Like the psalmist, we feel vengeful toward those we deem unworthy of prospering or toward those who abuse or punish us. We can relate to the cry in verse 18: "Surely you have set them in slippery places, you make them fall to ruin."

God addresses these laments, but in a surprising way. The spotlight in verses 21-26 swings from others to the psalmist: "When my soul was embittered, when I was pricked in heart, I was stupid and ignorant; I was like a brute beast toward you." In confession, God peels away the psalmist's hidden bitterness and pride.

In cleansing deeper layers, God cures the real ill—our overdependence on human flesh: "Whom in heaven have I but you? And there is nothing on earth that I desire other than you. My flesh and my heart fail, but God is the strength of my heart and my portion forever."

The tears of the peeling may hurt, but that "onion" becomes part of the healthy banquet God prepares for us. The menu avoids an overfocus on the failing performance of others or ourselves and includes huge portions of dependence on God's unfailing strength.

—*Laurie Oswald Robinson*

PRAYING AND WALKING IN THE WORLD:

- Make a list of those who have hurt you recently or in the past. Which hurts have you forgiven? Which are still festering? Which ones are you not sure about?

- Ask God to show you one hidden layer of resentment that still needs more cleansing. Peel away that layer in God's presence. Allow tears if there is grieving or relief. Ask God to become your strength and your portion.

- Seek out a friend, family member, or "enemy" with whom you have unfinished business, and finish what can be finished.

JULY 20

DIVINE FRONT-RUNNER

PLUNGING INTO THE WORD:

Psalm 75

PONDERING ON THE WAY:

As I write this devotional, the United States is twenty days away from midterm elections to determine who wins seats in Congress. I try to identify candidates who are most likely to work for justice and peace in our world, and I rely on voter guides in lieu of staying current on the issues.

Today's passage reminds me, however, that any human goodness, rightness, or integrity is no match for God's equity, stability, and judgment. Verse 3 says, "When the earth totters, with all its inhabitants, it is I who keep its pillars steady." We are reminded that neither the east nor west—nor the red or blue states—will determine the path of nations. It will be God, the divine front-runner, who ultimately executes judgment.

Today's psalm comforts and steadies us. We have the privilege of voting responsibly, but we must not fret the outcome. We must not take the weight of our imperfect nation on our shoulders nor lay blame on our nation's leaders, who are imperfect. Our greater responsibility is to give thanks for God's divine watchfulness of our world. And our greater privilege is to pray daily for God's peaceful and just reign to become ever more evident in all nations' governments.

—*Laurie Oswald Robinson*

PRAYING AND WALKING IN THE WORLD:

- Reflect on what portions of time you spend watching the news or reading news magazines versus the time you spend in devotional reading and prayer.

- Ask God to help you to take less seriously election outcomes and more seriously God's divine front-runner status and ultimate victory over the world's problems. Ask God to help you fret less and pray more.

- Seek out Christian reading or news sources that avoid the polarities of the "right" or the "left" but can help you stay focused on God's ways and the people who are most likely to follow in those paths. Seek out devotional books that can keep you centered in God's kingdom.

JULY 21 *(FOR CHILDREN AND FAMILIES)*

CHILDREN OF THE MOST HIGH

PLUNGING INTO THE WORD:

Psalm 82

PONDERING ON THE WAY:

Do you know what *adopted* means? Are you adopted, or do you know someone who is?

My nephew, Joel, was born to a mother who didn't have enough money to take care of him. She wanted a family that could love him and care for him. She found my brother, Neil, and his wife, Frances, and they adopted him as their own. Joel was born on the birthday of his adoptive father, June 23, which made it really special for both of them.

Today's passage says we all have a special bond with God. In a way, all of us are like Joel. We were born to a set of earthly parents. But God is the heavenly parent of everyone. Verse 6 says we are "all children of the Most High."

The psalm describes what God is like as a parent: God cares for the weak and those who don't have parents. God protects children nobody else cares about. And God often does this through adults who care about children.

God wants all children to have parents or caring adults to love them. Many of us live with our birth parents. Others are adopted like Joel. And still other children are cared for in foster homes. In every case, when we receive love from earthly parents or caretakers, we know that God loves us that much too—and even more!

—*Laurie Oswald Robinson*

PRAYING AND WALKING IN THE WORLD:

- In what ways do your parents or caretakers give you love and care? In what ways do they meet your needs? What does this show you about God?

- In your morning or bedtime prayers today, thank God for loving parents and caretakers. To express your thanks for their care, make them a thank-you card.

JULY 22

OPEN-MIKE NIGHT

PLUNGING INTO THE WORD:

Psalm 88

PONDERING ON THE WAY:

I can just picture that it's an open-mike night at a coffee house. A teenager dressed in black with long, stick-straight hair covering most of a heavily made-up face, steps up to the mike and reads this psalm. I'm guessing that very few in the audience would realize it was a Bible recitation. In fact, I can see the audience making comments about the mental stability of the writer and of teens in general.

Maybe we all need to be reminded that this passage is indeed in the Bible. It's stark and dark. But why not? After all, suffering and depression are part of most people's lives. Sometimes friends aren't loyal; sometimes we get a disease or get into serious trouble. Sometimes it seems like there is no hope. It feels like it's all God's fault.

Anger and sorrow are real and justified emotions. The trick is keeping our behavior appropriate despite them. Grieving with anger is an appropriate spiritual discipline. Instead of lashing out at friends or coworkers, the psalmist brings his troubles to God. Every night is open-mike night because God is always ready to hear what we have to share, whether it's a triumph and a joy or a crisis.

This psalm is not as negative as it may seem at first. It's true that, of all the psalms, this one is the only one without hope in it. But still the psalmist remembers God's ability to save people. He does believe in God's faithfulness, or else he wouldn't pray this prayer at all. He rails on and on because he knows that God can hear. This poem shows us that no matter how hard our problems may seem, God can help, although the Lord doesn't always come through immediately.

The poem also shows us that sometimes it's okay to sit in despair and rail at God. This is an honest expression of human emotion. Most people experience some pain and suffering and we, as Christians, should be open to hearing and sharing with each other. Maybe despair and anger should be welcome at open-mike night.

Maybe it's time for you to step up to the mike.

—*Michele Hershberger*

PRAYING AND WALKING IN THE WORLD:

- Think of a time when you were miserable or depressed. What did you do to cope with your feelings?

- What are some healthy ways to deal with anger, disappointment, frustration, sorrow, loneliness, etc.?

- How does this psalm show appropriate ways to grieve for a loss or sorrow?

- Find or make some ashes and mix them up with a bit of oil. Ask a friend to anoint you with this mixture of sorrow and healing balm.

JULY 23

MEANING

PLUNGING INTO THE WORD:

Psalm 90

PONDERING ON THE WAY:

20 years.
An eyelash drops and is brushed away.
A leaf falls only to be stepped on.
A firefly lights up its tiny space for a second.

A moment, a second, an instant.
Why does it matter which way I turn?
Why should you measure the work of my hands?

40 years.
I count my days.
I arrange my affairs.
I am an alien, a wanderer, a gypsy.
I have no home. I am a stranger.

Adonai.

A moment, a second, an instant and I am gone.
What is my gain?
A thousand years passes in the night and I am gone.

60 years.
You are a tsunami. I am a grain of sand.
You are a mountain. I am a pebble.
You are the ocean. I am a tear.

Adonai.
Adonai.

A moment, a second, an instant.

80 years.
Why does the grass grow?
Why do the flowers bloom?
They will only die.

Adonai.
Adonai.

Lord have mercy.

A moment, a second, an instant.

Why do you still love me?

I will only die.

If I mean nothing, why do you bother?

10,000 years.

You are the sun. I am a prism.

Yet you shine in me.

Adonai, shine in me.

—*Michele Hershberger*

PRAYING AND WALKING IN THE WORLD:

- Write a poem of your own, either on the meaning of life or the eternal might of God compared with our short lives.

- Think of people in your life who the world might consider insignificant yet who have made a huge impact on your life. Are you making a huge impact in someone else's life?

JULY 24

GUARDIAN ANGELS

PLUNGING INTO THE WORD:

Psalm 91

PONDERING ON THE WAY:

Some would say I'm not the safest driver. Yeah, I was a little reckless when I first got my license. I have more than one ticket on my record—at least three officially. There was the time I sped through a construction zone and the time I was playing cops and robbers (I was a "cop" and driving a friend's car) and was caught rolling through a stop sign. I realize it's highly ironic to be pulled over by a police officer while pretending to be a cop, but the officer didn't find it funny. My family and friends tease me about my driving record, though recently I've cleaned up my act considerably. Maybe it's because of my little keychain that says, "Don't drive faster than your guardian angel can fly."

I believe in guardian angels—not as winged spirits that bear a striking resemblance to their charges—but rather as an expression of the Holy Spirit watching over me. I believe my guardian angel was there the day I totaled my parents' car. I don't remember what happened, but the evidence showed we hit a mailbox, then a tree, then we spun into some bushes until a fence stopped us. The worst part was that I had friends in the car whose lives I had endangered.

As I sat there with my friends, frozen in shock, the person whose yard we'd just mowed called 911 and reported us as dead. We didn't even have injuries, yet for a few minutes the world thought we were gone.

And we should've been. The officers who inspected the crash site couldn't figure out why the vehicle didn't flip over. The physics of the accident, the velocity and momentum, all pointed to a caved in car. But it didn't flip. And somehow the car spun so we just landed in the bushes backwards. The axle was broken, but nothing came through the windows. There was no blow severe enough to activate the airbags.

It was one of the worst days of my life, and not just because I was grounded for a month. I did learn several lessons that day: Always wear your seatbelt. Obey the traffic laws. Never drive faster than your guardian angel can fly.

That day my life was saved. I could've died and over the radio it momentarily appeared that I did. I was saved. I have not yet fulfilled my purpose on Earth.

God doesn't promise that we won't get into trouble. Believe me, I got into lots and lots of trouble. I lost a car, insurance money, and some of my parent's trust. We will get into trouble. There will be consequences—some more serious than others. But God is with us.

> —*Tara Hershberger*

PRAYING AND WALKING IN THE WORLD:

- Think of a time when God performed a miracle in your life or saved the life of you or one of your friends or family members. Thank God again for that miracle!

- What does it mean to completely trust God? To abide in the shadow of the Almighty?

RUNAWAY EMMA

PLUNGING INTO THE WORD:

Psalm 100

PONDERING ON THE WAY:

This is a true story about a little lamb named Emma. Emma's mother had three babies, and Emma wasn't getting enough milk, so I started giving Emma a bottle of milk. She liked the milk, but she wasn't sure if she liked me. After all, I didn't look or sound like her real mother.

This meant that I sometimes had trouble catching Emma. When I caught her, she drank her milk. But when she was done, she was ready to run away to her real mother again.

One winter evening I took Emma and another lamb to our youth group meeting. We talked about sheep in the Bible that evening, and then I took the lambs back and put them into the trunk of the car. Just before I got the truck closed, Emma jumped out! And before I could grab her, she started running.

Here's the picture. Our church is in the country, with farms and fields and pastures all around it. Emma ran across the churchyard, across the road, and toward the farm nearby. I ran after her as fast as I could, crying out, "Emma! Emma! Please stop!"

But Emma was scared, and she kept running! She ran to the farm, across the yard, and into the tall grass. It was dark, and I could hardly see her, but I kept calling her name. "Emma! Emma!"

Do you know what happens to little lambs that get lost in the tall grass in Kansas? They can become breakfast for a coyote. I was desperate to get her back. But how?

Up ahead, I saw a creek. Emma was heading toward the creek. *I'll grab her when she goes into the creek,* I thought. I got to the creek just after Emma, jumped into the water, and ... just before I could get her, she jumped out on the other side.

Now I was cold, wet, and desperate, but Emma was still running.

I could see I had one more chance, and then Emma would be gone into the darkness. There was a wire fence she would have to go through, and if she did, she would cross the road and be gone. I had to catch her at that fence.

Emma ran into the fence, and I fell on top of her. I held her tight, gasping for breath.

And then ... then I felt a hard electric shock! Before I could move, another one! I was lying on an electric fence!

Still holding onto Emma as tightly as I could, I rolled off of the fence. Electric shocks or not, I would not let her go!

I took Emma home and gave her back to her real mother. And me? I celebrated with a long, hot bubble bath.

The Bible says that God is a good shepherd and we are God's sheep. God loves us even when we run away. God looks for us and wants to bring us back into God's pasture. And when we are together with God, we celebrate!

> —*Carol Duerksen*

PRAYING AND WALKING IN THE WORLD:

- Pretend to be sheep that are lost. Hide from your parents, but be sure to be in a place where they can find you. Bleat and act scared. Have someone pretend to be the shepherd and lead you to safety.

- Make instruments out of pots and pans. Play your instruments and sing. Make a joyful noise to God and march around having a parade in God's honor.

- **Adults:** perhaps you memorized this psalm as a child. Spend time with it now. Do what it says! Sing, be noisy, think of as many ways as possible to thank, praise, and bless God's name. Memorize it. Make it your morning mantra.

JULY 26

CHESED

PLUNGING INTO THE WORD:

Psalm 103

PONDERING ON THE WAY:

I'm an optimist. I think that life is wonderful. Now, I know it isn't always great. Sometimes it's awful. But on a day-to-day basis, I'm able to get up and have plenty to eat and drink and plenty to do, a job I love, and an awesome family. Yes, there are horrible things happening in the world, but as I see it, life is getting better. Sometimes we need to take a timeout and count our blessings.

My Blessings

1. Healthy family

2. Wide circle of friends

3. College education

4. Chocolate chip cookies

5. Supportive church family

6. Yogurt is now served in a tube

7. Indoor plumbing

8. Unconditionally loved by God

This is just a short list of the blessings I've received. The most important thing we all have been blessed with is number 8. We all are loved unconditionally by God.

This psalm is bursting with references to *Chesed* (pronounced "hesed"), a Hebrew word that means unconditional love, or covenant love. Every time "steadfast love" is mentioned, it's a promise that God will always, always love us.

The covenant here is a covenant between God and the chosen people, the Israelites. The Israelites were chosen to perform a mission and show God's love to the rest of the world, but they didn't always follow God's commandments. Every time the Israelites sinned, God had the right to walk away and leave them to their sin. The Israelites sinned a lot, but God never removed his hand from them. God never walked away. Even in the exile, God still sent blessings of hope. God is always ready to forgive.

That is the greatest blessing right there. We are always loved. That is Chesed. This psalm explodes with God's mercy. God's love is everlasting. Praise the Lord!

—*Michele Hershberger*

PRAYING AND WALKING IN THE WORLD:

- Count your blessings. Don't be afraid to make a longer list than I did.

- Think about times when you went astray and perhaps broke part of your covenant with the Lord. Did the Lord stop blessing you? Or were you forgiven? Praise God for forgiveness, second chances, and unconditional love.

JULY 27 *(FOR CHILDREN AND FAMILIES)*

HURRAY FOR FOOD!

PLUNGING INTO THE WORD:

Psalm 104

PONDERING ON THE WAY:

Ever wonder where the food you eat comes from? Where does cottage cheese come from? What about onions? Candy bars? Pudding? Macaroni and cheese? Worms? Wait, we don't eat worms. But they are food for birds and fish.

Where does food come from? Your parents? Your mom or dad probably make your food for you, but where did they get it? The grocery store. And where do they get it? You've probably seen farms, or maybe you even live on one. Then you know that food is grown on farms.

But nothing can grow without God. God made the world and all creation, and God still creates plants and animals and humans and helps them to be healthy and grow. God has made enough food for everybody in the world.

God made every animal and every plant, as well as the sun and the moon and the stars. God made everything that is good. God is in charge of everything, even things too small to see and things too big to imagine.

God creates everything. The creation is good and beautiful. When you see mountains or the ocean, or waterfalls or flowers, thank God for the wonderful creation. When you eat breakfast, lunch, and supper, thank God for the food you have. God provided it.

Even though there is enough food in the world for all of God's children, it isn't always available to everybody. Many people are still hungry. We have to share so that everyone can have enough to eat. If we take care of the earth and share our food, then the whole world will praise God for the wonderful creation and the food to eat.

—*Michele Hershberger*

PRAYING AND WALKING IN THE WORLD:

- What is your favorite food? Thank God for that food.

- Do you have a prayer that you say before you eat? What is it? What does it mean?

- **Adults:** Evaluate the role food plays in your life. Is it a healthy relationship? How can you both celebrate food and be responsible toward your body? How can you enjoy food while showing concern for those who don't have food?

JULY 28

HOLD ME LIKE A BABY

PLUNGING INTO THE WORD:

Psalm 131

PONDERING ON THE WAY:

Imagine a tiny baby. Babies are so dependent—they eat, sleep, make messes in their diapers—and turn hundreds of educated, well-mannered adults into cooing idiots. What else can barf into your face and get away with it? Yes, they're cuddly and cute, but other than swaying their parents into doing their bidding, infants are helpless. They depend on their cooing, idiot parents for everything.

Sometimes I wish I were a baby again. No taxes, no deadlines, no work. Babies are so content. They have no idea what is out in the world. They trust someone else to care for them. They eat and sleep and cry when they feel pain or hunger. They know they can't take care of their own needs.

Adults, on the other hand, think they are self-sufficient. They believe they can survive on their own, taking care of their own needs. But adults need a lot too. We can't do it all, as hard as we try. I often have been guilty of pride and vain ambition. I like to take on as many projects as I can, partly so others will know who I am. I like to be in the spotlight. I have a lot of desires, but I have to realize that some things are beyond my reach.

Just like mythical Greek heroes and mythical Victorian literature heroes and millions of real, regular people, David learns that humility and submission are the keys to happiness. Pride and ambition almost inevitably lead to a fall, certainly not to happiness. My own vanity and desires have not made me content.

Sometimes I wish I were a baby. You know … in some ways maybe I can be. Hold me like a baby, Lord.

Hold me tight.

> —*Michele Hershberger*

PRAYING AND WALKING IN THE WORLD:

- Think of times when your pride or ambition led to defeat or took you away from God.

- If you had positive childhood experiences with parents, thank God for the symbolism this provides of God's love for you. If you had more negative experiences, ask God to help you know and trust a loving heavenly parent.

- Find a childhood picture of you taken with a positive, significant adult in your life. Keep the picture in the space where you have quiet time with God to remind you of the peace that can be yours as you relinquish control and learn to trust. If you cannot find such a picture, find a picture of a child who is having a positive experience and draw strength from the image.

LOST IN BOSTON'S AND BABYLON

PLUNGING INTO THE WORD:

Psalm 137

PONDERING ON THE WAY:

When I was a little girl, my mom took me shopping for school clothes at Boston's. It was like a Wal-Mart, except it had five floors with an old-fashioned elevator operated by a woman. She slid the door open as mom and I and other shoppers squeezed into a tight, kind of smelly space. "Going up," she barked as the metal cage took us to the third floor.

I loved those shopping trips—except once when I got lost. I started crying and asked a woman at the cosmetic counter if she'd seen my mom. Pretty soon I heard my name being blared out on the store intercom. Mom was there within minutes, but those minutes felt like forever.

God's people also felt lost when they were in Babylon. It was where they were taken by the Babylonians, who had captured their city, Jerusalem, and taken them to a strange land. Today that region is Iraq, a violent part of the world. We read that the Israelites sat by the rivers of Babylon and cried when they remembered their homeland. They lived there for many years, but Jerusalem would always be home. It was where they worshipped God, their heavenly parent, and where they felt most connected to God.

The lost feelings of Boston and Babylon remind us that sometimes we are taken away from our parents, our home, and our church. But there is a place in our hearts we will always go back to that is our true home—the place in our heart where God lives.

—*Laurie Oswald Robinson*

PRAYING AND WALKING IN THE WORLD:

- Remember a time when you got separated from your parents. How did you feel? How did you feel when they found you again? Thank God today that you have parents or other adults in your life who provide a home for you.

- Draw a picture or write a one-page story about God's people crying at the rivers of Babylon. Then draw a picture and write another one-page story of how happy they felt when they returned to Jerusalem.

- Find a map and ask your parents to show you where Babylon would be located today. It is fifty miles south of Baghdad, the capital city of Iraq. Talk about how the people in that part of the world may be feeling lost, just like the ancient Israelites.

JULY 30

GOD KNOWS

PLUNGING INTO THE WORD:

Psalm 139

PONDERING ON THE WAY:

In my twenties I experienced a sad and troubled time when I was steeped in sexual sin. I was running from God and the church at that time, but I still clung to some Scripture passages I memorized when I was walking intimately with the Lord as a teenager. One of my favorites was today's passage, Psalm 139.

On the day I made the most costly decision of my life, I read this psalm for daily devotions. Only hours after reading how God created me and had plans for my life, I became sexually involved with someone off-limits. In that act, I damaged the self God lovingly crafted in my mother's womb, and I dashed the blueprint of God's plans. What had even more impact was that I broke another life with the brokenness of my life.

The juxtaposition of God's relentless love and my lonely rebellion taught me one of life's most important lessons: God doesn't abandon us, even when we abandon ourselves and God's ways. Even when we don't know who we are or where we are going, God knows. Even when we don't know how anyone could love us or heal us, God knows. Even when we think we will be lost in utter darkness forever, God's light and love finds us and searches us out.

—*Laurie Oswald Robinson*

PRAYING AND WALKING IN THE WORLD:

- Sit in silence, imagining God creating you in your mother's womb. Feel God's hand craft every part of you and plan every part of your life.

- Now silently pray these words from Psalm 139:23-24: *Search me, O God, and know my heart; test me and know my thoughts. See if there be any wicked way in me and lead me in the everlasting way.*

- Rent or purchase a DVD that depicts how a fetus grows within a mother's womb. Discuss how God's amazingly creative power, relentless love, and beautiful plans impact your life and the life of your loved ones and friends.

JULY 31

THE OPEN HAND OF GOD

PLUNGING INTO THE WORD:

Psalm 145

PONDERING ON THE WAY:

During a season of bitterness in my life, I vowed never again to darken the door of a church. In the midst of this godless time, I moved to New York City. After falling into deep loneliness, I was invited to a church called "The Open Hand of God." The church was nothing like my rural, Mennonite congregation, with its Swiss and German farmers. Its members grew up Jewish, Irish, Italian, and Asian and had never been on a farm.

Despite the strangeness, I found home. No one knew my family or my high school accomplishments; nor were they fooled by the happy-go-lucky image I'd hidden behind during my growing up years. They held the crumbling pieces of my life in their homes and hearts, and they guided me to God's open hands, which held and healed me.

The church's theme verse is found in today's Scripture passage, Psalm 145:16: "You open your hand, satifying the desire of every living thing." How comforting it was for those of us who experienced "closed hands" due to estrangement from former communities or to our faulty perceptions of God. Off-the-beaten-trail and beaten-down people gathered to worship a Lord who is gracious and merciful, slow to anger and abounding in steadfast love. The church was a haven of hope for those of us who stopped believing the Lord is good to all and had compassion on *all*—especially those creations who failed.

This church and today's psalm remind us that the Lord's faithfulness is not reserved for a successful few. It is available to all God's creatures who will receive it. "The eyes of all look to you, and you give them their food in due season. … The Lord is near to *all* … who call on him in truth." Whether we are among the beautiful people or the broken, it is not what we bring or don't bring in our hands that matters. What counts is what is in God's hands. And what is in God's hands is an open place—for you and for me.

—*Laurie Oswald Robinson*

PRAYING AND WALKING IN THE WORLD:

- Reflect on where in your life you are experiencing open and closed hands of God. What contributes to your perception of God's hands being closed or open? What people and communities have shaped those perceptions? Which personal decisions have shaped those perceptions?

- No matter what level of openness you experience today, pray for a further opening of your spirit to God and God's people. If you have a closed, wounded spirit, seek out a prayer counselor, a therapist, or a friend who can help you open your clenched fists a bit more.

- Take a walk in the country or on a nature path or bike trail. Open your senses to all the living things God has made. As you walk, pray you will see how God lovingly cares for *all* creatures, including you.

AUGUST 1

MAKE ME A VACUUM

PLUNGING INTO THE WORD:

Genesis 12:1-9

PONDERING ON THE WAY:

Most of us have no concept of what it means to pick up everything and leave our homeland. Some of us have ancestors who did it, and some of us are first generation North Americans who do know how it feels to pack up and make a transition to a totally new life in a new land. It's risky. It's a trip made because there is more to hope for in the new country than the old.

That's Abraham's story. Walter Brueggemann, in his *Interpretation Commentary* on Genesis, says that "the whole of the Abrahamic narrative is premised on this seeming contradiction: to stay in safety is to remain barren; to leave in risk is to have hope."

Brueggemann goes on to say that Jesus echoes that call when he declares, "Those who want to save their life will lose it, and those who lose their life for my sake, and for the sake of the gospel, will save it" (Mark 8:35).

In other words, we all need to be good vacuums. We need to empty ourselves of security and safety so we can be filled. We need to find ways to pour ourselves out so that God's blessings can come in. When God calls, we need to leave the comfort of home in order to travel to Canaan.

Personally, I find that difficult. I don't like being empty, and I don't like the unknown. The only vacuum I want in my life is the one that cleans the house. It sucks up the dirt, and when it doesn't work, I clean out the filter and pour the accumulated debris out of the canister. With the crud gone, it's ready to be filled again. And then it works.

Maybe it's time to clean out my spiritual filter.

—*Carol Duerksen*

PRAYING AND WALKING IN THE WORLD:

- What's the crud in your life? What needs to be poured out?

- Talk to someone who will keep you accountable. Tell that person what you are willing to do to become a vacuum. How will you empty yourself in order to be filled with God's calling and God's word for you? Agree to check in with each other.

- Talk to someone or read the story of a person who left home to come to a new country. Why did they do it? What were the risks? What were the blessings?

AUGUST 2

NOBODY'S PERFECT

PLUNGING INTO THE WORD:

Genesis 12:10-20, 13:1-18

PONDERING ON THE WAY:

Gabriel: Um, God, do you have a minute?

God: Of course! I have forever, you know.

Gabriel: I wanted to talk to you about Abram.

God: Ah yes, my man Abram.

Gabriel: You won't believe what he just did.

God: Try me.

Gabriel: He lied about being married to Sarai to save his skin.

God: Doesn't surprise me.

Gabriel: It doesn't?

God: (Sighs.) No. It's a human tendency—to want to save their skin.

Gabriel: But I thought, maybe, the man you chose to be the father of many nations might be … different.

God: Oh, he is.

Gabriel: How?

God: Watch this.

(Pause.)

Gabriel: He's letting Lot choose which land to own? He's giving him first choice?

God: Yep.

Gabriel: But that's huge! I've seen God-fearing farmers fight over land! I've seen families split up over their inheritance!

God: Exactly.

Gabriel: And Abram is letting Lot choose the best land. Why?

God: Because he trusts me.

Gabriel: Amazing! But … he didn't trust you earlier when he lied about his wife.

God: So it goes. I still have plans for him.

Gabriel: I guess nobody's perfect. *(Pause.)* Present company excepted, of course.

God: Of course.

—*Carol Duerksen*

PRAYING AND WALKING IN THE WORLD:

- Abram chose to foster good family relationships with Lot by letting him choose land first. With whom in your family do you need to foster a relationship? Are you willing to work on that?

- When have you tried to "save your skin" at the expense of your integrity? When have you stepped out in faith and been blessed as a result?

- Through our failures and faithfulness, God is always at work. What matters ultimately is God's faithfulness to us. Do you believe that? Have you experienced it? Or have you felt let down by God? Write your own psalm of lament or praise, or both.

AUGUST 3

PROMISES, PROMISES

PLUNGING INTO THE WORD:

Genesis 15:1-21

PONDERING ON THE WAY:

It happens to all of us. It happens to pillars of the church, as well as new Christians. We doubt. We don't feel close to God. We know with our brains that God is there and has made certain promises to us, but we don't feel it with our hearts. Not at all.

God had promised Abram land, and offspring to inherit the land. The land came through, but quite frankly, the offspring wasn't happening. So when the Lord shows up in a vision and repeats the promise, Abram isn't buying it. He knows what's possible between him and Sarah, and a baby isn't on the list. He knows he'll have to settle for second best—his heir will be a slave's son. He is not impressed with God's promises at this point.

But God repeats the promise. The God who can make countless stars is capable of keeping the promise of a baby. And Abram believes.

How? What changed? How did his heart believe when his head knew better?

First, perhaps we can read between the lines and see that Abram repented of his "I know better" attitude. In his repentance, he emptied his heart. The vacuum in his heart could be filled with faith.

Second, Abram's disbelief left because God gives miracles. God is all-powerful, and can do wonders inside people's hearts. Fast-forward to a disciple named Peter, proclaiming that Jesus is "the Messiah, the Son of the living God" (Matthew 16:16). Jesus affirms him, saying that "flesh and blood has not revealed this to you, but my Father in heaven" (Matthew 16:17).

Abram believed because God worked a miracle in his heart.

—Carol Duerksen

PRAYING AND WALKING IN THE WORLD:

- Write your own version of verses 1-6 in this passage, inserting yourself in place of Abram. What has God promised you? What do you doubt? What is your dialogue with God?

- While we don't view sacrifices as part of our relationship with God the same way Abram did, perhaps we have moved too far away from the idea of making a sacrifice. What sacrifice could you offer God to honor God's promises to you and your response?

- Go for a walk under the stars. For each star you see, thank God for a specific blessing. Impossible? Exactly.

AUGUST 4

THE EYES OF GOD

PLUNGING INTO THE WORD:

Genesis 16:1-15

PONDERING ON THE WAY:

Only one Old Testament believer is recorded as calling God "El-roi," or "the God Who Sees."

That one believer isn't a patriarch or matriarch like Abraham or Sarah. No, the person whose encounter with God was so personal that she called God "El-roi" was a woman slave named Hagar.

Hagar is told by God's angel that she will bear a son, a "wild ass of a man." This kid will be different, but that's okay. God promises both Hagar and Abraham that their son will become a great nation. God values their child, born through their desire to create an heir through "alternative methods." God values diversity and individuality among people.

Unfortunately, we seem to have more problems accepting diversity, and we don't understand how someone quite different from us can have a close encounter with God. We ignore obnoxious persons and gaze critically at clothing and bodies. We have trouble accepting persons with political beliefs or lifestyles different from ours. Our churches, for the most part, are homogeneous; yet even within our congregations, we argue about diverse worship styles and approaches to faith.

I wonder if "the God Who Sees" is also "the God Who Weeps" at the time we spend hassling with each other on the small stuff. I wonder if the God of Hagar and Sarah mourns when we disrespect the "wild ass of a man" in our midst. I wonder what it would take for me to see others through the eyes of God. A close encounter, perhaps?

—*Carol Duerksen*

PRAYING AND WALKING IN THE WORLD:

- Recall a time when a "close encounter" with someone quite different from you changed your opinion about that person. Can you plan for more opportunities like that?

- Spend some moments in meditation. Close your eyes and clear your mind. Imagine an encounter with God. How does it feel to be in God's presence? What does God say to you? What do you say to God?

AUGUST 5

HAVE I GOT A DEAL FOR YOU

PLUNGING INTO THE WORD:

Genesis 17:1-14

PONDERING ON THE WAY:

Dear Diary,

You won't believe what happened today. The Lord appeared to me. Yes, the Lord God. I couldn't quite believe my eyes or ears, but it's true. The Lord God came to me and changed my name to Abraham. Why? Because supposedly I am going to be the ancestor of a multitude of nations, and that's what Abraham means. God said we have a deal—a "covenant" in God's terms. Okay, that sounded good to me.

Then God said that, to seal the deal, I had to be circumcised. Not just me—every male in Israel. That didn't sound so good to me.

So tonight I'm sore. I'm really sore from my "non-elective surgery" and I'm a little sore at God too. I've kept my part of the deal, but Sarah and I are still without a son. And the way I feel tonight, even if I wasn't ninety-nine years old, it won't happen anytime soon.

> —*Carol Duerksen*

PRAYING AND WALKING IN THE WORLD:

- Do you get sore at God? Do you need to "vent" to God at times? It's okay—God is big enough to handle it.

- A covenant is serious business. Which covenants have you made? To a spouse? To children? To God? How are you doing in keeping your covenants? Spend time praying about your covenants and the challenges you face in keeping them.

AUGUST 6 *(FOR CHILDREN AND FAMILIES)*

A VERY OLD PRINCESS

PLUNGING INTO THE WORD:

Genesis 17:15-22

PONDERING ON THE WAY:

What does a princess look like?

Is a princess always young? Beautiful?

There was a woman in the Bible whose name was Sarai, (pronounced Sare-eye), and her name meant "my princess." She was married to Abram, and they didn't have any children, even though they really wanted to have a family. They got older and older, but they still didn't have any children. When they were old enough to be great-grandparents, God appeared to them and promised them they would have a baby. God also said that they would have new names. Abram would become Abraham, because that means "ancestor of millions." And Sarai would become Sarah, and that means "princess."

This is the difference between being called "my princess" and "princess." "My princess" means that she would be honored just by her family. But "princess" means she would be honored by many people. She would have a baby, and that baby would grow up and have children, and they would have children, and it would go on and on for many generations to Joseph and Mary, the earthly parents of Jesus.

A princess doesn't have to be young and beautiful for us to admire her, but there's more to the story of this Princess Sarah. You'll find out tomorrow!

—*Carol Duerksen*

PRAYING AND WALKING IN THE WORLD:

- Do you know what your name means or why your parents chose this name for you? Talk together about your name.

- Turn to Matthew 1 and trace the genealogy of Jesus. If you have a genealogy chart of your family, look at that together.

- Spend a few minutes guessing what might happen to Sarah in tomorrow's story. (Don't look ahead!)

AUGUST 7 *(FOR CHILDREN AND FAMILIES)*

SARAH GETS A BIG SURPRISE

PLUNGING INTO THE WORD:

Genesis 18:1-15

PONDERING ON THE WAY:

Remember yesterday we said that God promised Sarah and Abraham they would have a baby, but that they were getting really old? Well, more time went by, and they got older, and still no baby.

Then one day three messengers from God came to visit them again, and again they made the same promise. This time when Sarah heard what the messengers said, she just burst out laughing! "What a crazy idea!" she said. "I am way too old to have a baby now!"

The messengers heard her laughing, and they didn't like her lack of faith. They said, "Why is Sarah laughing? Is anything impossible for the Lord?"

That's a great question, isn't it? "Is anything impossible for the Lord?"

What do you think?

No, nothing is impossible for God. That doesn't mean that we can ask God for anything and it will happen right away, or even that it will happen at all. God knows what is best for us, and God's timing for answering prayers might be different from ours. It took a long time for Abraham and Sarah to have a baby, but they did. Nothing is impossible for God.

> —*Carol Duerksen*

PRAYING AND WALKING IN THE WORLD:

- Parents and caregivers, do you have stories to tell of times when God did something "impossible" in your life? If you don't have an "impossible" story, tell another story of a time when God answered a prayer for you.

- Watch the documentary video *Beyond Gates of Splendor* or the movie version, *End of the Spear*. In this story, five missionaries are speared to death by the Waodani tribe in Ecuador. A series of miraculous events unfolds that changes the lives of the slain men's families and the tribe as well. Based on a true story of love and forgiveness, this is a good example that, with God, nothing is impossible. Rated PG-13.

- Go to your church library together and find a book to read about God's "impossible" involvement in people's lives.

AUGUST 8

GRACE AND CONSEQUENCES

PLUNGING INTO THE WORD:

Genesis 21:1-21

PONDERING ON THE WAY:

We've all made mistakes. We've all made bad choices. Abraham should have waited. He should have trusted God more. He shouldn't have taken matters into his own hands. He shouldn't have listened to Sarah.

Because now there's a little boy involved—Ishmael. And a young woman, who didn't have a lot of choices—her only sin to be born a slave and a foreigner. He's a precious little boy, but also an extra heir to the promise. She's a faithful servant, but not the right mother, so now what do you do? The woman who wanted this arrangement now wants them gone—exiled—sentenced to slow death in the desert.

I've been there. I've been the jealous one, with regrets later. I've been the exiled one, innocent but screwed anyway.

I've been the guilty one, the one who should have trusted more, the one who set the whole mess into motion.

So what do you do? What in the world does God do?

God gave Abraham the freedom to make his own choices. And he blew it. So now God seems to be in trouble too.

Do I get God in messes? Do I break God's heart with my choices?

God finds a way out. The original promise is secure, and God's plan for Isaac and his future family stays intact. But God also cares for Hagar and Ishmael. They are chosen too, in their own way. God loves Hagar and her people, because God's original plan—the plan to bless every family on earth—is the reason for Abraham's chosenness to begin with (Genesis 12:3).

But the consequences of Abraham and Sarah's sin, their lack of faith, their quick takeover, still ripples today in the Middle East. Ishmael and Isaac are still fighting.

Grace and consequences. Grace and consequences.

—*Michele Hershberger*

PRAYING AND WALKING IN THE WORLD:

- Who are you in this story? In the desert? Feeling lousy in the tent? Wishing you could relive some certain events?

- What's strongest in your life now? God's grace or the consequences? Can you see grace within the consequences?

- Who are the Hagars in today's world? What would God have us do for them?

- Does God have favorites? What is the difference between being chosen and being God's favorite?

- Pray for the conflict in Israel and Palestine, the conflict in Iraq, the conflict in America, in Colombia, in Indonesia, in the world.

AUGUST 9

ULTIMATE SACRIFICE

PLUNGING INTO THE WORD:

Genesis 22:1-14

PONDERING ON THE WAY:

Sacrifice.
My son, my love.
How can You ask this?
Maybe I never should've had a child.

Let this cup pass from me.

I built up the fire.
Where is the lamb?
I built the fire with tears in my eyes.
My son, my love.

Couldn't you take my flock?
I have sheep, goats, land, a house.
Couldn't you just take me?

I built up the fire.
Innocence is realizing his fate.
Where is the lamb?
My son, my love.

This is my body, this is my blood.

Sacrifice.
How dare You ask this of me?
This is my only chance.
You promised.

You promised me my son, my love.
I trust as tears flow down. I hold nothing back and as I grit my teeth—
A ram; a way out. The Lord will provide.

Father, into your hands I commend my spirit.

I build up the fire.
The Lord does provide.
Here is the Lamb,
My son, my love.

> —*Michele Hershberger*

PRAYING AND WALKING IN THE WORLD:

- Do you believe that God would have really let Abraham kill Isaac?

- Is there anything you love too much to sacrifice? What would you do if God did ask you to give it up?

- Can you think of a time when you had to trust God completely and blindly? What happened? Did the Lord provide?

AUGUST 10

ROAD SIGNS

PLUNGING INTO THE WORD:

Genesis 24:1-49

PONDERING ON THE WAY:

Should I accept this new job, God? I don't know. Tell you what, if the person giving the interview cocks his or her head at a forty-five-degree angle while asking me if I really graduated summa cum laude, then I'll know the job is the right one for me.

Wouldn't it be great if life worked like that? All of those big decisions could be as simple as well-fated coin tosses. No more migraines, no big concern. I'd never have to worry whether to buy a new car or save for the kids' education.

However, I've never received glaring road signs to lead me to success. And a lot of other things about this story are different now too. No one marries their cousin, for one thing; and the method of swearing a vow also has changed. But you can still get a complete stranger to pierce your nose. And God's providence does still lead us to the right path, sometimes blatantly, sometimes not.

In this slightly repetitive story, Abraham has one wish. He wants his son to remain in Canaan, where he was destined to inherit the land, and yet not marry a Canaanite. He arms his servant with everything he needs. He has camels, servants, and gifts to prove his seriousness in the matter and his ability to support the new wife. He points the servant in the right direction, but without even simple road signs, it's far too easy to get lost in the desert.

And yet, not only does the servant find the right country and city, he lands at the very well used by Abraham's brother. The servant prays for a specific sign and it is granted. That's timing! Both Abraham and the servant take steps of faith and pray for signs, all the while believing in God' providence.

And the signs are there.

In a way this does still happen. The signs may not appear in neon, but they are there, if you look. If I go to the interview for a new job and find out that the job would require me to work weekends when I would ordinarily relax or go to church—that may be a sign that the job isn't for me. Or perhaps while in the office I see the boss yelling at an employee. Unless I like abusive worksites, this is another sign to decline the job.

But sometimes, in my life anyway, this doesn't seem to happen. No amount of believing seems to produce even a subtle hint. It is at these times that God is asking me to just start walking in faith. Sometimes God doesn't "open doors" for me. Sometimes I am asked to push them open.

It's always okay to ask. You may never get a message written in the sky, unless it's your birthday and you have a friend who flies blimps. But God honors the risk we take in looking for that message. And it's always important to trust. That's our job. And God, who is always faithful, will lead us to our wells—as well.

—*Tara Hershberger*

PRAYING AND WALKING IN THE WORLD:

- Do you have a friend who flies blimps? My birthday is July 22.

- Can you think of a time when God provided you with a sign that helped you make a good decision, or saved you from a bad one?

- Think about a big decision you are making, or will make soon. How can you more fully give that decision to God? Write a description of the situation on paper. Fold it up and put it in an envelope. Address it to God and put it away in a dresser drawer. Hear God saying to you, "Thanks. I'll take care of it."

AUGUST 11 *(FOR CHILDREN AND FAMILIES)*

REBEKAH OBEYS

PLUNGING INTO THE WORD:

Genesis 24:50-67

PONDERING ON THE WAY:

Leanne stared sadly out the window. This could be the last time she watched Alley the cat walk across the street, the last time she waited for the school to drop off her older brother, Matt, the last time she pressed her fingers to the glass window and made secret messages to her best friend, Rachel. The last time for so many good things. Why? Because tomorrow morning her family would move to another state, another house in a brand-new neighborhood. Daddy would drive the moving van, and Mom would drive their car. And Leanne would pout all the way there.

She was planning on it.

Mom said that Leanne would make new best friends and that Matt would really like his new school and that there would be other cats. She said that maybe they would get a cat. But Leanne still didn't want to move. Daddy said that this was something God wanted them to do, and even though it was really hard right now—hard to say good-bye to friends and hard to imagine meeting new ones—God would bless them for being brave. Daddy said that God knew it was hard, and that God would help them in ways that would be wonderful.

Daddy used the word *blessed.*

In our story today, Rebekah felt the same way. She knew that God wanted her to marry Isaac. The story of how Isaac's servant found her really surprised her. It helped her know she was to go with him to meet Isaac. She knew she needed to obey. Rebekah's mother and brother also obeyed God by letting her go.

But it might have been hard to obey God. It might have been scary to leave home, even though Rebekah was old enough to leave and get married.

Rebekah was rewarded for her obedience. She and Isaac loved each other and had a good life. They had two sons. God also rewards us for our obedience. And when we obey, God blesses us too, just like he did Rebekah. God doesn't take all the scary times away, but God helps us through the scary times.

> —*Michele Hershberger*

PRAYING AND WALKING IN THE WORLD:

- What has God asked you to do?

- How can you be obedient to God and to your parents?

- When has obeying your parents or God led to a good thing?

- Act out today's story. Pretend to be Rebekah or the servant or even the person who leads the camel to find Isaac.

AUGUST 12 *(FOR CHILDREN AND FAMILIES)*

QUARRELING BROTHERS

PLUNGING INTO THE WORD:

Genesis 25:19-34

PONDERING ON THE WAY:

Is it okay to fight with your brothers and sisters?

Sometimes Isaac and Rebekah's family had a hard time getting along with one another. Isaac and Rebekah had twins boys. The boys fought a lot with each other, and their mom and dad didn't know what to do.

The boys were named Esau and Jacob. Esau was born first. In those days it mattered very much who was born first. That person would become head of the family and would receive twice as much money and land as his brothers and sisters from the parents. It didn't matter if the second- or thirdborn was smarter or bigger—he still didn't get as many things as the firstborn did. Does that seem fair?

It didn't seem fair to Jacob either. Esau was a hunter, and Jacob liked to stay inside. One day, Esau came home very hungry, and Jacob had just made soup. Jacob did a mean thing. He didn't give his brother any food until Esau gave him his birthright. This birthright would give Jacob more money than Esau. Esau didn't care very much about his birthright, or the family traditions, so he gave it to Jacob.

What would you have done? Would you have kept the soup away from Esau? Have you ever kept a toy or food away from your brother or sister? How do you think that made them feel?

Jacob was mean to his brother. He knew that if Esau hadn't been so hungry, he wouldn't have given away his right to so much money. It wasn't a nice thing to do. God wants sisters and brothers to get along and to do nice things for each other. Brothers and sisters can become best friends, if the fighting turns into playing together nicely.

God can work through messed-up families too. In fact, the two boys both had a lot of children, and their children's children became two great nations of people, the Edomites and the Israelites. And God helped the world through these families even though they made many mistakes.

—*Michele Hershberger*

PRAYING AND WALKING IN THE WORLD:

- Name one nice thing you did for your brother or sister or friend today. Can you think of one mean thing you did to any of them? Can you say you are sorry?

- Have you ever cheated your brother, sister, or friend out of something? How can you say "sorry" and make it better?

- **Adults:** Have you ever pulled an "Esau"? Done something stupid when you felt desperate? Or "sold your birthright" by sinning and complicating your life so that God cannot fit in? Have you ever pulled a "Jacob"?

AUGUST 13

WORD MISSILES

PLUNGING INTO THE WORD:

Genesis 27:1-40

PONDERING ON THE WAY:

Have you ever wondered why Isaac couldn't give Esau the blessing too? Or why Isaac didn't simply reverse the blessing? Just say the words, Isaac, just give another blessing!

But it's not that easy. Words were considered very powerful in the ancient world, much more than we understand them to be in our modern context. In the beginning of the Bible, we read about God creating the world with a word. Jeremiah's and Isaiah's lips are touched as a symbol of the only tool they would ever need—the powerful word. In John, Jesus is the Word, and the Word is with God. In Revelation, Jesus comes to battle evil with words. The sword that comes out of his mouth in chapter 19 represents the might of the spoken word to destroy evil. It's impossible for Isaac to simply take back this blessing.

In my opinion, it shouldn't have come to that in the first place. Mother and son shouldn't have practiced deceit. God had already promised that the elder would serve the younger (25:23), and Jacob already had the birthright. This could've been made right without deception. Rebekah and Jacob could've appealed to Isaac on the basis of reason and justice. Even without the blessing, God would've taken care of Jacob.

Instead, mother and son deceive the cataract-ridden Isaac. The deception comes around to hurt Jacob. He has to leave, and he never sees his mother again. Furthermore, in his dealings with his uncle, he gets a helping of his own medicine (Genesis 29:15-30).

Words spoken to deceive also are powerful. But this time, the missile turns back on the source.

We've probably all been Jacob and Rebekah in this story. We've all told lies, hidden secrets, cheated, and even worn lamb wool (not just for fashion). We've also been Isaac and Esau, victims of deceit. It hurts a lot to be lied to, no matter what the situation is. Lying builds walls between people. Those walls are hard to break down.

Isaac never had quite the same relationship with any of his family members. He was angry with Jacob, betrayed by Rebekah, and his relationship with Esau suffered because of the misaimed blessing. The deceit not only hurt his feelings, it damaged every connection he had made. There would be no simple answer or easy solution. The power of words doesn't just apply to the blessing. The words Jacob spoke when he lied had huge power too—destructive power.

Sticks and stones may break my bones, but names will never hurt me.

Yeah, right.

> —*Michele Hershberger*

PRAYING AND WALKING IN THE WORLD:

- Isaac's words are irreversible. How closely do you monitor your words? Do you curse or bless easily?

- Have you ever practiced deception? Did it come around to bite you?

- Have you ever felt the pain of being deceived? What did you do?

AUGUST 14

REPETITION AND RENEWAL

PLUNGING INTO THE WORD:

Genesis 27:41—28:22

PONDERING ON THE WAY:

There sure is a lot of repetition in Genesis—a lot of barren women, firstborns getting gypped, husbands saying their wives are their sisters, God appearing to people in dreams, and first cousin weddings. And a lot of deception. Lots of deception. This time Esau schemes to kill Jacob as soon as Isaac dies and claim the inheritance after all. Rebekah is also at it again, planting the seed that provides for Jacob's safe removal from the jealous rage of his brother.

And let's face it—the repetition of sin and deceit can be discouraging.

But there is also a new thing or two. Amid the struggle and strife, there are … signs and dreams, blessings and promises. This is after all, the Beginning.

There is a ladder.

But what does the ladder mean? Is the dream a repetition or a new thing? The Lord was in that place, and still is. The promise is old—repeated—but the experience is new. Now this is Jacob's God. How many times do I rely on the faith of my ancestors? How many times am I afraid to climb the ladder, choosing to settle for stories from the past rather than face my own possibly terrifying experience with God?

The stories, the repetition, the recital of God's faithfulness—those are precious, important, faith-building things.

But I've got to climb the ladder—myself.

—Michele Hershberger

PRAYING AND WALKING IN THE WORLD:

• Are there lessons in life that you have learned several times?

• What dreams have you had, both literal and figurative? What vows have you made?

• What has been your ladder to heaven? What ladder is there in your dreams now?

THE OTHER LABAN GIRL

PLUNGING INTO THE WORD:

Genesis 29:1-30

PONDERING ON THE WAY:

I recently read *The Other Boleyn Girl* by Philippa Gregory. It depicts the bawdy court life of sixteenth-century Tudor England and King Henry VIII. The plot twists around sisters Mary and Anne Boleyn. Their family uses them as pawns in the family's rise to power. Mary is Henry's mistress and is replaced in his affections with power-hungry and deceitful Anne, who is the second of his six wives. After charges of witchcraft and adultery, Henry has her beheaded. Mary rebels against the deceitful games of courtly love and marries a common man whom she truly loves from her heart.

Today's story has its own brand of scandal and deceit. Jacob, who tricked his father, Isaac, into giving him Esau's inheritance, is sent away to find a wife from the clan of Laban, the brother of Rebekah, Jacob's mother. As Jacob enters Laban's territory, he waters his sheep, and meets Rachel, the younger daughter of Laban. Rachel runs home to tell her father of Jacob's arrival, and Laban takes Jacob into their home.

Jacob falls in love with the beautiful Rachel and asks for her hand in exchange for seven years of labor. After all the work, Laban tricks him and gives him the older, less beautiful Leah instead. An angry Jacob demands the hand of Rachel. So they worked out another deal; Jacob could marry Rachel if he agreed to work for another seven years.

Today's Bible story reminds us that extended families throughout all times have been prone to deceit, jealousy, and power plays. Jacob's life was marked by the cycle of trickery. He first tricks his own father and then is tricked by his beloved's father. We will never know what would have happened if Jacob or Anne Boleyn practiced honesty rather than deceit. But we can learn from them that we all reap what we sow.

—*Laurie Oswald Robinson*

PRAYING AND WALKING IN THE WORLD:

- When are you most tempted in your family system to practice deceit, or at least something less than the truth? Has this tendency become a pattern, or does it reflect an isolated incident?

- Confess this deceit to God—whether a "little white lie" or an all-out deception—and spend time at the foot of the cross. Take off your mask there and ask for new transparency.

- Seek out the person or persons you have harmed by deceit. Confess this deception and ask for their forgiveness.

AUGUST 16

THE SCIENCE OF SIBLINGS

PLUNGING INTO THE WORD:

Genesis 32:1-21

PONDERING ON THE WAY:

"The Science of Siblings," a July 2006 cover story for *Time,* discusses how after decades of research, psychologists claim that siblings are the most influential people in our lives. They even top parents, friends, and lovers in their ability to shape us, as they are often the longest running companions in our life's journey. As children, they teach us about the opposite sex and how to survive a fight with intimates and still end up friends. As we grow older, they also help cushion the rough edges with problem parents and stand by us when love, careers, and our own children disappoint us. If the relationships with siblings are rocky, they teach us that love hurts and that healing can be a lifelong struggle.

The writer of today's account in Genesis seemed to know this long before science, without the benefit of psychology. In this story, Jacob, who once bilked Esau out of his inheritance with their father, Isaac, desires to restore his relationship with Esau. So he journeys to his brother's region to find him and to give him gifts as a peace offering.

He sends these gifts ahead of his meeting Esau, in hopes they would appease his brother, from whom he has been estranged for years. He hopes the material goods will soften his brother's heart and woo him into accepting him. We don't read the end of the story for a few more days. But today, the text invites us to reflect on the power of the desire for restoration. No matter who did the breaking—whether we or our brothers and sisters—there is power in completing the "circle" set in motion by our families of origin.

—Laurie Oswald Robinson

PRAYING AND WALKING IN THE WORLD:

- Reflect on your family of origin. If you had siblings, do you experience close relationships with them, or are you estranged from your brothers and sisters? Or do you experience a "mixed bag" of emotional closeness and distance?

- Ask God to reveal a "circle" that needs to be closed or restored with a brother or sister in your family or origin. If you don't have siblings, reflect on the same question regarding a parent or grandparent, an aunt or uncle, or a cousin.

- In the next month, take another step in closing this circle.

AUGUST 17

THE LIMP OF BLESSING

PLUNGING INTO THE WORD:

Genesis 32:22-32

PONDERING ON THE WAY:

For years, my brother and I had outstanding issues from childhood that distanced us. At family gatherings our interactions tumbled into tense words and hurt feelings. But during one family reunion, my brother changed this unresolved "wrestling" between us. He confessed he'd been jealous of me, his little sister. He asked my forgiveness for the pain he had caused. His honesty helped me confess how I had become cold toward him. Many tears later, we were tired and "limping" from our work of reconciling. And yet we were ready to replace our bitter wrestling with a blessing of peace.

Jacob also wrestled with God in a dreamlike scene at Jabbock that symbolizes Jacob's anxiety about meeting his estranged brother, Esau. As he was alone in the middle of the night, he wrestled with a "man" until daybreak (v. 24). At the first crack of dawn, the wrestling match still had no winner. So God struck Jacob's hip socket and put it out of joint. But Jacob told God he wouldn't let go until he was blessed. Jacob won—but at a cost. He was given a new name—"Israel"—the prize for prevailing with God and humans. But he also limped, bearing the wound that came with the blessing.

Many of us experience wounds and blessings that come from wrestling with God and others. In the fray of righting our relationships, we can come away free people who "limp." It's a limping that reminds us we've battled interpersonal pain and come out on the other side, tired but at peace. It's a limping born of replacing our high-horse of self-interest with the humility of other-interest. It's a limping that slows us down to be more careful in our love, mindful that peace has a price tag.

—*Laurie Oswald Robinson*

PRAYING AND WALKING IN THE WORLD:

- Reflect on who you are wrestling right now. God, a family member, a friend? Take time to journal about the dynamics of this wrestling match.

- Pray for new humility to let God's way of peace and restoration become the winner in the fray. Pray for a sense of what your "new name" would be if you were to reconcile with the person or people with whom you experience conflict.

- When you are ready for God's way of peace to prevail, seek out the person with whom you are wrestling and be open to dialogue about your conflict.

AUGUST 18

RETURNING AND RECEIVING

PLUNGING INTO THE WORD:

Genesis 33:1-14

PONDERING ON THE WAY:

Fifteen years ago, I worked in two New York City nursing homes. In both jobs, I had the same supervisor. She taught me how to care for the elderly. She also taught me how to defend myself against her periodic cynicism. She mocked me about my trust in Jesus Christ. She had been a believer at one time but backtracked on her walk with God. I was a painful reminder of her broken commitment.

After no contact for years, she wrote in an e-mail that she had returned to a close walk with Christ. She asked forgiveness for the pain she had caused me. The e-mail shocked me out of forgetfulness. I had buried memories of those bad times and was simply joyful she was restored to a meaningful relationship with Jesus. This reunion included a phone call, in which we reaffirmed our love and our intent to move into the future as friends.

Perhaps similar dynamics were at work when Esau and Jacob reunited after twenty years of separation. Jacob bowed seven times before Esau, who ran to kiss and embrace him, after which they wept together. Jacob, perhaps uncertain of Esau's sincerity, gave gifts to ensure favor. But the gifts seemed of secondary importance to Esau, who said, "I have enough, my brother." He eventually accepted the gifts but went the second mile. He said, "Let us journey on our way, and I will go alongside you."

Like Esau, I knew the return of my friend would fall flat unless I graciously received her gifts of remorse and repentance. But the deeper reception was marked by a renewed commitment to walk into the future together. Because we are human, we will no doubt need to forgive each other for new wrongs. But the miles ahead will be less fettered because of our full-bodied reunion in the past.

—*Laurie Oswald Robinson*

PRAYING AND WALKING IN THE WORLD:

- What persons have been your "Esaus" in the past? Who most fully received your gifts of remorse and repentance with a renewal of friendship? Journal about how that positively impacted your life. On the flip side, journal about a person who did not receive you well. How did that impact your life?

- In extended prayer sometime this week, pray about one relationship that still needs to be fully reconciled. Ask for God's grace in making you ready to return to this person.

- Contact that person and complete the circle.

DADDY'S BOY

PLUNGING INTO THE WORD:

Genesis 37:1-31

PONDERING ON THE WAY:

Today we begin the story of Joseph. From the time he was born, Joseph was "Daddy's boy." In fact, he was probably a spoiled rotten brat. His father liked him more than the other eleven sons, and he gave Joseph special clothes and special attention. As you can imagine, the other brothers didn't like this at all. In fact, they pretty much hated Joseph.

It didn't help matters when Joseph told them about two dreams he had. In the first dream, all the brothers were working in the fields on the farm, making bundles of wheat. Joseph's bundle of wheat stood up straight, and the others that his brothers made bowed down in front of his.

In the second dream, the sun, moon, and eleven stars bowed down to Joseph. The sun and moon symbolized his father and mother, and the eleven stars were his brothers. You can imagine why the brothers hated to hear about Joseph's dreams.

One day, Joseph's father sent him out to the pastures to check on his brothers, who were taking care of the sheep. When the brothers saw him coming, they decided to kill him and throw him into a big hole in the ground. But one brother said they shouldn't kill him, so instead, they took off the special clothes from his dad, and threw him delete alive into the hole.

Not long after that, a group of men came by on their camels. They were on their way to Egypt, so the brothers decided to sell Joseph to them. That seemed like a good way to get rid of him. They killed a goat and put the goat's blood on Joseph's clothes and took them back to their father. They said a wild animal had killed Joseph, and their father believed them. He was very sad.

In the meantime, the men took Joseph to Egypt and sold him as a slave to a wealthy man in Egypt's government.

To be continued …

—*Laurie Oswald Robinson*

PRAYING AND WALKING IN THE WORLD:

- Begin to create a story board about the life of Joseph. You will need lots of white paper and crayons, markers or watercolors for the next few days of devotionals.

Each day draw or paint a scene or two about the story and then display them on the refrigerator or a wall or bulletin board in your bedroom or family room. Suggestions for today: Show how the brothers threw Joseph into the pit, or show a scene from one of the dreams.

- Ask God to help you not to be jealous of kids who seem to be favorites. Discuss your feelings with your parents or another trusted adult. And then ask God to help you see how special you are to God and to others.

- Rent a video, such as the *Prince of Egypt,* about the story of Joseph and watch it with your family or friends.

- **Adults:** Is jealousy a factor in your workplace or family? Do you deal with people who "lord it over" you and others? Or do you ever use your position of power to make others feel small? Where can you see yourself in this part of Joseph's story? Talk to God about it.

AUGUST 20 *(FOR CHILDREN AND FAMILIES)*

LIES

PLUNGING INTO THE WORD:

Genesis 39:1-23

PONDERING ON THE WAY:

Has anyone ever told lies about you? It didn't feel good, did it? That's what happened to Joseph in today's story.

After he was sold as a slave, Joseph ended up with a very important job in the house of the government man named Potipher. Potipher's wife saw that Joseph was handsome and good-looking. So, when no one else was home, she tried to get him to have an affair with her. He said, "No way!" When she tried to grab him, he ran away, but his clothes tore, and she had part of them in her hands. She used those torn clothes to tell a lie about Joseph. She showed them to her husband and said that Joseph had tried to have an affair with her, rather than the other way around. Potiphar believed her and threw Joseph into prison.

Even though Potipher's wife lied about him and Joseph ended up in prison, God was with Joseph and helped him. The chief jailor put Joseph in charge of all the prisoners. God was with Joseph so that everything he did turned out well, even when other people tried to hurt him.

—*Laurie Oswald Robinson*

PRAYING AND WALKING IN THE WORLD:

- Continue drawing a picture or two for your story board. Suggestions for today: show Joseph running away from Potiphar's wife, or show Joseph in prison.

- Ask God to help you forgive a person who has told a lie about you, or ask God for forgiveness if you have told lies about other kids.

- Pray for people who are in prison. Pray that they will experience God's love.

- **Adults:** When has God blessed you despite the negative energy of people around you? When has God rewarded your faithfulness? Praise God!

AUGUST 21 *(FOR CHILDREN AND FAMILIES)*

A SPECIAL TALENT

PLUNGING INTO THE WORD:

Genesis 40:1-23

PONDERING ON THE WAY:

Note to parents: read this yourself before sharing it with your children. The chief baker's death is somewhat graphic.

In our first story about Joseph, we read about Joseph's two dreams. Today we will find out how he told people the meaning of their dreams.

When he was in prison, Joseph met two other prisoners who had dreams that really bothered them. Joseph said that God could tell them, through Joseph, what the dreams meant. So the men told Joseph their dreams.

The first man had been a cupbearer—a servant of the pharaoh—before he went to prison. In his dream, there was a grapevine with three branches. As soon as the vine blossomed, the clusters ripened into grapes. The man pressed the grapes into a cup in his hand, which belonged to the pharaoh. Joseph said the dream meant that within three days the pharaoh would bring the man back to his job as his cupbearer.

The next man was the chief baker for the pharaoh. In his dream, there were three baskets of cakes and baked foods on his head for the pharaoh, but there were birds eating the food out of the baskets. Joseph said the dream meant that in three days the man would be killed by the pharaoh. His body would be hung on a pole, and birds would come pick on his body.

The dreams came true just as Joseph said. He had a special talent from God for understanding dreams.

—Laurie Oswald Robinson

PRAYING AND WALKING IN THE WORLD:

- Continue with your story board. Suggestions for today: Draw pictures of the two dreams of the cupbearer and the chief baker. Also, you may want to try a more difficult one—show God giving Joseph a talent for understanding dreams.

- **Adults and children:** What special talents has God given you? Thank God for the things you can do well. Give God a big round of applause for giving you those talents. (A round of applause is when you clap and make a circle in front of you as you clap.) Ask God to show you one new way to use your talents for the good of others.

AUGUST 22 *(FOR CHILDREN AND FAMILIES)*

JUST A DREAM?

PLUNGING INTO THE WORD:

Genesis 41:1-36

PONDERING ON THE WAY:

We all have dreams. Some of us remember them more than other people do. Some people pay a lot of attention to their dreams and try to figure out what they mean. Other people say, "It's just a dream" and leave it at that.

Today, as we follow the story of Joseph, he gets called out of prison by King Pharaoh because Pharaoh had two dreams, and he wanted to know what they meant. He called on Joseph because Joseph was known as a person who could explain dreams.

Joseph listened to what Pharaoh said about skinny cows eating fat cows, and thin ears of corn gobbling up big ears of corn. Then he explained that both of the dreams meant the same thing: There would be seven years of very good crops in the land, followed by seven years of no crops at all. Joseph told Pharaoh to find a leader who would collect all of the crops during the good years and save them for the bad years to come.

Pharaoh was very impressed with Joseph, but Joseph made sure to tell Pharaoh that it was God, not Joseph himself, who was giving answers to the dreams. He said that God was using him. Although he could easily have claimed the power for himself, he didn't. He gave God the glory for his special talent.

—Carol Duerksen

PRAYING AND WALKING IN THE WORLD:

- **Adults and children:** Talk about some dreams you remember. Do you know what they might mean?

- **Children:** Draw a picture that symbolizes today's story and add it to your storyboard. Hint: How about skinny cows eating fat cows and thin corn gobbling up fat corn?

- **Adults:** Do you give God the glory for what you do well? Is it a challenge to find the balance between being boastful and openly owning your gifts and abilities? How can you give God the credit for who you are and what you do?

AUGUST 23 *(FOR CHILDREN AND FAMILIES)*

PRISONER TO PRINCE

PLUNGING INTO THE WORD:

Genesis 41:37-57

PONDERING ON THE WAY:

When Joseph told Pharaoh he needed somebody to collect the crops during the good years and save them for the bad years, Pharaoh knew just who the right man was for the job—Joseph himself! So the pharaoh gave Joseph the job promotion of his life, complete with the best clothes, expensive jewelry, and even a rich, beautiful woman to be his wife. One day Joseph was a prisoner in a nasty dungeon, and the next day he was a powerful prince in a big, fancy house.

Joseph spent seven years gathering all the food he could throughout the land, because he knew what was going to happen in the next seven years. He also had two sons during those seven years, and he gave them names that talked about his own life. The first son was named Manasseh, which means "God has helped me forget the bad times and the loss of my family." The second son was named Ephraim, which means "God has given me good things in a land where bad things happened earlier."

Just as the dreams predicted, the seven good years ended and then the bad years started. But thank God, there was food stored up in Egypt for all of the hungry people.

—*Carol Duerksen*

PRAYING AND WALKING IN THE WORLD:

- **Children:** Draw a picture of a scene from today's story and add it to your storyboard.

- **Adults and children:** Think about the last several months or year of your life. What name would you give to that time period to describe it? Would it be Joy, or Winter, or Blessings, or Patience? Think of a word or a sentence to describe your life, as Joseph did when he named his sons.

- Our North American countries have plenty of food, yet people across the street and around the world are starving. How can you be involved in sharing from your abundance? Find a project to do with your children to share with those who are less fortunate.

AUGUST 24 *(FOR CHILDREN AND FAMILIES)*

JOE'S BRO'S SHOW UP

PLUNGING INTO THE WORD:

Genesis 42:1-17

PONDERING ON THE WAY:

While Joseph was in his palace eating and sharing the food that he'd stored up, things were not going well back on the family farm in Canaan. In fact, Joseph's family and other people were starving.

Father Jacob heard there was food to be had in Egypt, so he called a family meeting and said, "Look, guys, we've gotta do something. Why don't you go to Egypt and buy some grain?"

So they all headed for Egypt—all except the youngest brother, Benjamin. Jacob wouldn't let him go because he loved him the most—as much as he'd loved Benjamin's brother, Joseph, who Jacob thought was dead.

Guess what happened? Of course. They get to Egypt, and it's Joseph handing out the food. He looked so different, they had no clue it was their brother. But Joseph knew it was his brothers right away.

So he gave them all big hugs and said, "Look, it's me, your long-lost brother!"

Nope. Joseph remembered the dreams he had about his brothers bowing down to him. He decided to play games with them. He accused them of being spies. He gave them a really hard time. In fact, he threw them all into prison and said they'd all have to stay there except one. That one brother should go back home and bring Benjamin back, and then he'd let them all go free.

Why did Joseph do this to his brothers? For revenge? Because he was angry at them for what they had done to him? Because it was all part of God's plan? Stay tuned to see what happens next!

—*Carol Duerksen*

PRAYING AND WALKING IN THE WORLD:

- **Children:** Draw a picture of a scene from today's story to add to your storyboard.

- **Adults:** Was Joseph using his power to intimidate his brothers, or did he use his power in a healthy way to see if the hearts of his brothers had changed at all? What do you think? What power do you have? (Cultural, ethnic, male, female, financial, parental, personality, job, etc.) How do you use your power? Power itself is not right or wrong, but how it is used can be.

- Do we sometimes forgive too fast? Do Christians feel forced to forgive and forget in ways that are not healthy for either party?

AUGUST 25 *(FOR CHILDREN AND FAMILIES)*

LITTLE DO THEY KNOW

PLUNGING INTO THE WORD:

Genesis 42:18-38

PONDERING ON THE WAY:

Joseph puts his brothers in prison for three days and then brings them out. He says that he'll let them go home with grain on one condition: One of them has to stay in Egypt until the others bring their youngest brother, Benjamin, to see him.

What a position to be in! Now the brothers feel terrible, and they remember how terrible Joseph must have felt when they sold him into slavery. They figure that this is happening to them because they deserve it. Little do they know!

In fact, they actually said these things in their own language in Joseph's presence, because they figured he couldn't understand them. Of course he could, and hearing them talk really broke him up. He had to leave the room so they couldn't see him cry.

Joseph chose Simeon to stay, and the rest of the brothers went back home to their father. You can imagine Jacob's reaction when he saw them coming back without his son Simeon! Not only that, but when he heard that the only way to get Simeon back was to send Benjamin to Egypt to see the prince who had given them grain, he was heartbroken. And there was one more thing; the money they had paid for the grain had been put back in their sacks of grain!

What was going on? They had no idea.

—*Carol Duerksen*

PRAYING AND WALKING IN THE WORLD:

- **Children:** Draw a scene to add to your storyboard.

- **Adults:** How do you feel about your past and present relationships with your siblings? Have there been hurtful words and actions against one another? Do you want healing to happen in those relationships? If so, what are you willing to do?

- Are you confused or puzzled about something that's happening in your life right now? Can you surrender it in prayer to God and trust that God is in control?

AUGUST 26 *(FOR CHILDREN AND FAMILIES)*

JOSEPH THROWS A PARTY

PLUNGING INTO THE WORD:

Genesis 43:1-34

PONDERING ON THE WAY:

Jacob and his sons and their families lived on the grain they'd brought from Egypt. But when it ran out, they knew they needed to make another trip for more. The brothers reminded Jacob that they'd have to take Benjamin along, because the prince who'd sold them the grain had warned them, "No brother, no grain." The idea of letting go of his youngest, favorite son really stressed Jacob out, but they needed food, so he gave in. He sent his sons away with many prayers for their safety.

When Joseph saw that his brothers were back and had brought his youngest brother with them, he ordered that a wonderful meal be prepared to share with them. Now remember, they still didn't know that Joseph was their long-lost brother. They'd brought the money back that they found in their sacks of grain, more money to buy grain, plus some other special foods as gifts for him. They didn't know what was going on with this man. On the one hand, he'd treated them very well; but on the other hand, he'd made strange demands of them, and he seemed unusually interested in their father and youngest brother.

When they were all in the room together, getting ready to sit down to the big meal, Joseph saw Benjamin up close for the first time, and Joseph had to leave the room because he lost it again. He cried for what happened, the years that had gone by, and for the joy of seeing him again.

When Joseph pulled himself back together and returned to the room, they sat down to eat. Joseph did one more thing that had his brothers completely amazed—he had them seated in order of their age. They had no idea how he could know that, and he still didn't tell them who he was.

—*Carol Duerksen*

PRAYING AND WALKING IN THE WORLD:

- **Children:** Add a scene to your storyboard.

- **Adults:** Jacob did not want to let his treasured son Benjamin leave home. But he did, and you can imagine the prayers he offered as he saw his sons leaving and on the many days to follow. Without the means of communication that we take for granted today, Jacob had only his trust in God to depend upon. In which areas of your life do you totally depend upon God? Do you think it's harder for us to depend on God because we are able to "make things happen" for ourselves?

- Who do you find to be confusing because you don't know their motivation for what they do? Do these people behave differently than you, and that drives you crazy? Can you put yourself in their shoes?

- How is Joseph showing us the importance of true forgiveness? Real biblical forgiveness can't happen until the offending party changes his or her ways.

AUGUST 27 *(FOR CHILDREN AND FAMILIES)*

THE "STOLEN" SILVER CUP

PLUNGING INTO THE WORD:

Genesis 44:1-34

PONDERING ON THE WAY:

The brothers purchased their grain and began their trip back home to their father in Canaan—but not before Joseph pulled another trick on them. He put his silver cup in Benjamin's grain sack, and then, when the group was just a short distance down the road, Joseph sent his steward after them to accuse them of stealing the cup.

What?

That's exactly what the brothers said. They were so sure they hadn't stolen it, they told Joseph that if the cup was found in one of the sacks, that person should die and the rest would become slaves to Joseph. Joseph, knowing full well that the cup was in Benjamin's sack, said that the person who stole it would be his slave and the rest could go free.

They searched the sacks and found the cup. Now the brothers were really at their wits' end. If Joseph took Benjamin, and they returned home without him, they were afraid their father would die of a broken heart.

Judah, the unsung hero of the story of Joseph, stepped in. He told Joseph how horrible it would be if Benjamin didn't go back to his father. He explained that he promised his father he'd bring Benjamin back—that he'd be responsible and take the blame if anything happened. He offered to stay and be the slave—if only Benjamin could go back home.

And that's where we'll leave them until tomorrow.

—*Carol Duerksen*

PRAYING AND WALKING IN THE WORLD:

- **Children:** Think about the expressions on the faces of the brothers when the cup is found in Benjamin's sack. Draw a picture for your storyboard of those faces.

- **Adults:** From the beginning, the Joseph story includes physical and emotional abuse among the siblings. Pray today for people you know in abusive relationships. Pray for both the victim and the offender. Pray for God's grace and healing to be present in both lives.

- **Adults and children:** Talk about relationships within your family. How do you handle sibling disagreements? Does bullying happen? Talk about the Golden Rule: "Treat others the way you want to be treated." Can you try to do that?

AUGUST 28 *(FOR CHILDREN AND FAMILIES)*

A HAPPY REUNION

PLUNGING INTO THE WORD:

Genesis 45:1-15

PONDERING ON THE WAY:

Finally, Joseph couldn't pretend any longer. He told his brothers who he was, and he cried so loudly that everybody else in the palace heard him.

The brothers were scared to death that Joseph would punish them for what they had done to him. But he had no intention of hurting them. "God has been working in all of this," he told them. "I am here in Egypt for a reason—to save people's lives from the famine. Please, go get my father and your families and bring them here. I can't wait to see him again and show him my life here in Egypt."

When the brothers understood that Joseph wanted to help them rather than hurt them, they let their guard down. They cried with happiness and talked and talked— they had so much catching up to do!

> —*Carol Duerksen*

PRAYING AND WALKING IN THE WORLD:

- **Children:** Draw a picture of the happy reunion between Joseph and his brothers.

- **Adults:** In 1970, a movie came out based on a book by Erich Segal called *Love Story.* The most famous line from the movie was "Love means never having to say you're sorry." Although this quote sounds wonderful and romantic, the exact opposite is true. Love means you do have to say you're sorry. Love means seeking and receiving forgiveness. Joseph was able to forgive his brothers because he saw God's hand in what had happened. Forgiveness is what we all need from God, and what we all must offer each other. What role does forgiveness play in your life? Are you able to ask for forgiveness? Are you able to offer it to others?

- When in your life has something good come out of something bad? Did you see God at work in those situations? Share stories with one another.

AUGUST 29

PROMISE RESTORED

PLUNGING INTO THE WORD:

Genesis 45:16-28

PONDERING ON THE WAY:

Israel, where is your child?

Where once were twelve sons, twelve promises,
There is now only thirst and hunger.

One dead, one lost, the rest dying—
Joseph, gone, torn by animals
Benjamin, gone, in far-off Egypt
Other sons, gone from home, searching for food
O Israel, where is your hope?

The great promise seems a great joke.
What good is that great nation if it starves in its infancy?

One dead, one lost, the rest dying.
Egypt; the last hope, the last son.

Or is Egypt the final grave?
Will you lose them all, Israel?
Did you love too much?
Did you cling too hard?
They slip through your fingers like sand.

Rejoice, Israel, for the promise is restored!
The prayer is answered; a nation lives.

For the dead are alive. The lost are found.
The prodigal has returned.

Prepare the feast, Jacob, this is the promise.
Israel, here is your child, here is your hope.

Twelve sons, twelve promises.
Now there is abundance and dancing.

There is feast where once was famine.
This is the promise.

Israel, this is your child.

—*Michele Hershberger*

PRAYING AND WALKING IN THE WORLD:

- What impossible news would stun you today? Could God do this for you yet? Have you checked the horizon?

- God uses a pagan king, the pharaoh, to save Jacob's family from the famine and to make them a great nation. How does God use secular governments today to fulfill his will?

AUGUST 30 *(FOR CHILDREN AND FAMILIES)*

WORD HANDS

PLUNGING INTO THE WORD:

Genesis 49:1-27

PONDERING ON THE WAY:

Do you know what it means to bless another person? Blessings are hopeful, happy words that people say to other people to encourage them, which means giving them courage in their lives.

I like to think of blessings as "word hands." Have you ever used your hands to help someone? What are some ways your hands can be helpful to others? Have you ever had someone pick you up with their hands when you fell down? Have you ever had someone use their hands to help pick up toys from the floor? Has anyone made you a cake, mixing the flour and sugar and eggs with their hands?

Jacob gives all of his sons some "word hands" before he dies. Jacob and his whole family (more than seventy people) all had moved to Egypt—a big trip. The pharaoh gave them land, and the family was reunited with Joseph. After seventeen years of living in Egypt, Jacob turned 147. He was very old and knew that he would die soon, so he called his sons to him.

He spoke to each of his sons in turn. In his blessings to them, he was remembering how each son was a little bit the same as the others and a little bit different. Their blessings were right for who they were.

After Jacob had finished blessing his sons, he died. He felt more ready to die because he had taken the time to give words of love and encouragement to his children. Blessing people is a good thing to do.

—Michele Hershberger

PRAYING AND WALKING IN THE WORLD:

- Let's practice giving blessings to one another. Here are some ways to start a blessing. Face your mom or dad or others who are with you now and finish these sentences:

  1. I hope God gives you a _____.

  2. May all of your problems _____.

  3. May you have love for _____.

  4. I want God to help you with _____.

- **Adults:** Did Jacob give some sons unequal blessings because of favoritism or their personalities ? Or were they self-fulfilling prophecies? Have you been blessed with or suffered from words others have spoken over you? God can heal the wounds of unwise words. God can bring to fruition the words of blessing and honor that have been bestowed on you.

AUGUST 31

JOSEPH'S FORGIVENESS

PLUNGING INTO THE WORD:

Genesis 49:28—50:26

PONDERING ON THE WAY:

I can just picture that awkward moment. One of the brothers, maybe Judah or Levi, gets up the courage: "Hey Joe, remember that time when we threw you into a pit, then sold you into slavery and told Dad you were dead? Ha, ha, good times." *(Awkward pause.)*. "We're cool about that, right?" More silence while everyone nervously bites their nails. Naphtali edges toward the door. Asher feels sick to his stomach.

Now that Jacob, their father, is dead, Joseph may show his true feelings—feelings of revenge. The brothers squirm. They had been merciless to Joseph. What will he do to them?

It would've been easy for Joseph to wreak vengeance. He had all of Egypt's resources at hand. The whole country's devotion to him had again been demonstrated through their participation in his father's burial. Egyptian elders and officials, all of the servants of Pharaoh, traveled with the brothers to Canaan, at huge expense. And all of Egypt mourned seventy days—seventy days for a Canaanite shepherd! The Israelites had every reason to believe that they would be well cared for under Egyptian rule after seeing their loyalty to Jacob and Joseph. That is, unless Joseph still carried that grudge.

Joseph had every reason to punish his brothers, every right to throw the book at them. What would he do—now?

And then—it happens. Joseph starts to cry. It's just a sniffle at first, a small noise in his throat, but then he breaks down, weeping, tears flowing down as he lets go of something deep inside.

It's real. The forgiveness is real. Their own throats choking with emotion, the brothers come together as one, crying on each other's necks. This is the real reunion, a reuniting not by proximity, but by the spirit of forgiveness.

Years and years earlier, an immature Joseph bragged to his brothers about a dream, a dream in which they would worship him. He was playing God. And that wasn't good.

And now, when perhaps he really can justify playing God, at least a little, he doesn't. He forgives.

And in response to his love, to his forgiving heart, the brothers bow down, just as in the dream so long ago.

   —Michele Hershberger

PRAYING AND WALKING IN THE WORLD:

- Whom do you need to forgive? Really forgive? Can you call that person? Can you write it down?

- Can you think of times when God turned something bad into something good? When and how?

SEPTEMBER 1

BACK TO THE BASICS

PLUNGING INTO THE WORD:

Revelation 1:1-20

PONDERING ON THE WAY:

It's hard to turn down the chance to hear the end of a gripping story. Does the good guy or gal win? Does someone fall in love? Do people live happily ever after or crash and burn?

God understands that we grasp life's meaning through stories. Holy-Spirit-inspired authors used various literary genres to tell God's story. There's poetry in the Psalms, parables in the Gospels and teaching in the epistles. The beginning of this story is Genesis, which tells how creation began. The end of the story is Revelation, which tells what finally becomes of that creation. Revelation uses a literary genre called apocalyptic—a genre that used vivid word pictures and metaphors to describe visions about how God works in the world.

Revelation has been interpreted in a zillion ways. Some believe it maps out in literal detail what will happen in the end times. Others believe it spoke to the contemporary situation of the first church and we should read it through their experiences. Despite this, the first chapter is simple and direct. It reminds us that Jesus Christ is the beginning and the end of all things, Alpha and Omega. He is the one "who is, who was and who is to come."

We reel with Revelation's graphic and layered meaning. But today we come back to the basics: Jesus is the one character we depend on to be steady through the entire story. He came and left this world through his birth, death, and resurrection; he is here now in the presence of his Holy Spirit; and he will come again to take us to be where he is forever.

If there ever was a happily-ever-after ending, this certainly is it. But we have a few days of tough reading ahead before we can close the book. If we get overwhelmed, we need only to go back to the basics. They can comfort us and cheer us on our way.

—*Laurie Oswald Robinson*

PRAYING AND WALKING IN THE WORLD:

- Reflect on a time when you didn't know the end of the story of a particular season in your life. What emotion or action did this uncertainty evoke? If you are in such a season right now, how would going back to the basics help you cope?

- Pray for increased trust that God is the author of the plot of your life. Ask to more deeply trust the mystery and goodness of God's care for you in each part of your story—the beginning, the middle, and the end.

- Seek out a friend, relative, or coworker who feels anxious about not knowing the outcome of a particular season of life. Assure this person that God and you will be steady companions during the uncertainty.

SEPTEMBER 2

FIRST LOVE, FROZEN LOVE

PLUNGING INTO THE WORD:

Revelation 2:1-7

PONDERING ON THE WAY:

They told me it would happen. Someday, the honeymoon would be over. I didn't want to believe it. Surely the high of falling in love meant that my husband and I would be spared its falling out. But reality hit, and we've joined the masses in learning that it's easy to love well in the short run. It's much harder to love when a wrong word is spoken at a wrong time; when silence chills every corner of the home and heart; and a frantic schedule snuffs out family sit-down suppers.

This "first love" theme is part of the visions John, the writer of Revelation, received from the Holy Spirit. In one vision, he sees seven stars and seven golden lamp stands. The stars symbolize angels; the lamp stands symbolize churches. John is to write each angel a message from God, which is to be given to each of the seven churches. These messages include affirmations, warnings, or both.

In today's reading, the angel sent to Ephesus brings a "good news, bad news" message. The church gets kudos for being hardworking, patient, and discerning about false prophets. But it is also chided for abandoning its first love. It needed to remember from what it had fallen; it needed to repent; it needed to do the works that it did at first.

The angel warned that if the church at Ephesus wasn't willing to repent and return to this first love, the church's lamp stand would be removed. The removal of the lamp stand indicated a dying church. We might think lightly of falling away from our first love, but this was a serious warning; Ephesus was the only church to receive the dire threat of its removal as a church. Just as in a marriage, a church must practice renewed vigilance and intentionality in order for a first love not to become a frozen love.

—*Laurie Oswald Robinson*

PRAYING AND WALKING IN THE WORLD:

- How could your relationship to God, a marriage partner, or friend be in danger of a frozen kind of love? What are the steps that lead away from warmth and light into cold and darkness?

- Pray for wisdom on how to renew your relationships with God and others with intentionality and vigilance.

- Dig up old pictures that depict scenes from when you first met your spouse or a friend. Reminisce about what kinds of special touches or activities made your relationship so alive.

- How would you describe your congregation's relationship with Jesus? On the honeymoon? Living through stormy early years? Enjoying grandchildren? Heading for separation?

SEPTEMBER 3 *(FOR CHILDREN AND FAMILIES)*

OPEN DOORS, CLOSED DOORS

PLUNGING INTO THE WORD:

Revelation 3:7-13

PONDERING ON THE WAY:

When I was a little girl, my big brother locked himself inside his room to get away from me. No matter how hard I screamed or banged on the door, he would not unlock it and let me in. More often than not, I slunk away with red eyes, red fists, and a hoarse throat. He held the power, and unless he would open the door from the inside, I would not get in.

Today's Bible story tells us about how an angel took a message to one of the earliest Christian congregations. This church was in a city called Philadelphia. The angel told the church that Jesus—the holy one, the true one—has the key. It can open a door that no one else can shut; and it can shut a door that no one can open. Now, this isn't a real door with a metal key—this is a neat way of saying they are in trouble and God is going to help them.

In other words, God holds all the power in the universe. Even though the church itself has little power, God will supply the power. If the members of the church let God be powerful within them, they would get through their earthly troubles and go to heaven.

My brother eventually came out of his room, and the power struggle was over—at least for that day. This story reminds us that Jesus Christ wins the power struggle that goes on in our world between good and evil. When we know that Jesus holds the power, then we don't have to fight so hard to make things turn out right. We can wait for God to open the door to problems that have shut us out.

—*Laurie Oswald Robinson*

PRAYING AND WALKING IN THE WORLD:

- Have you ever been locked out of a room? How did it feel? Did you wish you could be an all-powerful Superman and burst through the door? Talk with your parents or another trusted adult about what God's power looks like. Is it always visible to your eyes?

- In your prayers today, ask to see God's power and give thanks for God's all-powerful personality.

- Seek out someone at school or Sunday school who has a disability that makes that person feel powerless. Go out of your way to be kind to her or him this week in words or actions.

- **Adults:** This tiny church had a special door they wanted open—the door of acceptance. As a Gentile congregation, they were looked down upon by the Christian Jews, and Jesus says, I'm the one "who has the key of David. ... I will make you a pillar in my temple." In other words—Jesus shows them acceptance. Who are the people feeling left out in your congregation?

SEPTEMBER 4

CHRIST AT HEART'S DOOR

PLUNGING INTO THE WORD:

Revelation 3:14-22

PONDERING ON THE WAY:

Nearly every house I went in as a child had the traditional painting of Jesus knocking on a closed door. The painting, "Christ at Heart's Door," was created by Warner Sallman. My first thought as a child was: *Why can't Jesus just open the door?* But in gazing at the painting longer, I'd see the door didn't have an outdoor latch. My second thought: *Why doesn't the person inside let Jesus in?* These musings went on for years before someone told me that the image depicted Revelation 3:20, a key verse in today's passage.

The church at Laodicea was neither hot nor cold but had grown lukewarm, which evoked the Lord's severe displeasure. To restore their faith, the church would need to accept the discipline of God by recognizing its lukewarm state and repenting. The church prided itself on being rich and prosperous in the world, but in reality it was poor, blind, and naked in God's kingdom. They would need to buy gold refined by fire—accept the purifying process, wear white robes to cover nakedness, shed shameful ways, apply salve to the eyes, and be healed from blindness.

Perhaps my childhood questions were right on. Even though God provides refining disciplines, only we can decide to receive these disciplines. It's the softening agents of the disciplines that make us willing to open our door from the inside. We are hungry, but we will not eat until we invite Jesus to sit at our table. He will not knock down our door. God will not force discipline on us. We must decide to let Jesus in and receive the loving disciplines.

—*Laurie Oswald Robinson*

PRAYING AND WALKING IN THE WORLD:

- **Journal about:** What door stands between you and the fullness of Christ's love? What are the characteristics of that door? What kind of loving disciplines would help you open that door?

- Pray for the Holy Spirit to reveal the "key" that will turn around the situation that keeps you locked away from the Lord in a particular area.

- Put a key near your Bible this week. Each day of devotions, hold the key in your hand as you open the door more fully to Christ's love and Christ's work in your life. Or, find a copy of Sallman's painting and place it in your devotional space.

SEPTEMBER 5

24/7 PRAISE

PLUNGING INTO THE WORD:

Revelation 4:1-11

PONDERING ON THE WAY:

As I write this, I am on a bit of a high—the kind of high that happens to parents when their son or daughter does something wonderful and outstanding. We just got back from watching our German exchange student, Lisa, run her way to a third-place finish in the state cross-country meet, and in the process, help her team grab second place.

Yes, we're celebrating. We're sending pictures to the papers, plastering the news on signs, placing long-distance calls to Lisa's family in Germany, and praising the accomplishments of a team whose hard work paid off. They earned it, and they are worthy—for this moment in time—of our praise.

What a minuscule example this is of the picture John paints for us in this passage. God is seated on a throne in the middle of the sea. The sea symbolizes horrible evil, and God's sovereignty is ruling in the midst of that evil. Around God are representations of all categories of animals and human life: wild animals, domesticated animals, humanity, and birds. They represent all of creation, and all of creation is consumed with a 24/7 activity: singing praises to God.

I'm trying to put this together in my mind—the reality of today when I find my praise going to the people I can see and know, and the nonstop praise going to God in this unusual book of Revelation. I wonder where those two intersect—my everyday life and John's vision. And where I come out is simply this: Can I carry the throne of God in my mind and heart through the drudgery of the day? Can I fall on my knees before my Creator and say "You are awesome" a million times over? Can I praise without ceasing?

Can I get as excited about God as a cross-country race?

—*Carol Duerksen*

PRAYING AND WALKING IN THE WORLD:

- Can you praise God day and night? Try it for twenty-four hours. Wear something like a bracelet or ring that you aren't used to, and that will be a reminder to praise God.

- How does your congregation praise God? How could you praise God more? Are you willing to work at that part of your congregational life?

- God created diversity, as symbolized in the lion, ox, eagle, and human being around the throne. Find a person or a group of Christians that is quite diverse from you and come together to praise God.

- What crowns do you need to cast down?

SEPTEMBER 6 *(FOR CHILDREN AND FAMILIES)*

WHO'S STRONGER—A LION OR A LAMB?

PLUNGING INTO THE WORD:

Revelation 5:1-14

PONDERING ON THE WAY:

Find pictures or stuffed toys of a lion and a lamb. Discuss with your children: Which one is stronger? What makes that one stronger than the other one?

The Bible talks about Jesus being like both a lion and a lamb. Jesus is like a lion because he is a powerful person—after all, he is the Son of God!

But more often than being called a lion, Jesus is called a lamb. Jesus is like a lamb because he died to take away our sins. In the Old Testament times, people would kill a lamb and offer it to God as a way to take away their sins. When Jesus came and died on the cross for us, he took the place of the lambs that had been offered to God. That's why he was called the Lamb of God.

It's hard to imagine that a lamb can actually be strong, but the love that Jesus has for everyone is stronger than anything else in the world. It is stronger than all of the bad things that happen, and it is stronger than the bad things that people do to each other. The love of Jesus, the Lamb of God, is the most powerful thing in the world. This love is the only thing that can take away all evil.

—*Carol Duerksen*

PRAYING AND WALKING IN THE WORLD:

- **Adults:** Power (as symbolized by the lion of Judah in this passage) is the way we are accustomed to getting what we want. Power makes things happen. Power overcomes. But it isn't the powerful lion that pulls it off in this passage—it is a slaughtered lamb. Jesus' voluntary death makes him both the slaughtered lamb and the conquering lion. Are there times in your life when you hope for the power of a lion, when it is the self-sacrifice of a lamb that is needed? Name those times and pray for the courage to be a lamb.

- **Adults and children:** Think of someone you know who is a bully and who tries to use power over you or others. Can you imagine Jesus putting his arms around that person and giving them a hug? Pray for that person. Ask Jesus to help you love him or her.

SEPTEMBER 7

REALITY CHECK

PLUNGING INTO THE WORD:

Revelation 6:1-17

PONDERING ON THE WAY:

John had visions; we turn on the evening news. It's not much different, really. Horrific killings, wars, famines, people dying for their faith, earthquakes, tsunamis, wildfires, pandemics. He saw it, and humanity has been living it.

Is it worse now? Are the end times near? Are we bringing these horrors upon ourselves, or is God manipulating the universe?

A God of love does not create pain. Sin causes pain. Being separated from God causes pain. Not respecting the Creator's creation causes pain. Humanity has been given choices, and quite frankly, there have been a lot of very bad choices.

Does that mean Hurricane Katrina was a punishment on New Orleans? No.

Does it mean our lifestyles have created global warming and weather patterns are changing? Probably. Does it mean humanity will be facing more catastrophes than ever before? Probably.

Will Christians be exempt from suffering? No. The execution-style murders of five innocent Amish schoolgirls in Pennsylvania in October 2006 shocked the world. The response of the Amish community seemed just as unbelievable. They attended the funeral of the killer. They offered forgiveness to his family.

Why? How? The Amish believe that God is in control. It's as simple as that. God is working God's purposes out in the world. Their role is not revenge. Their role is to give God's love and grace.

God uses earthly trials to bring about redemption—to bring people back to God. God can work through the worst events of human history. Nothing can happen that will deter God's purposes from being fulfilled—of that we can be assured.

—*Carol Duerksen*

PRAYING AND WALKING IN THE WORLD:

- Have you or someone you know been through a personal or community-wide catastrophe? How did you respond? With more or less faith in God? Did you feel the assurance of God's presence, or did you feel abandoned by the Creator?

- Take a newspaper or news magazine to a quiet place. Light a candle, and spend time praying your way through the news. Ask for God's purposes to be fulfilled in the midst of the chaos, violence, and destruction that is happening in your community and the world.

SEPTEMBER 8 *(FOR CHILDREN AND FAMILIES)*

THE HOG 'N' DOG

PLUNGING INTO THE WORD:

Revelation 7:9-17

PONDERING ON THE WAY:

Slickfester Dude is a very wise, observant cat who helped me write a book of stories about what he saw happening on our farm. This is one of his stories.

"I know where Reuben goes," he told me one day.

"You do? Where?"

Now I must explain here about Reuben. Reuben is a black pug dog. For the last few days, Reuben hadn't been around the house at all during the day, and when he showed up in the evening to eat, he looked and smelled bad. Actually, he'd been looking and smelling more like a pig than a pug.

Slick just looked at me, so I asked again. "So where does Reuben go?"

"Down by the creek, where that crippled pig is living in the mud. He sits there with that pig."

"Why? Why would Reuben spend days with a sick pig? Especially when his best friend is a chocolate Labrador. Who would leave a dog for a hog?"

"Maybe because the pig needs him." Slick looked especially wise when he said that.

Now it was my turn to think. Yes, that porker had been bullied by the other pigs in the pen. He'd been moved outside, away from the pigs that were hurting him. Somehow, he'd found his way down to the creek, where the shade trees and mud soothed his wounds. But what could Reuben do for him?

"But how?" I asked Slick. "How does the pig need Reuben?"

"He just needs him to be there. To sit beside him."

"Oh," I said. "You really think that makes a difference?"

"It always makes a difference to have somebody sit with you when you feel bad," Slick said.

And I knew he was right.

We all have bad things happen to us, and when they do, it's important to have somebody to sit with us, just like Reuben sat with the pig. People can sit with us, and even more importantly, God is with us. Even when it feels like we can't live through what's happening, God is there with us.

In a famous poem called "Footprints," a person dreams about walking along a beach with God. Across the sky, scenes of the person's life are flashing, and in each scene there are two sets of footprints—theirs and God's. But then the person notices that during their saddest and lowest times in life, there was only one set of footprints.

Can you guess why there was just one set?

Because, according to the poem, that's when God was carrying the person.

—*Carol Duerksen*

PRAYING AND WALKING IN THE WORLD:

- **Adults and children:** Read the poem "Footprints." Talk about times when God has carried you through tough stuff. Pray for the areas where you need God to carry you now.

- **Adults and children:** Who do you need to sit with?

- Send a note to a person who's been there for you when you needed someone.

SEPTEMBER 9

OUCH

PLUNGING INTO THE WORD:

Revelation 9:13-21

PONDERING ON THE WAY:

I've been looking at yellow cars lately. Yellow Mustangs, yellow VW bugs, yellow

Ford Focuses. The Mustang is out of my price range, and it doesn't get good mileage. The bug is cute, but I like Fords, and the Focus will probably win out when I'm ready to buy a new car.

I'm not admiring any used, boring cars.

Maynard and I dream of a glass sunroom on the south side of our house. And someday, when our old legs complain too much about the stairs, we'd love to have a big master bedroom on the main floor.

We aren't thinking about downsizing the house.

Then there's the motorcycle versus horse debate. Maynard thinks I should have a cycle so we can ride together. I think I should have a horse so I can ride with friends.

I'm not writing off either possibility.

Of course, I don't worship yellow cars, house additions, motorcycles, or horses. I am, however, just a little bit bothered by Ted Grimsrud's words in his book on Revelation, *Triumph of the Lamb:*

"We have to ask ourselves what values are calling the shots in our own decisions regarding how we spend our money, where we live, where we work, what (or even whether) we drive, how we spend our free time, what we say in public, and who our friends and associates are. These things say more than our words about what we worship."

Ouch.

—*Carol Duerksen*

PRAYING AND WALKING IN THE WORLD:

- If idolatry is defined as centering your life on anything but God, what's happening in your life?

- Meditate on this prayer: "Lord, have mercy on me, a sinner."

SEPTEMBER 10

THE SAME SUPREME SACRIFICE

PLUNGING INTO THE WORD:

Revelation 12:1-17

PONDERING ON THE WAY:

Several years ago, at a writers' workshop near Newton, Kansas, I heard a most interesting, profound comment from Duane Johnson of Topeka, Kansas. Duane's words had nothing to do with writing, but they had everything to do with faith, and with today's passage.

"We've chanted 'Give peace a chance' most of our lives, but what have we risked to bring it about?" Duane said. "The hard truth is that those of us who support nonviolence should be prepared to make the same supreme sacrifice as soldiers. But if we were to join groups such as Christian Peacemakers and inject ourselves between combatants in significant numbers, we would likely die in significant numbers.

"Those of us from the Baby Boom generation, having contributed to the conflicts that threaten to destroy humanity, should not expect our children, full of promise as they complete their education and begin careers of their own, to make that sacrifice. As we move into our 'golden years,' having already lived full lives, the time is approaching for us to live out what we have preached for so long and walk in the way of peace."

The most important statement in chapter 12 is found in verse 11: "They have conquered him by the blood of the Lamb and by the word of their testimony, for they did not cling to life even in the face of death."

Satan has been conquered, not by a violent force greater than his, but by the self-sacrificing death of the Lamb and those willing to die just as the Lamb died. Believers are safe, not necessarily from physical suffering, but from being separated from God. The dragon cannot destroy the church if it remains faithful.

Will being faithful mean a martyr's death for some of us? It seems improbable. But perhaps that's our challenge. Perhaps it shouldn't be such a far-fetched idea.

—*Carol Duerksen*

PRAYING AND WALKING IN THE WORLD:

- What do you think of Duane's words? Discuss them with your spouse, family, Sunday school, small group, coworkers, friends.

- Are you "martyr material"? Why or why not?

- Pray for Christians who are facing torture and death for their faith.

SEPTEMBER 11

THE ANTICHRIST WITHIN

PLUNGING INTO THE WORD:

Revelation 13:1-18

PONDERING ON THE WAY:

I am completing one of the toughest writing weeks of my life. Could you tell? Did you notice my need for a revelation on how to share about the Revelation to John?

I'm grateful for the insights gained from *Triumph of the Lamb* by Ted Grimsrud. More than once his words have offered not only helpful information on understanding the text, but also a challenge to what it means to my own life. It happened again as I studied this passage.

Grimsrud writes that the antichrist in this passage should not be seen as a specific person. Rather, the antichrist is "a spirit which is manifested every time people put their trust in values and institutions opposite of Jesus. The spirit of antichrist is present when people's loyalties to idolatrous nationalism leads them to take the lives of their 'enemies.' It is present when people's commitments to prosperity and the American dream causes them to close their eyes to others literally starving around them."

Gulp.

My husband Maynard is leaving in a month to go to Burundi, Africa, to follow the trail of the canned turkey that is handed out there from the Mennonite Central Committee meat canner. We are both excited about this opportunity. He will see people in situations he's never seen before. He will probably come back a changed man.

Just for a moment, one fleeting moment, the thought crossed my mind: What if he comes back and wants to give more money to the poor? What if it affects the dreams we have for our life?

I couldn't believe it. Why did that thought come to mind? What is wrong with me?

According to Grimsrud, this is the spirit of the antichrist. Suddenly, the beast is not somebody, something, or a nation "out there." The antichrist is the self-centeredness within my own heart. When my commitment to the American dream closes my eyes to my starving brothers and sisters, the spirit within me is anti-Christ. It is opposite the values of Jesus.

Sigh. It would have been easier to read Hal Lindsay's book or the *Left Behind* series. Less personally challenging, you know?

—*Carol Duerksen*

PRAYING AND WALKING IN THE WORLD:

- How do you feel about Grimsrud's interpretation of the antichrist? If you agree, do you see aspects of the antichrist in your life? If you don't agree, what do you think is the "mark of the beast" today?

- Read 13:9-10 again. Why do you think John is telling Christians not to fight against the beast?

SEPTEMBER 12

DRAGONS, ANGELS, AND WWJD

PLUNGING INTO THE WORD:

Revelation 14:1-15

PONDERING ON THE WAY:

Revelation has a real plague on it. How can a revelation, by definition a disclosure or an exposé, be so misinterpreted? It's just so hard to understand. There are so many symbols and so much imagery. Horse-heads, beasts, dragons, angels, multicolored horses, seals, Philadelphia, numbers, grapes—there are just too many confusing and unreal symbols.

Why couldn't the revelation be in layman's terms?

But here in this passage in the midst of flying angels and wine made out of anger and wrath (which doesn't go with pasta, fish, or chicken), there is a clear message. Follow the Lamb wherever he goes (Revelation 14:4).

Follow the Lamb. That's it. The ideal Christian is defined. Those who fall short will meet their fate in their own way, but the concern should not be on what color the scales of the Beast's left wing is, but simply on ... following. The saints are those who follow Jesus wherever he goes. And where did he go? To the cross by living the kind of life we all should live.

WWJD bracelets have passed their stage of popularity, but they were clever and catchy and true. We should do what Jesus did. How do I stop evil? What do I do when confronted with persecution? How should I live my life? How do I prepare for the end times, especially as I try to read an obscure book like Revelation? Follow the Lamb, follow the Lamb, follow the Lamb.

—*Michele Hershberger*

PRAYING AND WALKING IN THE WORLD:

- Think of some difficult decisions you may need to make. Look at the Gospels and ask yourself what Jesus would do.

- If you are not being persecuted for your faith, what does that mean? Does it mean no one knows you are a follower of Jesus? Is your understanding of Jesus so watered down that you don't offend any institutions? Or does it mean you're really lucky or blessed?

- Those who follow the Beast bear his mark, and those who follow Christ bear his. Whose name is on your forehead?

SEPTEMBER 13

EVIL DESTROYS ITSELF

PLUNGING INTO THE WORD:

Revelation 17:1-18

PONDERING ON THE WAY:

People do stupid things when they're drunk. We've all seen it. People get hurt, things are destroyed. Drinkers know that when they drink they could end up hurting themselves or others, or at the very least make fools of themselves through their loose tongues, uninhibited dance moves, or varying stages of sickness. Yet, thousands of people still drink every day.

In this passage, the inhabitants of Earth are drunk on Babylon's impressive powers and promises. They are intoxicated by the wonder and majesty of earthly institutions and creations. Humans know that the whore leads them into blasphemous idolatry and emperor worship (or in today's society, army or country worship) and yet, they still drink it in. The whore is responsible for the deaths of the martyrs and leads the people into her own brand of adultery. Here the people worship the dragon instead of God. Yet even the revelator is amazed by the whore.

You know, I never did trust Babylon. And as it turns out, neither does the beast. None of the evil creatures pictured here can trust each other. They are evil and therefore cannot fully cooperate even with each other. They wait until they can turn on each other, stab one another in the back so that one alone can have the power.

The "mystery" described here is more than things that were, aren't but will ascend, and then die. The mystery is that while the whore seems to rule over earthly kings and the beast, the beast hates the harlot and destroys her. Evil destroys itself. Evil hates and destroys itself. This is a kernel of truth about God's way of peace. God doesn't go to war. God's people do not go to war. Evil goes to war with itself! The beast, the sworn enemy of God, is carrying out God's plan without even knowing it. What an irony!

In this passage the writer is invited to witness the destruction of the whore to serve as a warning to those who are tempted to drink in the hallucinogenic that is power and might. He is there as a witness, as a truth-teller, as a warning to those who may want to party down.

But will we take the warning? We know all the horror stories about drinking. But will that stop us?

—Michele Hershberger

PRAYING AND WALKING IN THE WORLD:

- What are the Babylons of today? What idols are we asked to worship?

- What are ways in which evil destroys itself historically and continually?

- What happens when Christians try to destroy evil using some kind of an evil method? Do we become what we fight? Do the ends ever justify the means?

SEPTEMBER 14

THE POWER OF MONEY

PLUNGING INTO THE WORD:

Revelation 18:4-20

PONDERING ON THE WAY:

Some people just don't get it. It's one thing to be seduced by Babylon in all her glory, but the kings and the merchants are still mesmerized even as utter destruction rains down on the city. They weep. They can't see evil for what it is. They simply don't get it.

The Scripture is pretty clear here. Do not take part in Babylon's many, many sins, or you will fall with her. The city is down, down (in an earlier round) and the kings, merchants, and shipmasters (and butchers, bakers and candlestick-makers) go down with her, to a degree. They trusted in wealth and commerce over God, and it is their wealth that they lose. The people lamenting Babylon's fall do not die themselves. God doesn't want people to die, just the corrupt systems. God doesn't want people to die, but to repent.

And they are to repent from … a love of money. Money is dangerous. It may not be evil in and of itself, but it is a power. It longs to take the place of God, and in many people's hearts, it does. Money is dangerous on the outside and on the inside.

On the outside (in society) money widens the gap between the rich and the poor, leaving the poor oppressed. Money is a great temptation, and it brings with it the acceptance of cultural conformity. Finally, wealth brings a sense of overconfidence that blinds people.

On the inside, money and its comforts lull people into a sense of false security. People obsessed with money cannot see their own greed and the injustice of the disparity in its true light. They begin to worship money as a god. They start trusting money as their primary security.

But the god of money is a cruel taskmaster. In this passage, its true nature is revealed. In verse 11, there is a list of things that the merchants used to sell (of which they are mourning the loss). The cargo is listed in order of worth, starting with the most precious and ending with what is of least value.

The very last thing listed is human lives.

Don't be deceived. Don't let greed dehumanize you. Don't mourn for what surely enslaves you.

Let the beast go down.

—*Michele Hershberger*

PRAYING AND WALKING IN THE WORLD:

Take a hard look at your spending records for the last month. What story does your checkbook or credit card bill tell about what really matters to you? What would you mourn for in those records if they were destroyed? Holding your checkbook in your hand, speak to God. Listen for what God would say to you.

Works cited: *Triumph of the Lamb* by Ted Grimsrud (Wipf and Stock Publishers)

SEPTEMBER 15 *(FOR CHILDREN AND FAMILIES)*

WEDDINGS AND HALLELUJAHS

PLUNGING INTO THE WORD:

Revelation 19:1-10

PONDERING ON THE WAY:

Have you ever been to a wedding? Everyone is happy. The bride and groom are in love. Everything is decorated in pretty colors. There is music. There is yummy food. Sometimes there is dancing. People give presents to the couple.

There are a lot of traditions in weddings. There are groomsmen and bridesmaids, a flower girl and ring-bearer. The preacher asks if the two people will take care of each other for the rest of the lives. And the two people say "I do." There are traditions after the wedding too. There is a huge cake that the married couple cuts, and everybody gets a piece. The bride throws her flowers, and people try to catch them.

In some countries, weddings can last for days. In the Middle East, there are up to five parties given for a wedding. There are many other traditions that people use for weddings all over the world. For instance, wedding guests hold the bride and groom on chairs as they dance about the room in Jewish ceremonies, or shoot fireworks after a Chinese wedding. In America, the bride would wear white, but in Japan, a bride would wear a kimono with purple flowers.

In this passage, Jesus has triumphed over evil. Everyone in heaven is celebrating. Four times they sing, "Hallelujah." If you have ever heard a big choir sing the "Hallelujah Chorus," then imagine that song with a hundred times as many people singing. That is what heaven is like when Jesus is victorious.

Christians are the bride and Jesus is the groom. We will be united with God and live in happiness forever. There will be a huge party. We will eat and drink and sing and laugh. There won't be any more troubles—ever. Hallelujah! Praise God, hallelujah!

—*Michele Hershberger*

PRAYING AND WALKING IN THE WORLD:

- Have a pretend wedding with all the traditions that your family uses. Then have a party.

- Sing praise songs that have the word *Hallelujah* in them.

- **Adults:** The bride is clothed in fine linen, which represents the righteous deeds of the saints. If you were at the wedding, what would your clothes look like? What do your righteous deeds look like?

SEPTEMBER 16

NOT THE JESUS I KNOW

PLUNGING INTO THE WORD:

Revelation 19:11-21

PONDERING ON THE WAY:

I was reading through one of the *Left Behind* books, a popular series about the book of Revelation and the end times. While I realize, in humility, that Revelation can be a difficult book to understand and that I am in no position to claim myself an expert, I am fairly certain that something was wrong with the image of Jesus portrayed in this book.

It was the Jesus of Revelation 19. The authors did well to pick up on the detail of the sword coming out of Jesus' mouth in verse 15, and like me, they interpreted this as debar, or the powerful word that constitutes a major theme in the biblical narrative. But in the chapter I was reading, the words of Jesus—beautiful and true words— functioned as AK47s, riveting bullets that literally slaughtered the unfaithful.

That's not the Jesus I know.

I too believe in debar. Jesus is the Word, and there is no power greater than that of his word. As the writer of Hebrews says, this word is "sharper than any two-edged sword, piercing until it divides soul from spirit ... able to judge the thoughts and intentions of the heart" (Hebrews 4:12). In fact, his word is so powerful that it doesn't need to be a machine-gun bullet. That's not how the Word conquers evil.

That's not the Jesus I know.

But what if I'm wrong? I may be. But the proof is in chapter 19 itself.

In verse 13, Jesus is dressed in a robe dipped in blood. But the "battle" hasn't started yet. Where does this blood come from? It comes from the cross. The battle has already been fought.

The army following Jesus, here called the Word of God, is dressed in fine linen. This is hardly regulation military uniform. This is the same linen of Revelation 19:8, representing the righteous deeds of the saints. Is this a clue about how we are to fight evil?

And as the metaphors march on, we can see that there really is no battle anyway. The troops gather, and then it's over. And Jesus, in the end, fights evil in the same way he did when he walked the earth, by speaking the truth. By speaking the kind of truth that exposes evil for what it really is and thus destroys it.

The battle has already been won. And Jesus didn't need to use AK47s then either.

What if I'm wrong? I may be. But if I am, at least no one is getting killed because of it.

—*Michele Hershberger*

PRAYING AND WALKING IN THE WORLD:

- What do you think? Does Jesus change his character in the end times? Is part of worshipping the beast worshipping the efficiency and security of military solutions?

- Can the word of truth really defeat evil? If that seems impractical, think about this. Can Jesus defeat evil by using evil? Do the ends ever justify the means?

SEPTEMBER 17 *(FOR CHILDREN AND FAMILIES)*

NEW EARTH, NEW HEAVEN

PLUNGING INTO THE WORD:

Revelation 21:1-8

PONDERING ON THE WAY:

The end of the world seems like a scary time. When I used to think about the end, I thought that everything would be destroyed, but that was wrong thinking. In the Bible, God promised Noah that God would never destroy the world again. In this story, God promises that instead of destroying things and making new things, God will make the old things new again.

When you get your shirt dirty, you don't throw it away and buy a new shirt. Instead you wash it with soap and water, and it becomes clean. That's what God is doing with the world. Instead of throwing it away, God is making everything the way it should be—clean, strong, fresh, and new.

So instead of this being a scary time, it's very happy. There is no death, no crying or pain. God, who created the world and was there at the beginning, is still in charge of the universe at the very end. God is so powerful and good. We will be God's children forever and have everything we need.

Since God doesn't destroy the earth, it is clear that God really does love the earth and everything in it. All of creation, even though it has been polluted and damaged, can be saved and made new. If God cares for the earth, then we should too. If God won't destroy the earth, then neither should we. We are supposed to take care of the land and the animals, the plants and the air, so that the earth can be in the best shape possible when Jesus comes again.

—*Michele Hershberger*

PRAYING AND WALKING IN THE WORLD:

List things that make you sad. Then list all the things that make you happy. When Jesus comes back, all of the bad things will be made right, and the good things will last forever.

NEW JERUSALEM

PLUNGING INTO THE WORD:

Revelation 21:9—22:5

PONDERING ON THE WAY:

An impregnable city, a fortress.
A sword of fire blocks the only gate.

For millions of years we have walked through the wilderness.
Every night we dreamed of Eden.

Now is our chance.

Marked by sin, plagued at every turn,
But we survive with one dream in our hearts: Eden.

Jerusalem descends on a cloud.
A city pure as gold, its radiance dwarfs all other cities.

For millions of years we have walked through the fire.
Every day we dreamed of this city.

This is our chance.

A new city, a new bride.
O Death, O Babylon, where is your victory?

There is a light coming from everywhere and nowhere.
It shines off every jewel, through every person.

For millions of years we walked on this earth.
Every second we dreamed of this light.

Here is our light.

There is no night, there are no lies.
The new city is full of the glory of God.

The water of life flows as a river from the throne.
The tree of life blossoms, full of healing and forgiveness.

For millions of years we have walked with tears in our eyes.
Every day we dreamed of true life.

Now I kneel by the tree and weep.

For there is no more night, no more death.
The fortress stands open. The gates are open forever and ever.

—Michele Hershberger

PRAYING AND WALKING IN THE WORLD:

- Notice that the kings of the earth are included in the new church. What is God's ultimate goal—judgment or redemption? Destroying the sinner or the sin?

- The tree of life is used to heal all the nations, not just some. How is our society guilty of believing that God is only for one nation or people?

- Meditate on times when life has been difficult for you. Remember this passage when times become difficult again. It is a promise of the glory that awaits us.

SEPTEMBER 19

TRUSTWORTHY AND TRUE

PLUNGING INTO THE WORD:

Revelation 22:6-12

PONDERING ON THE WAY:

Are you really the Alpha and Omega
the first and the last
the beginning and the end?

The world's clouds disillusion us
our limitations depress us
weakness disappoints us

our souls groan with finite fickleness
we do not know where the mire and maze
begin and end.

We do not know how to begin to end
the confusion, the chaos, the lies
how to complete the healing;

the evil are still evil
the filthy are still filthy
the righteous still seek to do right.

The winds chill us to the bone
we long for the fire of your love
burning like sun above heavy hearts

we search skies for your return
a trustworthy and true promise
you are coming soon;

even as winter storms blow, your sun

breaks open our pain to unveil
a blue-skied forever of wholeness and worship.

Yes! You are the Alpha and Omega
the first and the last,
the beginning and the end.

—*Laurie Oswald Robinson*

PRAYING AND WALKING IN THE WORLD:

- Reflect on how knowing God as the beginning and end of all things helps you cope with your personal confusion and chaos.

- Give God praise and thanks that God's promises are trustworthy and true in a fickle world.

- Find a picture of the sun breaking through clouds and place it on your bathroom or bedroom mirror. Next to the picture, place the words from Revelation 22:6-12.

SEPTEMBER 20

BEARING THE BURDEN OF TRUTH

PLUNGING INTO THE WORD:

Amos 1:1-15

PONDERING ON THE WAY:

An unmarried friend of mine struggled to find a life partner. She finally met someone who seemed "perfect." But the Lord would not give her peace about the relationship. At the very least, she needed to give God time to work individually in their lives before they progressed as a couple. At the very most, it meant letting go of the relationship forever, leaving her free to meet someone else or to remain single.

I felt called to encourage her to "let go" of her immediate desires so she could fully grasp God's will, wherever it would lead. The message was uncomfortable to deliver and uncomfortable to receive. But we had built a strong bridge of trust in our longstanding relationship. I delivered the message in humility, and she received it with grace.

Amos was less fortunate in the trust category. He had no lineage of prophets in his ancestry and didn't come from Israel, where he prophesied. He was a herdsman of sheep and a tender of sycamore trees in Judah. God sought him out in the hills to send him to convey a warning of destruction to Israel. God's people were going through the motions of formal worship but were not living just and righteous lives that are the fruit of true worship. God would allow a total military disaster to strike the nation to punish the people and to shake up their denial that they had not kept their covenant with the Lord.

This wasn't the case with my friend. She walked close to the Lord, and her integrity was strong. Still, I bore the kind of burden that comes with speaking the truth in love. Truth often feels heavy, and, like Amos, we may not have the credentials that would make us feel worthy to speak out. But we learn from today's story that the crushing weight of falsity is much heavier than the burden of truth.

—*Laurie Oswald Robinson*

PRAYING AND WALKING IN THE WORLD:

- Reflect upon on a time when God called you to bring a heavy message to a family member or friend. Did you feel worthy to deliver that message? How was it received? Now, reflect on when you were called to receive such a message. What did you do? What was the result of heeding the message in humility and trust? What was the result of your disregarding the message?

- Prayer for increased courage to be a burden-bearer when God calls you to speak the truth in love to someone in your home or community.

- Have you been avoiding speaking the truth in love to someone recently? Seek an appropriate opportunity to do so.

SEPTEMBER 21

ANCIENT WARNINGS FOR TODAY

PLUNGING INTO THE WORD:

Amos 2:6-16

PONDERING ON THE WAY:

Since 9/11, the United States has fought wars in Iraq and Afghanistan in hopes of destroying terrorism. Left in the wake are dead soldiers and terrorists but also dead civilians. No statistics can tally all the loss of homes, communities, children, mothers, and fathers that come with the "gains" of making a more secure world. A military campaign that leaders called "just" has borne the bitter fruit of injustice.

Amos's ancient warnings are eerily relevant today. In verses 6 through 8, he tells the Israelites that God is deeply displeased. They have acted unjustly toward the poor, committed religious corruption, and denied good legal process. God led the Israelites out of Egypt's tyranny into a promised land of new freedoms. But they squandered this mercy in merciless acts, and they must answer to God for this misuse. In verses 13 through 16, Amos reminds them that their military might is no match for the power of God's righteous judgment.

First-world nations and leaders in workplaces and churches can be tempted to value the "muscle" of power over people. They need to practice power-sharing in just ways. People living in freedom are responsible for how they use that freedom. Will it be used to free people from fear—or to fetter them to new fear? Closer to home, will we use our personal power to better our loved ones and communities? Or will our hidden insecurities bring insecurity to others? In verse 16, Amos reminds us that people who dress themselves in a wrong use of power will become "naked." They will be exposed to their Creator, the one who has shown them justice and compassion and asks them to respond in kind.

—*Laurie Oswald Robinson*

PRAYING AND WALKING IN THE WORLD:

- Reflect on when you are most tempted to use the power of outward status, privilege, and rank to get your way. In what ways do these methods put you at odds with God's desires for justice and compassion?

- Pray for new insight about the power plays you pull in your relationships. When you become aware of these patterns, confess them and ask for forgiveness.

- Identify one person over whom you hold power. Do one activity with that person this week that brings a new level of mutuality and safety.

SEPTEMBER 22 *(FOR CHILDREN AND FAMILIES)*

FAMILY FUN, FAMILY FIGHTS

PLUNGING INTO THE WORD:

Amos 3:1-15

PONDERING ON THE WAY:

It's fun when our families go on vacation or enjoy a Saturday evening feast of pizza and ice cream at our favorite restaurant. It feels like the fun will never end.

Everybody's getting along and having a great time.

But sooner or later, disagreements pop up and somebody gets grouchy. Little fights—sometimes big fights—break out between family members. It's all part of being in a family.

God has a family too. Some of the first people in that family were the Israelites, who are part of today's Bible story. Amos, a man who brought God's message to the Israelites, told them that God was upset. God had treated them like family by providing for their needs. These people had been abused by a bad leader in a place called Egypt, but God helped them escape. But once the Israelites got to a new place, they treated people unfairly, just as they were once treated. Amos told them that this unfairness would backfire on them, and they would once again be surrounded by a new enemy.

God, as their heavenly parent, was hurt that they didn't pass on some of the love and care they received to the people around them. It's like when we fight with our brothers and sisters right after we get home from vacation. Our parents may give us that eagle eye that says, "We just gave you a special trip. Can't you show some thanks by getting along?"

We won't stop disagreements and fighting completely, but we can try to remember all of the good things we've been given and pass on more caring and kindness to other people.

—*Laurie Oswald Robinson*

PRAYING AND WALKING IN THE WORLD:

- Draw a line down the center of a blank sheet of paper. On one half, draw a picture of your family having fun. By drawing a smiley face, pretend God is smiling in the background. On the other half, draw a picture of your family fighting. Draw a frowny face. How did you feel when you drew the happy side? The unhappy side?

- In today's prayers, thank God for caring for you as God's child. Thank God for your earthly parents or guardians. And then ask God to help you care for others.

- Make a list of ways God has been kind to you and ways you want to be kind to others. Put it someplace where it will remind you to find one person at school or at Sunday school to whom you can show kindness this week.

SEPTEMBER 23

DEGREE-BY-DEGREE

PLUNGING INTO THE WORD:

Amos 4:1-13

PONDERING ON THE WAY:

After watching PBS programs on global warming, every weirdly warm day in December can send my thoughts into a tailspin. *We're in big trouble. We're going to "fry" or drown or be blown away.* Our local PBS TV station has featured documentaries on global warming, an increase in the temperature of Earth's atmosphere and oceans. Climatologists say an increase in the burning of fossil fuels in the last fifty years is the cause of increasingly severe weather, including more and larger floods, droughts, heat waves, hurricanes, and tornadoes.

Unfortunately, my fears about global warming have not caused me to change my lifestyle. I drive less than a mile to work when biking is very doable. I make unnecessary trips to the supermarket. And I join my fellow Americans in eating and buying more than is needed. Scientists warn that if we continue to deny what is happening, we will heat up the Earth degree by degree until we have destroyed our creation as we know it.

Amos says a series of disasters sent by the Lord failed to persuade Israel to return to God. Degree by degree, God tried to convince them to repent of their ways: a lack of bread, a lack of rain, and blight and mildew in gardens and vineyards. God intensified the warnings through pestilence and violence, but still, the people chose not to turn to God. So Amos told them to prepare to meet God—a God who is done with warnings.

In any age, people fail to heed intensifying signals that something is amiss. The saddest fact of this failure is not the impending destruction but the degree-by-degree denial that leads to destruction. But if denial is degree-by-degree, change also can be degree-by-degree. That is our hope, and that is our choice.

—*Laurie Oswald Robinson*

PRAYING AND WALKING IN THE WORLD:

- Reflect about a time when you received a series of increasingly intense warnings about a life situation. What happened when you heeded them? When you denied them?

- Ask God to help you turn toward and not away from God on a particular issue you have been avoiding.

- Rent the DVD, *An Inconvenient Truth,* a film about global warming featuring former Vice President Al Gore.

SEPTEMBER 24 *(FOR CHILDREN AND FAMILIES)*

BIG DIPPER AND A BIG GOD

PLUNGING INTO THE WORD:

Amos 5:4-17

PONDERING ON THE WAY:

Have you ever camped outside and searched the night sky for star pictures, called constellations? Perhaps parents or camp counselors pointed out the Big Dipper. Perhaps it felt so close in the clear night sky that you felt you could touch it or climb down its long handle into the dipper.

In today's Bible story, Amos, chosen by God to take messages to the Israelites, talks about how God created the constellations, such as the Big Dipper. Amos mentions two others—Pleiades and Orion. Orion, "the Great Hunter," is the largest of eighty-eight pictures in the sky. But Amos wasn't discussing the size of these constellations. He was describing the bigness of God, who created not only these star wonders but all of creation. God controls all of nature—night, morning, and the sea.

Amos told the Israelites they failed to listen to this big God. God had told them to try to do good things and not bad things. But many of the people chose to do the bad. People who had money treated poor people unfairly. God was very sad and angry about this. So God would allow these people who had everything to feel the pain of losing some of those things. They had made others cry. Now they would cry too.

God doesn't want anyone to cry. But sometimes, human beings choose not to listen to what would make them and others around them happy. Whether God speaks through the wonders of the skies or in the whispers of our own hearts, God wants us to listen. A big God deserves a big ear.

—*Laurie Oswald Robinson*

PRAYING AND WALKING IN THE WORLD:

- Draw a crayon picture of the Big Dipper. Or write a song or poem about a time when you and your friends and/or family enjoyed gazing at the night skies.

- In today's prayers, thank God for creating the skies, Earth, and all the peoples of the Earth. Ask the big God to give you a big ear to hear how God wants you to treat people who are close to you.

- Ask your parents or Sunday school teachers to take you to a planetarium where you can learn about the stars and the heavens. After you visit, talk about how a big and awesome God created all these wonders. Then offer a prayer of praise for God's bigness.

SEPTEMBER 25

LET JUSTICE ROLL DOWN

PLUNGING INTO THE WORD:

Amos 5:18-24

PONDERING ON THE WAY:

The ancient prophet Amos would have found good company with John Perkins, a modern-day African American from Mississippi. Perkins experienced oppression by whites, including the murder of his brother. Perkins wrote a book about his journey, *Let Justice Roll Down* (Regal Books, 1976). The phrase is a theme woven through Amos's message to the Israelites, and the oft-quoted Amos 5:24.

Perkins grew up in Mississippi in dire poverty and dropped out of school in the third grade. He fled to California when he was seventeen after his older brother's murder at the hands of a town marshal. Perkins vowed never to return to his homeland. But in 1960, after his conversion to Christ, he returned to share the gospel of Christ with his people. His outspoken support and leadership role in civil rights demonstrations resulted in repeated harassment, imprisonment, and beatings.

Amos didn't target racism specifically in his warnings but rather voiced the global theme of injustice. He did, however, target specific sins of the Israelites in verses 21 through 24. They committed many injustices. Yet they participated in religious events and gave God their offerings. But God would not accept their outward show of religiosity. God did not want a people who sang praise songs but did not touch the pain of the poor. God did not want the melody of harps but the melody of justice rolling down like waters, the sounds of right living flowing like a stream.

We may not have the name recognition of Amos or Perkins. But God knows our "name"—both the person we show to the world and the person we are when no one is looking. May the ancient and modern-day prophets inspire us to let the sound of "justice rolling down like waters" be the backdrop for all our public and private relationships.

—*Laurie Oswald Robinson*

PRAYING AND WALKING IN THE WORLD:

- If you were alive then, how old were you and where did you live at the height of the civil rights movement? Who most impacted you during that time? How does that person exemplify Amos's messages to the Israelites?

- Pray for a deeper integration of your public and private selves, asking God for new and creative ways to allow justice-keeping to become more of a priority in your worship and your work.

- Read *Let Justice Roll Down* aloud with a friend or your family. Discuss the relevance of its story and its message for your life today.

SEPTEMBER 26

ENOUGH ALREADY!

PLUNGING INTO THE WORD:

Amos 6:1-8

PONDERING ON THE WAY:

I read this passage
Mulled it over
Decided
"It's about materialism,
Being comfortable,
No worries,
Feeling secure,
And God's not impressed
With those attitudes."

I read the commentary
On this passage:
Same interpretation.

Enough already!
I screamed silently.
Why do so many parts of Scripture
Address the same theme?
Why do I have to keep writing about this?
Enough already!

And God said,
"Touché."

—*Carol Duerksen*

PRAYING AND WALKING IN THE WORLD:

- Do you think the Bible addresses materialism too much? What are your thoughts and feelings when you read those passages?

- Another theme addressed in this passage is the "pride of Jacob and his strongholds." The people had placed their security in the city strongholds they built, and they were proud of these strongholds. What are our contemporary strongholds? Do we depend on them for our security?

- Pray for the leaders of the country and the nationalism that seems to be inherent in our country's attitude toward others.

SEPTEMBER 27 *(FOR CHILDREN AND FAMILIES)*

A PLUMB LINE

PLUNGING INTO THE WORD:

Amos 7:1-9

PONDERING ON THE WAY:

Familiarize yourself and your children with a plumb line by using online resources, a local hardware store, or a contractor. You can even make your own plumb line by using a string and a heavy weight.

A plumb line is a simple tool used for determining whether or not something is perfectly vertical or upright. Used since very ancient times, a plumb line is just a line and a weight of some sort, at first just a stone, but later a weight made from lead. The weight will point directly to the earth's center of gravity, and that will determine the vertical from a given point.

In today's Scripture passage, Amos had a vision of God standing beside a wall with a plumb line, symbolizing that God was measuring how "upright" the people of Israel were. Had their lives been aimed directly at their center of gravity—God?

Nope. They were crooked.

God was very upset at the children of Israel for being crooked. Just like parents who get upset when their child disobeys them, God gets frustrated when we don't obey God's words. Sometimes, our disobedience gets us into trouble, or something bad happens. It's like building a house without using a plumb line. It's not where we want to live.

—*Carol Duerksen*

PRAYING AND WALKING IN THE WORLD:

- What happens when we don't have God as the center of our lives? How is that like living in a crooked house?

- A necklace with a stone on it can be a symbolic plumb line. Wear one as a reminder to keep your heart centered on God.

- Pray this centering prayer:

    God be in my head and in my understanding.

    God be in my eyes and in my seeing.

    God be in my ears and in my hearing.

    God be in my mouth and in my speaking.

    God be in my hands and in my holding.

    God be in my soul and in my believing.

    Amen.

SEPTEMBER 28

NO PROPHET

PLUNGING INTO THE WORD:

Amos 7:10-17

PONDERING ON THE WAY:

I am no prophet
Daughter of a Kansas wheat farmer
And a stay-at-home mother.

I live on a farm
Tending sheep and other critters
My husband works with trees

One evening in the darkness of a car
Traveling to a family gathering,
We talked.
I wondered out loud about writing a devotional book
Noting
The impossibility of doing a year by myself.

And Maynard said:
"Then you need to get some other people to help."

And God said to three women
In the midst of multitasking
Overbooked lives
"Go, write a book.

"Read the Word of the Lord,
Listen
Write."

    —Carol Duerksen

PRAYING AND WALKING IN THE WORLD:

- Whether or not you feel like a prophet, God has called you to a ministry. Ministry happens whenever you touch another life with God's love. How are you a minister of God's love?

- Someone has said that authentic ministry involves comforting the afflicted but also afflicting the comfortable. What do you think?

- Listen to your inner voice. What is God calling you to do that would be impossible without God?

SEPTEMBER 29

ELEPHANT IN THE ROOM

PLUNGING INTO THE WORD:

Amos 8:1-14

PONDERING ON THE WAY:

I believe there's a bigger issue for congregations to be talking about than all of the things thrown together that we disagree on. It's something we don't talk about because it is very personal, and because it affects all of us. We don't talk about it because every one of us would have to examine our hearts and our motives, and how they match up with God's Word. We don't talk about it because we know we wouldn't agree. We don't talk about it because we don't view it as a "sin." We view it as a personal choice, and heaven forbid that we should counsel each other on what to do with that choice.

The "elephant in the room" is the almighty dollar. Is it okay to make a lot of money? Is it okay to spend it on ourselves? Is it okay to pray for prosperity? Is it true that there is abundance available for everyone—we just have to discover how to access it?

Is it wrong to own a luxury car when people in Africa don't have enough to eat, or is it a good thing because the car builders are feeding their families too? If I can afford something, why not own it?

The issue of money—how it's obtained and how (or if) it's shared just keeps coming up, doesn't it? In this passage, we see that the business practices of the children of Israel were deplorable. They sought wealth at the expense of the poor. They couldn't wait for the Sabbath to be over so they could sell wheat. They actually changed the scales to balance products more in their favor.

I know someone whose business practices seem to be just the opposite of those in this passage. He sells things to people who have trouble paying for them, and then he doesn't pursue them to collect the money. He's not wealthy—he could use the money. He just doesn't hassle people for payment. Why? That's what I want to know. If I sell something, I want my money. I don't want people to take advantage of me.

I have a lot of questions about the role of money in our lives. I hear good sermons about it, but we don't talk about it over dinner at the Pizza Hut after church. I doubt it will ever spark the heated discussions in our conference that some other issues have. And, in light of how many times wealth is addressed in the Bible, I wonder why.

—*Carol Duerksen*

PRAYING AND WALKING IN THE WORLD:

- Invite several people over or go out for a meal together and discuss the questions posed in this devotional: Should our goals include making a lot of money? Is it okay to spend it on ourselves? Is it okay to pray for prosperity? Is it true that there is abundance available for everyone—we just have to discover how to access it? Is it wrong to own a luxury car when people in Africa don't have enough to eat, or is it a good thing because the car builders are feeding their families too? If I can afford something, why not own it?

- Pray for God's guidance in the money issues of your life. Do you *need* more money? Do you *want* more? Is anyone taken advantage of when you make money? How do you share your money?

- Pray the Lord's Prayer. Although the word money isn't mentioned, how do you think the topic is addressed in the prayer?

SEPTEMBER 30

A GOD PLANTING

PLUNGING INTO THE WORD:

Amos 9:11-15

PONDERING ON THE WAY:

The small hills of my Kansas farm don't drip wine like the mountains in this passage, but when the setting sun kisses the prairie grasses and the world turns golden, I am drunk with pleasure. Some of the sweetest apples and apricots I've ever tasted come from fruit trees just outside my door. I can walk through our 120 acres of forest, hilltops, creek, pond, alfalfa, natural grass, and pasture, and every time I do it I am amazed that this belongs to us. This land is ours. This is where I am planted.

Is there anything sweeter than planting your own vineyards and fruit trees and enjoying the harvest? Is there anything more satisfying than turning over your ground with a plow? Is there anything more beautiful than tall rows of lush, green corn soaking up a humid Iowa day? If farming is in your blood, the answer is no.

In today's passage, God promised the children of Israel their heart's desires. Not only will they plant vineyards and drink of the wine, but God will plant them upon their land, never again to be plucked up. If there's anything better than being planted in your land, it's having God do the planting.

I believe God planted us here. The circumstances surrounding the purchase of this farm were amazingly "coincidental." In the past eleven years, Agri-Urban and the youth group from Tabor and Goessel Mennonite churches have used our farm and animals to entertain and educate thousands of people of all ages. What happens here at the "Day on the Farm" in August and the living nativity "Night in the Barn" in December is way beyond what people can plan. It's a "God planting." And for me, it's as amazing as mountains dripping with wine.

> —*Carol Duerksen*

PRAYING AND WALKING IN THE WORLD:

- How and where has God planted you?

- Are you experiencing God's harvest in your life? How has God blessed you beyond what you could ever imagine? Do you praise God and thank God for those blessings?

- Pray for the persons in this world who are displaced—those who are not in their land due to conflict between countries and civil wars. Pray for those in refugee camps, and for the people who are giving their time and energy to minister to them. How is God calling you to help them?

OCTOBER 1

THANKS IN THE MIDST OF MESSINESS

PLUNGING INTO THE WORD:

1 Corinthians 1:1-17

PONDERING ON THE WAY:

"If we do not give thanks daily for the Christian fellowship in which we have been placed, even where there is no great experience, no discoverable riches, but much weakness, small faith, and difficulty; if on the contrary, we only keep complaining to God that everything is so paltry and petty, so far from what we expected, then we hinder God from letting our fellowship grow according to the measure and riches which are there for us all in Jesus Christ. ... The more thankfully we daily receive what is given to us, the more surely and steadily will fellowship increase and grow from day to day as God pleases" (Bonhoeffer, _Life Together_, 29-30).

Well said, Dietrich Bonhoeffer. I don't know if you read this well-known German theologian or not. If you do, you know the power of his words. If you don't, it's not too late in your faith journey to start. I can almost guarantee his writing will impact your life.

Take the quote above for example. Set it alongside Paul's words to the Corinthians, and we get instructions to give thanks for God's presence in our fellowship of believers, and to do that first and foremost. Before Paul shares his concerns and admonishments with the church at Corinth, he praises God for them and he affirms them. Despite all of the difficulties, divisions, and disagreements the Corinthian church is facing, Paul sees the church as the work of God in the world. The body of believers is God's body in the world—God's hands, feet, eyes, and ears. Broken and scarred though we may be, we are all God has.

Scary, isn't it?

"Has Christ been divided?" Paul asks, and we could ask the same question. In the midst of our quarrels and denominational divisions, we belong only to Christ. Christian community, according to Bonhoeffer, is "not an ideal which we must realize; it is rather a reality created by God in Christ in which we may participate" (30).

—_Carol Duerksen_

PRAYING AND WALKING IN THE WORLD:

- If you are part of a church, thank God for each member. Pray your way through the church directory. (This may take more than a day! Keep the directory with your Bible and devotional materials.)

- First Corinthians 1:4-9 are great verses to commit to memory. Go for it! Hear God saying them to you. Put the name of your congregation in place of each "you" in the passage.

OCTOBER 2 *(FOR CHILDREN AND FAMILIES)*

TOOT YOUR HORN

PLUNGING INTO THE WORD:

1 Corinthians 1:18—2:5

PONDERING ON THE WAY:

Do you know what it means to "toot your own horn"?

If not, here are some possibilities for you to choose from:

    A. Buy a trumpet and blow it.

    B. Brag about yourself.

    C. Play a kazoo.

    D. Play a French horn instrument.

The answer is … all of the above.

Let's look at the answer, "Brag about yourself." If you "toot your own horn," it means that you talk about how good you are in something. You make a big deal about yourself. You tell people that you are really smart, or an awesome soccer player, or the best singer in your class. "Tooting your own horn" means it's all about you, and you want to make sure everybody knows it!

The Bible says that God chooses people who aren't necessarily "the best" at anything. Why? Because God loves everybody equally, and because God wants our faith to be based on God's power, not on our own goodness.

"If you're going to brag, brag about God," the Bible says.

It's wonderful to be good at something, and those abilities are gifts from God to you. Rather than tooting your own horn, though, toot a horn for God!

—*Carol Duerksen*

PRAYING AND WALKING IN THE WORLD:

- **Adults and children:** Play kazoos together as a praise song to God.

- **Adults:** Do you feel wise? In which areas do you feel as if you have wisdom, and in which areas do you feel like a fool? Spend time in prayer, thanking God for the wisdom you have, and for God's ability to use you both as a wise person and as a fool.

- Read chapter 2, verses 1-2, again. Are there times when you or other Christians you know spend too much time in lofty words, polished speeches, and theological debate and not enough time focusing on Jesus? What would it mean to change that?

OCTOBER 3

ODE TO A FOOLISH WOMAN

PLUNGING INTO THE WORD:

1 Corinthians 2:6—3:4

PONDERING ON THE WAY:

That's what they would have called you
Did call you, behind your back, at least some
> Foolish
Foolish to not pursue a better career
Foolish to squander your intellect,
for pete's sake, the church?
Mission work?
Where is that gonna get you
Except a dingy room in Hanoi
One lousy lightbulb
To grade your papers by.

So much potential.

You look at me with those eyes.
Yes, I understand
Children in Puerto Rico need to learn English
Children in Cambodia
Children in inner-city Philadelphia
and Vietnam

But when they captured you
For teaching from a British newspaper
Did you think it was a wise choice then
Teaching English in the armpit of the Communist regime?
Where'd it get you
Sleeping on a jail cot between three guards.
What were they afraid of—that you'd hit them
Over the head
With the Bible and escape?

They were afraid of you
Tiny Kansas woman

For the foolish way the students clung to you
For the irrational way you loved
Living among them
They were afraid of you
Tiny Kansas woman
Armed with a wisdom they could not know.

So much potential.

You had a secret
A calmness during the interrogation
Offering warm tea to the men ransacking your apartment
Refusing to go to breakfast at the jail because
You would not miss your time of devotion and prayer.

You foolish wise woman.

In that moment
In that instant between "I will not go to breakfast" and the moment
They backed away staring
Did your heart clutch in fear?

Or were you wise enough to know
That even if they killed you,

You still would have won.

So much potential.

O tiny Kansas daughter, in your foolishness
In your wise foolishness

You won.

—*Michele Hershberger*

This poem is in memory of my sister-in-law, Miriam Hershberger, who served in Vietnam under MCC. She was arrested, interrogated, and deported in the early 1990s.

PRAYING AND WALKING IN THE WORLD:

- What does it mean to be "of the flesh"? Are you mature or still an infant spiritually?

- Are you ready for solid food? Are your ears and eyes ready and receptive to the Spirit?

- What are ways that human wisdom and true, divine wisdom seem to contradict each other?

OCTOBER 4

Y'ALL ARE THE TEMPLE OF GOD

PLUNGING INTO THE WORD:

1 Corinthians 3:5-23

PONDERING ON THE WAY:

"Y'all come back now, y'hear!" I was born in Missouri, and yes, people actually said that to me. I spent every summer of my childhood in a tiny town where the biggest tourist attraction was a half-sized Wild West village set up in someone's front yard.

But *y'all* isn't just for Missouri folk. It's also good Greek. Here too, it's not given its proper due, at least in English. Verse 16, in Greek, contains a plural you. As in, "you all are God's temple."

I cannot count how many times I've heard that my body was a temple and that I should therefore treat it with respect. (That's true; see chapter 6.) But it's also true, and maybe even more important to Paul, that all local believers—together—form God's temple. God's Spirit dwells where multiple believers come together in peace and love.

Let's be honest. It's easier to preach against drinking beer than against quarreling in the church. But Paul here says that if we destroy God's temple—that is, the local community—God will destroy you. Pretty serious. I think we need to hear more sermons on the importance of our congregational life together.

We all are God's temple. We keep up maintenance through shalom living. We destroy God's temple by arguing, hypocrisy, bickering, gossip, and backstabbing. Our community, when it functions in love, is where the Spirit dwells. The foundation is in Jesus. The walls are built up with prayers, good works, service, peace, and justice. The church is not a building, and it's not the leaders either, but the people who serve and worship in it.

God's temple is holy, so take care of it.

—*Michele Hershberger*

PRAYING AND WALKING IN THE WORLD:

- How does a new interpretation of this passage affect your opinion of people who abuse alcohol? What about people who argue and fight?

- Give your church a careful inspection. How are you building on the foundation of Jesus? Where do you spend your time and energy?

- Notice in verse 15, even if the work doesn't survive, the builder will still be saved. We cannot earn salvation with good works. What then is the purpose of doing them? To earn salvation or rewards, or to glorify God?

OCTOBER 5 *(FOR CHILDREN AND FAMILIES)*

FOOLS FOR CHRIST

PLUNGING INTO THE WORD:

1 Corinthians 4:1-13

PONDERING ON THE WAY:

Once there was a boy named Dave. Dave couldn't run very well. One of his legs was shorter than the other. He couldn't see very well either. He had to wear glasses. Plus, he had asthma. He sat out in gym class, even though he loved to play games. It was hard for Dave to do what he loved because he would run out of breath or lose his glasses. What's worse is that the other kids picked on him. Instead of trying to make him feel better, they called him names and pushed him around on the playground.

One day, the kids decided to play baseball. The captain of one team, Adam, went to Sunday school every Sunday, and he heard that we are to love everybody. So he picked Dave for his team. Adam felt funny inside when he picked Dave. Would the other guys laugh at him, like they did at Dave?

Dave didn't suddenly become a great baseball player. In fact, their team lost. But there was a miracle, even if it didn't happen on the field. Adam had shown Dave that he was accepted, and that made Dave feel like a superstar.

The kids on the other team made fun of Adam because he picked Dave. The kids on Adam's team were mad at him. They called him a fool for giving Dave a chance, but Adam knew that's what Jesus would've done.

Sometimes being a Christian means looking a little silly, or doing something unpopular. Sometimes you may be tired or hungry. Sometimes people will call you a fool, but what is foolishness to the world is wisdom in God's eyes.

> —*Michele Hershberger*

PRAYING AND WALKING IN THE WORLD:

- Are there people you have judged before you really got to know them? Maybe now is a good time to give them another chance.

- What are some things that Jesus did or asks us to do that may seem foolish?

OCTOBER 6 *(FOR CHILDREN AND FAMILIES)*

ROLE MODELS

PLUNGING INTO THE WORD:

1 Corinthians 4:14-21

PONDERING ON THE WAY:

There are many people in our lives who teach us what it means to serve God. They are courageous, loving, kind, and generous people. They are role models. God sends people into our lives to help us live like Jesus. We need other people to help us understand what God wants us to do.

I have lots of role models in my life, just in my own family.

My dad used to sell propane. Even when people couldn't pay, he still took them the propane because he knew that the people would need it when the weather got cold. He showed kindness and generosity, without expecting anything for it. He knew that God would take care of him and his family.

My Great-Grandpa Kropf taught me how to stand up for my beliefs. He refused to pay special taxes for the government to go to war, because he believed that the war was wrong. People came to put hot tar and feathers on him so he would look like a big chicken. The tar would burn his skin and hurt him badly. But when they got close, they saw something or someone that Great-Grandpa Kropf couldn't see. They screamed with fear and ran away.

My husband's parents had a visitor at their house named Victorino. He was a refugee. His family lived in another country, but he couldn't live there and he didn't have a home. My mother and father-in-law let him stay at their home for three years. They taught me a lot about what really matters—people.

Timothy was sent to the church in Corinth (which is in present-day Greece) to be a role model. He showed the people there how to be good Christians. People like Timothy are around in my life and in your life too. We should be very grateful to have people to help us live right.

—*Michele Hershberger*

PRAYING AND WALKING IN THE WORLD:

- Who are role models in your life? Write one of them a letter, thanking them for showing you how to be a good person.

- Think of stories of people you know or have read about who did something extra special for someone else or who were extra brave in doing what they believed was right. What is your favorite story?

- How can you be a role model for others?

OCTOBER 7

YEAST IN THE MIX

PLUNGING INTO THE WORD:

1 Corinthians 5

PONDERING ON THE WAY:

I don't know a lot about yeast. I use it to make bread. I watch in fascination as it interacts with warm water and sugar.

It grows.

So tiny and yet so strong.

I guess that's how sin works too. Sexual misconduct, especially in this chapter, doesn't seem so tiny, but on the other hand, it isn't the only sin in town. Paul speaks against quarreling and discord in the church as much as he speaks against inappropriate sexual practices (that's what "being of the flesh" means in chapter 3). But you don't hear that sermon much these days.

But back to our topic—yeast—sin. Any sin. Paul says that we can't tolerate sin in our midst. The brother or sister in Christ who won't repent must be kicked out. It seems harsh, but that sin, left unchecked, works like yeast and infiltrates the whole batch of dough.

You have to expel the sinner to save the church.

But it also, ironically, may save the sinner. What if being on the outside, says Paul, is the only thing that will help this person want to get back in?

Sometimes you don't know what you've lost until you lose it.

> —*Michele Hershberger*

PRAYING AND WALKING IN THE WORLD:

- Is there yeast in your congregation? Do you love your sisters and brothers enough to hold them accountable? It's not right to kick them out immediately

(Matthew 18), but it also isn't right to pretend nothing's wrong just to avoid conflict.

- Is there yeast in your life? Can you find someone who can help you get rid of it? For your own sake?

- Reread verses 9-13. Paul is not advocating that Christians stay away from all persons who sin—only other believers. Ironically, some congregations do the opposite. They look the other way while people in the congregation have affairs, embezzle, or waste away from alcohol abuse. But the new people better quit smoking and cover up those tattoos before they attend the ice cream social. What about you? Your congregation?

OCTOBER 8

CHRISTMAS TREES AND TRUSTING GOD

PLUNGING INTO THE WORD:

1 Corinthians 6:1-11

PONDERING ON THE WAY:

"What should I do?" Dave asked. He crossed his arms and sighed. Forty thousand dollars was a lot to lose just because another Christian wouldn't pay up. Christmas tree farming wasn't that lucrative.

My husband, Del, and I didn't know what to say. As his pastors, we knew the "right" answer. Don't file a lawsuit against a brother in Christ. It didn't need to be spoken. We all knew what had to be done. Or rather, not done.

But it was so hard. Dave had four children. This loss represented a year's salary. What if next year's crop of trees failed? Or the price of fuel increased? Or the market went soft?

Yes, Paul's right. Christians shouldn't take each other to court.

But Paul, Christians shouldn't live in such a way that anyone would want to take them to court.

Exactly, says Paul. But two wrongs don't make a right.

God was asking Dave to trust him.

But the man got off scot free!

Trust me.

But how will I pay my bills?

Trust me.

But what if it happens again?

Trust me. Trust me.

>   —*Michele Hershberger*

PRAYING AND WALKING IN THE WORLD:

- Note that chapters 5 and 6 are put together for a reason. Should we expel the Christian who is unjust instead of taking him to secular court?

- Does your congregation work this way? What would you have said to Dave?

OCTOBER 9

WHY DO THAT?

PLUNGING INTO THE WORD:

1 Corinthians 6:12-20

PONDERING ON THE WAY:

You can almost hear the debate going on among some of the Corinthian believers and Paul. They say, "Hey, God gives grace, right?" And Paul says, "Well, yes, but—why would you want to do that?" They say, "But, aren't we free? Aren't you the big champion of freedom from the rules of Jewish law?" Paul says, "I hear what you're saying. But in one way, you are not free; you have been bought with a price." They say, "We don't want to get legalistic here." And Paul says, "No, we don't. But again, if you have truly become a new person, why would you want to do that?"

For the Corinthian church, the struggle was about prostitution, a practice not only legal but a widely accepted social convention. Couldn't Christian men participate?

We may not struggle in our congregations with this particular issue, but the deeper issue that Paul raises is as important to us as it was to them. The Corinthians claimed that every sin was outside the body. In other words, it didn't matter what you did with your physical body. What matters was spiritual health alone. Paul refutes that heartily. God created our bodies as good things. We are to take care of them. Even more, we belong to God and to one another in the church, not to ourselves. Fornication, or any other sin, affects the whole local body of believers, and it threatens the intimate union we have with Christ.

Paul says to us, "If you truly have become a new person, why would you want to do that?"

—*Michele Hershberger*

PRAYING AND WALKING IN THE WORLD:

- If prostitution isn't the issue today, what is? Or do we still struggle with this type of sin?

- Do you feel the tension between God's grace and our call to discipleship? How would you explain this balance to a new believer?

- In what ways do you harm part of God's good creation—your body? What do you need to ask forgiveness for? In what ways can other believers help you stay accountable?

OCTOBER 10

MARRIAGE BUILDERS

PLUNGING INTO THE WORD:

1 Corinthians 7:1-9

PONDERING ON THE WAY:

During engagement and my first year of marriage, I devoured books on relationships between spouses and the genders. After each book read, I called my sister to share its gems. It became a standing joke, as she exclaimed, "You could be a marriage counselor by now!" The jab in her joke is that reading about glorious possibilities in marriage wouldn't exempt me from needing to apply these ideals in the demands of the daily grind.

Every book in one way or another agreed with Paul: Wholesome and exclusive sexual relations are marriage builders that fight against marriage busters in secular culture. Biblical commentators agree that Paul was radical for his day when it came to sexual relations. It was assumed a husband had authority over his wife but not the wife over the husband. But Paul counteracts this in verse 4 by saying that the wife and husband have mutual authority over each other's bodies. She belongs to him, and he belongs to her.

That belongingness counteracts attitudes of our culture, rife with individualism and pleasure-seeking. We may faithfully observe the boundaries of marriage but chafe at the sacrifices of love. We delight in the honeymoon days. But as years grind on, our once-frequent rushes of romance trickle into infrequent and mechanical sexual relations. If we don't nurture regular sexual intimacy within marriage's monotonies and responsibilities, the desire we once had for pleasing our beloved turns into mere pleasure release for self.

Paul encourages couples, whether newly married or celebrating decades-long anniversaries, to nurture belongingness by uniting sexually. Achieving this unity is neither automatic nor easy and takes a lifetime of failures and recommitments. But it can help hold together what our world tries to pull apart.

—*Laurie Oswald Robinson*

PRAYING AND WALKING IN THE WORLD:

- Reflect together with your spouse about how monotony squelches sexual passion. Talk with each other about how you can rekindle some passion. If you are single, find trusted others with whom to talk about what this passage means for those who are not free to express their sexuality in genital union.

- **Married couples:** Pray that the Holy Spirit's fruits of love, joy, and peace, as well as skills of communication and kindness, would help reinvigorate your desire for sexual union. **Single persons:** Pray that God would help direct your sexuality toward wholesome relationships.

- Read a book about building a strong marriage. Possibilities include: *Fighting for Your Marriage* by Howard J. Markman, Scott M. Stanley, and Susan L. Blumberg; *The Mystery of Marriage: As Iron Sharpens Iron* by Mike Mason; and *Theology of the Body for Beginners* by Christopher West.

OCTOBER 11

TWO SPIRITUALITIES, ONE COUPLE

PLUNGING INTO THE WORD:

1 Corinthians 7:10-24

PONDERING ON THE WAY:

A growth curve in my marriage is realizing that Alfonso's spirituality is different from mine. Because he doesn't often verbally express his devotion to Christ, I'm tempted to think he doesn't experience a vibrant relationship with God. But I'm realizing how wrong I am. As an extrovert, I talk about God a lot. But Alfonso forgives more easily than I do, more effectively living that love in practical, down-to-earth ways. When it comes to human weakness, he is more patient with me than I am with him. He expresses his devotion in loving deeds, a style that maintains a needed equilibrium in our home.

These differences give me an understanding of Paul's theme in today's passage, even though our examples are dissimilar. He's discussing a believer and nonbeliever trying to live under the same roof—not just a style difference in Christian discipleship. But a parallel can be drawn. He counsels us to bear with differences. Verse 15 says that it is to peace that God has called us. A marriage stamped with God's peace has a saving, preserving quality even amid differences that run the gamut from food preferences to faith perspectives.

In verses 20-24, Paul reminds us that we must let each other live the life God calls us to live as individuals. He discusses slavery and circumcision, topics far from our modern-day experience. And yet he expands on the idea of slavery by saying that a slave is a freed person belonging to the Lord, and a free person is a slave of Christ. No matter where our spouses are in their relationship with God, we all need grace and freedom. We all need to grow as we will, not as another one wills for us.

—Laurie Oswald Robinson

PRAYING AND WALKING IN THE WORLD:

- Reflect on your style for expressing your relationship with God. How about your spouse? Do your differences cause conflict? How does God's peace bridge the gap? If you are single, how does the nature of your walk with God impact your close friends and extended family?

- Pray for the grace to focus on your need for growth rather than on the needed growth of those in your close circle. Journal about what you experience as you concentrate on your own quality of spirituality.

- Take a personality test and compare it with a spouse, friend, or family member. What does the test reveal about your differences in spirituality?

OCTOBER 12

SINGLES IN A MARRIED WORLD

PLUNGING INTO THE WORD:

1 Corinthians 7:25-40

PONDERING ON THE WAY:

During my forty-six years of singleness, my other single friends and I often lamented about being single in a married world. Our most acute pains came not from secular society but from our congregations. Many church activities revolve around families and couples. And when single ministries do begin, they often flourish for a short time and then die a slow death. *Singles* covers such a broad spectrum of people. It is complex to minister to a crowd that includes those who have never been married and those who are single again because of the death or divorce of a spouse.

In today's passage, Paul's take on singleness is much more positive. He says singleness can be superior to marriage in its ability to allow one to focus on the concerns of the Lord rather than on the concerns of one's spouse or children. Biblical commentaries say that in Paul's day Christians believed the end times were near, as is suggested in verses 29-31. So being unencumbered as a single person was considered a plus in days of uncertainty.

Perhaps the deeper counsel from Paul isn't about one's single or married state as much as it is about the need to establish a servant-hearted commitment to one's calling, no matter what it is. In either the single or married state, one is not to be self-centered, but other-centered (vv. 32-35). Caring about others is not the exclusive privilege of those who live in families under the same roof. God desires a caring attitude from all of God's people.

Because caring requires time, single persons can find more freedom in ministering to others. Our congregations must recognize the preciousness of singleness. We must name it as the reputable vocation it is and that many make it to be.

—*Laurie Oswald Robinson*

PRAYING AND WALKING IN THE WORLD:

• If you are single, reflect on what most keeps you from using your freedom to care about others. If you are married, reflect on how you can be less self-centered in your home and with others in your church family. Reflect especially on what can keep you from caring more about singles. How open and caring is your church toward singles? If you are married, how open and caring are you?

• Pray for God to help you develop a deeper commitment to be a servant-hearted person, whether single or married.

• If you are single, invite a family over for dinner or dessert, or make plans to meet at your favorite restaurant. If you are married, invite a single person to enjoy an extended family gathering with you and yours.

OCTOBER 13 *(FOR CHILDREN AND FAMILIES)*

YOUR BEDTIME, THEIR BEDTIME

PLUNGING INTO THE WORD:

1 Corinthians 8:1-13

PONDERING ON THE WAY:

Are you the oldest, middle, or youngest child in your family? Depending on where you are in the lineup, your bedtime or your other privileges may not be the same as that of your brothers and sisters. When I was eight years old, my brother was just becoming a teenager. I had to go to bed earlier than he. He also got to go to the movies with his friends. But I could go only with my parents. Because of our age difference, he got more freedom than I did, and that didn't always feel fair.

Today's Bible story talks about how we can be tempted to act like "big shots" with those who don't have as much freedom as we do. We may rub their faces in the fact that we are older and bigger and that we know a lot more than they do. But verse 1 of today's Bible story says that "knowledge puffs up, but love builds up." As loving Christians, God wants us to make sure our freedom doesn't hurt someone else. Rather, we are not to take advantage of our extra privileges. Perhaps we could even give up a privilege so we could play with a little brother or sister. Sure, a movie with friends is *a lot* more exciting. But for a small sacrifice, you can make a big difference in a little one's day.

Today's reading reminds us that it is not how big in age or how much we know that matters most. What makes us big in God's eyes, and causes God to really know and relate to us, is how big our love is for God and others.

—*Laurie Oswald Robinson*

PRAYING AND WALKING IN THE WORLD:

- Talk with your parents and brothers and sisters about what feels fair and unfair around your house. Honestly air your feelings.

- Pray together about finding new and creative ways to engage in family activities that include all ages.

- If you are a big brother or sister, give up an afternoon or evening with friends to play with the little ones in your home. If you are a younger child in your family, invite your big brother or sister to do a special activity with you this month.

- **Adults:** The big issue for the Corinthian congregation was whether to eat meat placed before idols. Paul cautions those who have the "right" theology (it's just meat) to really love the brothers and sisters who have a different theology. In other words, having the right love trumps good theology. What's the issue in your church?

OCTOBER 14 *(FOR CHILDREN AND FAMILIES)*

ADULTS ARE PEOPLE TOO!

PLUNGING INTO THE WORD:

1 Corinthians 9:1-14

PONDERING ON THE WAY:

As a little person, it's sometimes easy to forget that big people have needs too. It's the job of parents, teachers, and pastors to take care of you. God gives you adults to guide you and to make sure you grow up well. But it's also good for you to recognize that when good things come your way, it's important to say "thanks."

For example, in today's Bible story, the apostle Paul encouraged people to thank those who shared the gospel with them. He suggested they should help the ministers to have enough food, clothing, and other necessary items to live healthily.

You can do simple things to show thanks. You could give your dad a hug for helping you learn to ride bike; make a thank-you card for a Sunday school teacher who taught you about Jesus; or bake chocolate chip cookies for your teacher's birthday. And because October is the month set aside in the United States to show appreciation for pastors, you could do something for yours. Perhaps your family could invite the pastor and his or her family over for supper. Or, you could treat them to an ice cream outing or give them a gift for their office or home.

Adults don't expect you to take care of them. But they would feel great if you showed them some special kind of kid-caring. Big people need love too.

—*Laurie Oswald Robinson*

PRAYING AND WALKING IN THE WORLD:

- Talk with your parents or other adults about what kids can do to make them feel special.

- In your prayers today, ask God to make you more aware of all the good things adults provide for you. Thank God for giving you caretakers.

- Get out your crayons and construction paper and make thank-you cards for your parents, one of your school teachers, and one of your Sunday school teachers. Thank them for something special they have done for you lately.

ADJUSTING YOUR RACE PACE

PLUNGING INTO THE WORD:

1 Corinthians 9:15-27

PONDERING ON THE WAY:

A college coach in my community created a conditioning program for people who wanted to exercise after work. Every evening, a handful of us met at the college stadium for "dog days," when we did a half hour of squats, sit-ups, jumping jacks, and laps. When the coach left for another school, one of the more fit women in our group took leadership. She was a former high school sports star and was in great shape. She could lap us several times over. But when she was done, she joined the slower ones and ran the last laps with us at our pace. She never failed to cheer us on, "Great job. Good work. Keep going." We wanted to die, but she gave us the courage to doggedly finish the course.

Her motivational gifts are how I visualize Paul's spirit in today's passage. In verses 19 through 23, he describes what it means to "coach" those in spiritual training. To the Jews, he became a Jew in order to save the Jews. To the weak, he became weak so he could win the weak. He became all things for all people so that he might save some. He sacrificed his pace to help others take their first baby steps toward God.

While he mentored others, Paul also kept in spiritual shape himself. He modeled what it means to run in such a way as to win the spiritual race. Paul trained doubly hard and gave up some of his freedom so he and others could win the eternal prize.

—*Laurie Oswald Robinson*

PRAYING AND WALKING IN THE WORLD:

- Reflect on what it means to be a parent or mentor. What does it mean to adjust your pace for the good of another's "race"? When is it most difficult to do this? When do you receive the most joy in doing this?

- During some moments of silence, close your eyes and visualize running your last laps around a tough "track" in your life with Jesus at your side. How do you feel? What is he saying to you? How does he encourage you to finish?

- Even though it is an old film, hunt down *Chariots of Fire* and watch it with your family and friends. How does it exemplify today's passage?

OCTOBER 16

FALLEN AND FAITHFUL

PLUNGING INTO THE WORD:

1 Corinthians 10:1-13

PONDERING ON THE WAY:

During this test, my wilderness is hot, dry, difficult
to find comfort, I feast on idol delicacies—
too much food and too many things,
too much searching for human approval,
too much complaining.
After days of this feasting,
I hunger anew for Moses and Christ,
for the eating of the lean desert food
of my Israelite ancestors,
for the drinking from the hard rock of Christ.
But like my former brothers and sisters,
just when I think I stand, I fall.
In this failure, I search
for God's baptizing tears
in the cloud and in the sea.
I cannot feel God's comfort
but in the midst of this heat
I hear a stream trickling beneath sand.
Soon Jesus will quench my thirst;
soon Jesus will make a way.

—*Laurie Oswald Robinson*

PRAYING AND WALKING IN THE WORLD:

- Reflect on your most intense spiritual test at this time. What kind of temptation is it evoking?

- Pray for new perseverance to rely on God's faithfulness to provide a way through your fallen human patterns.

- Share your temptation with a trusted spouse, friend, or clergy person. Ask that person to pray for you daily and to meet with you weekly or biweekly until you have passed the "test."

OCTOBER 17 *(FOR CHILDREN AND FAMILIES)*

"I" IS FOR IDOL

PLUNGING INTO THE WORD:

1 Corinthians 10:14-22

PONDERING ON THE WAY:

What is an idol? Look it up in the dictionary.

One of the definitions I found is "an object of extreme devotion." An idol is something we worship and love more than God.

It's easy for us to say, "I don't have any idols. I don't love anything more than God." It's easy to say that. It isn't so easy to *practice* it.

For example, imagine that you are driving past a Wal-Mart. Wal-Mart has a toy or video game you have been wanting, and you are just *dying* to go in there and buy it. You start begging to go get it, and then your parent says: "How about if you put that money in the offering at church for the school kits we're sending to children in Africa?"

You want to help those children in Africa—you really do. But you want that toy too. It's a tough decision, isn't it?

Those children are children of God just like you are. They have so little compared to what you have. Buying toys isn't wrong. But if having more and more toys is keeping you from sharing with others, then it is harmful. It's possible that a toy or video game you want is an idol if you consider it to be more important than helping others.

Talk about it. What might be the idols in your life?

—*Carol Duerksen*

PRAYING AND WALKING IN THE WORLD:

- **Adults:** Is busyness an idol for you? Do you have "so much on your plate" that you don't have time for God's work? God's people?

- **Adults and children:** Are sports an idol for you?

- Pray for your eyes to be opened to the idols that take your worship away from God.

OCTOBER 18

BLACK AND WHITE OR FULL COLOR

PLUNGING INTO THE WORD:

1 Corinthians 10:23—11:1

PONDERING ON THE WAY:

My husband grew up Amish. His mother and half of his siblings are still Amish, and we see them at least once a month for family get-togethers. They use a horse and buggy for transportation, don't have electricity, don't attend school past eighth grade, and their predominantly homemade clothes follow a certain pattern. Years of traditions and religious standards have given them clear lines to follow regarding acceptable behaviors. From the outside, it would appear that theirs is a world of black and white choices.

Guess again. The horse and buggy is used for transportation in the Yoder, Kansas, community, but tractors and trailers are a much quicker mode of getting around, even for entire families. In Missouri, where Maynard's Amish brother is a dairyman, electricity is allowed in the dairy barn but not in the house. In certain communities in Indiana, stocking caps and enclosed buggies are forbidden. As consistent as the Amish may appear to the outsiders' eyes, there are many variations from community to community as to what is lawful.

And why, we might say, is an enclosed buggy or a stocking cap wrong? Why does the barn get electricity but not the house? It's all a matter of each bishop and his group deciding what is lawful for them.

The issue of what is lawful was the challenge presenting itself to the Corinthians in this passage, and it presents itself to us today. How do we determine when we place limits on our own freedom for the sake of others? This is not a black and white issue—it wasn't for the Corinthians and it isn't for us. We decide—as individuals, as churches, as denominations—what is lawful for us. Paul gives us a bottom line: Whatever we do, it all must be done for the glory of God. He moves us from thinking about *what I can do* to *how God can be glorified.*

I know that we intend to glorify God in our choices and decisions, but I have to wonder what would happen if we specifically used that guideline as a measuring stick. Maybe if we became less focused on drawing lines and more intent on pointing all lines toward God, our lives would break out in a celebration of Spirit-infused colors.

—*Carol Duerksen*

PRAYING AND WALKING IN THE WORLD:

- Recall or locate a hymn or contemporary praise song with the theme of glorifying God. Bring that song to mind often—let it "play in the background" as a theme for your daily life.

- Where do you need to let go of black and white lines so you can praise God with full-color joy?

- Where do you need to set boundaries so your freedom isn't a stumbling block for others?

OCTOBER 19

CHEW ON THIS ONE

PLUNGING INTO THE WORD:

1 Corinthians 11:2-16

PONDERING ON THE WAY:

Okay, here goes. The woman with quite short hair who kept her name when she got married twenty-six years ago is going to write about one of Paul's controversial passages on women and men in the church. I take a deep breath …

For starters, I'll say I don't understand it all, and neither do many scholars who have spent much more time studying the Scriptures than I have. We know that there are obvious cultural differences between Paul's day and ours. Paul was addressing specific problems at Corinth. What we need to know is: What does that have to do with us today? What do I take out of this for my life?

One commentator I read said that Paul was talking about honor and shame issues in verses 4-6, and that it might be the same as saying to today's church: "Men shouldn't come to church wearing dresses, and women shouldn't come to church topless."

I laughed at that, and then I thought: But what if it was a church in Scotland, and the men were wearing ceremonial kilts? Or what if it was a congregational meeting of an African tribe where topless women were the norm?

Even the interpreter's attempt to put it in modern-day language wasn't one hundred percent successful.

I took the passage to Michele and Laurie in one of our book-writing meetings. Michele reflected on the fact that although cultures and contexts change, eternal truth doesn't, and the eternal truth in this passage is: "Are we honoring one another?"

Laurie shared that she'd done some journaling recently that might help in our interpretation of this passage. I asked her to send that journal to me, and here it is:

This morning, I was thinking about how I am really a free spirit and how even though my nature is highly creative, it also can drive others crazy at times. I want to do what I want to do when I want to do it. But life and marriage and job and ministry often require more structure, discipline, and accountability. My prayer this morning is that I would not so much be a "free spirit," but that I would be a spirit who is free to follow and obey God.

Yes. The Spirit who spoke to Paul and the church at Corinth is the same Spirit who helps us discern the truth for us today. The eternal truth here, I believe, is that the Spirit calls us to honor and respect one another even as we are postmodern "free spirits." May our unchanging God guide us in a changing world.

—*Carol Duerksen*

PRAYING AND WALKING IN THE WORLD:

- Read the passage one more time and choose a nugget of truth with which you can resonate. What stands out that supersedes cultural differences?

- Pray for humility—in hearing God's word, in your relationships with men and women, in your relationship with God.

OCTOBER 20

THE NOD

PLUNGING INTO THE WORD:

1 Corinthians 11:17-34

PONDERING ON THE WAY:

Communion is being served at Tabor Mennonite Church near Goessel, Kansas. The deacons pass the trays of bread down the rows, and when everyone is served, we partake. Then the cup. Round silver trays of tiny juice glasses are passed down the pews. I take a cup and turn toward my sister in Christ seated next to me. Our eyes meet, she nods, and I partake.

"The Nod" is a tradition at Tabor—a simple, powerful tradition that I believe would receive the apostle Paul's nod of approval. It's one thing to take communion as a symbol of Jesus' sacrifice for me. It's another thing to physically acknowledge my relationship with other Tabor members when I take the cup.

What if I disagree theologically with the brother next to me? What if the sister seated beside me said something that hurt my feelings? What if, when our eyes meet, we both know that we don't always see eye to eye?

The Nod gives me a choice. I can chicken out and choose to sit beside someone I know is "safe." Or I can choose to sit beside someone who pushes my comfort level. I can choose to "examine myself, and only then eat of the bread and drink of the cup."

As a Mennonite, my *Confession of Faith* states that in the Lord's Supper, we remember how Jesus laid down his life for his friends, and as his followers, we recommit ourselves to the way of the cross. We confess our sins to one another, and we receive forgiveness, coming as one body to the table of the Lord.

May we all know the cleansing power of The Nod in our hearts and souls. May we truly come to the Lord's Supper as one body.

—*Carol Duerksen*

PRAYING AND WALKING IN THE WORLD:

- Is there a Christian brother or sister with whom you have issues? Can you, with integrity, take communion with them? If not, what are you willing to do about it?

- What are the traditions that make the Lord's Supper meaningful for you?

- Prior to the next time you participate in the Lord's Supper, take some significant time to pray and prepare your heart, both in relationship with Jesus and with your sisters and brothers in Christ.

- Paul warned of great judgment for persons who do not "drink worthily." This verse is not so much about doing communion in a wrong way, but about social inequalities in the fellowship. The free and wealthier Christians were not waiting for the Christians who were slaves. Are there social barriers in your church?

OCTOBER 21

BUT HIS GIFTS ARE SO ... DIFFERENT

PLUNGING INTO THE WORD:

1 Corinthians 12:1-11

PONDERING ON THE WAY:

A former youth pastor friend of mine—I'll call him Les—tells the story of inviting congregational members to assist him in the youth ministry program of the church. "See me after church if you'd like to help," Les announced one morning. After the worship service, as people filed by him, he looked hopefully into the eyes of those with whom he'd like to work, and then Les noticed someone we'll call Mike who was … well … different. "Please God, don't let it be Mike," he prayed silently.

Yes, Mike was the only one to stop and talk to Les.

And so the partnership was formed. And they disagreed on almost every approach to every program and situation. But they survived the first year.

The second year, Les put out the plea again. Surely others would volunteer. But at the end of the worship service, Mike alone stood in front of him again.

For five years, Mike and Les worked on youth ministry together. Les admits he never did understand Mike's ideas and his way of doing things, but he is also quick to say that Mike was called by God just the same. The same Spirit lives within both of them, although it was obviously expressed in different ways.

We can read this familiar passage from Paul and affirm what it says, but living it out is often another challenge. What if a person's gifts are not only different from ours, but they affect the way we want to see things happen? What if the amazingly creative pastor has such a cluttered office, she can't find important papers? What if the highly organized secretary finds herself steaming every time the pastor makes a last-minute change in the bulletin?

What if the children's Sunday school teacher offers a child-size altar call every Sunday, and you don't believe in "child evangelism"?

This isn't easy. Being followers of Jesus doesn't cure our humanity—our tendency to think negative thoughts, gossip, and disagree. But our declaration of "Jesus is Lord" offers hope for our humanity. Because we agree on this, we pray for the patience to do God's work alongside each other, appreciating the different Spirit-gifts within our sisters and brothers.

> —*Carol Duerksen*

PRAYING AND WALKING IN THE WORLD:

- Do you have people like Mike in your life? Resolve to pray God's blessing upon that person every day for the next month.

- This passage mentions the gifts of speaking in tongues and interpretation of tongues. Visit a congregation where those gifts are manifested in worship services. How do you feel about those manifestations?

- Use the words "Jesus is Lord" as an internal mantra when you find yourself in disagreement with a brother or sister.

OCTOBER 22 *(FOR CHILDREN AND FAMILIES)*

WHEN FEET SMELL AND A NOSE RUNS

PLUNGING INTO THE WORD:

1 Corinthians 12:12-31

PONDERING ON THE WAY:

Depending on the age of your children, read today's passage to them from the Bible, pausing to talk about the practical applications of our bodies needing many different parts to work together.

Discuss:

- What can each part do that other parts can't do?

- A nose smells, and feet run. When do feet smell and a nose runs?

- Do you like where ears and eyes are located? What would happen if their places on the head were switched around?

- What is a really tiny part of the body that is very important?

- What is a part of the body you keep covered most of the time? Why?

- What is your favorite part of your body? Why?

- What is it that your body can do that you think is the most amazing?

Continue this discussion based on your children's interest.

Just as our bodies are unique and made up of many different parts, as children of God we are all different but important to the work of God in the world. For example, think about the many different people in a church. Some people are great singers, and some keep the church building clean and comfortable. Some people love to make food, and some would rather be teachers. Some people are really good at visiting other people, and some people give money. There are many things to be done in God's church, and it takes everyone doing their part to make it work.

If you are part of a congregation, talk with your children about what roles different people play. What roles do children play? What do your children enjoy about being in the church?

—*Carol Duerksen*

PRAYING AND WALKING IN THE WORLD:

- **Adults:** Statistics say that twenty percent of the people do eighty percent of the work in most congregations. Where do you fit in? Do you need to share more of your gifts? Do you need to set aside priority time for your family and your own spiritual growth?

- What do you enjoy doing that hasn't yet been shared with God's kingdom? How can you make that happen? Pray about it.

OCTOBER 23

LOVE LESSONS

PLUNGING INTO THE WORD:

1 Corinthians 13:1-13

PONDERING ON THE WAY:

Paul did not write these words for weddings. He didn't intend for them to be associated with starry-eyed couples and pastors trying to find new ways to talk about the same words. He wasn't talking about people who were "in love," floating on an emotional high.

Quite the contrary. Paul was addressing the church community—people like you and me who find that feelings don't cut it when it comes to loving each other day in and day out. Feelings come and go. Love stays around. Love sticks it out. Verses 4 through 7 give the specifics. If you can do these things and think these thoughts as you relate to the body of believers, you are truly a lover.

But being this kind of lover is tough. Love has to be practiced. It's hard work—work that we can't do on our own. God's transforming power isn't so much about a feeling of love as it is giving us strength to stick with it—to keep on practicing. We need to "work out what God has worked within."

If we truly can learn to live with and love a brother or sister who drives us crazy, our congregational life would change, and so would our marriages. These words may not have been written for weddings, but they certainly apply to marriages—probably more so after twenty-five years than on the wedding day. You need these words because, after twenty-five years, you've heard his same jokes a hundred times. You've heard her embarrassingly loud snoring every night. You've experienced the changes that menopause brings physically and emotionally. You've taken "outgrown" clothes to the secondhand clothing store. You've survived his annoying habit, and you've noticed that sex isn't what it used to be.

You're learning what it means to bear all things, believe all things, hope all things, and endure all things. You're learning what the "love chapter" is really about.

—*Carol Duerksen*

PRAYING AND WALKING IN THE WORLD:

- Locate a book that elaborates on the characteristics of love in this passage. Read it, study it with others, put it into practice.

- Memorize this passage—or at least verses 4-7. Say it every day. Let the words become your actions and attitudes.

OCTOBER 24

A DOMESTICATED SPIRIT?

PLUNGING INTO THE WORD:

1 Corinthians 14:1-25

PONDERING ON THE WAY:

If you could describe the gift God has given you as a musical instrument, what would it be? Lead trumpet? The bass clarinet that lays the foundation? The melodic flute? The soulful sax? The cymbals that strike a dramatic note or clash around a bit?

Whether brass, woodwind, or percussion, Paul says in chapter 12 that we need to play in the band and appreciate the other band members. And, he adds this important note (small pun intended): The music needs to make sense. The flute and harp need to make distinct notes, the bugle a clear call.

Hey, Paul, haven't you ever heard of improv jazz?

I do appreciate Paul's words here. And I agree that everything we do in our congregational setting needs to build up other believers. That's part of pursuing love. There is a clear need for order and clarity in the church. Yes.

But I sometimes wonder if we've taken Paul's words further than he would have intended. Paul knew God to be a God of order, not disorder; and he understood the importance of using minds as well as emotions. But the worship services I participate in are at times so head-centered, so orderly, that my emotions aren't stirred at all. The order is so dominant, so pervasive, that the Spirit isn't welcome. The Spirit gets domesticated, and we like that because we like things safe and predictable.

Now, maybe that's my own fault. Maybe this is part of my culture.

Or maybe some of us are afraid to let go a little. Should there be an interpreter when people pray in tongues? Yes. Should there be tongues? Yes.

> —*Michele Hershberger*

PRAYING AND WALKING IN THE WORLD:

- If you could give yourself a grade on how open you are to change, what would that grade be?

- Would Jesus say you need more order in your life or more flexibility? Can you pray about this and ask for help?

- Do you appreciate the other "instruments" in your congregational orchestra? Write a letter to the "musicians" you take for granted the most.

OCTOBER 25

CONFESSION TIME

PLUNGING INTO THE WORD:

1 Corinthians 14:26-40

PONDERING ON THE WAY:

Confession time. I am a woman who has spoken in church, who speaks in church regularly, and I'm not just referring to potluck directions in the back kitchen.

And I also consider myself a lover of Scripture, a committed Christian who believes in the inspiration of Scripture.

Even this passage.

So how do I dare make both of these statements with any kind of integrity? Believe me, I struggled long and hard with this.

I could give you all sorts of logical and even biblical reasons justifying the permission I feel to teach and preach in church. First Corinthians 11:5 comes to mind, where Paul gives specific cultural instructions to women *when* they pray and prophesy in church. The arguments are many and varied.

But I'd rather just say this. I feel called by God. I say this with great humility and even a little fear—I really do want to honor the Scripture as the highest authority in my life—but I must respond to this calling. I have a burning in my soul to speak the truth God has given me. Like Jeremiah, I can't keep quiet.

I can't keep quiet.

I write this devotional with tears. My local congregation has outwardly affirmed my call to speak, and I try to be sensitive to those who view 1 Corinthians 14 differently than I do—those who give this Scripture greater weight than the passages that affirm female leadership in the church. But I know this is a painful subject for some of my dear sisters and brothers, people who love Jesus and the Scriptures as much as I do.

And so we continue the dialog. We commit to loving one another. We pray.

We confess.

> —*Michele Hershberger*

PRAYING AND WALKING IN THE WORLD:

- What do we do when the Bible seems to speak with different voices on a subject? A Christocentric way of interpreting the Scriptures would advocate for looking closely at the life and teachings of Jesus. How did Jesus treat women and others who were considered marginal?

- How does this Scripture fit with the earlier verses of chapter 14? Was there a need for order as Paul and the early Christians tried to live the tension of being in a specific culture and trying to live the timeless truths of the gospel?

- Who is a Christian woman who has impacted your life for good? Have you ever thanked her for that?

OCTOBER 26 *(FOR CHILDREN AND FAMILIES)*

HE'S ALIVE!

PLUNGING INTO THE WORD:

1 Corinthians 15:1-11

PONDERING ON THE WAY:

Jesus is alive! After being dead, he's alive again! First Corinthians 15:3-11 is a great summary of the resurrection event. Read the Scripture passage to your children, then review these facts and ask the corresponding questions.

- Jesus died for our sins. What is a sin? Do you know how Jesus died?

- Jesus was buried in a tomb. What is a tomb? Jesus' tomb was in a cave. Can you tell me what really big thing was rolled in front of the cave like a door?

- God raised Jesus back to life. Do you know which day God did this? How do you think Jesus got out of the cave? How would you have felt if you saw Jesus alive after he had been dead?

- Then Jesus appeared to Cephas. Cephas is another name for Peter, one of Jesus' special friends. Sometimes these friends are called "the Twelve," and sometimes they are called "the disciples." Can you name some of the other disciples of Jesus?

- Jesus appeared to more than five hundred people and then to James and then to more of Jesus' friends. Can you guess how many people all together saw Jesus? (We can't really know for sure.)

- Last of all, Jesus appeared to Paul. Paul is very thankful that Jesus came to him because he didn't feel as if he deserved it. Before he met Jesus, what did Paul do that was bad?

Now, give your children a chance to ask any questions they might have. It's important that they are encouraged to process this important story. It's okay if they can't understand everything.

—*Michele Hershberger*

PRAYING AND WALKING IN THE WORLD:

- Take time to pray, thanking God for making Jesus come alive again.

- Hand out modeling clay to the children. Have them make figures of Jesus, the cave, the stone, Peter, and the other friends of Jesus. Act out the story with the clay figures.

- **Adults:** Has Jesus appeared to you as "one untimely born" (see v. 8)? Do you consider yourself an apostle (a sent one)? Would you call yourself the least of the apostles or some other title? Why?

OCTOBER 27

ONE OF THOSE MOMENTS

PLUNGING INTO THE WORD:

1 Corinthians 15:12-34

PONDERING ON THE WAY:

There are those moments, singular moments, when time seems to stand still and you know your next decision, your next move, is crucial. You could go one way or the other, say one thing or its opposite, and one way would lead to light and the other darkness.

I had one of those moments with Florence. Florence was a dear friend, almost a second mother to me. She was dying of liver cancer. And I was a young pastor. Her pastor.

Florence looked at me with big brown eyes framed in pain, and asked, "What's going to happen to me when I die?"

A thousand words, at least five different explanations, all straight from seminary or good books, a watershed of emotions—all flooded my brain. What do I say? "Well, theologians disagree on what exactly happens. It depends on how you interpret ..."

No. That wasn't the thing to say.

She continued, clarifying herself, having no idea that my head was frozen with ideas. "I'm not afraid of death, just a little worried about the transition."

And then the moment came. I suddenly found the words to say. It didn't matter to Florence or me that we knew exactly what happened at death. I knew, with a clarity I have seldom felt since, that Jesus was going to come and help her make that transition.

And that's what I told her. We made a plan. She was to tell us when death was near, if she could still speak. If she couldn't speak, then somehow she would try to signal us as best she could. And our job, as family or close friends, would be to remind her to take the hand of Jesus. This was our grace-filled way of giving her permission to die and a way of reminding all of us that she would not be alone on this journey.

The morning of her death, she made a noise. We drew near. Her eyes opened wide. She did something she had not been able to do for days. She lifted her hand off the bed … and clasped a hand we could not see. She smiled. And then her hand went limp. She was gone.

I have never been the same.

I know something I cannot prove.

I don't really care about how all the details work out.

I know hope.

—Michele Hershberger

PRAYING AND WALKING IN THE WORLD:

- What would you have said to Florence?

- Thank God for his resurrection power.

OCTOBER 28

DORITOS IN GLORY?

PLUNGING INTO THE WORD:

1 Corinthians 15:35-49

PONDERING ON THE WAY:

Should I eat this bag of Doritos? What a crazy question to ask when working with this Scripture! What do tortilla chips have to do with the resurrection of our bodies?

Maybe a lot. We know we all will be changed. The big question of this passage is, How will we be changed?

How will we be changed? That is the question Paul struggles to help us understand. How is a seed similar to and also different from the plant that grows when the seed dies? What is the difference between an earthly body and a heavenly body? What will my imperishable body look like someday? Is the spiritual body still a "body"? Will I be a spirit, or will I be able to pinch myself for joy at the resurrection?

I don't know for sure, and maybe it doesn't matter.

Actually, I think it does matter. Paul says we will be resurrected as Jesus was.

I see two options. I could be a spirit or a ghost, still talking, still thinking, and responding but without a physical body per se. The second option is a truly "new" body, where I can be touched and I still have freckles (we can only hope), but I won't get sick or feel pain.

Paul says we will be resurrected like Jesus. So will I able to walk through walls like Jesus did after his resurrection? That would be different from my present body. Will I eat fish like Jesus did after his resurrection, something I do every day (not the fish part)?

I vote for this new kind of physicality. Why? Because God in the biblical narrative has consistently affirmed the physical body. Creation is good, says Genesis 1, and while it is not divine, it is to be cared for and nurtured. Nature, including my physical body, is something wonderful that God created.

This is where the Doritos come in. How we decide on this issue affects our ethics. If my body will not be redeemed in any way, then why not treat it like trash? Why not party on the weekends? Why not eat the whole bag?

But … if my body is an integral part of my life with God after death, if my freckles will accompany me to glory, if my new body bears even a trace of resemblance to my earthly body—then I need to care for it. Not that God won't cure the physical problems I have or will have someday. The point is, however, that it will still be physical in some way.

How I treat my body matters.

> —*Michele Hershberger*

PRAYING AND WALKING IN THE WORLD:

- Take some time to thank God for your body. Pray like this: Lie on the floor and isolate different muscles in your body. For example, tighten the muscles in your fingers for fifteen seconds and then release. Work from your feet up to your head. As you tighten a certain area of muscles, thank God for your body and everything you can do physically.

- Take the next three days and keep a body journal. Write down everything you eat, how much you exercise, and what you do to help yourself relax. The point is not to lose weight but to help you become aware of how you treat your body.

- Do you struggle to believe in the resurrection? Talk to God about this in prayer. Ask for help, for guidance, for peace.

- Enroll in an exercise class. Pilates is great!

OCTOBER 29

O DEATH, WHERE IS YOUR STING?

PLUNGING INTO THE WORD:

1 Corinthians 15:50-58

PONDERING ON THE WAY:

I remember with fondness a certain plaque on the wall of the babies' room at Zion Mennonite Church. It read, "We will not all die, but we will all be changed." The verse was placed, appropriately so, above the changing table.

Joking about death in the church nursery is always pretty easy. Toddlers crawl up to you and stretch out their chubby hands. You feel their smooth skin and breathe in that wonderful baby smell. They wiggle and cry and touch everything. Their tiny red cheeks move ever so slightly as they breathe their baby dreams. They are so alive. They are so alive.

But right outside the window of the baby nursery at Zion Mennonite, you can look out over the field and parking lot and into the cemetery. It has its own beauty. It's a green, lush carpet, dotted with ornate stones in various shapes and conditions. Some have begun to crumble from the rains and beating sun, from a hundred years of watching others living. What does the phrase, "We will not all die, but we will all be changed" mean in this place?

I think it means this: We can still laugh. We can still laugh in the face of death. Resurrection means that the worst enemy of all, the hardest tyrant, the last dreaded word, the final blow—isn't final. Death has been swallowed up in victory. The sting of death, sin, has been defeated. Jesus fought the most powerful enemy and won!

Sin may still change a baby's smooth face into an old man's wrinkles, and sin may still take a young mind and make it confused, but that's as far as sin gets to go.

The final say belongs to Jesus.

—Michele Hershberger

PRAYING AND WALKING IN THE WORLD:

- What makes you more comfortable? A nursery or a cemetery? Why?

- Reflect on your life in this way: What are some of the actions you do that are indirectly (or directly) ways to avoid death? How are these actions related to sin in your life? What would you change about your life if you had no fear of death?

OCTOBER 30

PAUL'S BLOG

PLUNGING INTO THE WORD:

1 Corinthians 16:1-12

PONDERING ON THE WAY:

I feel that, in a way, Paul's letters are like a blog, an Internet diary of sorts. People log on to their respective websites and write the things they did, or the things they plan to do, or the thoughts they've had recently. What really sets a blog apart from a traditional private journal is that almost anyone can read it. Even if the intended audience is a select group of people, it can fall into anyone's hands.

Basically, this is true for Paul's letters. Meant for certain churches in a certain time, millions of people throughout the world now read and study them. Paul was way ahead of his time on this one, much to the benefit of the whole world.

Of course, there are glaring differences between the average blog and Paul's letters. For one thing, a blog can be written by anyone who knows how to type, whereas Paul was a learned man, a miracle-worker, a pastor, a church planter extraordinaire, and author of a huge chunk of the most-printed, most-read, and most holy book in the known history of humanity.

This is what a blog might look like, if Paul were here today:

> Hey Epaph (Epaphroditus), I haven't writen ina long time, bc I been really busy. Timothy finally came down to see mehere in prison. Supa siked to start to get out and GET TO ROME!! J an so my LAST CONVO WITH Priscilla and Apollos was rockin awesome an I got a new *computer* (which I am usin rite now!!). Woot, woot. Me and Onesimus are heading toward Philemon's place we are going to rock that house church soon! Peace and grace out.

Unlike a blog, Paul's writing has value to more people than just the latest readers on FaceBook. These are specific instructions to a real, living congregation. Even though we are eavesdropping on a two-thousand-year-old conversation, there is so much we can learn: I need to follow the directions of my pastor better. I need to save more money. I need to tithe more money. I need to invest more into a relationship. I shouldn't count on anything—it is only and always if the Lord permits. Wide doors for effective work in the kingdom have opened up for me. There are many adversaries. I hope the church doesn't eat up my friend. Someone I know is being stubborn …

Basically, he's saying: Behave yourselves; and sometimes things don't work out.

They seem like fortune cookies, these pithy phrases, but they each reflect truths in each of our lives at one point or another. That's more than I can say for most blogs, but more on that later. It's time to update my Myspace.

> —*Tara Hershberger*

PRAYING AND WALKING IN THE WORLD:

- Which statement is the most like you? Which is the least like you?

- How can reading the works of righteous people show us how to emulate them? Are you really reading all of Paul?

- If you had to write a set of instructions to your congregation, what would it say? What if someone from your congregation wrote to you?

OCTOBER 31 *(FOR CHILDREN AND FAMILIES)*

LOTS OF LETTERS

PLUNGING INTO THE WORD:

1 Corinthians 16:13-24

PONDERING ON THE WAY:

Paul wrote a lot of letters. Half of the books in the New Testament are letters that Paul wrote to churches he worked with. The book of Corinthians is a letter Paul wrote to the church in Corinth. This passage is the very end of the letter.

Have you ever written a letter? Letters can make people feel braver and can help them remember to be good. Letters can make people laugh and also can cheer people up when they're sad.

Work with your family and fill in this letter. They'll ask you for a word and will write it in the blanks. Then they'll read the letter. It may be a funny letter, so get ready to laugh.

Dear *(name a cartoon character or an animal)* _____,

Greetings from warm and sunny *(name a place)* _____! I'm writing you so that you will be encouraged. That means you'll remember to *(name something you do in church)* _____. I also want you to be brave when you *(name something you do at school)* _____.

Remember to be friends with *(name a friend)* _____ and also with *(name someone you don't know very well)* _____. And always be sure to eat your *(name a funny food)* _____.

When are you going to come see me? Will it be before *(name a holiday)* _____? When you come, be sure to bring *(name a silly thing you have in your closet)* _____.

And remember that Jesus loves you! And I love you too!

Grace and peace,

Paul

Now read your letter!

    —Michele Hershberger

PRAYING AND WALKING IN THE WORLD:

- Pretend you are a preacher, and write a letter to your church. If you can't write yet, have your parents or an older brother or sister write it.

- **Adults:** What would you say to your church if you were writing a letter?

- Look at your mom or dad. How would you finish this sentence if you were talking to them? "May God give you _____ today." That's what it means to give a blessing to someone.

BITTER WATERS MADE SWEET

PLUNGING INTO THE WORD:

Exodus 15:22-27

PONDERING ON THE WAY:

As a writer, I am very familiar with the bitterness of deadlines. Because of my procrastination tendencies, I've often had to write on deadline at 3 a.m. I fight sleep, pleading that the Holy Spirit will help me connect with my readers. This often means slogging through writer's block and fighting the feeling that I have nothing significant to say.

But the sweetness of a job completed cancels out the bitter taste of hard work. Even though it often feels impossible to fill up a blank page with words that can bless others, time and again God's presence has made it all possible.

In today's passage, the Israelites also experienced the contrast of bitterness and sweetness. In the verses preceding today's Scripture, Miriam led the Israelites in a victory dance for having passed through the Red Sea. Only three days later, as they left the Red Sea for the wilderness, their sweet sense of God's provision was tainted by having only Marah's bitter waters to slack their thirst.

Again, God uses a source of water—this time a bitter spring rather than the Red Sea—to convey that God is the one who will provide. They could not push back the wall of water threatening to kill them, and they could not make bitter waters sweet. In their sojourn from bondage to liberation, God would be their source of stamina and guidance. They learned that the sojourn was a series of junctures that would replace their human independence with the humility of dependence.

Whether you are meeting deadlines, building a solid marriage, or tackling an addiction, God makes bitter places sweet when we take our rightful place as frail humans in relationship to a faithful God. God makes the impossible possible.

—*Laurie Oswald Robinson*

PRAYING AND WALKING IN THE WORLD:

- What challenges are embittering the waters of your life right now? Write down several aspects of the situation that uncover your frailty and dependence.

- Pray that you will become more willing to imbibe God's provision that makes your bitter waters sweet. In your prayer, open up your palms as a symbol of receiving the sweet waters of God's faithful help, of relinquishing the impossibilities and accepting new possibilities.

- Is a close friend, relative, or coworker facing bitter waters? This week, through a small kindness or gesture, remind that person of the sweetness of God's providing and prevailing presence.

NOVEMBER 2

THE FLESH POTS OF *IF-ONLY* THINKING

PLUNGING INTO THE WORD:

Exodus 16:1-12

PONDERING ON THE WAY:

During the adjustment of my new marriage, I read *The Lies Women Believe* by Nancy Leigh DeMoss. During our first marital conflicts, I thought *if only* Alfonso was different, then I would be different. But Nancy reminded me of a lie: People and situations make me something different from what I am. The truth: People and situations uncover who I really am. And I was a new bride who wasn't prepared to face the fact that sacrifice and suffering is as much a part of true love as are comfort and kudos.

The Israelites also swallowed an *if-only* lie in today's Bible story. The hungrier they became in the wilderness, the more they desired the familiar food, or flesh pots, of Egypt. *If only* they could have better food, they would get on with their journey. The situation revealed their true character; they were filled with cowardice and addiction to past comforts. Rather than face the future with God's provisions, they fantasized about the past—albeit a past infected with injustice and despair.

This story shows we can be as afraid of new freedoms as we are of bondages left behind. For example, a woman starving herself to death won't let go of an eating disorder. Or a man drinking himself to death won't let go of an alcohol addiction. People are hungry for spiritual infilling but often fill that emptiness with unhealthy substances or behaviors.

In tomorrow's reading, we discover how God fed the Israelites. But no matter what kind of sustenance they received or we receive today—and no matter what shape our fantasies or addictions take—God desires we face life as it is, not as we would like it to be. It's in the reality of life that we uncover who we are and who God is shaping us to become.

—*Laurie Oswald Robinson*

PRAYING AND WALKING IN THE WORLD:

- When you daydream about the past, what "flesh pots" cause nostalgia? Which present challenges cause you to fantasize about past comforts, even if they are harmful to you? What truth have you discovered about yourself amid challenges that make you pine for earlier days—days that brought you the strange comfort of familiar bondages?

- Pray for a transformation of *if-only* thinking into the ability to embrace reality as it is and not as you would like it to be. Pray for the grace to accept yourself, both your sunny and dark sides. Pray you can move into a future freer of false expectations of yourself and others.

- Find someone to join you in reading and discussing one of DeMoss's books. Other titles include *Walking in the Truth,* a companion guide to *Lies Women Believe; A Place of Quiet Rest;* and *A 30-Day Walk with God in the Psalms.*

NOVEMBER 3 *(FOR CHILDREN AND FAMILIES)*

WHAT IS IT?

PLUNGING INTO THE WORD:

Exodus 16:13-21

PONDERING ON THE WAY:

When I was a girl, my mother sometimes prepared a dish that on first glance looked like hamburger. But the minute I stepped into the kitchen with a hungry, growling stomach, the smell told me it was *not* hamburger, even though it was the same color.

I'd curl up my nose and say, "What is it?" Mom replied, "It's like hamburger, only better for you." And because mom cooked only one main dish, I had no choice but to sit down to a plate of liver and onions, full of iron but also full of strange tastes.

The Israelites in today's story also turned up their noses at what God chose to feed them in the wilderness. It was a white, flaky substance that looked like frost on the ground. It was "manna," which means "What is it?" It covered the ground fresh every morning. But there was one rule: They were to gather up all the manna and not leave any of it on the ground for the next day. They didn't follow this rule, and the food got wormy. They wanted food, in their way and their time. But God was teaching them to trust God's way.

Like Mom, who fed me good food to make me grow strong, God fed God's people with the food God knew they needed. Sometimes, we think our parents or God aren't treating us right. But they love us in the best way they can. I still like McDonald's hamburgers better than I do liver. But every time I smell liver cooking, it brings back the smell of love.

— *Laurie Oswald Robinson*

PRAYING AND WALKING IN THE WORLD:

- When are you most tempted to think your parents or other adults aren't treating you right?

- Pray for God to help you trust that adults care about your welfare. Thank God today for your parents or caretakers.

- In a Bible dictionary, research different foods eaten in the Old Testament, and draw pictures of these foods. Put the picture on your refrigerator as a reminder that God provides what you need, including parents who cook for you.

NOVEMBER 4

THE SMELL OF WORSHIP

PLUNGING INTO THE WORD:

Exodus 16:22-36

PONDERING ON THE WAY:

It wasn't until middle age that I returned to an old family tradition: filling a slow cooker with a roast, carrots, potatoes, and onions. I created the dish Saturday night and stored it in the fridge until Sunday morning when I slid it into the stove to cook during church. This "ritual" connected me to the faith formation of my childhood. The roast created an aroma that teased and taunted the taste buds as we waited to feast at our simple but heavily laden table. And the Saturday evening roast prep created an aroma that will always stimulate my sense of Sunday as being a special, set-apart day for God.

The Israelites had their own food experiences, including their forty-year diet of manna, the white, flaky substance that tasted like wafers made with honey. Whether it smelled delicious or not, I don't know. But like the Saturday evening roast prep, Moses told the people they were to gather two days' worth on Friday so they would have enough for Shabbat, or Saturday—the Sabbath for the Jews. Some of the people didn't believe God and tried to gather some on Saturday only to find the ground bare. The other interesting thing about the manna was that it would stay good from Friday through the Sabbath, but on any other day, it would spoil overnight. This was God's miraculous way of teaching the Israelites to trust God for their sustenance.

The manna was so pivotal that God wanted the people to keep a sample of it for generations to come. It would remind them of God's provisions in the wilderness (v. 32). The return to the roast ritual reminds me that Sunday is when I break normal routine to honor and thank God for God's feast of provisions that nurture me with food, feed me with faith, and witness to me of divine faithfulness.

>   —*Laurie Oswald Robinson*

PRAYING AND WALKING IN THE WORLD:

- Reminisce on the rituals and traditions that surround your family's Sabbath. If you were not part of a church-going or worshipping family, think about rituals or traditions you've read about or friends who observed a set-apart day as a time to rest from labor and reflect on God.

- Confess to God those things that keep you from observing Sabbath. Ask for forgiveness, and receive God's grace.

- If you are part of a family, call a family conference to decide together what Sabbath will mean in your home. If you are single, ask another person to keep you accountable for new Sabbath habits and commitments.

NOVEMBER 5

BOTTLED WATER AND BADGERING MOSES

PLUNGING INTO THE WORD:

Exodus 17:1-7

PONDERING ON THE WAY:

Most people in the Western world have access to tap water, but the bottled-water business reaps millions of dollars. Just in the last decade, bottled water sales have increased fivefold. We can buy more than seven hundred brands of bottled water, and supermarkets shelve whole aisles with these bottles. The overabundance of choices can confuse health-conscious people searching for the best water for their buck.

People in today's Scripture passage also were confused over issues of water but for an opposite reason—its lack. They turned on Moses, accusing him of bringing them to the desert to die of thirst. Moses fought back. "Why do you quarrel with me? Why do you test the Lord?" And when that didn't work, he cried out to the Lord, "What should I do with this people? They are almost ready to stone me!" As always during a wilderness crisis, the Lord surprised the people. He told Moses to strike the rock of Horeb with the same staff Moses used to part the Red Sea. As Moses struck the rock, water gushed forth. The miracle met the people's test with an unexpected provision.

As bottle-watered North Americans, we can't identify with a life-threatening physical thirst that causes panic. But we still test the Lord and his leaders in other ways. For example, one can find many disgruntled people in congregations or organizations who turn on their leaders. They thirst to get spiritual or emotional needs quenched and believe the leader is not satisfying their thirsts in the right way.

But today's passage reminds us it's futile and inappropriate to manipulate our leaders or our God. The Lord's living water of hope and healing cannot be contained like bottled water. It is wild and miraculous, always found in surprising places and surprising times.

—*Laurie Oswald Robinson*

PRAYING AND WALKING IN THE WORLD:

- Reflect on a time when you sought to control someone or something to get your needs met. What happened? Did it work? For how long? How did you feel once you succeeded?

- During prayer today, ask God for new insights about how you can lower your expectations of human leaders and raise your expectations of the Lord.

- Identify a leader who most recently disappointed you. Find a way, either overt or hidden, to honor and support the leader's guidance.

NOVEMBER 6 *(FOR CHILDREN AND FAMILIES)*

WISE GRANDPA, WEAK GRANDPA

PLUNGING INTO THE WORD:

Exodus 17:8-16

PONDERING ON THE WAY:

My grandpa, John Egli, was one of the world's most wonderful storytellers. After holiday feasts at his home shared with Grandma Ella, his grandchildren fanned around his feet as he created stories on the spot. But when he got older, he barely could speak and his storytelling days were over. The man who once had delighted us with his stories was the same man who grew frail, leaving only memories of his tales. Instead of expecting him to tell us stories, we sat and held his hands and told him our stories.

Grandpa John grew weak because of age. Moses, the leader of the Israelites in today's Bible story, grew weak because of being involved in a long military battle. When Amalek attacked the Israelites, Moses stood on top of a hill with God's staff in his hand. When he held it up, Israel's army, led by Joshua, won the battle. When he lowered the staff, Amalek won. After several times of this, Moses grew weary. And so Aaron and Hur stepped in to help. They held up his hands, one on each side. When they did that, Joshua and his army finally defeated the enemy once and for all.

It's easy to forget that at one time, old people were wise, active, and strong. We can remember and honor their years of strength and their worth by visiting them and caring about them. We even can help them do what they no longer can do for themselves. Sometimes, in the case of grandparents who were part of our lives, we can give them back the gift of time or listening that they once gave to us.

—*Laurie Oswald Robinson*

PRAYING AND WALKING IN THE WORLD:

- Do you still have grandparents who are living? If so, are they still alert and able to talk with you? If not, what were they like before they died?

- Thank God for older or handicapped people in your life. Use crayons and construction paper to create a card that thanks them for all they mean to you.

- Visit your grandparents. Or, if you don't have living grandparents, ask your mom and dad to take you to a local nursing home where you can visit an older or weaker person who needs a friend.

- **Adults:** Our passage today is a Holy War story. We have evolved from original Holy War, where only God does the fighting, to the people fighting with God. But there is still the strong element of the terror of the Lord where it is a miracle of God that determines the victory. What does this story have to say about fighting wars today?

BLENDING FAMILIES

PLUNGING INTO THE WORD:

Exodus 18:1-12

PONDERING ON THE WAY:

A recent *Time* article discussed the challenges of blending families of divorced and remarried couples. The article suggests it takes at least five years for the families to truly blend. I saw this verified recently when my sister and her husband—married about five years—had their two sets of kids gathered around the Christmas tree. As we sang carols and read Luke, familial bonds glowed. The article didn't address whether Christian blended families fare better than non-Christian ones. But an unspoken peace prevailed in that living room. By focusing on Jesus and honoring him as Emmanuel—"God with us"—two very different families became unified.

Today's Scripture passage depict two very different families—Moses, from the Israelites, and his wife, Zipporah, who came from the Midianites. This difference did not stop Jethro, her father, from visiting Moses when he heard all that God had done for Moses and his people in the exodus.

Moses responded well. He greeted Jethro with a kiss and told him about God's deliverance. Jethro rejoiced with Moses over God's acts and even declared that "the Lord is greater than all gods" (v. 11). They worshipped together—Jethro brought a burnt offering and sacrifice, and Moses and his elders shared bread with Jethro.

The love of God, the parent of all peoples, can make us one family within our immediate and extended circles, with our church families, and with all peoples. This unity takes the hard work of human cooperation with God. Jethro traveled many miles to see his son-in-law and to honor Moses' God. And my sister and husband sacrificed time and emotional energy to focus their blended family on Christ. But as people share their bread and their hearts, the hard work becomes a holy work.

—Laurie Oswald Robinson

PRAYING AND WALKING IN THE WORLD:

- Reflect on what kind of family you come from—original, blended, adoptive. What brings unity to your family? What causes disunity? Reflect on your part in helping to forge unity.

- As the Thanksgiving and Christmas holidays approach, pray that the peace of Christ and the love of God prevail within your family gatherings.

- Identify one family member who is estranged from the extended family in large or small ways. In some kind of gesture—an e-mail, a snail mail card, or a face-to-face visit—demonstrate God's unifying love.

NOVEMBER 8

DO IT MYSELF OR DELEGATE

PLUNGING INTO THE WORD:

Exodus 18:13-27

PONDERING ON THE WAY:

Am I the only one with this problem? I stew silently around the kitchen, putting dishes in the dishwasher because other household members leave theirs on the counter. I heave a big sigh as I pick up clothes left where they were discarded on the floor. I grumble to myself as I throw trash away that was just left lying around.

I have a choice: delegate chores or do it myself. It's a tough choice. Delegating can mean they won't get done the way I'd do them. They may not get done as soon as I'd do them. Doing it myself makes me crazy because there are other things I need to be doing and because these are the kinds of chores that can be shared among all household members.

Moses was used to doing everything himself. It took an outsider—his father-in-law who wasn't a part of the Israelites—to see that something had to change. "Get a life, Moses," he said. "You're going to have to delegate! You can't do all of this by yourself."

Much to Moses' credit, he listened. He didn't have control issues. He didn't flinch at giving responsibility to other people. He didn't lose sleep wondering if so-and-so got a fair judgment. He didn't look over the shoulders of the people he appointed to the new roles.

I'm guessing, however, that Moses wasn't totally a hands-off manager. I bet he found ways to train and instruct, offering wisdom and encouragement to the leaders he appointed. I bet he found a balance between overworking himself and "working over" the men under him.

My home is small stuff compared to the Israelites. But it's where I live, and it's where I need to find and share peace.

—*Carol Duerksen*

PRAYING AND WALKING IN THE WORLD:

- Do you have control issues? Whom do you need to give more space? Where do you need to delegate so you feel less stress?

- What does it mean to trust the people in leadership in your congregation? Your church denomination? How do you know when to trust and when to challenge?

- Pray for Christian leaders you admire. Pray for Christian leaders with whom you have issues.

NOVEMBER 9 *(FOR CHILDREN AND FAMILIES)*
CONNECTORS

PLUNGING INTO THE WORD:

Exodus 19:1-9a

PONDERING ON THE WAY:

Do you play with Thomas the Tank Engine trains? Maybe you did when you were smaller, or you know someone who has a collection of Thomas and his friends.

How do the engines and train cars connect to each other?

Without a way to connect engines and train cars together, you couldn't have a train, could you? You would have just a bunch of engines and train cars sitting around by themselves. But when you hook them together, you have a train!

Our story today is about Moses being a connector between God and the people of Israel. The Israelites needed to hear some rules and messages from God. Moses listened to God and then told the people what God had said. The people answered, and Moses told God what they said. Moses connected God and the people together.

Who are the connectors between people and God today?

Teachers, preachers, parents—anybody who tells us about God is a connector for us. Connectors teach us about God, just as schoolteachers help us learn reading, writing, and math. That doesn't mean we can't talk to God directly; we can pray to God anytime and God hears us. Connectors just help us learn more about God so we can love God more.

—*Carol Duerksen*

PRAYING AND WALKING IN THE WORLD:

- Next time you see a train, think about how it's connected together, and thank God for people who teach you about God.

- Draw a train. Draw God in the engine, you in a train car, and then draw somebody in between the engine and the train who is a "connector" between you and God.

- **Adults:** Who connects you with God? For whom do you play that role? Pray specifically for someone who has given God's message to you. Pray for someone to whom you have been God's messenger.

NOVEMBER 10

MINI MOSES

PLUNGING INTO THE WORD:

Exodus 19:9b-25

PONDERING ON THE WAY:

"I accepted Jesus as my Savior at Camp Washunga."

"The time when I felt the closest to God was at youth convention."

"I remember when we went to Acquire the Fire—there were so many kids there worshipping God, and that's when God became real to me."

Through the years, as baptism candidates in our congregation shared their testimonies, inevitably we'd hear words like these. Most of the close encounters with God remembered by these teens occurred in worship settings outside their normal environment, often in large groups. These mountaintop spiritual experiences stood out for them above the daily and weekly connections with God fostered by their families and congregation.

Mountaintop experiences with God go way back, as we read in this passage. There's something about coming together, expecting to experience the power of God, worshipping in awe of the Spirit's movement, and sharing it with other people of God. This outpouring from God's self to God's people is one of the miraculous aspects of our faith journey.

This is good news for convention planners. But what does it say to Sunday school teachers, pastors, youth leaders, and Bible study leaders? Wouldn't it be nice to hear a teenager say that your sermon or your youth group session impacted them in a life-changing way? Wouldn't it be humbling in a cool kind of way to know that God spoke through you in a mini-Moses fashion?

And that is one of the mysteries I love the most about God. God *does* speak through mini-Moses folks today. God *does* come to the camps and conventions, youth group sessions, and worship services. God uses still small voices in retreats and rockin' praise bands in concerts. God is so big and unfathomable, yet so intimate and personal. And while teenagers may remember the mountaintop experiences when sharing a testimony, God and God's people walked with that young person up the mountain and will walk with them on the trip down too.

—*Carol Duerksen*

PRAYING AND WALKING IN THE WORLD:

- Pray for the camps, conventions, and weekend retreats that you are familiar with. Put them on your calendar for future reference when they are in session and pray for those leading and those attending.

- Recall your mountaintop spiritual experiences. Thank God for the special connection you felt with the Creator, the Holy Spirit, and Jesus at that time.

- Make plans to give yourself the opportunity for a special spiritual experience. For example, attend a convention or spend twenty-four hours in a silent retreat.

NOVEMBER 11 *(FOR CHILDREN AND FAMILIES)*

GOD RULES

PLUNGING INTO THE WORD:

Exodus 20:1-17

PONDERING ON THE WAY:

You've probably heard about the Ten Commandments. The Ten Commandments were rules to live by, given by God to the Israelites. Let's take a look at them and how they might apply to your life.

1.   Worship God and only God.

2.   Don't have any "fake gods."

3.   Don't use God's name in a wrong way.

4.   Rest every seventh day.

5.   Honor your parents.

6.   Don't murder.

7.   Don't cheat on your husband or wife.

8.   Don't steal.

9.   Don't lie about your neighbor or friend.

10. Don't wish you had what your neighbor or friend has.

Some of these apply more to adults than children, but some of them are good rules for children of all ages. For example, what do you think "fake gods" might be?

A "fake god" is anything in your life that is more important than God.

Don't use God's name in a wrong way. We often think that just means "Don't cuss." But it's more than that. Using God's name in a wrong way happens when you say, "I am God's child," and then you turn around and act like a jerk.

Now let's talk about the Sabbath. The Sabbath was the seventh day of the week—a day of rest for everyone. As Christians, we now celebrate the first day of the week, Sunday, as our day of rest. But here's the question: Do you rest on Sunday? Talk about this with your family. What do you do on Sunday?

Honor your parents. That means respect and listen to your parents. How are you doing in that area?

Don't steal. That's pretty obvious, isn't it?

Don't lie about your neighbor or friend. Don't make up stories about people you don't like. Don't say bad things about them.

Don't wish you had what your neighbor or friend has. Oh, that's a tough one. If somebody has a toy you really like, don't wish it was yours.

You might wonder why these rules are important, and the answer is that God knows what is best for our lives, and these rules from God make life better for everyone. Look at the rules again. How do you think life is better when we follow them?

—*Carol Duerksen*

PRAYING AND WALKING IN THE WORLD:

- **Children:** Make a poster for your room with these rules on it. Put them in your own words and draw pictures to go with them if you want to.

- **Adults:** Which commandment is the biggest challenge for you? Are you willing to work on it? Would your life change if you took this commandment seriously?

- **Adults:** Did you notice verse 1? God acted first in grace, by saving the Israelites from slavery. Then God gave them these ten ways to respond—in gratitude for what God did for them.

NOVEMBER 12

BOOTS BEHIND THE PULPIT

PLUNGING INTO THE WORD:

Exodus 20:18-21

PONDERING ON THE WAY:

Sheree's a horsewoman.
From belt buckle to braided hair,
From Banamine in her fridge to bridles in the barn,
Sheree looks and lives the role of a horsewoman.

So when God spoke in a dream one night
And Sheree woke up to tell her husband
"I think I'm supposed to be a preacher,"
It's hard to say who was more surprised.

Today she's a pastor.
Messenger from God
To her congregation.
Sharing God's Word with them.
Sometimes her words are tough to hear.
Challenging.
Sometimes … they can be downright scary.

Because God doesn't specialize in keeping people comfortable.
And Sheree doesn't specialize in mincing words.

But then
God only knows
How to call
How to use
Shepherds
Fishermen
Horsewomen

> —*Carol Duerksen*

PRAYING AND WALKING IN THE WORLD:

- How much of what your pastor says on Sunday challenges you? Do you accept the challenges?

- When has God called you out of your comfort zone? Did you listen? What happened?

- Thank God and ask for God's continued presence in the lives of pastors you know.

NOVEMBER 13

AARON'S JOURNAL

PLUNGING INTO THE WORD:

Exodus 32:1-6

PONDERING ON THE WAY:

I know it sounds bad, but well, we got tired of waiting for Moses today. He'd been up there on the mountain so long, and, like the people said, who knows what happened to him. He might never come back, the people said, and I couldn't argue because I didn't know. Without Moses, everybody was feeling really lost. They needed somebody to lead them. Our neighbors all have gods they can see, so I figured, maybe this was the time for us to have a god like that too. It's not that it would replace Yahweh … this god would just be a visual representation of Yahweh.

So we melted the gold from everybody's earrings and made a golden calf. It was a good-looking calf, if I do say so myself. Then I declared it was time for a festival—we needed one to get everybody's minds off of Moses not coming back and to celebrate the new god. Wow—I haven't partied like that in a long time. Maybe having this gold calf will bring us good luck. We could use some.

—*Carol Duerksen*

PRAYING AND WALKING IN THE WORLD:

- The Israelites got tired of waiting. When have you grown impatient with God? When have you tried to take things into your own hands?

- Pray for patience in the area(s) of your life where you need it the most.

- Making the golden calf was a big mistake—a sin of huge proportions. God had no more than given the Ten Commandments than the Israelites flagrantly violated one of them. What are the sins of your life? Your community? Your country? Repent.

NOVEMBER 14

MOSES' JOURNAL

PLUNGING INTO THE WORD:

Exodus 32:7-14

PONDERING ON THE WAY:

Call me in "shock and awe." I'm up on the mountain, in the middle of my amazing experience with God, when God suddenly tells me I have to get back to the Israelites. "They've really done it this time," God says. "They've built themselves a golden calf to worship. I'm fed up with them. If they don't need me, I don't need them. I'll wipe them out. They'll be history. I'll start over with you."

I didn't like the sound of that at all. After everything we'd been through—coming out of Egypt, the Lord leading us and delivering us with miracles. After all that, I couldn't imagine having the whole nation wiped out. I understood God's anger, but destroy everybody? Please! No!

Dare I argue with God? I did. I pleaded for the lives of the Israelites. I told God it wouldn't look good for the Lord to bring them out of Egypt and then destroy them on a whim. I recalled God's promise to Abraham, Isaac, and Jacob about the descendants they would have. I pulled out all the stops.

And God listened. God reconsidered. The Lord didn't destroy them.

So I sit here tonight, in shock at people who can sin so blatantly and in awe of a God who listens to the heart of a mere mortal, pleading on their behalf.

—*Carol Duerksen*

PRAYING AND WALKING IN THE WORLD:

- What are your thoughts as you read this passage? What do you think of the idea of God's mind getting changed by Moses' pleas? How does that fit into your idea of who God is?

- When have you "made deals" with God? What happened?

- Praise God for being a just God—a God who doesn't "let anything go," yet a God who doesn't let go of us.

NOVEMBER 15 *(FOR CHILDREN AND FAMILIES)*

ONE SIN, THEN ANOTHER

PLUNGING INTO THE WORD:

Exodus 32:15-24

PONDERING ON THE WAY:

Ryan was happy with his baseball card collection—most of the time. He had great cards: Sammy Sosa cards, Cal Ripken Jr. cards, and even a George Brett from 1985. He kept them clean and safe in plastic card protectors. It was a great collection.

But he didn't have a Johnny Damon card. And Kaitlyn, his neighbor next door, did have one, a card made especially for the World Series. And every once in a while, she would look at Ryan and sing, "Ha, ha, ha, I have a card that you want! I have a card that you want!"

So Ryan did something that was wrong to do. Kaitlyn was singing her annoying little song again, and he was so mad he could almost burst. So when Kaitlyn wasn't looking, he tore her Johnny Damon card. He didn't even keep it for himself, which might have been a smarter thing to do. But he was so mad that he didn't even want it. Ryan just wanted the card to be ruined.

When Kaitlyn couldn't find her card, she asked Ryan about it. He said, "I don't know where your card is, but I bet Chad took it." Chad was Kaitlyn's little brother. So Kaitlyn went and told her mom that Chad took it, and Chad got in big trouble. He cried and cried, but nobody listened to him when he said he didn't take it.

But then Kaitlyn found the torn-up card in the trash can at Ryan's house. She went to Ryan, her face all red with anger. "Well," said Ryan, "I have no idea how that card got torn up. Maybe … maybe … " Ryan searched for words to say. "Maybe the vacuum cleaner picked it up and that's how it got ruined." But Ryan's mom, who was standing right behind him, said, "But Ryan, I didn't run the vacuum cleaner today. Do you think there might be another real reason why the card got torn?" Ryan started to cry. His one bad thing led to another bad thing, and now all his lies were catching up with him. One sin led to more and more sins. Ryan was miscrable.

In the Bible story about the golden calf, the same thing happens. One sin leads to more and more sins. What do you think we can learn from this story?

—*Michele Hershberger*

PRAYING AND WALKING IN THE WORLD:

- What should Ryan do? What would make Ryan feel better? What would make Kaitlyn feel better?

- Have you ever had to tell one lie to make up for an earlier lie? What happened? Did the lies get bigger and bigger?

- **Adults:** God forgave the people, but there were still dire consequences for their behavior. This is more the nature of sin, rather than the nature of God's judgment. Can you think of examples of this in your own life?

NOVEMBER 16

3000 DEAD IN IDOL FIASCO

PLUNGING INTO THE WORD:

Exodus 32:25-35

PONDERING ON THE WAY:

"This is Bezalel son of Hur, reporting from the Israelite camp where chaos seems to be the order of the day. It appears that when their leader, Moses, left, they didn't know how to act. Let's talk to a person on the street. Excuse me, sir. What exactly is going on here?"

"It's crazy! People literally have been running mad in the streets! It looks like the Levites are trying to bring about some order, but I don't know … "

"What exactly are the Levites doing?"

"They're sweeping through the camp, killing people!"

"Why?"

"Moses told them to. They're killing at will—friends, family, neighbors. It's a massacre!"

"But I don't understand. Why?"

"It's a long story. Basically, they really screwed up bad. They blatantly defied God. They're paying the price."

"I see … I guess. Oh, excuse me—I see Moses over there. I need to get a word from him. … Moses? Could I have a comment from you? What's going on here?"

"It's not a pretty picture. I came down from the mountain, and the people had gone crazy. While I was meeting with Almighty God, they were building a golden calf idol. God was not pleased, to say the least. I tried to intercede on their behalf. I tried to take the blame for their sin and asked for the punishment myself. But God said the people had to take responsibility for what they did and suffer the consequences. That's it in a nutshell. Now you'll have to excuse me."

"Thank you, Moses. Just one more quick question. Would you say that the future of the Israelites looks uncertain at this point?"

"We are still moving toward the Promised Land. We have a covenant. We have the presence of God with us. We will survive."

"From the Israelite camp, this is Bezalel son of Hur, reporting."

—Michele Hershberger

PRAYING AND WALKING IN THE WORLD:

- Which way would you have chosen had you been a leader during this time? Would you have chosen to take God's place—to mete out revenge, take the rap on behalf of the people—or just to wait and hide? Which method of leadership worked the best then? Which would work the best now? Which is right?

- The slaughter of the Levites is hard to swallow. How can Moses have asked them to do this horrible deed? Was it really the desire of the Lord? On one hand, the people were very young in their understanding; perhaps what seemed appropriate then is not appropriate now. Yet this is a part of the Bible, and we must deal with it as such. What is right?

THE PRESENCE OF GOD

PLUNGING INTO THE WORD:

Exodus 33:1-11

PONDERING ON THE WAY:

Know any stubborn people? I do. Sometimes I get so angry at friends, as well as enemies, when they are being stubborn. It is indescribably frustrating to witness their blind stupidity. Compared to them, I feel quite enlightened, and sometimes I just have to get away from them.

God also can get frustrated by stubborn and disobedient people. Though God loved the Israelites and brought them to the Promised Land, they were warned through Moses that, from here on out, God could not accompany the people directly. God understood about removing oneself from a situation. The Israelites' sin was too great, too painful to bear. Perhaps the Israelites had not taken their sin seriously enough, and only through God's harsh refusal to travel with them would they see the error of their ways.

The fact that the Israelites took this news so hard says several things about their relationship with God. First of all, God's presence must have been a very powerful force in their daily lives. They may not have understood God, because the full revelation was not shown until Jesus lived and died, but they did actively know God.

Second, God had been present with them in a very real way. For all of Israel's sin, God was intimately close to them. The pillar descended. God spoke to Moses face-to-face, as a friend! This happened often and each time the people, filled with awe, bowed down to acknowledge the presence of God. Yes, the Israelites were stubborn. They created a golden calf immediately after witnessing the miraculous power of the Lord firsthand. But they experienced the Presence. God was with them.

God was with them.

Nowadays, we have the entire gospel. We are no longer infants in the faith, but have centuries of theology to fall back on. And we are still stubborn. We are still stiff-necked. We still fall short of God's plan for us. We go to church, we listen to the right people, but ultimately we do as we please. I can't even imagine what would happen if God came to my church during the service, or after, at the bring-your-own-casserole potluck. I can't imagine what would happen if God made us accountable for our WWJD bracelets. Nowadays God is more of a Sunday thing. Back then, God was everywhere and God was everything with incredible, incomprehensible closeness.

Hmm … suddenly I don't feel so enlightened after all.

—*Michele Hershberger*

PRAYING AND WALKING IN THE WORLD:

- Who are the stubborn people in your life? How can you be sure who is enlightened and who is stubborn? Who has the open mind?

- Does God's wrath consume us still today? What is the line between judgment and grace? Does grace keep us from being consumed? Do you take sin seriously?

- How close is your relationship with God? Is it an everyday relationship? Once-a-week? Or is it a constant one? What can you do to improve that? Does the pillar of cloud and fire go before you?

NOVEMBER 18

PRAYER THAT TAKES GUTS

PLUNGING INTO THE WORD:

Exodus 33:12-23

PONDERING ON THE WAY:

Moses prays in a way I seldom pray. In this passage, Moses asks God to change his mind. And he doesn't even use nice words or say please. Moses instead throws some of God's own words back up into God's face. You said your presence would go with us. Now, because of the golden calf incident, you are going back on that promise. No deal.

No deal, Lord.

Now, Moses doesn't say those exact words, but it's close. And even after God promises his presence will go with them, Moses still persists, still pushes his argument. Does Moses know with whom he is dealing?

Apparently so.

And then, after God grants this bold request, after God changes plans in a 180-degree turnaround, not once but twice, Moses does it again. Moses asks for something else. And it's not just any request, not even the brave request of God's presence among his people.

Moses asks to see God's glory! Moses asks to see what no human had ever seen before. The moment between Moses' prayer and God's response to it must have been the most terrifying moment in Moses' life. What would God do to a man who asked like that? Slay him right there and then? Fry him in holy fire? Moses doesn't even say, "If it be your will …"! He just asks. Will this brave prayer be his undoing?

Or will it be the most wonderful moment one can know? The Lord keeps his mystery and power—"I will be gracious to whom I will be gracious, and will show mercy on whom I will show mercy"—but at the same time grants Moses a wonderful view. God makes sure to protect Moses—the glory is surely enough to kill him—and then reveals to Moses God's back, but not the face of God. That is too much.

So, like the pillar of cloud and fire that both revealed and concealed the Lord, so too is the glory of the cleft rock.

Moses survives his brave prayer. He is a different man for it.

Maybe I need to rethink prayer.

—Michele Hershberger

PRAYING AND WALKING IN THE WORLD:

- Moses doesn't use the words, *If it is your will* or *Your will be done.* Is that because Moses already knew God's will? Is it wrong to use these words?

- Are there times when you feel called to pray in a brave way like Moses and you don't? What holds you back? What are you afraid of? God? Or your own lack of faith?

- Do you really want a more intimate relationship with God? What would have to change for you to have that kind of relationship? Is it worth it, or are you content to travel to the Promised Land with just an angel leading the way?

NOVEMBER 19

SLOGANS AND PARADOXES

PLUNGING INTO THE WORD:

Exodus 34:1-10

PONDERING ON THE WAY:

"Tempus fugit" was a favorite saying of one of my high school teachers. "Tempus fugit. Time flies, so work as hard as you can in the time that we have." I think he saw *The Pajama Game* one too many times. On the other hand, I had a teacher who frequently said, "Haste makes waste." Everyone has a credo that they live by. For some, it's simple and short, for others it may be a manifesto. Corporations have mission statements. Businesses have slogans.

However, I believe it is the church that began the creed craze. Though churches might not be as good at making snappy jingles, they are the foremost authority on encapsulating beliefs, whether in huge canons of teachings or in Veggie Tale segments. Our best slogan is "Slow to anger, and abounding in steadfast love and faithfulness." This may sound familiar because it was used in about every psalm ever written. This and its surrounding verses comprise a *Reader's Digest* version of Judeo-Christian theology. Needless to say, it's important. Catch phrases don't catch on for nothing.

God is one hundred percent holy. There is no letting the guilty get off free. In fact, God punishes, or allows sin to manifest itself for up to four generations. This doesn't seem right. God punishes the great-grandchildren of the sinner in question? Yikes!

Yet, God is one hundred percent merciful. God's undying, faithful love goes to the thousandth generation. Is this a paradox? At what point does grace trump judgment or vice versa? One thousand generations is greater than four. One thousand is much greater than four.

Still, this whole visiting iniquity thing does not seem fair. It's like the time my sister wrecked the car, yet I was the one who could suddenly only drive to and from school. Does God really punish us, or is that just the reality of sin?

A parent's sin does affect the child's life. That's just how life is. But sometimes, God's judgment is merciful. Paradox again? Consider the above car situation. My parents loved me enough to restrict my driving privileges. Ouch. It hurts even now to admit that my parents were right. God loves us enough to show us the right way to go and keep us from destructive patterns.

So it's true. God can be one hundred percent divine judge and one hundred percent forgiving, loving Father. That's two hundred percent. Only you, God. After all, anything is possible. Isn't that a slogan for something?

—*Tara Hershberger*

PRAYING AND WALKING IN THE WORLD:

- Do you relate more to a God who punishes or a God who forgives?

- Which is more important, judgment of wrongdoers or grace? How can God be both completely merciful and completely divine at the same time?

- What sins have your parents or grandparents done that have hurt you? Why doesn't God just erase all that? Can you find it in yourself to be gracious to them? Can you forgive?

NOVEMBER 20

DILEMMA

PLUNGING INTO THE WORD:

Exodus 34:11-16

PONDERING ON THE WAY:

When Joe first came to our church, I really liked the guy. Friendly but to the point, assertive without being obnoxious. He had, well, charisma.

But that was part of the problem. Wherever Joe went, he was a natural leader. And when he came to our congregation, he felt called to lead. Specifically, he wanted to teach Sunday school, and as you can guess, our Christian Ed department was always looking for new volunteers.

But Joe didn't believe that Christians should be pacifists. Joe liked going to our church, and he was in dialogue about what it meant to be nonresistant to evil, but he didn't buy it yet. And he was forthright in reminding us that not everyone who grew up in the church accepted this theology either.

He wanted to teach Sunday school.

Now Joe is not exactly one of the inhabitants in the land that the Lord promised to drive out so that they wouldn't influence the young people of God into idol worship. Nor has my congregation ever had an atheist or even someone who practices another faith ask to teach Sunday school for us. On the other hand, my congregation wasn't even considering driving Joe out. They wanted him there. They wanted to have this healthy dialogue with him as a fellow follower of Jesus.

But way down deep, the issues are similar. At what point—because your people feel "young" in the faith—do you hunker down and just keep to yourselves? And when is it appropriate to interact with others who have different beliefs, so you can learn from them a better way to serve God and so you can teach them a better way too?

It goes both ways. We have been called to be missionaries, to be conduits of God's blessings to the whole world. We are also fragile humans who tend to compromise way too much, who let the world shape us instead of the other way around.

It's a dilemma.

—*Michele Hershberger*

PRAYING AND WALKING IN THE WORLD:

- The contemporary examples of this dilemma are myriad. Do you let pre-Christian youth play in your worship band? Do you go into bars to build relationships with people so they will hear what you have to say about God? Do you let your kids watch R-rated movies if those films really make some powerful statements about life? Discuss these situations with others. Can you see both sides of the argument?

- Do you have a desire to interact with those outside the faith? Can you pray and ask God to give you more of a desire for this?

- In what ways do you compromise too much?

NOVEMBER 21 *(FOR CHILDREN AND FAMILIES)*

OFFERINGS

PLUNGING INTO THE WORD:

Exodus 34:17-28

PONDERING ON THE WAY:

Every Sunday in church there is a special time. Ushers come down the aisles and pass baskets or bags down every row. This is the offering time. People put money in the baskets. The money goes to help the church and people around the world.

Why do we give the money? God asks us to give back the first of everything we have. This means the first of our money, the first of our time, and the first of our talent.

God doesn't need our money or our toys or our food. God has everything in the world already. God asks us to give our first because it is a way to honor God. By giving back to the Lord, we say thank you. God gave us everything we have, so it's only right that we should say thanks.

Offering money, time, and talent to God is also a good way to show we trust God to take care of us. It might be hard to trust that God will provide for all of our needs, since we can't see God. Giving God the first and best shows a lot of trust.

The Israelites were herders and farmers. They gave the firstborn calf without knowing if there would be more calves. Farmers gave the first part of their crop, not knowing if more would grow. Maybe your mom and dad give the first part of their paycheck from work. Our "firsts" represent our own survival. In order to give the first calf or the first crop, you have to believe the Lord will give you the rest.

Besides, since God gave us everything we have, that stuff isn't really ours. Everything we have belongs to God. So when God asks us to give back our first and our best, God is only asking for a little bit of what really belongs to God. We are so thankful for God's love and care that we gladly give our first and best in our offering. It's not just for the church; it's to thank God for our blessings and to say, "I trust in you."

—*Michele Hershberger*

PRAYING AND WALKING IN THE WORLD:

- What are the gifts God has given you? How can you give the first of them back?

- Do you trust God enough to give God the first of everything?

- Get a fancy basket or box and have an offering time. If you don't have any money to give to God, maybe you can draw a picture for God and write down some words that tell God what you will give him.

- **Adults:** Do you give the first of your paycheck? Look over your checkbook. Who or what do you worship? Do you give the first of your time? Look at your day planner or blackberry. Whom do you worship with your time?

NOVEMBER 22

LUMINARIES

PLUNGING INTO THE WORD:

Exodus 34:29-35

PONDERING ON THE WAY:

No sooner is Thanksgiving turkey done than homes become ablaze with icicles on eaves, reindeers on lawns, and stars on roofs. As spectacular as these well-lit homes are, my favorite home is one that skips humongous electric bills for humble paper bags. Along their walkway, my neighbors place two dozen paper bags filled with sand, into which they place a candle to be lighted at evening. These luminaries are beautiful in their simplicity.

In a sense, Moses was a luminary. Today's portion of the story starts when Moses comes down from the mountain after fifty days spent with God renewing the covenant between God and the people. In his hands are two tablets filled with the Ten Commandments. He was not aware that his skin was ablaze with the reflected glory of God. The Israelites became afraid of this man who they thought had become a "god" in his trips up the mountain.

To quell their fears, every time he relayed God's words to the people, Moses veiled his face. And when he returned to speak with God, he removed the veil. This sensitivity to the people indicates that Moses didn't desire hero worship. He knew he was simply a luminary reflecting the light. This light didn't make him a god but allowed him to focus the people's sights on the light of the one true God.

In the coming holiday season, true radiance doesn't have to be about outward show but about shine from the inside out. Perhaps this year it's time to keep the icicles veiled in their boxes and to uncover the simplicity of candlelight.

—*Laurie Oswald Robinson*

PRAYING AND WALKING IN THE WORLD:

- Reflect on what hinders you from keeping Christmas simple. Maybe it's family expectations, keeping up with the Joneses, covering up an inner emptiness that seems out of sync with a "holly, jolly Christmas."

- Pray for renewal of a humble spirit that will substitute the inner glow of Christ for the outward show of Christmas.

- Invite family and/or friends over to create luminaries for your yards for the holidays.

NOVEMBER 23

FREE OR FORCED?

PLUNGING INTO THE WORD:

Exodus 35:1-29

PONDERING ON THE WAY:

Many Christians are realizing that passion, not programs, enlivens people to be the hands and feet of Christ in the world. Congregations are changing the way they do church to reflect this new insight. Some programs that have been operational for decades are being replaced by short-term ministries that last only months. People who have a specific passion and pursue it are those who create the ministries for a particular "season."

Moses, who led God's people long before our twenty-first-century ministry models took hold, didn't have formal ministry training. But he did have direct contact with God, from whom he received instructions for the building of the tabernacle. Moses didn't rely on prodding or pushing to get the job done. Instead, people's passions drew them to the task. Verse 21 says, "And they came, everyone whose heart was stirred, and everyone whose spirit was willing, and brought the Lord's offering to be used for the tent of meeting and for all its service, and for the sacred vestments." The tabernacle was built and furnished because of freewill offerings, not forced service.

This Old Testament community shows us that today's passion-based ministries have precedent. These ministries reduce ambivalent involvement, and they free people to be creative and fully engaged. How about you? Are a stirred spirit and willing heart motivating you to be all God is calling you to be, to give all God is calling you to give? Or are you filling an obligation to perform or a service for which you are not gifted?

—*Laurie Oswald Robinson*

PRAYING AND WALKING IN THE WORLD:

- Reflect on the above questions. What most motivates you to serve in your community and/or congregation?

- Pray for a deeper awareness of your gifts. If you feel passionless, ask God why this is the case. Ask for the light of the Holy Spirit to stir your spirit and rekindle a willing heart.

- Talk with friends in your church family about what it means to be led by passion rather than driven by performance.

- An excellent book to read is *When There's No Burning Bush: Following Your Passions to Discover God's Call* by Gary Morsch and Eddy Hall, published by Baker Books. Order from www.bakerbooks.com, Amazon.com, or your local bookstore.

NOVEMBER 24 *(FOR CHILDREN AND FAMILIES)*

EYES BIGGER THAN STOMACH

PLUNGING INTO THE WORD:

Exodus 35:30—36:7

PONDERING ON THE WAY:

Have you ever been really hungry, filled your plate with food, but then couldn't eat everything? Maybe it happens to you at Thanksgiving, when the turkey, mashed potatoes, pumpkin pie, and all of the other food looks so good! But before your plate is clean, you feel like a stuffed turkey yourself! You can't eat another bite! That's when your parents might say, "Your eyes were bigger than your stomach."

In today's Bible story, Moses felt stuffed too, in a different way. It wasn't turkey that was overflowing on his plate. As he led God's people to build a huge church, people brought so many offerings to help build it that Moses had to tell them to stop bringing their gifts. They had enough.

This was not a bad problem for Moses—it was wonderful! And it's not bad to enjoy a big meal at Thanksgiving or other times with friends and family. Having food, money, and things is good when we know how to use them without wasting them and when we thank God for them.

As we sit down at tables filled with food, let's be sure to thank God for everything we have. Let's also find ways to care for people who don't have enough, and to share with them because we have too much.

—*Laurie Oswald Robinson*

PRAYING AND WALKING IN THE WORLD:

- Ask God to help you share your toys, time, and love with other children.

- Do you know kids who belong to families who don't have a big feast at Thanksgiving? Talk about ways you and your family can provide something special for them this season.

- **Adults:** What's happening in your fellowship of believers? Is the passion so strong that your leaders have had to ask you to stop giving?

NOVEMBER 25

THIN PLACES

PLUNGING INTO THE WORD:

Isaiah 9:1-7

PONDERING ON THE WAY:

Author's note: There is a term in the Celtic spiritual tradition called "thin places," where the spiritual and the natural world intersect. It's a place where it's possible to touch and be touched by God and to experience a deep sense of God's presence in our everyday world.

THIN PLACES

There is a place where the lonely
who have lived in a land of deep darkness
see a great light.
It is the place where blue-black sleep of fear
flutters open to the orange-fuschia eyes of dawn
and new sight.
It is the place where estranged lovers and friends
decide that time is too short
to fight.
It is the place where a son
touches his troubled family
with peace and might.
It is a place where a throne of power
reigns with justice
and makes wrongs right.
It is a place where the Wonderful Counselor,
Mighty God, Everlasting Father, Prince of Peace
brings morning out of night.

>   —*Laurie Oswald Robinson*

PRAYING AND WALKING IN THE WORLD:

- Identify three thin places in your life.

- As an experiment, spend time in prayer early tomorrow morning and late at night. How does communing with God at these times make you more receptive to the intersection of your humanity with divinity?

- Buy or borrow a book about Celtic spirituality and journal about some of its aspects.

NOVEMBER 26

THE BADGE OF POLITENESS

PLUNGING INTO THE WORD:

Isaiah 40:1-11

PONDERING ON THE WAY:

In the church family where I grew up, many of us wore badges of politeness. I may have just fought with my brother, or my family may have had a stressful week. But once we came to church, we, like others, were polished in our Sunday best and wore sunny smiles. When I got a little older, I remember thinking, *How are these people really feeling?*

Only later did I learn that this politeness existed throughout the wider church. And later still, I learned to be more transparent. I now regularly confess that storms trouble the blue skies of my life. My journey has potholes and dead ends. And I walk through many valleys. It isn't until I take off my badge of politeness that I experience God's comfort in confession.

It is the kind of comfort found in today's Scripture verses. The prophet foresaw that God's people would break their covenant with God, a choice bringing exile. The road ahead would be roughened with the rocks of disobedience, ambivalence, and estrangement. But after their suffering, God would prepare the way of the Lord in their wilderness, make straight in the desert a highway of their God, and lift up their valleys. Their mountains and hills would be made low, their uneven ground would become level, and their rough places would become plain. The glory of the Lord, in the midst of the gore of their humanity, would be revealed.

Believers can have this comfort, but it comes with a price. We must turn in our badges of politeness in exchange for honest confessions of our pain and struggle. Only when we shed our exterior prettiness can the Lord's word dress us. By confessing our humanity, that withers like grass and flowers, we can allow the Lord's glad tidings to strengthen us.

—*Laurie Oswald Robinson*

PRAYING AND WALKING IN THE WORLD:

- Reflect on when you are most tempted to wear your badge of politeness? How is that badge impeding your spiritual growth? How is it impeding the spiritual growth of others?

- Pray for God's help to trade in your badge of politeness for honest confession of pain and struggle. If you are feeling strong right now, pray for spiritual eyes to see how the word and life of the Lord is providing this strength in the fleetingness of your humanity.

- Identify one friend or family member who needs a confidant so they can take off their badge of politeness. Bring the Lord's comfort to them, just as the prophet brought God's comfort to the Israelites.

NOVEMBER 27 *(FOR CHILDREN AND FAMILIES)*

FALLING AND FLYING

PLUNGING INTO THE WORD:

Isaiah 40:27-31

PONDERING ON THE WAY:

When a baby eaglet is old enough to learn to fly, her mother takes her for a wild ride on her back. While she's flying, the mother eagle flips over, and the eaglet begins to try to fly. The papa eagle oversees this flight school. If an eaglet can't fly, he'll swoop down at a high speed to catch the baby before it hits the ground. Most eaglets do not learn how to fly the first time they try. They continue the flight process until they learn.

The parent eagles have five main feathers on each wing. This is so they can adjust their wings during long training fights to keep the eaglet from falling to the ground. The eaglet is always under the close care of the mother and father during training. Once the eaglet flies, the papa and mama eagle fly around in a circle in celebration.

Today's Bible story tells us that God, like a father and mother eagle, sees our every move and cares about every little or big thing in our lives. More than that, God never has to go to sleep or take a break. Today's verses even compare us with baby eagles learning to fly! Verses 21-32 say that even though youths will faint and be weary, those kids who wait on God's strength will mount up with wings like eagles.

When we are learning to ride a bike or make a new friend or move to another town, God helps us do these hard or new things. When we get tired or afraid, God, like a mother or father eagle, scoops us up when we are about to fall and carries us through the hard times.

—Laurie Oswald Robinson

PRAYING AND WALKING IN THE WORLD:

- **Adults and children:** The following passages also refer to God as a mother eagle: Deuteronomy 32:10-12; Psalm 17:8, 36:7, 57:1, 61:4, 63:7, 91:4. Read them. How does it feel to you to imagine God as an eagle carrying you on its wings? When do you need that assurance the most?

- Go online to this website: *http://animal.discovery.com/convergence/spyonthewild/birdtech/birdtech.html.* On this site you can actually take a ride on the wings of an eagle!

- Pray this prayer, filling in the blank with your own words: Carry me, God, on your swift, strong wings. I need you to carry me through _____ right now. Hold me up. I can't do this alone. I am tired and troubled. Give me the lift I need. I need you, God. Amen.

NOVEMBER 28

WHERE'S WALDO?

PLUNGING INTO THE WORD:

Isaiah 42:1-4

PONDERING ON THE WAY:

Where's Waldo? is a series of children's books created by the British illustrator Martin Handford. Readers are to find Waldo in a busy picture full of people. Waldo wears a red and white striped shirt, carries a wooden walking stick and wears thick glasses. He loses things, including books and even his shoes. The challenge also is to spot these items in the illustrations of hundreds of tiny people doing various amusing things. The reader searches hard to find a well-hidden Waldo among the group, but his distinct character gives him away.

Today's passage identifies a person whose character is marked by servanthood. These four verses comprise the first of four of what biblical scholars call "servant songs" in Isaiah. Scholars don't agree on whether the servant in these passages is Israel, a figure such as Moses, or Christ himself. But they do agree the songs describe a servant of the Lord: someone who carries out justice, who lights the way to eternal life, who bears the burdens of others and provides encouragement, and who brings forth righteousness.

Verses 2 and 3 describe the nature of this justice-keeping servant. He will not cry or lift up his voice or make it heard in the street; this servant will not break a bruised reed; this servant will not quench a dimly burning wick. In other words, this servant is a humble person who deals gently with broken and weak people.

In the end, these songs contain lyrics that describe who we are to become as God's servants. Can other people spot us in the unjust and self-seeking pages of our world?

—*Laurie Oswald Robinson*

PRAYING AND WALKING IN THE WORLD:

- Reflect on the characteristics that define who you are. Do they contain elements of today's passage?

- Pray that God will transform you into someone identified as a servant in our self-seeking world. Pray for new intimacy to develop between you and the supreme servant, Jesus Christ.

- Just for fun, buy or borrow several of the books in the *Where's Waldo?* series and share them with family and/or friends.

NOVEMBER 29

HARRIED-NESS AND HOLINESS

PLUNGING INTO THE WORD:

Isaiah 42:5-9

PONDERING ON THE WAY:

We are entering Advent, the four weeks during which we prepare to welcome Christ into our world. Everywhere we go this holiday, we will be confronted with a choice: Will we heed the "idols of harried-ness" or the "angels of holiness"? In other words, will we grab the spirit of commercialism with its jingle and jangle? Or will we embrace the spirit of quietness that allowed humble shepherds to hear angels proclaiming the coming Savior?

Articulating this choice between commerciality and spirituality has become a cliché. We don't want to be trite. So, we don't talk about the guilt we feel when we eat too much, shop too much, go too much—all of which can woo us into idolatry. But today's passage doesn't let us off the hook that easily. Verse 8 tells us that God's servant will be a light to the nations, will open the eyes that are blind, and will bring prisoners out of the dungeon. The power for this liberating justice comes from the fact that God's servants give glory only to God and do not praise idols.

Fleeing after the season's idols may bring us temporary excitement. But that flight could dull the ability of Christmas "angels" to pierce through the dungeons and blindness of our lives with eternal light and love. The choice is ours—prisons or power.

—*Laurie Oswald Robinson*

PRAYING AND WALKING IN THE WORLD:

- Reflect on what comprises your idols of harried-ness. What comprises your angels of holiness? What or who shapes your tendency to choose one over the other?

- Pray that the Holy Spirit will quiet your spirit in the harried-ness of your environment so you can better focus on the holiness of the season.

- Place an image of Christmas angels on your refrigerator, your car dashboard, or your work desk as a reminder to slow down and to listen for the angel songs of joy announcing Christ's coming and coming again.

NOVEMBER 30

SPRINGING UP

PLUNGING INTO THE WORD:

Isaiah 44:1-5

PONDERING ON THE WAY:

This devotional is a mountaintop in my life as a writer. It is the last devotional I write out of the 125 assigned to me for this book! (Yes, I have some in December, but we didn't write everything in chronological order.) The moment brings nostalgic smiles and sighs as I remember the hours and hours spent the last twelve months in praying, reflecting, reading, and writing. Time after time, just when I feared my well was running dry, God's flow of new life sprang up once again to bring insight and strength.

To my delight, today's passage in Isaiah 44 parallels the theme of our book, "Now it springs forth" (Isaiah 43:19). In today's passage, the prophet reminds us that God is the one who has formed the people of Israel and each one of us in the womb. And it is God's Spirit who will pour water on the thirsty land, and streams on the dry ground of our lives. It is God's Spirit who will be poured out upon our descendants, and God's Spirit will bless our offspring. The blessing will cause this offspring to spring up like a green tamarisk and like willows by flowing streams.

I don't have children, but I have a sense that one of my "descendants" is this book.

In the sometimes dry journey of late night and early morning writing, God's creative energy brought buoyant, fresh streams. This book is a witness to the springing-up power of God. Created and chosen by God to be servants, Carol, Michele, and I desire to minister this new life to others. I invite you, the reader, to join the flow, as you allow the Spirit of God to spring up within the thirsty lands of your soul.

—*Laurie Oswald Robinson*

PRAYING AND WALKING IN THE WORLD:

- Reflect on where you need God to spring up afresh within you. Name the dry grounds of your life and the specific thirsts of your soul.

- In prayer today, ask the Lord to water those dry places with holy streams. Thank the Lord for being the source of all that nurtures and blesses your soul and the lives of your loved ones—children, other relatives or friends, and church family.

- Within the next month, make time for a half-day or daylong retreat. Use the time to invite God's springing-up power to revive you.

DECEMBER 1

NOSES IN THE AIR

PLUNGING INTO THE WORD:

Isaiah 45:14-19

PONDERING ON THE WAY:

Few animals can portray arrogance like a llama. When I sold my llama, Hunter, to a guy down the road to guard his sheep, I had no idea Hunter would hold it against me. I'm sure he doesn't have anything against his new home—he just has an attitude about the fact that I did it to him. When I stop by, he comes running to the fence to see who it is, his long banana ears forward with curiosity. Then, when he realizes it's me, those ears go straight back, his nose shoots up in the air, and he literally turns his butt to me. At that moment, it's all about him, and he is one stuck-up llama.

Religious arrogance or snobbery has been a pitfall for people of faith from the beginning. In this passage, we can see the Israelites walking the fine line between having their noses in the air because God is with them, and acknowledging with humility that God is indeed with them. The difference between religious snobbery and faithful confession can be summed up in the phrase, "It's not about you. It's all about God."

It's not about other nations coming under our control. It's not about making a lot of money. It's not about your son or daughter getting a full-ride scholarship to college.

It's all about the God who created the heavens, formed the earth, organized it to be habitable, and who speaks the truth. It's all about God doing what God does, and when we benefit from that, when blessings come our way, our response is faithful confession.

Rick Warren, author of *The Purpose Driven Life* and other books that have made him a millionaire many times over, has responded to God's blessings by doing reverse tithing. He gives away ninety percent of his income and lives essentially the same lifestyle he did before fortune and fame hit. His nose isn't in the air. Arrogance has not been a byproduct of his success. He seeks to be a faithful steward of his resources.

May God bless us, and may we respond with faithful confession that the Lord and the Lord alone is our God.

—*Carol Duerksen*

PRAYING AND WALKING IN THE WORLD:

- Do you get arrogant about people who are arrogant? Do you consider yourself better than those who are religious snobs? Repent.

- Do leaders in your country believe that God is on the side of your country? What do you think?

- Pray for humility.

DECEMBER 2

THE ONLY AWESOME ONE

PLUNGING INTO THE WORD:

Isaiah 45:20-25

PONDERING ON THE WAY:

I heard the other day that the people who work editing dictionaries were talking about taking out the word *awesome*. I don't think they really wanted the word to become officially nonexistent; I think they were just rebelling against the huge overuse it's been experiencing over the past few years. Even now, as I'm writing, I'm hearing a television commercial for pizza, and the word *awesome* was used twice in a few seconds.

"Our God is an awesome God." There's that word again, only this time it's attributed to someone who truly deserves it. This Isaiah passage resounds with the power of God!

Hey ya'all!
Come here!
You who don't have a clue—
Praying to deadwood
(with emphasis on the dead!)
State your case!
You won't get far.
Because if I've said it once,
I've said it a thousand times
I am the One and Only God!
Read my lips—
I am the One and Only God!

So get a life!
Get it from me,
With me
Through me!

Get a life
Get on your knees
Declare it loud!
Awesome!
I am the Only One who deserves the word!
Awesome!

    —Carol Duerksen

PRAYING AND WALKING IN THE WORLD:

- Sing or listen to a song like "Our God Is an Awesome God" or "All Hail the Power" as you contemplate what that means. What does it mean in terms of the universe? The earth? The nations of the world? Your life?

- Pray on your knees. Humble yourself physically and spiritually before God.

- Pray the alphabet, praising God with twenty-six different words.

- Promise to tell someone about the awe you feel for God, but don't use the word *awesome*. Find other words to describe God.

DECEMBER 3

SALVATION FOR OSAMA

PLUNGING INTO THE WORD:

Isaiah 49:1-7

PONDERING ON THE WAY:

The Servant's salvation is for Osama bin Laden.

Jesus loves Dennis Rader, the serial killer from Wichita, self-proclaimed as BTK because he would bind, torture, and kill his women victims.

God's plan includes redemption for the Hutus who massacred eight hundred thousand of their Tutsi neighbors in Rwanda.

Really?

Let's be honest. Don't we often picture God within the confines of our community, our kind of people, our nation? One of my mind-pictures of Jesus is the kind shepherd because … well, because I've seen pictures of him like that and because I have sheep. I understand that image of Jesus.

I do not understand terrorists and their way of thinking. I do not understand how people can do unspeakable things to other human beings—I can't even put my old cats to sleep. I don't understand the connection between a God of love and persons filled with hate.

I understand the verse that says, "I am honored in the sight of the Lord, and my God has become my strength."

But then verse 8 says, basically, "It's not enough. The plan is much bigger. The plan is for all nations—for salvation to reach the ends of the earth."

The picture in my head is salvation somehow spreading sweetly across a world map, smothering it with goodness and joy. But I don't see how it soaks into Osama, Dennis, and Hutus.

The picture needs to change. Isaiah 40:13: "Who has directed the spirit of the Lord, or as his counselor has instructed him?" Paul recalls Isaiah's words in 1 Corinthians 2:16, and then he adds this: "But we have the mind of Christ."

There it is. We have the mind of Christ. And when we don't, we'd better be on our knees.

—*Carol Duerksen*

PRAYING AND WALKING IN THE WORLD:

- How do you see salvation reaching the ends of the earth? What is your role?

- Pray for the mind of Christ. What does that mean specifically for you?

DECEMBER 4

MAKE NOISE, FOR GOD'S SAKE!

PLUNGING INTO THE WORD:

Isaiah 49:8-13

PONDERING ON THE WAY:

Wouldn't it be fun to give this passage to a film animator?

Imagine: Little animated people—all you see is eyes—shut away in total darkness. Suddenly, a door swings open. Light! The little people tumble out, falling over one another in their hurry to escape their despair.

A smooth, winding path (think yellow brick road) invites them on a road trip, and they set off. Through towering mountains and lush valleys they trek, stopping at sparkling streams to drink, delighting in the treats set out along the roadside just for them. The sun caresses the travelers, the breeze kisses them softly, and suddenly they break into song.

And it isn't just tiny high-pitched voices singing! A low bass rumbles from somewhere deep in the earth, a hallelujah chorus explodes across the sky, and snowcapped mountains are harmonizing in glorious song!

Can you imagine? Animators and children can. Unfortunately, many of us adults have lost much of our ability to imagine scenes like mountains singing.

But it's not just a lack of imagination—I think it's a lack of gratitude. If we were overflowing with praise and thankfulness for God's deliverance and presence in our lives, we'd be singing so loud that the mountains and plains would reverberate with us. It's time for us to make some noise, for God's sake!

—*Carol Duerksen*

PRAYING AND WALKING IN THE WORLD:

- Use your imagination to draw, write, sing, or dance the story of God's compassion and presence as you know it.

- Pray out loud! Praise out loud!

DECEMBER 5 *(FOR CHILDREN AND FAMILIES)*

PALM PILOTS

PLUNGING INTO THE WORD:

Isaiah 49:14-21

PONDERING ON THE WAY:

Do you or your parents use a palm pilot to help keep track of schedules, things to buy, places to be?

I do. Like right now my palm says "Adam" because I saw Adam yesterday, and seeing him reminded me that I owe him some money. So I wrote "Adam" on my palm to remind me to pay him when I got home.

Yes, I use the "original palm pilot"—writing on my hand with a pen.

Did you know God uses a palm pilot like I do? Yep. In Isaiah 49:16, God says, "See, I have inscribed you on the palms of my hands."

Why would God say that?

Because God wants to remember us.

Of course God doesn't actually have to write something down in order to remember it. But in this story from the Bible, the Israelites think that God has forgotten about them. They are complaining, thinking that God has forsaken them. But God says in response, "No way could I forget you! See, I've even written you on the palms of my hands."

God's people are written on God's hands—now *that's* a palm pilot I want to be on. And by the way, it won't ever need upgrading!

—*Carol Duerksen*

PRAYING AND WALKING IN THE WORLD:

- **Children:** Trace around your hand. Write "I love you. God" on the hand. Cut it out and put it someplace you'll see it often.

- **Adults:** Put a message in your electronic scheduler or on your calendar that will remind you of God's love for you.

- Write someone's name on your hand for one day and pray for that person every time you look at your hand.

DECEMBER 6

WAITING WITH A GOOD BOOK

PLUNGING INTO THE WORD:

Isaiah 49:22-26

PONDERING ON THE WAY:

I hate to wait. The only thing that makes waiting bearable for me is a good book. If I can read, I can wait. But just passing time, waiting, does not sit well with me.

God's people have spent years waiting. They waited to reach the Promised Land. They waited for deliverance from their enemies. They waited for the Messiah.

One thing that made the waiting bearable was having a good book to read. For thousands of years, that "book" was oral history, which eventually was written down. Today, our Good Book is the Bible. And just like God's people of the past, we experience God's faithfulness, at the same time waiting and yearning for the fulfillment of God's promises. We read the Good Book not only to pass the time, but to help us understand the passing of time. God's timing is not our timing, and quite frankly, that doesn't always sit well with us.

The last part of verse 23 tells us that "those who wait for me shall not be put to shame." Eugene Peterson's translation in *The Message* is, "No one who hopes in me ever regrets it."

So whether it sits well with us or not, we find ourselves waiting and hoping. Whether our oppressor is cancer or clinical depression, an addiction or a government, physical violence or mental trauma, we turn to God for hope and deliverance. We wait with a Good Book. We wait with a Great God.

—*Carol Duerksen*

PRAYING AND WALKING IN THE WORLD:

- Talk to God about your "waiting issues."

- What is your favorite passage of hope? If you don't have it committed to memory, do so.

DECEMBER 7 *(FOR CHILDREN AND FAMILIES)*

JESUS STANDS WITH ME

PLUNGING INTO THE WORD:

Isaiah 50:4-9

PONDERING ON THE WAY:

If you push me
And I don't push back,
It's not because I can't.
It's because I won't.

If you say bad things about me
And I don't say bad things about you,
It's not because you didn't hurt me.
It's because I refuse to hurt you.

If you call me names
And I don't call you names in return,
It's not because I'm a softy,
It's because I'm strong.

If I say I have a friend who helps me—
It's not because he's imaginary or make-believe.
It's because my friend Jesus has been there, done that.
It's because my friend Jesus stands with me.

And that's the truth.

    —*Carol Duerksen*

PRAYING AND WALKING IN THE WORLD:

- **Adults and children:** Talk about times when you have been bullied and pushed around physically or with words. How did you react?

- Next time you are being bullied or treated badly, sing "Jesus Loves Me" quietly in your head (or aloud if you want to) but change it to "Jesus Loves You."

DECEMBER 8

CINDERELLA, TAKE ONE

PLUNGING INTO THE WORD:

Isaiah 52:13-15

PONDERING ON THE WAY:

There are a lot of Cinderella stories; rags to riches, servant to king. Most popular recently are sports stories. There was even a boxing movie recently called *Cinderella Man*. In this movie genre, the team or individual suffers, but then they get a new coach, a new star, a new chance to be something, or even a new yellow lab who can play basketball/football/volleyball/Roller Derby/mah jong with the greatest of ease. Without fail, these teams succeed. They are exalted over their rivals. It may have taken a miracle, but the *Angels in the Outfield* sure aren't *Bad News Bears* anymore since they learned to play *Hardball* and emerged triumphant as *Mighty* um … *Ducks*.

The point of the movies is that the normal people can succeed, even if they live as servants to their evil stepmothers. The movies are meant to make us feel better about ourselves. Because truly, anyone can succeed.

The prophecies of Isaiah are meant to comfort the Israelites. The Israelites were suffering. They had not won a game in years. They needed new uniforms. They needed a dream to follow. Israel is the suffering servant. They were the vessels of God's blessing to the whole world, and yet as a people they had undergone many hardships; so many, in fact, that their appearance was marred beyond recognition.

What does it mean that they would prosper? The suffering servant in this passage can also be Jesus. Jesus humbled himself. Jesus suffered, but God exalted Jesus above any nation and any person. True followers can expect the same thing. Now, this exaltation may look different from what the world offers. Prosperity in God's kingdom has a different feel than prosperity in the world. God has an upside-down kingdom.

But then again, who wants celebrity status when you can feel true joy?

Followers of Christ can expect some suffering. They may look foolish in the world— marred. Who would give up a lucrative career to be a missionary? Who would give up prestige to work with inner-city kids for almost no pay and certainly no fame? Who would even talk about nonresistance or laying down arms? That's crazy. That's a risk. That smacks of trusting in an almighty deity for ultimate protection.

Who will reign in the end? The humble, the crucified, the marred—ah, they will startle many nations. The humble, the crucified, the marred—truly they are the Cinderellas of this world.

—*Michele Hershberger*

PRAYING AND WALKING IN THE WORLD:

- What is the world's definition of *success* or *prosperity*? How does that differ from God's definition? Which definition does your life resemble more?

- Think of things that would create a "marred appearance" for the Israelites, for Jesus, and for Christians in today's society. What are foolish things that to God make perfect sense?

DECEMBER 9

WHO HAS BELIEVED

PLUNGING INTO THE WORD:

Isaiah 53:1-6

PONDERING ON THE WAY:

Who has believed what we proclaim
>   Every day from November 24 to December 25

That the one who can save us all
>   Most powerful, most glorious
Is the same one
>   Who was balding slightly
>   Fairly plain and surely not a snappy dresser

And despised no less
>   Rejected
>   Poked fun at—
Why, we saw him as a nobody
>   Has-been
>   No-account
>   Under-achiever.

Then there was the arrest
>   the flogging
"If you are the Son of God, then defend yourself"
>   the brutal hanging on that tree
>   (the real Christmas tree)

And we have all turned to our own way
>   We have all turned our backs
Because he's not the Messiah we want.

If you are the Son of God
Come down from there and make our lives pretty

And we really don't believe what Isaiah proclaimed
      And we've made a Jesus in our own image
A Jesus who nods approval as
      We kill Arabs in his name
Fighting for democracy as if it's
      next to godliness
A Jesus who despises sexual sins
      but sleeps peacefully in his
Suburban two-story
while others lie in the streets

Pretty Jesus
Nice Jesus
Cuddly Jesus

Who has believed what we have been shown
—the real Jesus.
      —*Michele Hershberger*

PRAYING AND WALKING IN THE WORLD:

- Which Jesus are you more comfortable with? The baby in the manger? The kind and wise teacher? Or the bleeding criminal on an execution stick? Are you tempted to keep Jesus in safe places like the manger bed?

- The kind of Jesus you believe in determines the kind of Christian you will be. If Jesus was an outcast because he challenged unjust systems and refused to use military power, then what does that mean for your ethics?

DECEMBER 10 *(FOR CHILDREN AND FAMILIES)*

WHEN BAD THINGS HAPPEN

PLUNGING INTO THE WORD:

Isaiah 53:7-9

PONDERING ON THE WAY:

Once, when I was in fifth grade, I was playing basketball on my elementary school playground. Suddenly, for no reason, someone from my class came over to me and knocked me down. I was so surprised, I didn't even think to run away or defend myself.

I had done nothing wrong. I couldn't figure out why she would hit me so hard. I hoped there had been some mistake and that somehow it had been an accident. But when I went to get my things and run inside, I found that my homework and the folder it had been in was ripped up. I was scared. I felt very sad.

Sometimes bad things happen to good people. The Israelites were good people, or at least they tried to be good people. But bad things happened to them anyway. They were sent away to live in a new place, a place they didn't like called Babylon. How would you like to be forced to move to another country and learn a new language and new customs? They didn't like it one bit! They thought God had left them.

Even Jesus, who is perfect, suffered. He was innocent, but bad things happened to him too. When bad things happen to us, Jesus understands. What's more, God promises that the suffering and bad things will not last forever, but a reward in heaven will last forever.

Jesus rose from the dead and saved us all. The Israelites came back from Babylon. And the person who hurt me on the playground? I forgave her, and we eventually became friends. Even though bad things happen and we can't change that, we can control how we react to it. What would Jesus do? Pray and forgive them, or plot revenge?

—Michele Hershberger

PRAYING AND WALKING IN THE WORLD:

- Has something bad ever happened to you that you didn't deserve? Have you known nice people who got hurt?

- What can you do about bad things that happen in the world? Talk to your parents about this. What did Jesus do when people were mean to him?

DECEMBER 11

PROMISE OF HOPE

PLUNGING INTO THE WORD:

Isaiah 53:10-12

PONDERING ON THE WAY:

During Advent, I like to reflect on what the world was like when Jesus was born. A part of me wants to believe in the syrupy sweet scenes of a clean, sleeping baby in the glowing barn, the entire world at peace, even the faces of the cows and the doves are all aglow. But part of me knows better. It wasn't like that at all.

The world in which Jesus was born was full of pain and hardship. There were brutal massacres, heavy taxes, a corrupt government. Most Jews were bonded servants. Thousands of men were crucified in Sephoris, a town four miles from Nazareth, just a couple of years before Jesus was born—crucified right along the main road so everyone could benefit from the object lesson. It was really a horrible time, a time not unlike the Palestine of today.

"Out of his anguish he shall see light." In a terrible, cold world, wrought with violence, poverty, and corruption, there was a light. On a dark night when two young, impoverished people were forced to sleep in a small barn, the hope of the world was born. What does it mean that our salvation is a seemingly illegitimate baby?

It means that out of darkness and pain comes light.

                                                          —*Michele Hershberger*

PRAYING AND WALKING IN THE WORLD:

- How does God help us see the light even in the midst of darkness?

- Are you going through a difficult time right now? Or do you have a close friend who struggles in the dark? Pray that God can help you see the light.

- What can you do to bring about light in the midst of anguish?

DECEMBER 12 *(FOR CHILDREN AND FAMILIES)*

SONG OF TRIUMPH

PLUNGING INTO THE WORD:

Isaiah 60:1-9

PONDERING ON THE WAY:

Act out the following passage. Read the sentences below and do the actions suggested in parenthesis, or make up your own actions, as you feel led.

Stand up and shine. *(Stand up from a kneeling position and spread out arms.)* Your light has come. *(Be the sun or a candle.)*

It is very dark. *(Cover eyes with hands.)* But the Lord has given you light. *(Open eyes.)*

People will come from everywhere to see the light of God's glory. *(Walk toward "light.")* Kings will come to kneel at God's throne. *(Be kings and march to a throne.)*

Everyone in the family will come together. *(Move together.)* The lost shall return and everyone will be safe again. *(Hug one another.)*

Everyone will be very happy. *(Jump for joy.)* You will have everything you want.

You will have camels. *(Pretend to be camels and go to the throne.)* You will have gold and frankincense. *(Be wise men and bring gifts.)*

You will have sheep. *(Pretend to be sheep.)*

No one will be afraid or run away. *(Run away, then come back.)*

Even people who live far, far away will come. *(Continue marching as from a long distance.)* They will be happy and joyful too *(Jump for joy again.)*

Everyone will praise God because God brought all that is good to you and to everyone. *(Bow or fold hands to pray.)*

> —Michele Hershberger

PRAYING AND WALKING IN THE WORLD:

- What things make you the happiest? God can make you even happier than those things can.

- Can you think of ways in which God's glory has been shown on Earth?

- Can you think of examples of people from many nations bringing glory to God? Is your church service like this?

DECEMBER 13

IN THE LORD'S WAY AND TIME

PLUNGING INTO THE WORD:

Isaiah 60:10-22

PONDERING ON THE WAY:

I love those Bible passages where the prophet says that my people will get their just deserts. *Your enemies will bow before you. They will come bearing gifts. All who despise you will come begging. They will kiss your feet.*

Oh yeah, I love it when they kiss my feet.

Lots of people love this passage for that same reason. I imagine that the religious descendants of Isaiah, the Jews, find much hope here. Their history has been smeared with the blood of their martyrs, choked by the fumes of Auschwitz. And some would say, because of passages like this one, that the United States and Canada should always support the nation-state of Israel, for God is in the business of blessing this specific government.

But what about the blood of others? What happens when people, fighting in the name of God, kill other people to make their superiority a reality, to make this passage come true?

Who are God's people? A certain ethnic group? A certain denomination? Or a people chosen for a mission, the mission to bless all the families on the earth, just like Abraham? Who is Zion? Is it not a mixed group, people from every tribe and nation, a people united in their obedience to the Lamb? (See Revelation 5:9.)

I love it when my team, my side, my people—win. But I must be careful to let God define who my people are.

"I am the Lord; in its time I will accomplish it quickly" (Isaiah 60:22).

It will happen—in the Lord's way and in the Lord's time.

>   —*Michele Hershberger*

PRAYING AND WALKING IN THE WORLD:

- When you hear the word *chosen* as it relates to the people of God, what do you think of? Specifically the Jews? The church? Anyone who will obey the Lord? Who are these blessings for?

- How do you balance the need for justice to reign with the understanding that we can't take that justice into our own hands? Can you wait for the Lord to make all things right? Can you imagine true justice in our world that is so full of innocents who suffer?

- Which of the lines of this passage should you be using as your prayer tonight for your city? Your state or province? Your country? Your world?

DECEMBER 14

AT THE HOMELESS SHELTER

PLUNGING INTO THE WORD:

Isaiah 61:1-9

PONDERING ON THE WAY:

A couple of nights ago, I slept at the homeless shelter. I serve there occasionally as an overnight host. It's a relatively easy job, helping fix supper for around twenty or thirty of us, spending the evening playing cards or watching TV, and then sleeping in the office next to the front door so I can hear the doorbell in the middle of the night.

A group of Christmas carolers came to sing for us, and one of the residents, affectionately named Snowball, went out of his way to disrupt the singing. He turned up his Walkman so loud that everyone could hear it through his earplugs. He could have played it in the men's sleeping room, but instead he paraded through the main room where we were singing—not once, but three times.

I don't know why Snowball had to act that way. Maybe he couldn't handle the sympathetic looks from the carolers. It's hard not to feel like you are on display at the poor person zoo.

Or maybe he couldn't stand to hear the words:

> *He comes the prisoners to release, in Satan's bondage held.*
> *The gates of brass before him burst, the iron fetters yield.*
> *He comes the broken heart to bind, the bleeding soul to cure,*
> *And with the treasures of his grace to enrich the humble poor.*

Jesus read from Isaiah 61 in his first appearance as a rabbi in his hometown synagogue in Nazareth. These verses speak of the Messiah, the Lord's Anointed, and what Messiah's job was to be:

Bring good news to the oppressed

Bind up the brokenhearted

Proclaim freedom for captives and

Release to prisoners. And …

Proclaim Jubilee, the year of the Lord's favor.

In this year, land was allowed to rest, slaves were freed, debts canceled, and land was returned to its original owners.

Jubilee is about giving people a second chance.

Most Christians spiritualize these verses in Isaiah, so that the Messiah's role is to free us from the bondage of sin ... and that is true, but—that's not all. If we really followed Isaiah 61, if we really followed the Messiah, there would be no homeless shelters. There would be no need.

But I still live in a broken world, a world of bankruptcy, drug addiction, abuse, and depression. So we fix supper, and laugh, and play cards at the shelter.

"Hark! The glad sound! The Savior comes, the Savior promised long ..."

—*Michele Hershberger*

PRAYING AND WALKING IN THE WORLD:

- Jesus came to heal us both spiritually and physically. How do you need his healing touch today?

- We are to be the hands and feet of Christ in the world. What debts do you need to cancel? What broken hearts are you to help mend? Who needs a second chance that you can help give?

- How can you help your government start to live out Jubilee principles? Pray and ask God's guidance.

DECEMBER 15

WAITING FOR LIGHT AND FIRE

PLUNGING INTO THE WORD:

Isaiah 64:1-4

PONDERING ON THE WAY:

When mother put on *Messiah* during my childhood and began baking Russian teacakes, I *knew* Christmas was coming. The faster the violins played Handel's masterpiece, the faster she stirred the batter. Following the cookie-baking concert was the concert of the Fort Dodge, Iowa, symphony, which performed the music each December.

As a small girl, some of the lyrics confused me. I think of two librettos taken from Malachi. The first was a solo, "He Is Like a Refiner's Fire." The second was sung by the chorus, "And He Shall Purify the Sons of Levi." These words didn't jibe with the sweet comfort of baby Jesus of our coffee-table crèche, lit by soft lights. How was it that the gentle light of the Christ child also contained a purifying fire of a heavenly king?

Isaiah 64 clarifies on this point. The prophets told people that waiting for God's deliverance would include the tough stuff as well as the tender. In verses 1-2 we read, "O that you would tear open the heavens and come down, so that the mountains would quake at your presence—as when fire kindles brushwood and the fire causes water to boil." God guided them out of seventy-plus years of Babylonian captivity back to their home by the preserving light of grace and acceptance. But that light also contained the purifying heat of suffering and judgment.

The music that once confounded me now makes perfect sense. Over the years, God has revealed God's self through light and fire, comfort and challenge. Advent, and any season of waiting for God, includes salvation and repentance, toughness and tenderness, gentle candlelight of comfort and huge brushfires of change.

—*Laurie Oswald Robinson*

PRAYING AND WALKING IN THE WORLD:

- Reflect on what you have been waiting for this Advent season—deliverance from a personal problem, help for a relative, a new depth to your spirituality, peace in your home?

- Share your hopes, dreams, and anticipations with the Lord. Write in a journal what you hear from God after you have unburdened your heart. What guiding light or what purifying fire is God speaking into this situation?

- Share Handel's *Messiah* with your family and/or friends this Advent season, either on a CD or at a live concert. Discuss how the masterpiece presents both sides of God's nature, the guiding light and the purifying fire.

DECEMBER 16 *(FOR CHILDREN AND FAMILIES)*

WOLVES AND LAMBS TOGETHER

PLUNGING INTO THE WORD:

Isaiah 65:7-25

PONDERING ON THE WAY:

Do you have a dog or a cat as a pet? How about a bird? Would you let a bird and a cat be in the same cage together? Probably not. Cats are known to eat birds—they are natural enemies.

Wolves and lambs are also natural enemies. Wolves eat lambs. But today's Bible story talks about wolves being kind enough to sit beside lambs and share a meal together! It's like they will be friends at a birthday party, sitting side by side and sharing ice cream and cake!

This idea of a wolf and lamb being friends gives us hope of a peaceful future that will last forever for those who believe and serve God. For these people, God will make a new heaven and a new earth—a place where strange but good things happen, like wolves and lambs being friends, like no more kids crying, like no more grandparents dying.

The next time you see two animals being friends—like a dog and a cat—remember that this togetherness is nothing compared with the future God has planned!

—*Laurie Oswald Robinson*

PRAYING AND WALKING IN THE WORLD:

- Talk to your parents or another trusted adult about what it means to be friends with everyone—even people you think are your enemies.

- In your prayers today, thank God that there will be a time someday in the future when everyone and all of the animals will get along with each other.

- Draw a picture of a wolf and lamb eating together. Can you think of other animals that are natural enemies? Draw a picture of them taking a nap together.

DECEMBER 17

THE ROSES AND THORNS OF *GUADETE*

PLUNGING INTO THE WORD:

Isaiah 66:18-24

PONDERING ON THE WAY:

Alfonso, my fiancé, brought me roses during our engagement. They filled my house with sweet aromas and the color of deep red. They also filled my heart with the aroma of a promise; he would come into my life in a way no one had ever done before and no one would ever do again in the same way. His coming would transform my life forever as we upheld our promise to love each other in good times and bad, for better or worse.

Engagement, with its anticipation, is a lot like Advent, which is now in its third week. I was filled with joy and wonder of all that was to come—our marriage, our honeymoon, our home. And in Advent we relive with joy Christ's first coming as a child and reflect in wonder on his second coming as King.

The third Sunday of Advent is called *Gaudete,* Latin for "rejoice," when many churches switch from lighting red candles in the Advent wreath to lighting the one pink candle—its color symbolizing the intensifying nearness of Christ's coming and coming again.

The book of Isaiah also is filled with themes of rejoicing over the Lord's coming to transform our world into a new heaven and a new earth. The Lord has come and will come again not only for Israel but for all nations. The Lord is coming "to gather all nations and tongues; and they shall come and shall see [God's] glory. "All flesh shall come to worship before" the Lord. A price will be paid by those who refuse to wait in faith for the Lord's coming. The prophet likens rebels to those who will itch and burn with worms and fire, rather than shine with God's glory.

This painful image doesn't fit with cheery holiday smells and bells. But Isaiah encourages us to remember that in any committed relationship, whether in our human commitments or our covenant with God, roses of love include the thorns of sacrifice.

—*Laurie Oswald Robinson*

PRAYING AND WALKING IN THE WORLD:

- Reflect on the "roses" and "thorns," and the rejoicing and the suffering, of your committed relationships. How can this Advent season of waiting help you embrace the fullness of your fidelity to God and to your loved ones?

- Close your eyes and imagine you are holding the soft Christ child and smelling the sweet hope of his incarnation. Then, imagine yourself beholding the Lord's second coming. Smell the incense of glorious reward awaiting the faithful and the acid smoke of purifying love for those who refuse to wait in faith. Journal your reflections.

- Read more about the historical roots of Advent and today's expressions of this season. If you are a person who observes Advent with a wreath at home, share what you learn with your family or friends. If you haven't used a wreath, find one on sale at the end of December or create one and use it next year.

DECEMBER 18

FABLES OR FOR REAL?

PLUNGING INTO THE WORD:

Luke 1:1-4

PONDERING ON THE WAY:

When I was a small child, my father read to me nearly every evening after supper. This half hour was our ritual: the same chair, the same books, the same smell of his whiskery face, the same lessons learned. What Peter Cottontail and other characters taught me about life were not fables but were for real, as real as my father's embrace and the time he spent loving me in a way I understood.

As a girl, I was just as impatient as I am today. Make a beeline for the story. Learn the lesson. Close the book. Open another. So it's with consternation that I read the first four verses of Luke. All the talk of writing an orderly account for Theophilus feels a bit like chaff blowing in the wind. Give me the grain, please.

But on deeper reflection, we can see that the writer of Luke wanted to assure us that God's incarnation in Jesus was not a fable. In verses 2-3, the writer reminds us that even though he was not an eyewitness to the events, they were for real. The following accounts were not made-up tales told by long-oppressed Jewish people who imagined deliverance from their centuries of bondage. A real baby in real history was bringing real salvation.

How about us this Christmas? Are we fostering a childlike spirit that embraces the story of God's incarnation as truth? Or are we so jaded by skepticism and intellectualism that we struggle to experience real comfort in the arms of a real God who sent us a real baby?

—*Laurie Oswald Robinson*

PRAYING AND WALKING IN THE WORLD:

- Reflect back to when you were a child. What elements of the Christmas story were most captivating? How about as an adult? How has the story changed for you over the years?

- Pray that God will restore your childlike openness not only to the truths of the story but to Christ, the real person in real history who brought real salvation.

- Share an evening meal sometime during Christmas with family and/or friends. Read the Christmas story aloud. Discuss what elements of the story fill you most with childlike wonder.

DECEMBER 19

TOO GOOD TO BE TRUE

PLUNGING INTO THE WORD:

Luke 1:5-25

PONDERING ON THE WAY:

The character of Zechariah in today's passage and in *The Nativity Story*, Hollywood's portrayal of Christ's birth, reflect seasons of my own disbelief. The screen's powerful depiction of the fear-ridden priest scratched open scars from my darkest Christmas.

In my twenties, I ran from the Lord because I acted in ways that made me disbelieve that God could still love me. To fill the resultant void in my soul, I engaged in a string of failed relationships. One Christmas day, I took a walk by myself in the snowy woods, nursing wounds incurred by yet another broken relationship. The woods' silence—punctuated only by the lonely *whoosh* of snow brushing off of trees—reflected the barren silence of my own heart. Disbelief in God's love had left me lost and loveless. My broken bond to Christ had broken me. His love was just too good to be true.

The filmmaker showed this same kind of brokenness in Zechariah. The camera zoomed in on his face, filling with pain the moment he lost his voice. This symbolized the loss of his faith that God would grant him and his wife, Elizabeth, a child in their old age. This child, like Elijah, would be a prophet of the Lord, turning Israelites toward God in repentance. But after years of infertility and unfulfilled waiting for the Messiah, he couldn't receive a message that seemed too good to be true.

Devotionals in the coming days will depict how Zechariah takes a journey from silence to words and from disbelief to belief. But as people who also struggle with disbelief, we can identify with today's dead end. Though it feels barren, it is a place filled with the grace of a God who dares bring us messages of joy in our jaded world. And because of this grace, perhaps we, like John, the son of the once-disbelieving Zechariah, can declare that a Messiah, who seems too good to be true, is true.

—*Laurie Oswald Robinson*

PRAYING AND WALKING IN THE WORLD:

- Reflect on what you are experiencing in your life right now that leaves you hungering for a too-good-to-be-true message. How is it similar or dissimilar to Zechariah's experience?

- Pray for the Lord to heal wounds incurred by disbelief in God's love, goodness, and provision. Ask God to lift this burden of jadedness and disillusionment and to replace it with the buoyancy of joy and delight.

- Rent *The Nativity Story* and watch it with your family and/or friends during Christmas. Discuss the character of Zechariah and how his disbelief is similar to your own. Also discuss how the return of his voice conveys God's grace.

DECEMBER 20

YES

PLUNGING INTO THE WORD:

Luke 1:26-38

PONDERING ON THE WAY:

MAGNIFICAT: A CHRISTMAS PRAYER OF *YES*

Lord, I don't understand where
my *yes* will lead.
I only know I must say it.
The winter is cold,
The night is dark.
There is no Star of Bethlehem to guide me
on the Kansas prairies.
But the memory of Mary blazes
a trail through my heart,
and the ever-living
Christ child is born afresh.
She was decades younger than I
when she said her *yes* that changed the world.
How I long to say a *yes* that will also change my world.
In the fear, the frailty, the faults
of myself and others,
a faithless *no* beckons me to speak,
but I refuse.

There is loveliness in a *yes*
that is frail and yet fearless
in the face of so much uncertainty.
I do not hope to be called blessed as Mary,
and yet in my willingness to pray
to the one light of love
in the endless abyss,
I feel your blessing—
warming my cold,
bringing royalty to my rough places,
becoming simple presence in complex mystery,
making a young and hopeful girl of me again
when I feel aged and jaded,
shaping out of this Christmas prayer a blessed peace.

    —*Laurie Oswald Robinson*

PRAYING AND WALKING IN THE WORLD:

- Reflect on your resistance to saying *yes* to God about a particular area of your life. What is most tempting you to say *no*? What about the model of Mary could embolden you to agree with God's plan, even though you don't understand it?

- Pray for renewed courage and faith to say yes, even though a *no* may seem to make more sense and would be less risky.

- Befriend someone you know who has suffered because they said *yes* to God, causing others to doubt their motives or their judgment.

DECEMBER 21 *(FOR CHILDREN AND FAMILIES)*

VISITING RELATIVES

PLUNGING INTO THE WORD:

Luke 1:39-45

PONDERING ON THE WAY:

Family members often travel to visit one another in the summertime or on holidays. When I was a girl, my father woke me up at 4:30 a.m. to make the long trip from Iowa to my cousins' Pennsylvania farm. Eighteen hours later, I jumped out of the car and happily greeted Uncle John, Aunt Alice, and Cousin Johnny. The pain of the long roadtrip was soon forgotten as I helped milk the cows, rode Johnny's pony, and ate fresh sweet corn until I was ready to burst.

Today's Bible story tells us about when Mary, pregnant with the baby Jesus, took a long journey to visit her relative, Elizabeth. Elizabeth was also pregnant with a baby boy. When Mary arrived, Elizabeth's baby jumped inside her tummy, and Elizabeth believed that this meant her baby was saying "Hi!" to Mary's baby. Years later, when the babies had grown up, Elizabeth's son would be known as John the Baptist, and he would tell people about Jesus, his cousin and the Son of God.

Your visits with relatives may not be exciting in the same way that Mary and Elizabeth's visit was, but your trips can be filled with lots of good times with cousins, grandparents, aunts, uncles, and other special people. Trips can be special times to remember how John the Baptist and Jesus grew from being babies to being important people in God's plan to bring us a Savior.

    —*Laurie Oswald Robinson*

PRAYING AND WALKING IN THE WORLD:

- Draw two pictures: one of a fun visit to the home of a relative and the other of Mary's visit with Elizabeth.

- In your bedtime prayers, thank God for sending Jesus into the world to be your friend and Savior.

- **Adults:** Have you ever felt a "Holy Spirit connection" with another person? Has your "heart jumped within you," even as Elizabeth's baby jumped within her womb at the sound of Mary's voice?

  Here's a story from Maynard Knepp, Carol Duerksen's husband: While he was in Burundi, Africa, on a trip with Mennonite Central Committee, Maynard met a man named Cassien. Cassien had a spirit about him—a quiet, strong, unquestionable Holy Spirit that Maynard had never encountered in anyone before. He felt it when they talked, and he felt it when they shook hands. Maynard knew, both from hearing Cassien's stories and from being in his presence, that this was indeed a man of God. Maynard's heart "jumped within him" when they spent time together, and that interaction has changed Maynard's life.

DECEMBER 22

SINGING MARY'S SONG

PLUNGING INTO THE WORD:

Luke 1:46-56

PONDERING ON THE WAY:

The Christmas season is full of music: "Glory to God in the highest," the song of the angels in Scripture; beloved Christmas hymns; and the tradition of caroling at homes of friends and relatives. But of all the season's songs, Mary's song, or the "Magnificat," is one of the most profound and impacting.

In the song, we find a pattern for Christian discipleship. *She gives glory to the Giver of Christ, not to herself.* Rather than focus on the merits of her cooperation, she focuses on the one who makes her cooperation with God's plan possible. "My soul magnifies the Lord, and my spirit rejoices in God my Savior. ... The Mighty One has done great things for me, and holy is his name."

She joins God in working for truth and justice in the world. "He has shown strength with his arm; he has scattered the proud in the thoughts of their hearts. He has brought down the powerful from their thrones, and lifted up the lowly; he has filled the hungry with good things, and sent the rich away empty." She cooperates with this justice-keeping God by giving birth to the ministry of Emmanuel, or "God with us."

She accepts her giftedness from God, neither downplaying nor inflating her significance. She acknowledges that God's favor and not her ability is what gives her life meaning. But neither does she let a sense of unworthiness reject that favor: "He has looked with favor on the lowliness of his servant. Surely, from now on all generations will call me blessed."

No matter what our theology about Mary, we can agree that her *yes* changed the world forever. May we emulate and echo her song as we sing our *yes* in our way in our world.

—*Laurie Oswald Robinson*

PRAYING AND WALKING IN THE WORLD:

- Reflect on Mary's *yes* and list ways her song can help you say your *yes* to God. How does this song reflect the balance of contemplation and action, of humility and favor, of praise and penitence?

- Pray for a deeper awareness and openness of how Mary is a model for your own Christian discipleship.

- Read *The Prayer of Mary: Living the Surrendered Life* by Keith Fournier with Lela Gilbert.

- Listen to or sing the song, "My Soul Is Filled with Joy (And Holy Is Your Name)." This song uses the words from Mary's Magnificat. It can be found in the songbook *Sing the Journey* from Herald Press, and the CD can be ordered from Mennolink.org.

DECEMBER 23 *(FOR CHILDREN AND FAMILIES)*

WHAT'S YOUR NAME?

PLUNGING INTO THE WORD:

Luke 1:57-66

PONDERING ON THE WAY:

What's your name? Say it out loud right now.

More than anything you will get for Christmas this year—a doll, a bike, a computer game—your name is one of the most important gifts you have ever received.

Hearing your name helps you know when it's time to stop playing and come to the table for dinner, or when to answer a teacher's question. It's also the one word that will remain with you always. It is on your birth certificate, and it will be one of the last words mentioned at your funeral. Most of all, it is the one word given to you by your parents, who brought you into this world. It ties you to your family forever.

Today's Bible story tells us about a baby given the name "John." John's father, Zechariah, gave him that name because an angel told him to. When the angel told Zechariah that he and his wife were going to have a baby, Zechariah didn't believe the angel because he thought they were too old. And because he didn't believe the angel, Zechariah suddenly couldn't talk anymore. In fact, he couldn't say a word until his son was born.

When the baby was born, the rest of the family wanted to name him Zechariah, after his father, but his mother, Elizabeth, said, "No, he is to be called John." And as soon as Zechariah wrote the name down on a tablet, he could talk again! This moment was so powerful that the family accepted the name. Baby John became a special man who led many people to believe in Jesus.

—*Laurie Oswald Robinson*

PRAYING AND WALKING IN THE WORLD:

- Create a picture with crayons and pencil by writing your name in many different sizes and colors. Ask your parents or another adult to help you frame the picture and put it in your room.

- Discuss with your parents how they chose your name. Ask them how your name holds special meaning for them, and look at a book of names to see what various names mean.

DECEMBER 24

ONE CHRIST, ONE CANDLE

PLUNGING INTO THE WORD:

Luke 1:67-80

PONDERING ON THE WAY:

I have attended many Christmas Eve candlelight services. They never fail to mesmerize me with the soft glow of dozens and dozens of candles progressively lighting up a dark sanctuary. From grandchildren to grandparents, from husbands to wives, from friends old to new, each solitary candlewick is set aflame.

My heart beats faster as the heat and light reach my unlit candle. In awe, I humbly receive Christ, the light of the world. As we sing "Silent Night," I am aware of how frail my little candle is by itself but how full it becomes when it joins a community of light. But first, this entire room of light was set on fire, just one candle at a time.

Zechariah embraced this mystery by eventually embracing his personal mission in his faith community. After a period of disbelief, he accepted his role of fathering John, the prophet of the Most High. Because Zechariah opened himself to the Holy Spirit, he could proclaim God's mercy and favor in a merciless and fearful world. Because Zechariah kept his personal covenant, he witnessed to a covenant-keeping God. Because Zechariah let God light his one little candle, he contributed to the dawn from on high that was breaking upon God's people. That dawn gave light to those who sit in darkness and in the shadow of death.

Zechariah's life modeled a truth that the late peace prophet Mahatma Ghandi penned, "Be the change you want to see in the world." If we want to fan the flame of Jesus' light in the world, we must be the light we receive.

—*Laurie Oswald Robinson*

PRAYING AND WALKING IN THE WORLD:

- Reflect on what personal mission you sense God calling you to in the year ahead. Also reflect on how you sense God wants you to become more engaged in your faith, business, or extended-family community.

- Pray that you will become more open to receive the light of Christ in the dark places in your life. Pray also that you will be more willing to carry the Christ-light into the dark places of your community—including church, the marketplace, and your home.

- Attend a candlelighting service this evening with your friends and family.

DECEMBER 25 AND 26 *(FOR CHILDREN AND FAMILIES)*

DONKEY'S STORY

PLUNGING INTO THE WORD:

Luke 2:1-20

PONDERING ON THE WAY:

My name is Donkey. I don't have a real name. Just Donkey. Is it because I'm not worth even having a name of my own? Maybe. It can't be because of Shrek—he hasn't been invented yet.

I'm just Donkey. I was born with crippled back legs. I walk funny, except it isn't really funny. I can't carry packs, and I certainly can't carry a person. I hang out with the shepherds and the sheep because there's nothing else for me to do. Even with them, I feel worthless.

The night it happened, that's just what I was doing—hanging out with the sheep and shepherds. Dozing off and on. Watching the stars. Listening to the night critters. Listening for any unusual sounds in the flock. I sensed what happened next before I actually saw it.

Read: *Luke 2:8-14, sing "Hark the Herald Angels Sing"*

You can't imagine the excitement among the shepherds! The next thing I knew, they were gone! Just like that! Gone! And I'm standing there thinking, *Okay, so who's going to "keep watch over the sheep by night"? Who's going to make sure a coyote doesn't sneak in and steal a lamb? Who?*

Donkey. Me. I was all they had that night. So I checked out the herd. I knew them all. I knew which lambs belonged where. I counted sheep—I don't mean so I could fall asleep. I counted sheep and came up one short. So I counted again. Still one missing. I walked slowly through the herd and looked at each ewe chewing her cud. And I found out who was missing. The big ewe named Martha had triplets, but only two lambs were curled up beside her. One of Martha's babies was missing.

Great. Just great. Now this crippled donkey gets to go looking in the dark for a missing lamb. I have to—if I don't, that baby will be a midnight snack for a coyote. I started walking. And while I walked, I wondered what the shepherds were finding in Bethlehem. I hoped they were having a better time than I was!

Read: *Luke 2:15-18*

Suddenly, I heard a tiny cry. Over there, to the left. I tottered toward the sound, put my head down to the ground, and there she was … the missing lamb. Her leg was caught under a rock—she couldn't get away.

Now what's a donkey to do? Go back to the cozy safety of the herd or stand out in the dark with one little lamb and wonder who will show up first—the shepherds or a coyote?

I knew. I slowly moved over until I was standing directly over that lamb, with my crooked legs crossed over her body. I can still kick—a coyote would have to face those legs before he'd get his meal. And that's where I stood.

I guess I dozed off. Because I dreamed I was with the shepherds in Bethlehem. I dreamed we were in a barn. There in the barn stood a man, and beside him, a teenage girl was sitting in the straw. A newborn baby boy was wrapped in a soft blanket on the straw beside the girl.

Sing: *"Away in a Manger"*

The baby opened his eyes, and he looked around until he found me—me, the worthless donkey. He looked into my face with his large, dark eyes, and then … and then it was like he was a grown man, standing right beside me, there in the dark, standing with that lost little lamb.

"Well done, Donkey," I heard him say. "A good shepherd leaves the herd to look for the one sheep that is missing. I am the Good Shepherd—I came to seek out and to save those who are lost. I came so they can have life, and have it abundantly!"

I woke up to hear singing. The shepherds were back, singing and praising God for what they had seen in Bethlehem. They found me standing over that lamb. They called me "Good Donkey" and carried the lamb back to its mother. And me? I sang and danced my way back to the herd, and I've been singing and dancing ever since.

—*Carol Duerksen*

PRAYING AND WALKING IN THE WORLD:

- When it comes to worshipping Jesus, with whom do you identify—the shepherds who hurried to see him or the donkey who was left behind?

- Do you ever feel sorry for yourself like Donkey did—upset because you're stuck with the work while others are having fun? Can you see that Jesus is with you too?

- Offer a prayer of praise that Jesus came for everyone!

- Sing and dance today in the joy of Christmas!

DECEMBER 27

JESUS

PLUNGING INTO THE WORD:

Luke 2:21-24

PONDERING ON THE WAY:

The God who became flesh
screamed
a loud healthy
baby boy cry
of pain and anguish.
Circumcision.

The firstborn male
of Mary and Joseph
dedicated
designated
as holy to the Lord.

Human boy child
suffers
in physical pain.

Divine God-son
consecrated
as God's own.

One
and the same:
Jesus

  —*Carol Duerksen*

PRAYING AND WALKING IN THE WORLD:

- What is the most amazing thing to you about the paradox of Jesus being both human and divine?

- Do you tend to think more about the divine or the human aspect of Jesus?

- Today, focus on the "other side" of Jesus. If you usually think of him as divine, put Jesus into the everyday aspects of your life. See him doing what you do. If you usually think of Jesus as human, focus on his divinity.

DECEMBER 28

BITTERSWEET

PLUNGING INTO THE WORD:

Luke 2:25-35

PONDERING ON THE WAY:

Simeon
You praise our son
And we revel in your words
Then you bless us
And we feel so good.

But you're not done—
What's that you say?
Shadows lurk ahead
A sword will pierce our souls?

How are we to feel then?
Bittersweet words
Ringing in our ears
Are we blessed or cursed
To be the parents
Of this baby we call
Jesus?

    —*Carol Duerksen*

PRAYING AND WALKING IN THE WORLD:

Being connected to Jesus is a blessing, but it isn't all joyful. If we are truly following him, we will cry in the shadows as well as dance in the light, and the sword will pierce our hearts. Jesus invaded comfort zones and crossed status quo barriers. How comfortable is your journey with Jesus?

DECEMBER 29

SENIOR WISDOM

PLUNGING INTO THE WORD:

Luke 2:36-40

PONDERING ON THE WAY:

She's old, a woman, a widow, and a prophet. Anna "just happens" to show up in the part of the temple where Joseph, Mary, and Jesus are and adds her prophetic praise to what they have already heard from Simeon. What a testimony to God's continual interest in using people of all ages, marital status, and gender to proclaim redemption to the world.

The wisdom that senior citizens can offer us is sometimes lost in our impatience with their long-winded stories, their failing memories, and their inability to understand our technology. But just because "times are changing" doesn't mean our older friends and family members are outdated. Some things don't change, and one of those things is the wisdom accumulated through the years by our elders. Another thing is that people still need people. While cell phones have increased our ability to talk to each other, our real communication has probably decreased. Perhaps more than ever before, people need people who will look them in the eyes, talk with them face-to-face, listen with attentive ears, and not always be in a hurry to move on to the next activity.

Seniors citizens can be those people in our lives, calling us to hear their wisdom, take a break from our busyness, and discover what redemption means in our day-to-day living.

                                        —*Carol Duerksen*

PRAYING AND WALKING IN THE WORLD:

- How does God speak to you through older persons? How does your congregation tap the resources of wisdom and experience available in the lives of senior citizens? How do you work at connections between the young and old?

- As this year draws to a close, contemplate the relationships you and your family have with people in their seventies, eighties, nineties. Consider setting some personal or congregational goals to foster those connections.

- Schedule a regular time to spend with an elderly person. Put it on your calendar. Consider it equal in importance to the other things you consider "must do's."

DECEMBER 30

PRE-TEEN JESUS

PLUNGING INTO THE WORD:

Luke 2:41-50

PONDERING ON THE WAY:

Jesus as a preteen. I love it. He's old enough to hang out with his friends more than with his parents. He's got his own agenda. His parents apparently had the same philosophy my husband and I have with the teens in our home: We trust you until you prove to us that we can't.

And that's just what Jesus did—at least in the eyes of his panicked parents. He broke their trust. He wasn't with the group going home the way he was supposed to be.

When they finally found him, the words flew. His mom was really upset, and let him know, probably embarrassing him in front of all his scholarly friends.

"Jesus, where have you been? Your dad and I have been looking all over for you! Do you have any idea how worried we've been? How could you do this to us?"

And the typical preteen answer: "What's the problem? I know what I'm doing. Give me a break."

Mary and Joseph didn't get it, and Jesus didn't push the issue. That would come with time.

The issues and challenges our youth face today are certainly more complicated than those faced by Jesus. Nevertheless, Jesus walked in youthful shoes, and he is a prayer away when you need to talk to him about the young people in your life.

And yes, you can trust him.

—*Carol Duerksen*

PRAYING AND WALKING IN THE WORLD:

- Pray for teens you know. Pray for Jesus to walk with them in the tough choices they face in today's world.

- Consider being a mentor for a teen in your congregation or through the Big Brothers Big Sisters program. It could easily be life-changing for both of you.

DECEMBER 31

A NEW THING WITHIN YOU

PLUNGING INTO THE WORD:

Luke 2:51-52

PONDERING ON THE WAY:

Here we have eighteen years of Jesus' life packed into two sentences. Don't you wish you knew more? I do. On the other hand, it's all there. Jesus matured. He learned life lessons. He grew in his relationship with God, and with his family and friends. What more should a person do with their life?

What would it mean for you to put your name in verse 52? "And Carol increased in wisdom and in years, and in divine and human favor." What would it mean to set goals for the New Year based on this verse?

How would you like to gain more wisdom? Read more good books and watch less reality TV? Attend events with speakers who broaden your perspective? Get to know someone who is very different from you?

Get to know someone who is very different from you?

How would you like to increase in favor with God? Join a Bible study? Listen to inspirational tapes while driving to work? Resolve to read through the Bible in a year? Teach Sunday school? Do you have a secret addiction from which you need healing?

How would you like to increase in favor with others? Do you have unresolved issues with someone? Have you been putting off spending time with someone? How's your marriage? Are you working so hard to give your children things that you don't have time to be with them?

Put your name in that verse. Set goals for the New Year, and then determine a plan of action. Invite God to do a new thing within you—one day at a time.

"See, I am doing a new thing! Now it springs up ..." (Isaiah 43:19a, NIV).

> —*Carol Duerksen*

PRAYING AND WALKING IN THE WORLD:

Fill in the blanks:

- I want to grow in wisdom through _____.

- I want to grow physically through (let's think exercise rather than actually getting bigger) _____.

- I want to grow in my relationship with God through _____.

- I want to grow in my relationship with others through _____.

This is just a beginning. Develop the outline. Share it with others. Be accountable. And may you grow with God!

MICHELE HERSHBERGER serves as Chair of the Bible and Ministry Division at Hesston College, where she teaches Bible and youth ministry classes. She has authored *A Christian View of Hospitality* and *God's Story, Our Story*, the catechism resource for Mennonite Church USA and Mennonite Church Canada. Michele also enjoys preaching, touring as a speaker for The Giving Project and speaking at several Mennonite youth conventions and conferences. Michele graduated from Hesston College with an AA, Goshen College with a BA in communication and Associated Mennonite Biblical Seminary with a Masters in Biblical Studies. She is married to Del Hershberger and they have three children. Michele is a member of Hesston Mennonite Church.

LAURIE OSWALD ROBINSON is editor for Mennonite Women USA and its publication, *timbrel: women in conversation together with God*. She formerly served as news service director for Mennonite Church USA, and before that as assistant editor for *Mennonite Weekly Review*. Laurie graduated from Goshen College with a bachelor's degree in communication, English minor. She completed creative writing courses from the University of Iowa and seminary classes at the Great Plains extension of Associated Mennonite Biblical Seminary. She grew up and was baptized at Manson (Iowa) Mennonite Church. She is married to Alfonso Robinson, and they live in Newton, Kansas . She is a member of First Mennonite Church in Newton.

CAROL DUERKSEN is a freelance writer. She lives on a farm between Goessel and Hillsboro, Kansas, along with her husband Maynard Knepp, a large assortment of animals, and a different exchange student each year. She is the editor of *With*, a magazine for Christian teens; has co-authored nine Amish novels with her husband; and collaborated with her cat, Slickfester Dude, in writing a children's book. Carol is a Hesston College graduate; a semi-retired youth minister; shepherd during lambing season on the farm; and a coordinator for foreign exchange students. She is a member of Tabor Mennonite Church near Goessel.

Jonas Series

The Jonas Series was the brainchild of Maynard Knepp, a popular speaker on the Amish culture who grew up in an Amish family in central Kansas. Knepp and his wife Carol Duerksen, a freelance writer, collaborated to produce their first book, *Runaway Buggy*, released in October, 1995. The resounding success of that book encouraged them to continue, and the series grew to four books within 18 months. The books portray the Amish as real people who face many of the same decisions, joys and sorrows as everyone else, as well as those that are unique to their culture and tradition. Written in an easy-to-read style that appeals to a wide range of ages and diverse reader base — from elementary age children to folks in their 90s, from dairy farmers to PhDs — fans of the Jonas Series are calling it captivating, intriguing, can't-put-it-down reading.

RUNAWAY BUGGY

This book sweeps the reader into the world of an Amish youth trying to find his way "home." Not only does *Runaway Buggy* pull back a curtain to more clearly see a group of people, but it intimately reveals the heart of one of their sons struggling to become a young man all his own.

HITCHED

With *Hitched*, the second installment in the Jonas Series, the reader struggles with Jonas as he searches for the meaning of Christianity and tradition, and feels his bewilderment as he recognizes that just as there are Christians who are not Amish, there are Amish who are not Christians.

PREACHER

Book Three in the Jonas Series finds Jonas Bontrager the owner of a racehorse named Preacher, and facing dilemmas that only his faith can explain, and only his faith can help him endure.

BECCA

The fourth book in the Jonas Series invites readers to see the world through the eyes of Jonas Bontrager's 16-year-old daughter Becca, as she asks the same questions her father did, but in her own fresh and surprising ways.

SKYE SERIES

A spin-off of the much-loved Jonas Series, the Skye Series follows Jonas
Bontrager's daughter Becca as she marries and becomes the mother of twin
daughters, Angela and Skye. While Angela rests on an inner security of
who she is and what life is about, Skye's journey takes her to very different
places and situations. Through it all, she holds tightly to one small red piece of
security—a bandanna her Amish grandfather gave her as a child.

TWINS

In the first book of the Skye Series, Becca and her husband Ken
become the parents of twin daughters through very unusual
circumstances—circumstances that weave the twins' lives together
even as they are pulled apart by their separate destinies.

AFFAIR OF THE HEART

Not long after rock star Skye Martin settles into
the Wellsford Amish community, the tongues begin to wag. She's been
seen a lot lately with Ezra Yoder, an Amish man who always did seem
to have secrets of his own.

SWEDE

Against his wishes, Henrik Svensson leaves Sweden and comes to the
United States as an exchange student, thinking he can make the year
bearable by chasing girls and ignoring the rules.

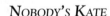

NOBODY'S KATE

From the authors of the well-known Amish novels in the Jonas Series
and the Skye Series, an extraordinary new novel of personal discovery,
faith journeys, and unique relationships.

WHO'S KATE

Kate Weaver's best friend is a car dealer who blesses
her with spiritual direction and encourages her growing attraction to
the owner of a golf course. She uncovers the dark secret of another
Amish family and challenges the Amish bishop to confront his abusive
son. Pushed to open her heart and mind to new thoughts and beliefs,
Nobody's Kate discovers she belongs to God, herself and those she
meets on her journey of faith.

Slickfester **D**ude **T**ells **B**edtime **S**tories
Life Lessons from our Animal Friends

by Carol Duerksen (& Slickfester Dude)

WillowSpring Downs is not only a publishing company — it's also a 120-acre piece of paradise in central Kansas that's home to a wide assortment of animals. Slickfester Dude, a black cat with three legs that work and one that doesn't, is one of those special animals. In a unique book that only a very observant cat could write, Slickfester Dude tells Carol a bedtime story every night — a story of life among the animals and what it can mean for everyone's daily life. This book will delight people from elementary age and up because the short stories are told in words that both children and adults can understand and take to heart. Along with strong, sensitive black and white story illustrations, the book includes Slickfester Dude's Photo Album of his people and animal friends at WillowSpring Downs.

SLICKFESTER DUDE VISITS THE AMISH
A storytelling cat, Slickfester Dude takes his friend Kent to visit an Amish farm where they find out how much fun they can have without all of their worldly gadgets.

ORDER FORM

All titles are $9.95 each.
Jonas Series:

_____ copy/copies of *Runaway Buggy*

_____ copy/copies of *Hitched*

_____ copy/copies of *Preacher*

_____ copy/copies of *Becca*

Skye Series:

_____ copy/copies of *Twins*

_____ copy/copies of *Affair of the Heart*

_____ copy/copies of *Swede*

Other:

_____ copy/copies of *Nobody's Kate*

_____ copy/copies of *Who's Kate?*

_____ copy/copies of *Slickfester Dude Tells Bedtime Stories*

_____ copy/copies of *Slickfester Dude Visits The Amish*

Contact information:
phone
620-367-8432
fax
620-367-8218
email
willowspringdowns@juno.com
website
allamish.org

Name _____

Address _____

City _____ State _____ ZIP _____

Phone # _____

Email _____

_____ Book(s) at $9.95 = Total $ _____

Add $3.50 postage/handling if only one book _____

Add $6 postage/handling if two or more books _____

Total enclosed $ _____

Make checks payable to WillowSpring Downs and mail, along with this order
form, to the following address:
WillowSpring Downs • 1582 Falcon • Hillsboro, KS 67063-9600